Bunbury of Maida

Bunbury of Maida

A History & Personal Experiences of the Campaigns in Holland, Egypt & Italy by a British Staff Officer

Memoir and Literary Remains of Lieut.-General Sir Henry Edward Bunbury, Bart.

Edited by his son
Sir Charles J. F. Bunbury

Narratives of Some Passages in the Great War With France, from 1799 to 1810

Sir Henry Bunbury

With an Account of the Battle of Maida
by Charles Oman

Bunbury of Maida
A History & Personal Experiences of the Campaigns in Holland, Egypt & Italy by a British Staff Officer
Memoir and Literary Remains of Lieut.-General Sir Henry Edward Bunbury, Bart.
Edited by his son Sir Charles J. F. Bunbury
Narratives of Some Passages in the Great War With France, from 1799 to 1810
by Sir Henry Bunbury
With an Account of the Battle of Maida
by Charles Oman

FIRST EDITION

Leonaur is an imprint of Oakpast Ltd
Copyright in this form © 2022 Oakpast Ltd

ISBN: 978-1-915234-20-9 (hardcover)
ISBN: 978-1-915234-21-6 (softcover)

http://www.leonaur.com

Publisher's Notes
The views expressed in this book are not necessarily those of the publisher.

Contents

Memoir and Literary Remains of Lieut.-General Sir Henry Edward Bunbury, Bart. 7

Narratives of Some Passages in the Great War With France, from 1799 to 1810 33

The Battle of Maida 361

Memoir and Literary Remains of Lieut.-General Sir Henry Edward Bunbury, Bart.

(1778-1799)

Henry Edward Bunbury was born in London on May 4, 1778: the younger of the two sons of Henry William Bunbury, and Catharine Horneck, his wife.

My grandfather, Henry William Bunbury, born in 1750, was remarkable for his talent as an artist: his humorous sketches of men and manners (*Bunbury's Caricatures*) were celebrated in his time, and are well known to lovers of art: but he was not less distinguished for the grace and refined beauty of his designs of a different class of subjects. These are less generally known, although some numbers of his designs from Shakespeare, very characteristic examples of his manner, were published in 1792-6. I possess a large collection of his original drawings, and several small paintings in oil; amongst these, a curious caricature of himself, and several of his associates at Rome.

It is worth noticing, that amongst all his humorous and satirical designs, I have never seen any that bore the least reference to a political subject; although he lived in times of great political excitement. In his twenty-second year he married the younger sister of his intimate friend Charles Horneck; and after his marriage, he lived for several years at Barton, in a small house near the Hall, which was occupied by his brother, Sir Thomas Charles Bunbury. (Mrs. Bunbury, and her sister Mrs. Gwyn, were celebrated for their beauty. Sir Joshua Reynolds painted them together, and separately; at a later time, their portraits were painted by Hoppner.) Here Oliver Goldsmith was a frequent and welcome guest; he had been on terms of friendly intimacy with the Horneck family before my grandmother's marriage, and continued to be a cherished friend of both the husband and the wife.

Goldsmith's charming letter to Mrs. Bunbury, on receiving an invitation to Barton, was first published in Prior's edition of his works, from a copy sent to the editor by my father, and has been republished in subsequent biographies of the poet, as well as in the appendix to the *Correspondence of Sir Thomas Hanmer*. *(Goldsmith's Works*, ed. Prior, vol. iv. Irving's *Life of Goldsmith, Correspondence of Sir Thomas Hanmer*.)

Garrick also was an intimate friend of my grandfather, and some playful verses addressed to him by the great actor, will be found in the collection already referred to (*Correspondence of Sir Thomas Hanmer*, &c.). Nor was Samuel Johnson a stranger; the 'family Bible' at Barton bears this inscription (in my grandfather's handwriting):

'Purchased by Dr. Samuel Johnson for Catharine Bunbury, 1778.'

My grandfather was very ready with his pencil, and fond of using it. For an instance: when he was in command of the Suffolk militia, a young private in the regiment came to him one day (as I have heard), to ask for a pass, that he might visit his sweetheart; Mr. Bunbury signed the pass, and on the same paper drew a comical sketch of the young man walking with his beloved, to the great amusement of the authorities and others to whom the paper was shown.

My father's elder brother, Charles John Bunbury, born November 2, 1772, gave early promise of brilliant talents, which excited the most ardent hopes of his parents. At Westminster School he was the intimate companion and friend of Robert Southey, who seems, as we may infer from a remarkable passage in his 'Letters,' to have been deeply impressed by the brilliant and attractive qualities, and the wasted life, of Charles Bunbury.

In a letter of March 30, 1804, after speaking of Coleridge, he adds:

> I knew one man resembling him, save that with equal genius he was actually a vicious man. If that man had had common prudence, he must have been the first man in this country, from his natural and social advantages, and as such, we who knew him and loved him at school, used to anticipate him. I learnt more from his conversation than any other man ever taught me.... and I learnt more morality by his example, than anything else could have taught me, for I saw him wither away. He is dead and buried at the Cape of Good Hope, and has left behind him

nothing to keep his memory alive. (*Life and Correspondence of R. Southey*, ed. C. C. Southey, vol. ii.)

From Westminster, where he seems to have left the reputation of one who *could* do anything he pleased, but who would seldom take the trouble to excel in the ordinary studies of the school, Charles John Bunbury went to Cambridge (to Catherine Hall, I believe). Here, as at Westminster, he at first gained a brilliant reputation among his contemporaries. But he unhappily fell into habits of intemperance, which were too prevalent in those times; he wrecked his health, his fame, and his prospects, and caused deep disappointment and grief to his parents. He was obliged to quit the University, and his uncle, Sir Thomas Charles Bunbury, who had hitherto treated him as his heir, and had paid for his education at Westminster and Cambridge, refused to do anything more for him. Colonel Gwyn, who had married his aunt, advised that he should be put into the army.

A commission was obtained for him in the 52nd Infantry, and in a few months, he was promoted to a troop in the 25th Light Dragoons, with which regiment he went out to India in 1796. Very soon after landing there, and on a very short acquaintance, he married Miss Frances Davison; a marriage which seems, I know not why, to have still further increased the displeasure of his family. He had not been long in India before he fell into bad health; and was on his way homeward on sick leave, when he died at the Cape of Good Hope in May 1798, in the twenty-sixth year of his age. (His widow married Mr. Sydenham, a man of great ability and varied accomplishments, who afterwards held an important diplomatic post at the Court of Lisbon.)

The portrait of Charles John Bunbury, painted in 1780, (exhibited in 1781), is one of Reynolds's most charming pictures of children. (See *Life and Times of Sir Joshua Reynolds*, by Leslie and T. Taylor, vol. ii.) It is now at Barton, and has been more than once exhibited in the British Institution.

I have been told by my father, that Sir Joshua while painting it, to prevent the boy from becoming weary and restless, entertained him by relating fairy tales; and the look of pleased and wondering attention in the child's face is in accordance with this statement.

In 1778, when the critical state of the war with America made it necessary to call out the whole military force of the kingdom, and to form camps in various parts of the country, my grandfather, holding a commission in the Suffolk militia, joined the camp at Coxheath, in

Kent. Several sketches of camp life, now in the collection at Barton, remain as records of the time he passed there. (He also, as it appears, exhibited some of his camp sketches in 1780, in the exhibition at Somerset House; see Leslie and Taylor's *Life of Sir J. Reynolds*, vol. ii.)

During this time his wife remained in London, in lodgings in Pall Mall; and there her younger son, Henry Edward, was born on May 4. Sir Joshua Reynolds, an intimate friend of the family, was one of his godfathers.

I will here insert a fragment of my father's reminiscences of his early days, which he began to write very late in life, but of which, unfortunately, he left nothing but this mere beginning.

RECOLLECTIONS OF CHILDHOOD.
By Sir Henry E. Bunbury.

I was born in London, on May 4, 1778. The first things which I can recollect were the being sent to school at Bury before I was five years old; disgusted with Gray's *Elegy* by being obliged to get it by heart, without understanding its meaning; and flogged for a lie which I did not tell. These matters fixed themselves strongly on my memory, but they were not particularly well calculated to improve my temper or open my heart. My only brother was my senior by five or six years, and was going to Westminster School, after having been under Mrs. Barbauld's care, when I was doomed to cry over the Country Churchyard in Mr. Priest's little academy, so that I had no playmate or confidant.

My sorrows there, however, were short, for my father left Suffolk, and, at the earnest desire of my mother's sister, the wife of Colonel Gwyn, I was left to her care, and went to live with her at Mildenhall. The next event which remains upon my memory was the breaking of our windows by the village mob, because the colonel would not illuminate his house on account of the peace of 1783—a peace which threw him upon half-pay, and checked all his hopes of promotion in the army. I well remember how his Welsh blood was roused by the smashing of the glass, and how he mustered his footman and gardener, and the gardener's labourer, and made a sortie sabre in hand, and took a prisoner, and kept him in the dim great hall of the old mansion all night; and with what curiosity and timidity I peeped at the audacious lad who had dared to throw stones at uncle's windows.

My father had embarrassed his circumstances by the generosity of his nature, and a carelessness about money which did not befit a younger brother. He was poor, and the Gwyns were now poorer. My uncle, Sir Charles Bunbury, was satisfied with paying the expenses of Westminster for my brother, whom he looked upon as his heir; so that my education was in a fair way of being left to the chapter of accidents. However, the curate of Mildenhall, a very poor but zealous young man, took the direction of a humble school, and thither I repaired every day to learn writing and arithmetic. My master taught these things well; and I had a turn for figures, and made a good progress. For schoolfellows and companions, there were the sons of the blacksmith and the tailor, and other patricians of the village. How well do I recollect running about in the summers of the first years of my living at Mildenhall, in a tight jacket and trowsers made out of my aunt's old chintz or printed cotton gowns; coming round the bowling green or about the paddocks, mouthing scraps of Shakespeare, or inventing wonderful stories or scenes of futurity in which I was the hero.

This indulgence of my childish imagination in every sort of wild vagary was a great amusement through the many long months and even years of comparative solitude, but it had mischievous effects: it became so deeply rooted a habit, that I could not throw it off till long after I had grown up; it prevented my mind from becoming properly regulated, and hindered my application to useful things. Colonel Gwyn had exhausted his fortune in very early life, and had afterwards served gallantly in America. He was now unemployed and poor, but he was fond of hunting and shooting, and still loved Newmarket, though he abstained from play. But he had no turn for books, and my aunt had no means to procure them for herself. The collection, therefore, at Mildenhall, to which alone I could have access, was not calculated to make my private studies very profitable.

However, I devoured all I could, and some of them over and over again. Well do I remember where they stood, and a great part of the contents of those old shelves. An incomplete set of Pope's *Shakespeare* was the treasure to which I was never tired of returning; *Don Quixote* stood next in my affections; then there were a few odd volumes of Swift, a translation comically called *Scarron's Comical Romance*, *The Devil on Two Sticks*, part of *The Turkish Spy*, and a few other English books, besides my uncle's depot of works on farriery and racing, and some Italian poetry and Spanish plays that profited my aunt alone.'

★★★★★★

Colonel Gwyn, who had married Mary Horneck, Mrs. Bunbury's elder sister, was (as his name indicates) a Welshman; a very little man, but smart and active, and with so good an air and bearing, that he looked much taller than he was. Madame D'Arblay, who saw him frequently when he was equerry to the king, says that he was considered a very handsome man. He had distinguished himself in the American war by his courage; and after he was thrown out of active employment by the peace, was noted for his skill as a horseman, and for his knowledge of horses. He was appointed one of the equerries to George III. (succeeding Colonel Manners) in July 1787; and as, in this capacity, he often attended the king in his rural expeditions, his name figures in some of the droll satires of *Peter Pindar*. Mrs. Gwyn always acted the part of a mother to her younger nephew, Henry Edward; for his own mother, entirely wrapped up in her hopes for her promising elder son, cared little for the younger, and willingly resigned him to her sister's charge. After the time to which my father's fragment refers, but in what year I am not aware, he was sent to a preparatory school near Eton, from which he ran away.

At nine years of age, through the interest of Lord Harcourt, who was a friend of his uncle and aunt, he was appointed a page to Queen Charlotte; and he would sometimes talk, in his latter days, of the fashions of ladies' dresses, as he had seen them at the drawing-rooms which he attended in this capacity. Not long afterwards he was sent to Westminster School; and here he saw more of his father and mother than he had hitherto done, as they were then living in Whitehall, opposite to the Admiralty. Mr. Bunbury was at this time equerry to the Duke of York: some amusing notices of him will be found in the diary of Madame D'Arblay, who met him now and then when he was acting in this capacity, and who seems to have been considerably alarmed by his reputation as a caricaturist, and by the satirical turn of his conversation.

The headmaster of Westminster School was Dr. William Vincent, afterwards Dean of Westminster, a man of great learning, (see his Life in *English Cyclopaedia*), and author of a very valuable contribution to ancient geography in *The Commerce and Navigation of the Ancients in the Indian Ocean*. But I imagine that the younger Bunbury received little of his personal attention. Of my father's life at Westminster, I can find no record; but I do not remember to have heard him say anything which could lead me to infer that he had profited much by it, or remembered it with much pleasure. The fact that all his own sons were educated at home, seems to show that he was not deeply impressed with a sense of the advantages he had himself derived from Westminster. He was probably not a zealous student, and acquired no more than the usual superficial knowledge of Latin and Greek.

Of his schoolfellows, the one, I think, for whom he had the greatest regard, and with whom in after life he kept up the most intimate and cordial intercourse, was the late Lord Colborne (Ridley Colborne). The Marquis of Lansdowne, the venerable statesman who was so lately removed from among us, was another of his acquaintances at Westminster. Another was John Archibald Murray, the most intimate friend of Francis Horner, and ultimately a Scottish judge by the title of Lord Murray. After leaving school, my father never met Mr. Murray again till late in life, and I remember his speaking of the pleasure he had had in renewing the acquaintance.

Southey was still at Westminster when my father went thither; and though there never was the same intimate friendship between them as between the poet and the elder Bunbury, yet they were thrown much together. I find this MS. note by my father in his copy of Southey's *Life*:

> Wynn (Mr Charles W. W. Wynn), Southey and I were lodged in the same room at Clough's. I was four years their junior.

Southey left Westminster early in 1792, and did not meet Henry Bunbury again till 1811; a passage in a letter to Mr. Wynn, in the latter year, expresses vividly the emotion with which he met his old schoolfellow after such a lapse of time. (*Letters of Southey*, ed. Rev. J. W. Warter, vol. ii.)

Charles John Bunbury was at Westminster when his younger brother came thither, but showed him no kindness, and contributed nothing to his comfort. Indeed, the two brothers were almost strangers; owing to the difference of age, and to the younger one having been brought up almost entirely by his aunt, they scarcely knew each other; and all that my father remembered to have ever received from his brother was a *thrashing*, administered very soon after his first arrival at Westminster. A few months afterwards, Charles was dismissed from the school on account of a boyish riot.

In January 1795, before he had completed his seventeenth year, Henry Edward Bunbury received an ensign's commission in the Coldstream Guards. (January 14, 1795.) I have heard him speak of the sudden and dangerous transition from the restraints of a public school to the laxity of military life, in times when study of any kind was not only not required, but was rather discouraged, in that profession, and when superior officers thought it unnecessary to bestow the slightest care on the morals of their subalterns. During the summer of that year his regiment formed part of the force encamped on Warley Common in Essex.

Of this and the three following years of his military life, my father left no record, beyond some slight and rough notes of his professional employments year by year, from which he had probably intended to compose a narrative of his military career; an intention which, unfortunately, he never carried out. In these notes, under this year 1795, I find an allusion to a curious fact, of which one might wish to have more information:

> Mr. Dundas's wish to send the Guards to the West Indies. Veto of George III.

This he may probably have learned in the course of his subsequent acquaintance with Dundas; and if he was correctly informed, it is a striking illustration of the extent to which the Ministry of that time were willing to sacrifice our military resources to their passion for the acquisition of 'sugar islands.'

Later on, in this same year, 1795, my father was appointed *aide-de-camp* to his uncle General Gwyn, and served with him in the camp which was formed at Weymouth. In the winter he was detached, on the recruiting service, to Exeter, and lived there with the officers of the 25th Light Dragoons, then under the command of Lieutenant-Colonel Stapleton Cotton, that gallant and famous Lord Combermere who died the other day in extreme old age, and at the head of his profession. In the following year, he rejoined General Gwyn, who was then employed on the general staff in the neighbourhood of London, and who had the special charge of inspector of the cavalry in England; an appointment for which he was peculiarly fitted by his thorough knowledge of horses.

My father attended General Gwyn on several journeys to different parts of England, for the purpose of buying horses for the cavalry. In August 1797, he purchased a troop in the 16th Light Dragoons; and during that and the following year he continued on home service, partly with his new regiment, and partly with his uncle, whose *aide-de-camp* he remained. His father and mother had now removed to the neighbourhood of Weybridge, and were living in a small house in a very pretty spot, close to the Duke of York's park at Oatlands. The duchess took a great fancy to Mrs. Bunbury, and seemed fonder of her company than anyone else's; and this intimacy had an important influence on my father's career.

In the spring of the year 1798, he lost his brother, who died (as I have already mentioned), on his way home from India; and towards the close of that year his mother was attacked by the painful illness which proved fatal to her. She died on July 8, 1799, at the age of forty-five, and was buried in the church of Weybridge; in which same church were afterwards interred her friend, the Duchess of York, and her sister, Mrs. Gwyn. (There is a description of her tomb, and a copy of the inscription on it, in Brayley and Britton's *History of Surrey*, vol. ii.).

(1799-1805)

It was in the year 1799, that Henry Edward Bunbury had his first experience of active service; and that of an important nature. Having been appointed *aide-de-camp* to the Duke of York, he attended that general through the short, but severe and unfortunate, campaign against the French in North Holland. Of this campaign he wrote, in later years, a full and very interesting narrative, which was embodied in his published work, *Narrative of some Passages in the Great War with France*, which follows this *Memoir* in the second part of this book.

He there points out very clearly the errors, both in the original plan, and in the conduct of the campaign, which led to its failure; he shows that this failure was owing to a deficiency of military judgment in the designers of the scheme, to faults of the generals commanding, and above all, to the division of authority, and to the want of harmonious co-operation between the allied commanders; not in any degree to a deficiency of courage, or of high soldier-like qualities in the British troops.

As the Duke of York did not land in Holland until September 13, my father did not himself witness the brilliant commencement of the operations: the landing at the Helder, in the face of the Dutch troops; and the repulse of the French in 1805, their attack on the position of the Zuype, on September 10.

But, on the evening of the 18th, he was despatched to accompany the column which, under the command of Sir Ralph Abercromby, was directed upon Hoorn and Alkmaar, with the intention of turning the French position, at the same time that it was to be attacked in front by the main army of the Allies. In the work already mentioned, he has related a curious example of those strange panics that sometimes seize the bravest troops;—when two of the best regiments in our service, startled by an incautious shout, 'broke like a flock of sheep, plunging into the deep mud at the sides of the causeway, and dreaming for some minutes that they had been surprised and charged by a sortie of cavalry.'

He was despatched from Hoorn by Sir Ralph Abercromby, at an early hour on the 19th, to apprise the Duke of York of the state of affairs on that side; but though he was well mounted, and took short cuts across the marshes, he was not able to join His Royal Highness till the Allies were repulsed—'the Russians in full retreat, and Dundas beginning to fall back.' On this occasion he witnessed, and has recorded in his book, a very striking instance of the unyielding courage and energy of British soldiers. He was present also at the battle of October 2. Having at the close of that day, lain down to rest on the wet ground, the continual rain converting his resting-place into a pool of water, in which he passed the night, he was attacked by severe rheumatism, which crippled him for some time.

When the fighting was renewed on the 6th of the same month, he, being thus disabled for active movement:

> .... was carried up and perched on the top of the tall steeple of Alkmaar, with a spying-glass, to try to ascertain for the duke what was the direction, and where were the main points of the fight. But all was confusion, and, in fact, the troops were intermingled.

After the forces employed on this disastrous expedition had returned to England, (1800), Henry Edward Bunbury continued for some months on the personal staff of the Duke of York, and in constant attendance on him at Oatlands and in London. His opinion of the duke he has recorded in the work already quoted. Stating frankly his conviction that 'he (the duke) was not qualified to be even the ostensible head of a great army on an arduous service,' he has at the same time warmly expressed his personal feelings of affection and gratitude to him, and his appreciation of many good and amiable qualities in his character.

The duchess made a great impression on him: I have often heard him speak with warmth of her charming character and the irresistible fascination of her manners, which acted like a spell on all who approached her.

Nevertheless, my father always felt in after life that this period, spent in attendance on the duke at Oatlands, and elsewhere, had been a time of idleness, unimproving, and unsatisfactory. The duke, though a sedulous and zealous administrator, was neither himself disposed to intellectual activity, nor likely to encourage habits of study or application in those under his influence. Nor, as it seems, was the general tone of his society favourable to such habits. He was addicted to indulgence in wine and play, and to irregular hours. My father used to ascribe the dyspepsia from which he suffered in middle life to the very late, very long, and very heavy suppers which were customary at Oatlands: suppers beginning near midnight, and protracted to an indefinite length. The duke also encouraged him in high play, and even (as I have heard), used to lend him money for the purpose. At the same time, he felt that these evils were compensated by no opportunities of real improvement in either the theory or the practice of his profession.

At length, sometime in the course of this same year, he formed the determination to waste no more of his life, but to devote himself to the earnest study of his profession, and make himself really fit for its higher grades. This was the crisis, the turning point, of my father's career; it determined the whole subsequent course of his life. I have heard that what gave him the immediate impulse into this new course, was his accidentally looking into the *Meditations of Marcus Aurelius*, which made a great impression on him. The impression was lasting. He applied for, and obtained, leave to resign his post on the Duke of York's staff, and to enter as a student into the Military College at High Wycombe, then newly established.

From this time, he never relapsed into habits of idleness, nor ceased to attend to the cultivation of his mind. Hitherto his advantages in the way of education had been scanty. He had indeed gone through the usual routine of a public school, but it does not seem to have imbued him with much love of learning; and neither at his home, nor (as far as I have heard) in the army, had he yet met with any who were willing and qualified to excite and direct the activity of his intellect. But having once entered on the career of mental improvement, he did not relax his efforts; but continued to profit by every opportunity of adding to his knowledge and of improving his faculties, till he became as remarkable for the extent and accuracy of his information, as for the strength and soundness of his judgment.

He entered the senior department of the Royal Military College at High Wycombe in August 1800, being still a captain in the 16th Light Dragoons, and continued there through the greater part of the following year, 'working hard,' according to his rough notes. The 'senior department' was under the direction of General Jarry, an old French officer, who had served under the great Frederick, and was well acquainted with the Prussian system of war. The course of study:

> Embraced mathematics, fortification, castrametation, military topography, reconnaissance of ground, estimation of the military resources of a country, disposition and movement of troops under the different circumstances of offensive and defensive warfare, French and German. (From information obtained for me by Major-General William Napier.)

My father certainly studied diligently while at Wycombe, but though he is said to have 'finished his studies' on the 30th of November 1801, I hardly suppose that he mastered all those subjects in the time. With respect to German, certainly, I know that his ignorance of that language was a subject of regret to him in his latter years.

Late in 1801, his studies were interrupted by a severe attack of ague, which obliged him to go to his uncle's house at Barton in Suffolk, to recruit his strength.

In the following spring, (March 11, 1802), he became, by purchase, a major in the 9th West India Regiment, and immediately went on half pay.

It was during the leisure time afforded by the Peace of Amiens, if I am not mistaken, that my father attended a course of lectures on chemistry and mineralogy, given by the noted Frederick Accum; and thus, acquired a taste for studies which were afterwards a great source of pleasure to him.

The speedy renewal of the war, (1803), however, recalled him to strictly professional occupations; and as his studies had now qualified him for the more important staff employments, he was appointed (April), one of the assistants in the Quartermaster-General's Department; and was stationed for the first few months at Hastings, afterwards at East Bourne. In the early part of the next year he succeeded Colonel Willoughby Gordon in the Kent district, with the rank of lieutenant-colonel, (January 21); and during the greater part of that year he remained at the famous camp at Shorncliff, near Hythe, where Sir John Moore was then training a select force to a degree of discipline and efficiency unrivalled in our service, and probably never surpassed in any other.

Shorncliff must have been an interesting station in those days, when Napoleon was known to be mustering his formidable army, for the invasion of England, on the opposite side of the narrow strait; when his camps were actually within view, and our officers were daily watching on the cliffs with their telescopes directed towards Boulogne, in constant expectation of seeing the French flotilla putting to sea. My father would often, in later life, talk of those times, and I remember with what interest he read the details published in Thiers' *Histoire du Consulat et de l'Empire*, of the vast preparations made for the invasion, which showed how thoroughly Napoleon had been in earnest. He observed that, owing to the different rates of drifting of the vessels, as influenced by the tides and currents, the divisions of the French armament would probably not all have reached the same part of our coast. (Note of conversation, Feb. 6, 1858.)

But there was one choice division, of 4,000 picked grenadiers, under Lannes, which was to have been embarked in rowboats, and might probably have come directly across to Folkstone or Sandgate; here they would have been met by Sir John Moore, who had about an equal number of the best troops in the British service; 'and there would have been such a fight as has rarely been seen.' Moore's plan, he said, was 'to fight them in the water'; to charge them with his infantry while in the very act of leaving them boats, and before they had time to form. He (Sir John Moore) had seen with what difficulty *our* best troops had withstood a very partial attack made in this manner by the French, at the time of the landing in Egypt, and he did not think that the French would be so well able to sustain it.

My father was at this time the senior officer of the Quartermaster-General's Department in that district, and, enjoying much of the confidence both of Sir David Dundas and of Sir John Moore, had the advantage of hearing all the plans of attack and defence, the probabilities of the invasion, and all the prospects of the expected campaign, continually discussed by them. He has given us in his *Narrative* the results of these discussions, and the measures upon which the generals had determined. Before the end of the year, however, he was withdrawn from the Kent district, being recalled to the Quartermaster-General's Department in London.

It was during this winter (1804-5) that he made the acquaintance of the famous Henry Dundas; and the following note, found among his papers, records his impressions of that celebrated statesman:—

In the winter of 1804-5, I saw a good deal of Henry Dundas, Lord Melville, first at the house of his brother-in-law, General

Alexander Hope, and afterwards at his own. Both at the one and the other table I saw him quite *au naturel*, for there were seldom more than two or three other persons present, and those his most intimate friends. Lord Melville was a particularly agreeable man in such a society, notwithstanding his advanced age, his strong Scotch accent and Scotch peculiarities. There was a sort of jovial, fearless *abandon* about him that entirely removed from one's mind at the time all thought of the deep, astute, and wily character which was assigned to him in political life. I recollect asking him one day whom, amongst the eminent men he had known in his time, he considered to be the ablest statesman. To my surprise (for I had felt little doubt that he would name Mr. Pitt), Lord Melville answered, "I think Lord Bath was the best statesman I have known. He always saw the main point, and threw away the rubbish of a complicated question quicker than any other man." On another evening Lord Melville spoke much of his earlier career. One thing in particular made a strong impression on my memory.

"When I came up to London as Lord Advocate," said he, "I came determined to fight the battle for Scotsmen, and to win for them their proper place in public estimation, and their proper share of power and influence. Before that time Scotsmen had been looked down upon in England. They were regarded with dislike and distrust." (My father said that Dundas added, in his slow deliberate manner, and with his Scottish accent: 'And I think I have succeeded'.) Certainly, Harry Dundas did succeed, during his thirty years of political influence, in winning for his countrymen an ample share in the power and emoluments of the State. It is not without reason that the citizens of Edinburgh have set up his statue in St. Andrew's Square.'

(1805-1809)

In March 1805, Henry Bunbury received orders to prepare to join an expedition which was to proceed to the Mediterranean, under the command of Lieutenant-General Sir James Craig. He left England accordingly, in April, being at the head of the Quartermaster-General's Department of the expedition, while his friend Colonel James Campbell had the appointment of Adjutant-General. He says, in the work which I have so often quoted:

We were both entire strangers to Craig, and his manner to us at first was not engaging or conciliatory; but when he came to find we were disposed to do our duties actively and carefully, he warmed to us by degrees; and in the latter and more difficult times of his command I found Sir James Craig one of the kindest men I have ever had to transact business with, and one on whose just and honourable feelings I could always place an entire reliance.

The expedition sailed on April 19, 1805, but information of the French fleet having passed the Straits of Gibraltar obliged it to take shelter for some days in the mouth of the Tagus; and at Gibraltar it was again detained for a considerable time by orders from home, so that it was not till July 18th that it arrived at Malta. There Sir James Craig, whose health had been very precarious, recovered all his strength and spirits, and 'set to work indefatigably, inspecting regiments and departments every morning at four o'clock, writing despatches and transacting business all day, giving great dinners every evening.' The staff officers of his force were no doubt in constant activity; and that Colonel Bunbury had already established a claim to his confidence, is evident from the following passage:—

Extract of a 'Secret and Confidential' Letter from H.R.H. the Commander-in-Chief to General Sir James Craig, dated Horse Guards, October 12, 1805.

I have much pleasure in expressing my gratification in the very favourable report you have transmitted of the troops under your command, as well as of the reliance you are enabled to place in the officers composing your staff, particularly in the Deputy Quartermaster-General, Lieutenant-Colonel Bunbury, of whose intelligence I have always entertained a very favourable opinion.

******

Colonel Bunbury had become a regimental Lieut.-Colonel (Newfoundland Fencibles) on March 28 in this year, having received the same rank by Brevet on Dec. 31, 1803.

******

General Craig and the corps under his command remained at Malta till the beginning of October, while negotiations were going on for joint action with the Russian forces, and while the Queen of Naples was weaving a complicated web of treacherous intrigues, to betray alike the French Government and the Allies.

The British forces at length put to sea on November 3, effected their junction with the Russians coming from Corfu, and, after being much delayed by unfavourable weather, landed in the neighbourhood of Naples on the 20th of the same month. They were placed at first in cantonments in the neighbouring villages, and in December were moved forward to the line of the Lower Garigliano. Here they were intended to form the left wing of the line of defence against the expected French attack; while the Russians occupied the centre of the line, with their headquarters at Sulmona; and the Neapolitan troops, under the Comte de Damas, formed the right.

The winter proved uncommonly severe; and I have heard my father tell that the snow fell fast in the streets of Naples, and that the *lazzaroni*, who had never seen it before, were running about, catching the flakes as they fell, and laughing and screaming like children.

It must have been during this same period that, while one day riding in the meadows on the banks of the Garigliano, he was attacked and chased at full speed for a considerable distance by a herd of buffaloes, irritated by the sight of a little dog which accompanied him.

He was present, as he has recorded, at a council of war held at Naples on January 4, 1806, when it was resolved, in conformity with a plan proposed by the Russian General Oppermann, that the allied armies should retire on the advance of the French to the mountains of the Principato, and defend the two Calabrias. He says (*Passages*):

> The only dissentients were Sir James Craig and Brigadier Campbell. Major-General Stuart and I concurred with the Russians, and I have not a doubt now that I was wrong in my opinion. But I was a young man, eager for active service, and ignorant of the important objects which were involved in securing Sicily from the French before it was too late.

The plan, however, was not carried into effect, for the Russian troops were recalled by their own government, and the British were thereupon withdrawn to Messina, that they might be in readiness to defend the island. Their reception by the Neapolitan authorities there was not, at first, very friendly; and it was not until after the irresistible advance of the French had obliged the Court of Naples to fly for refuge to Palermo, that:

> The tardy invitation came to Sir James Craig to disembark, and a reluctant authority to occupy the citadel of Messina. The British troops were landed on February 17, and every exertion

was immediately made to put the fortress into a condition to resist the enemy.

The following extract of a letter from Sir James Craig, about this time to the authorities at the Horse Guards, shows how highly he estimated the services of Colonel Bunbury:—

> Extract of a Letter from Sir James Craig to Colonel (Willoughby) Gordon.
> February 14, 1806.
> From the unfortunate situation of my health, a more than usual share of business has fallen on Brigadier-General Campbell and Lieutenant-Colonel Bunbury; both have answered my fullest expectations. The diligence, intelligence, and activity of the latter, who has had a wider field for displaying these qualities, call upon me in a particular manner to mention them to His Royal Highness.

Soon after this, Sir James Craig's health broke down entirely; he resigned the command to Major General Sir John Stuart, and sailed for England.

When Sir John Stuart planned and carried out the brilliant little expedition to the coast of Calabria, my father was the principal officer on the staff, being not only quartermaster-general to the force, but having the temporary superintendence of the adjutant-general's department, in the absence of Brigadier Campbell. He and the Military Secretary, Captain de Sade, were the only officers to whom the design was communicated by the general, and with whom the arrangements were concerted. At the Battle of Maida, of which he has given such a clear and animated account in his *Narrative*, he played an active part.

At the beginning of the action he was with the right wing of our army, and rode by the side of Colonel (Sir James) Kempt as he led forward his light infantry to that celebrated bayonet charge which instantly overthrew the French brigade opposed to them. Having seen that the enemy were routed in that quarter, and receiving no orders from Sir John Stuart, he rode to our left wing, which was engaged in a more doubtful fight; and as he relates, he was anxiously watching the French sharpshooters, who were stealing farther and farther round the left of Cole's brigade, when one of his assistants brought him the welcome news that the 20th regiment had landed and was approaching. He rode instantly to meet them, and explained to their commanding officer, Colonel Foss, how matters stood; and the spirited advance of that regiment decided the fate of the day.

Sir John Stuart, in his official despatch describing the battle, says:

> To the several departments of the army, every acknowledgment is due; but to no officer am I bound to express them so fully, on my part, as to Lieutenant-Colonel Bunbury, the Deputy Quartermaster-General, to whose zeal, activity, and able arrangements in the important branch of service which he directs, the army as well as myself are under very marked obligations.

Sir James Craig, in a private letter to my father, dated November 3, 1806, says:

> You do me justice in supposing that I should take a warm interest in the transactions of your Calabrian adventure, but in nothing, I assure you, has it been more gratified than in the ample justice that has been done to the share you had in it; nor have I failed to take some credit to myself, for having on all occasions foretold the merits I was assured you would display, whenever the moment arrived for more active exertions than were required while I was with you.

For this service he received a medal.

Before the Maida expedition was known in England, the government had appointed General the Hon. Henry Edward Fox (younger brother of the second Lord Holland, and of Charles James Fox), to the chief command in the Mediterranean; and when the forces returned to Messina, they found General Fox already arrived there.

This circumstance had a permanent influence on the course of my father's life. General Fox, the youngest son of the first Lord Holland and of his wife Caroline, eldest daughter of the second Duke of Richmond, was born March 4, 1755, (Collins's Peerage, edition of 1812), and was therefore at this time fifty-one years of age; he had served with honour in the American War, and in the unfortunate campaigns of 1793-4-5, in Flanders; but was now much broken in health. He was not gifted with brilliant talents, but had an ample share of that kindly, generous, and affectionate nature which Lord Macaulay has celebrated in others of the same family. (See the Essay on Lord Holland, in Macaulay's *Critical and Historical Essays*, vol. iii. ed. of 1843.)

At the same time, he was free from those follies and vices which had dimmed the splendid qualities of his brother Charles. He was married to Marianne, daughter of William Clayton, of Harleyford, and was accompanied to Sicily by his wife and his two daughters, the elder of whom, Louisa Emilia, had not yet completed her eighteenth year. My father, as may be supposed, made a very favourable impression on the general, and was soon received on a friendly footing in the family; an attachment grew up between him and the general's elder daughter; and on the 4th of the following April they were married. There could not be a happier union than this proved.

Charles James Fox, to whose influence, no doubt, his brother's appointment to the Mediterranean command is to be ascribed, had been dead some months when his niece's marriage took place; he died on September 13, 1806. My father had seen him but thrice, although his uncle Sir Thomas Charles Bunbury, had formerly been a zealous political follower of the great orator, and had indeed been one of those who were called 'Fox's Martyrs.' He remembered having once, when a little boy, travelled as *bodkin* in a post-chaise to Newmarket, between Charles Fox and Lord Carlisle.

Not long after, when he was a Westminster schoolboy, he had one day got out of bounds, and hurrying back, was nearly run over by a hackney-coach while crossing a street. Mr. Fox happened to be passing, stepped forward and pulled him out of the way of danger. He did not know the boy whom he rescued, but the boy knew him. Once afterwards, they were formally introduced to each other in the streets of London; but this was the extent of their acquaintance.

To return to Sicily:—

Sir John Moore had arrived at Messina shortly after General Fox, to whom he was to act, ostensibly, as second in command; and as the commander in-chief was in infirm health, and was moreover charged with diplomatic as well as military business, the effective military command devolved in fact on Moore. My father, who had previously been under Moore's command at Shorncliff, enjoyed his esteem and confidence, and, on his part, fully appreciated the noble and heroic qualities of that great man. He was not, however, one of those who, in after years, were inclined to exalt Moore to a level with Wellington. The following fragment, written long afterwards, expresses vividly his recollections of the person, the manners, and the character of Sir John Moore:—

> I knew him well, and loved him, and he was always kind to me. His figure, the expression of his countenance, are now before me; and the tones of his voice seem to play upon my ear.

Sir John Moore was a man on whom Nature had set her favouring signet. In person above the middle height, broad-shouldered and muscular, yet formed light and agile. His features fine, and his keen penetrating eye seemed to look through one's brain. The play of his countenance was very remarkable; expressing alike, and without effort, the open, familiar, and bantering humour with which he greeted those whom he esteemed, and the chilling contempt, or the frown of darkness, with which he visited the objects of his dislike. He was thoroughly honourable, just, and generous; far above all sordid motives, and hardly to be swayed by any passion from what he felt to be his duty.

When speaking of him as a soldier, it were superfluous to touch upon his intrepidity, of which there were but to evident proofs afforded by the many wounds which he received in battle. As a commander, Moore excelled all others I have seen or known of, in teaching both officers and men their several duties. (Remains unfinished.)

Soon after his marriage, on May 5, 1807, he set out with his bride, on a long tour of Sicily, with the view of thoroughly examining, in the first place, its military resources and condition with a view to defence, and moreover the general state of the country and its inhabitants. He had already, in the previous autumn or winter, made a first military tour through part of the island; but he now explored it much more completely, employing the time from May 5 to June 18 in this investigation. From Messina he went first by the usual coast-road to Taormina, a route, indeed, with which he was already well acquainted.

Of that place I cannot find among his papers any detailed description; but I have often heard him, in later years, speak with enthusiasm of the beauty of its scenery; and after he had become acquainted with the most beautiful parts of England and Wales, France and Italy, and the Alps, he used still to say that the view from the ancient theatre of Taormina surpassed all that he had ever beheld. From Taormina, he and my mother turned inland, and skirted the lower region of Etna on three sides, by Francavilla, Bronte, and Nicolosi, returning to the coast at Catania; thence they proceeded by Lentini to Syracuse, and then, turning westward, by Terranova and Alicata to Girgenti, where they visited the sulphur mines, and admired the beauty of the Grecian temples.

Thence they went northward, across the island, to Petralia, an insignificant place at the foot of the Madonia mountains, noted for a natural spring of naphtha or petroleum; and then turning to the north-east, traversed the mountain forest of Caronia, from whence they enjoyed a magnificent view, and descended to the northern coast of the island of St. Agata. At this place they hired a boat which conveyed them to the Lipari Islands; they explored Volcano, Stromboli, and Lipari; and finally returned by the same conveyance to Messina.

The result of this and the previous tour was a very careful and comprehensive report, drawn up by Colonel Bunbury, on the resources and circumstances of the island, principally in a military point of view.

The *Letters of Sicily* (unfortunately incomplete) were compiled late in his life from his own notes and reminiscences, and my mother's journals, of this and subsequent tours. But I may add, what is not there mentioned, that he and my mother were diligent in collecting natural curiosities, especially minerals, and formed in these journeys a valuable collection of the mineralogy of Sicily. They obtained a great variety of the lavas of Etna, the beautiful crystallizations of sulphate of strontian, and sulphur, from the mines near Girgenti, specular iron from Stromboli, interesting specimens of obsidian and pumice in great variety from Lipari, and a rich series of the beautiful sulphur and salts formed by sublimation within the crater of Volcano.

In this last locality they collected specimens of a peculiar mineral, which, on being afterwards examined by scientific men in London, was found to be native boracic acid; a mineral described by Smithson Tennant, in the first volume of the *Transactions of the Geological Society*, in 1811, from specimens obtained in the same place.

General Fox was recalled from the Mediterranean command in July of the same year; and his newly-married daughter had not only the sorrow of parting at once with her father, mother, and sister, but the deeper grief of knowing that both her parents were in a very precarious state of health, and that it was doubtful whether she might ever see them again. (Mrs. Fox, in fact, died, after much suffering, on October 15, 1808.) The command in Sicily devolved on Sir John Moore, 'a man to whom every officer and soldier looked up with an entire confidence.' He applied himself at once with his usual energy and ability to the devising an effectual plan of defence against the overwhelming forces by which he might expect to be attacked.

In my father's *Narrative* will be found the system on which he determined, and the considerations on which it was based. But in September, Moore also was removed from Sicily, being ordered by his government to proceed to Lisbon; and although his successor, General

Sherbrooke, was a man of great resolution and vigour of character, the defenders of the island were reduced in numbers, and disheartened by the apparent indifference shown to them by the government at home. The treachery of the government which they were immediately defending was still more embarrassing. My father has recorded how, under the very eyes of General Sherbrooke, some Neapolitan gunboats were delivered into the hands of the French by the treason of the Neapolitan commandant. The enemy were thereby enabled to obtain possession of the fortresses of Scilla and Reggio, and to proceed with security to collect artillery and materials for the invasion of Sicily.

Thus threatening, as they did, so closely the position of our small army, they kept it constantly on the alert, and rendered continual vigilance necessary on the part of all who held commands in it.

On February 10, 1808, the first child of my father and mother was born—a son, who received the name of Henry Edward; but this infant lived only until the 8th of June following. Almost exactly a year after, February 4, 1809, another son was born to them, and was christened Charles James Fox—the eldest of those who have survived to mourn the loss of those admirable parents.

A remarkable eruption of Etna, which began 1809, towards the end of March 1809, excited in a high degree the attention and interest of Colonel Bunbury. Being first warned of what was happening by a shower of volcanic dust which fell at Messina (sixty miles from the volcano) in the morning of March 27, he immediately obtained leave of absence, and set out for the mountain, in company with Colonel Coffin, Captain A'Court, and Sir John Dalrymple, all on horseback, with his wife and her intimate friend Lady Dalrymple, who travelled in a litter.

His interesting description of this journey, and of the great eruption which he witnessed, will be found in the present volume. It made a deep impression, as may be supposed, on his memory, and he delighted to talk in after years of the incidents of that expedition: the narrow escape of the two ladies from falling over a precipice; the procession of penitents at Randazzo, and the grand scene beheld from the convent there; the preaching at Piedimonte; and the visit to the stream of lava.

He has omitted in his description two particulars which I find mentioned in my mother's journal: the one, that in skirting the northern base of the mountain by Francavilla, they were for some time enveloped in a thick cloud of extremely fine volcanic dust, which obscured the view, covered them entirely, penetrated all veils, irritated the skin, and was intensely painful to the eyes. The other, that while they were watching the river of fire, they felt large heavy drops of water, strongly *salt*, and mixed with fine ashes, incessantly falling on them, while the sky was without a cloud. No doubt these proceeded from the condensation of the watery vapours thrown up by the new crater, and mingled with the saline vapours which were likewise continually ejected by it.

I am tempted to extract from the same journal the lively description of the *fondaco*, or village inn, at Lingua Grossa, showing the style of accommodation for travellers in Sicily in those times:—

> It was the most curious place I ever saw—a low hovel, with the walls of loose lava stones, not in the least smoothed or plastered; a fire on the ground in one corner, without any vent for the smoke, so that the whole place was completely black. Barrels of wine were ranged all along one side of the wall, and close to the fire was the bed, with a small screen of reeds before it. We sat on low stools round the fire, above which hung the kitchen utensils. It was much more like the hut of a savage than anything else.

It appears, however, that it was but seldom, and only in exceptional cases, that they were reduced to avail themselves of the shelter of a *fondaco*. In general, in their various journeys about the island, they were sure of a hospitable reception at the numerous convents. The monks seem to have been very well disposed towards the English, and their circumstances enabled them, as their institutions and habits inclined them, to be liberal in their hospitality.

Colonel Bunbury had scarcely returned from this visit to Etna, before he began to prepare for joining an expedition which Sir John Stuart, now commanding in Sicily, had organised against the French Army at Naples. (Sir John Stuart, Count of Maida, had been appointed Commander of the Forces in the Mediterranean, and had arrived at Messina in that capacity in April 1808.) He had, indeed, already applied to the Horse Guards for leave to return to England on urgent private affairs, and he received the desired leave before the expedition sailed; but of course, this did not withhold him from going on a service which promised to be of some importance.

In the meantime, however, a spirit of discontent against the general, and almost of contempt for him, had grown to such a height among the officers under his command, as to threaten very serious consequences.

The most unbecoming language was known to be current, and at length Sir J. Stuart, who had long avoided conversation with his Adjutant-General, James Campbell, or myself, suddenly sent for me. I found him extremely agitated, and he poured forth his complaints apparently with full confidence. He told me that a general officer had come to him, seemingly as the spokesman of several others, and had held to him a language of remonstrance and censure so strong and unbecoming, as to lead him to apprehend an open resistance to his authority, and a disobedience to his commands, if he should order the troops to embark.

At Sir John's desire, Campbell and I bestirred ourselves to ascertain the extent of the mischief; and we soon found out that, though the spirit was bad, and the language in common use was indefensible, there was no danger of an open mutiny. Under the circumstances, however, the best thing to be done was to disperse the caballers, to get the troops on board their ships, and to sail away from Sicily. (*Passages*.)

My mother accompanied her husband to Milazzo, where the force destined for the expedition assembled, and from whence it sailed on June 11. The history of this expedition is fully related by my father in the *Narrative* already quoted. It made a brilliant show, and started with the fairest promise; but the results were insignificant, almost ignoble.

The force under Sir John Stuart, amounting to nearly 13,000 men, obtained possession, almost without resistance, of the islands of Ischia and Procida, and there they remained, from June 25 to the middle of July, without attempting anything further, although officers and men were alike eager for action.

The position they had taken, indeed, occasioned great agitation at Naples, and caused considerable uneasiness to the French. Nor was this uneasiness without a cause. Soon after the British forces had settled themselves in Ischia, two gentlemen arrived and solicited an interview with the general, announcing themselves as accredited delegates from the '*Patriotti*' of Italy. Sir John Stuart declined to see them, but commissioned Colonel Bunbury to hear and report to him what they had to say. They told him that they were delegated more particularly by the patriotic societies in the kingdom of Naples, but were in connection also with similar associations all over Italy; that their special business was to inquire the intentions of the British general; that if his object was simply to drive out the French, they would help him to the utmost of their power, which was great; but if he aimed at restoring Ferdinand and his queen to the throne of Naples, they would join the French against him.

Sir John Stuart declined to give any answer to this overture: perhaps his instructions withheld him from entertaining such offers; but, in spite of the representations of his staff, he appeared determined not to attempt anything further against the enemy on the mainland.

Finding, at length, that there seemed to be no chance of active operations, my father availed himself of the leave of absence which he had previously obtained, and returned in a boat to Messina, in order to catch the packet for England. But he had scarcely been at Messina more than two days, before, to his great astonishment, General Stuart and his whole army arrived there likewise.

Colonel Bunbury, with his wife and infant child, embarked on August 1, and sailed for England, not without regret, especially on my mother's part, at quitting a place where she had spent three happy years, and where she left many friends to whom she was warmly attached. Neither of them ever saw Sicily again, but they always delighted to call up the recollections of it, and my father felt an especially warm interest and sympathy in the noble struggle of the Sicilians for their liberties in 1848.

The homeward voyage was rough; they were delayed many days at Gibraltar by contrary winds; and it was not till towards the end of September that they landed at Falmouth.

Colonel Bunbury's services in Sicily had not been unobserved by some who were well qualified to appreciate them; and he had not been a month in England before he was surprised by an offer of the post of Under Secretary of State for the War Department.

Narratives of Some Passages in the Great War With France, from 1799 to 1810

Contents

Preface	37
Introduction	39
Narrative of the Campaign in North Holland, in 1799	50
Observations and Inquiries	72
Military Preparations 1800	84
Campaign in Egypt in 1801	101
Appendix to the Campaign in Egypt, 1801	148
Military Transactions in the Mediterranean, 1805-1810	159
Military Transactions in 1805 and 1810	167
Appendix: Papers Referred to in Military Transactions in the Mediterranean	309
The Battle of Maida	361

Preface

This volume is composed of two *Narratives* of transactions with which I had personal acquaintance, and of the outlines of our military history in Europe during the years which connect the periods of the narratives.

The campaign of the British and Russian Armies in North Holland in the autumn of 1799, forms the subject of the first personal *Narrative*. It is no more than a slight sketch of a great, but unfortunate, undertaking. I was then a very young man; but as one of the *aides-de-camp* of His Royal Highness the Commander-in-Chief, I enjoyed opportunities of seeing and hearing much that was unknown to the officers in general of my own age. There is no good account of this campaign, which was projected on a great scale, and from which great results had been anticipated. In the absence of better and more ample information as to the disastrous expedition of 1799, the present account is submitted to the public.

The second *Narrative* relates to the military and diplomatic measures pursued by England on the shores of the Mediterranean from the spring of 1805, to the close of 1810. Of these transactions I can venture to speak with more authority, because I was then at the head of the Quartermaster-General's Department, and enjoyed the confidence of successive commanders of the army. It is with regret that I have felt myself obliged to speak severely, and to condemn some passages in the conduct of two or three brave men, whose reputation has been cherished by their countrymen; but I could not tell my tale truly, nor could I show the causes of our failures, without unveiling the weaknesses of these individuals.

The two *Narratives* were written many years ago; and a few copies of each were privately printed in 1849, and 1851. The connecting out lines of our military operations have been written more recently; and

I feel it incumbent on me to express my regret that I have not been able to give a more satisfactory account of the Egyptian campaign in 1801. Brilliant and important as brief service was, there are scarcely any documents of importance to be found which come from high authority. The first commander, Sir Ralph Abercromby, was mortally wounded only thirteen days after the landing of his army; and all the correspondence and papers of Lord Hutchinson, who succeeded to the command, are supposed to have been lost at sea on their way to England. I had gathered some facts from conversations with military friends in past days, and particularly with Sir John Moore; and for matters of detail I have had recourse to the two ponderous quartos published in 1802, by Sir Robert Wilson and Major Walsh.

For the account which this volume contains of the Court of Naples and Palermo I offer no apology. That Court was too bad to be represented worse; but there was in it some consciousness of its want of faith towards the kingdom which was protecting by its forces those degraded sovereigns, and lavishing on them vast sums of money, which were shamefully misapplied. One instance of the anxiety of the court that the whole truth should not reach the ears of the British ministers may be here mentioned. I came to England on my private affairs in the autumn of 1809. Just as the packet was sailing from Messina, a messenger from Palermo was put on board.

Shortly after my arrival in London, I was surprised by a visit from the Prince Castelcicala, the Sicilian Ambassador, who had received instructions to tender for my acceptance the Order of Saint Ferdinand, or Saint something. The offer was declined with the courtesy which was due to the character of Castelcicala; but with unaltered sentiments as to his sovereigns and the Court of Palermo. It happened that a few weeks afterwards I was appointed Under-Secretary of State for the War Department; and I continued to hold that Office till it was abolished in 1816,

Henry Edward Bunbury.

Barton Hall,
June, 1854

Introduction

We have been so long accustomed to measure the efficiency and conduct of British troops by the standard, of that noble army which fought and conquered in the Spanish Peninsula, that men of the present generation can hardly form an idea of what the military forces of England really were when the great war broke out in 1793. Our army was lax in its discipline, entirely without system, and very weak in numbers. Each colonel of a regiment managed it according to his own notions, or neglected it altogether. There was no uniformity of drill or movement; professional pride was rare; professional knowledge still more so. Never was a kingdom less prepared for a stern and arduous conflict; and this fact may be fairly taken as a proof that Mr. Pitt had entertained no design of engaging in a war with France.

However, in the autumn of 1792, a sudden and fearful alarm had gathered over England. The events in Paris during the months of August and September had excited horror, and had aroused antipathy towards the French, while the increased audacity of revolutionary factions in Great Britain inspired a dread of immediate rebellion. The Republican armies of France had conquered the Austrian Low Countries, and were menacing our Allies in Holland. Our merchants were alarmed for their commerce; our landowners were anticipating invasion or revolution. There arose a general cry for measures calculated to meet the perils of the time.

In December, 1792, the militia of England was embodied, and additional recruits were ordered to be enlisted for the regular service, but to an amount far from adequate to the greatness of the occasion. The British Government still hoped to evade hostilities and was content to remain in a defensive position. All doubts, however, were soon terminated. In February, 1793, the French declared war against Great Britain and Holland, and they followed up their declaration by the immediate invasion of the latter country. Their general, Dumourier, broke into Holland in February at the head of not more than 13,000 men. But he knew how totally the Dutch were unprepared, and how generally they were disinclined to resist his attack.

Their military means were contemptible; their fortresses were unprovided, and they were deprived of one of the chief means of defending Holland by the severity of the winter, Dumourier reckoned on the effects of his audacity and promptitude; on the ease with which his cannon could pass the frozen waters; and on the disaffection which was borne by a large proportion of the people to the *Stadtholder's* government Within a fortnight the French made themselves masters of Breda, Klundert, and Gertruydenburg; nor did they encounter any serious resistance till they attacked Wilhelmstadt. Here a brave old soldier, Count Botzlaer, was in command. He infused spirit into his little garrison, and he brought the enemy to a stand.

In the meantime, the English ministers were trying, with the miserable means at their command, to afford some assistance to the House of Orange. About 1,700, of the foot guards, with a few scores of artillerymen, were all that could be mustered for this service in the first days of the crisis. But of proper vessels to transport them across the sea there were none. The troops wore huddled on the 25th of February on board of such empty colliers as could be found in the Thames, and by great good fortune they reached the coast of Holland without loss.

General Gerard Lake, with his brigade of Guards, brought ample strength to the garrison of Dort, and English gunboats gathered in the waters of Wilhelmstadt. Here, then, were the colours of Britain first waved in defiance of Republican France, and thus began the Great War.

Dumourier found himself baffled in the audacious hope of penetrating rapidly to Amsterdam. He at once retraced his steps, and fell back to Antwerp. In spite of the celerity both of his advance and his retreat he yet returned too late. The centre of his army had been engaged unsuccessfully in the siege of Maestricht. His right wing had been posted near Aix-la-Chapelle. It was attacked on the 8th of March by the Austrians, who, slow and cautious as they were, had yet been encouraged by the exposed position of this part of Dumourier's army, to risk a battle.

The French were completely defeated, the siege of Maestricht was immediately raised, and Dumourier arrived just in time to effect his junction with the retreating portion of his army. He rallied them, and restored some order and confidence; and strove by a series of obstinate, though partial actions, to arrest the march of the Austrians. But his struggle was vain: on the 18th of March he was defeated in a general engagement at Neerwinden; his soldiers were utterly disheartened, and the wave of war was rolled back to the frontier of France.

It is no part of my design to write a history on the war. But I wish to sketch, however slightly, the first services of our British troops in Europe, and to shew the inefficiency to which our military means had been brought through the neglect of our government during ten years of peace. The results may be painful to contemplate, but they afford a lesson which ought not to be forgotten.

When Dumourier quitted Antwerp, Lake advanced with his brigade of Guards to that city, and he there met three weak battalions of the line, which arrived from England under the command of Ralph Abercromby. The whole (barely mustering altogether 3,000 rank and file) moved onwards to Bruges and Ghent, while large bodies of Hanoverians and Hessians in British pay were arriving successively in the same neighbourhood. Thus, was formed an army of about 17,000 men, which was placed under the command of the Duke of York. Six or seven squadrons of light dragoons and some artillery arrived from England in May, and the columns then moved forward to co-operate with the Austrians on the frontier. But such was the condition of the British infantry at this time, that two of Abercromby's regiments were left behind, as being unfit to appear in the presence of an enemy!

As the British and Hanoverian troops were involved in the disasters which fell upon the Allied Army in the campaigns of 1793, and 1794, a popular outcry was raised in England against the Duke of York. Men were ready to attribute our failures to his unfitness for command, and even our ministers appeared to assent tacitly to a judgment which served to throw upon the shoulders of His Royal Highness much of the blame which ought to have rested on themselves. Theirs was the fatal plan of besieging Dunkirk; theirs the shame of its failure.

★★★★★★

Our government had promised to the duke the co-operation of a squadron, which should attack and bombard Dunkirk from seaward, while he assaulted the time-worn fortifications from the land side. Admiral Macbride was lying with this squadron in the Downs; but so far was the duke from meeting any assistance from the navy, that his lines, during the fortnight which he spent before the town, were exposed to a cannonade from half-a-dozen gunboats and Dunkirk privateers! Lord Chatham was then at the head of our Admiralty.

✶✶✶✶✶✶

Insisting on this selfish project, they drew off not only the Duke of York's force, but some 13,000 subsidised Austrians likewise, from the great army of the Allies, which had been up to that time successful in its operations, and was pressing with an overpowering strength upon the defeated and disheartened enemy. With this fatal separation of the armies began the tide of disaster which swept the Allies, within twelve months, beyond the Rhine.

After our defeats near Dunkirk, the troops of several nations which composed the Duke of York's *corps d' armée* recovered by a circuitous march their connexion with the main army, under the Prince of Saxe Coburg. They bore their parts handsomely in the actions which fell to their share in the latter part of 1793, and the spring of the succeeding year. Indeed, there was no lack of gallantry whenever our handfuls of British troops were allowed opportunities of closing with the enemy. The Guards, under General Lake, at Lincelles; the Fifteenth Light Dragoons at Villars-en-Cauchie; the weak brigade (Fourteenth, Thirty-Seventh, and Fifty-Third Regiment's) led by General Fox at Pont-à-chin, afforded brilliant examples of their national valour. But it must be remembered that the Duke of York never had more than 3,000 British infantry and about 700 Light Dragoons during the year 1793.

✶✶✶✶✶✶

In the first moments of alarm after the failure at Dunkirk our government sent three regiments of infantry to Ostend, and said they would have sent more but that they had no transports! However, within a month the three regiments were recalled and despatched to the West Indies!

✶✶✶✶✶✶

In 1794, he had many squadrons of our horsemen, but little more infantry, though by this time there had been large and efficient forces at the disposal of our ministers. They preferred sending a great proportion of their troops to encounter the yellow fever in the West Indies, and keeping another body at home to threaten an invasion of Brittany, which was never carried into effect.

The main strength of the Duke of York's division lay in the Hanoverians, and good and brave troops they were; but repeated actions soon wore down their numbers. It should be remembered also that the duke never held an independent command, with the exception of the unhappy attempt on Dunkirk. Before and after that lamentable project of the British cabinet His Royal Highness was subordinate to the Prince of Saxe Coburg. Of the latter it seems necessary to say a few words. Affable and courteous in his manners, this commander-in-chief of the allied armies was popular with his troops, and made himself agreeable for the time to those who were engaged to obey his orders; but this prince possessed few of the qualities necessary for the chief of a great army. Slow and cautious to an extreme, he never knew how to follow up success, or to rally under defeat.

It would have been less mischievous if he had been merely a bad general, but the weakness of his character led him to subserviency. In 1794, he became the tool of an Austrian faction, of which the minister Thugut was the chief. This Thugut had risen gradually from a low position till he had acquired a great influence over the young Emperor Francis. He worked slowly and cautiously, but he worked successfully, to bringing about a complete change in the policy of Austria. Instead of attempting to maintain the imperial sovereignty in the Low Countries, Thugut had woven in his dark mind a scheme by which the empire might gain advantages at the expense both of unsuspecting friends, and of the allies who were lavishing their money and shedding their blood in support of what they yet believed to be the views and interests of the cabinet of Vienna.

The provinces which now form the kingdom of Belgium were to be gradually abandoned to the French, in the base hope that, with their connivance, Austria might rob her German neighbours of an equivalent territory. While the contingent forces, commanded by the Duke of York and the Prince of Orange, were still fighting by the side of the Austrians, the measures by which the interests of England and of Holland were to be sacrificed, were carried silently into effect.

The consequences soon became apparent. The Duke of York's corps, now reduced to 13,000 or 14,000 men, had been detached from the Austrians under the pretext that he was to cover the country between Tournay and Ghent. In the latter days of June, 1794, His Royal Highness suddenly found himself in a very critical position, without support or connexion on either hand. The Austrians were in full retreat from the Sambre, and heavy columns of French were pressing forward on every side.

Even with Ostend the duke's communications were intercepted, though just at this time there arrived at that port 7,000 British infantry under the command of Lord Moira. The French were in possession of Courtrai, and were pointing towards Ghent. The duke, abandoned by the Austrians, had no course left but to make a rapid and difficult retreat between the advancing columns of the enemy, and endeavour to reach the Scheldt. He accomplished his object, after having been joined by Lord Moira with 5,000 of his men. This general, who had been sent from England to secure Ostend, had found on his arrival that the position of the Duke of York's little army was extremely dangerous. With great promptitude and much skill, Lord Moira passed to the northward of Ghent before the enemy arrived there in force; and he effected his junction with the Hanoverians and the British in the neighbourhood of Alost.

The treachery of the Austrian ministers had been equalled, if not surpassed, by those of Prussia. According to a treaty ratified by the cabinets of London and Berlin, there ought to have been by this time an army of 62,000 subsidised Prussian soldiers on the Meuse or the Scheldt, for the defence of Holland.

The Prussian ministers had received 300,000*l*., in advance, but they sent not one soldier. The chance of doing more than save the British and Hanoverian Army seemed to be nearly at an end. The people of Holland were known to be thoroughly disaffected; and their troops, and even most of their officers, were unwilling to fight. Yet the English, having received large reinforcements, still cherished a hope that positions on the Meuse and the Waal, flanked by the Dutch fortresses and inundations, would retard the progress of the enemy, and that the winter would put an end to the campaign. But the French, under Pichegru, were not to be arrested in their victorious career by waters or by winter. When the latter came, a frost of unusual severity rendered the former passable on every side; while it inflicted dreadful sufferings on our retreating and disheartened columns.

Many partial actions were fought without any heavy loss of men on our side, but the numbers who perished from hardships of every kind, and from the inefficiency of our hospital establishments, were deplorably great; and seldom has an army endured a more fearful trial than that which struggled through the intense severity of the winter of 1794-5, while making good its retreat from the Waal to the Weser.

After this rough sketch of the disheartening service on which the British troops were first employed, I must trace some of the features which unhappily characterized our military men more than half a century ago. I have already, said that during the campaigns of 1793 and '94, our officers and soldiers distinguished themselves frequently in battle, but if we are to consider the Duke of York's corps as an army, it will be found to have been lamentably defective. Every department of the staff was more or less deficient, particularly the Commissariat and Medical branches. The regimental officers in those days, were, as well as their men, hard drinkers; and the latter, under a loose discipline, were much addicted to marauding, and to acts of licentious violence, which made them detested by the people of the country.

Some of the cavalry, dashing fellows in a fight, piqued, themselves on being "rough and ready;" to which might justly have been added "drunken and disorderly." But most of the infantry, while under the leading of Abercromby, Lake, and Fox, were kept in better order. On the sad retreat, indeed, through the Dutch provinces, and under the various miseries to which our troops were then exposed, the discipline of the whole gave way, and it was with great difficulty that any subordination was preserved.

※※※※※※

The army was at this time commanded by the Hanoverian General Walmoden, but the British troops were under the immediate orders of General Harcourt. Lord Moira had returned to England shortly after he had joined the Duke of York; and the latter had resigned his command in December, apparently to meet the wishes of the British cabinet.

※※※※※※

In the spring of 1795, the shattered remains of the British troops returned to England, The results of their campaign had been ill calculated to improve their discipline, or to excite a military spirit in the country. Not had our aims acquired reputation on land in any other quarter. In 1793, a short attempt to defend Toulon had ended in our expulsion, and a few regiments, afterwards employed in Corsica, found no opportunities of gaining distinction. So inefficient were the means even in the naval service of England, that, small as our army was, it was required to furnish battalions to serve as marines on board our fleets. With the year 1794, began the fatal passion for carrying on the war in every part of the West Indies, though the Bulam fever was raging in all quarters.

Multitudes of brave men perished in this and the two succeeding years, for the sake of grasping more sugar-islands, and particularly in the vain attempt to hold St Domingo, Our infantry and artillery were drained to the lowest point, by the incessant demands of our War Minister for fresh supplies of men to replace the victims of the yellow fever. To the mania for prosecuting this ill-omened service is to be ascribed, more than to any other cause, the inefficiency of the British Army during several years.

******

Some idea of the dreadful waste of men may be formed by looking to the returns laid before Parliament. From these it appears that in the year 1794, there were "killed, or *dead in the service*," 18,596 soldiers. And that in the two succeeding years there were discharged, "on account of wounds or *infirmity*," no less than 40,639 men.

******

Even those regiments which returned from that fatal climate were long unfit for service: they consisted of feeble, worn-out invalids. Nor, while sketching the condition and general character of the British Army in those days, can I omit to mention the manner in which (the ordinary recruiting being found insufficient) men were obtained, in order to fill up the enormous void occasioned by the deaths in the West Indies. It is useful to note this matter, because it serves to account in part for the degraded state of the service, and the odium which long attended it I will not dwell on the political jobs which characterized the raising of many regiments in Ireland, though I cannot forget that faith was often broken with the men who had been thus enlisted.

The officers, having obtained their steps of rank, were contented; the nominal corps were reduced; and the men were drafted into regiments in India or St. Domingo. But the most crying infamy was that which resulted from the employment of crimps on a very large scale. Our government made contracts with certain scoundrels (bearing the king's commission!) who engaged to furnish so many hundred men each for such and such sums of money.

The deeds of atrocity, to say nothing of the frauds, which attended the working of this scheme, could hardly be credited in the present times. They occasioned many serious riots, and they spread the taint of disaffection to the service.

There is little to be told of our military achievements during the years 1795-96, and '97. The Cape of Good Hope was captured, and Ceylon, and some of the Indian spice-islands. These were valuable acquisitions; but still they required garrisons to retain possession of them, as well as of the sugar-colonies which we had taken from France; and thus the members of our regular British infantry were always kept down to a lower level at home than the main objects of the war demanded. One material improvement, however, is to be dated from this period: an uniform system of drill and movement, both of the cavalry and infantry, was introduced and carried into effect.

General David Dundas had the merit of having compiled these regulations (which were mainly founded on those of the Prussian Army), and they were warmly patronised by the Duke of York, who was now Commander-in-Chief. The administration of our army improved gradually in every respect; and at the same time the pay of the soldiers, which had been shamefully low, was augmented. Camps of instruction were formed during the summers of several successive years; and an uniformity of drill and of movement was established throughout the service.

In May, 1798, Sir Home Popham, commanding a squadron on the coast of Flanders, unfortunately imagined that it was desirable to destroy certain sluice-gates near Ostend. He was a clever man, and he persuaded our War Minister to send over a brigade of picked troops under General Coote for this service. They landed; blew up the gates; and then found that a heavy surf (no uncommon circumstance on those shores), made their re-embarkation impracticable. These fine fellows, after fighting gallantly against the great force which gathered from every side to assail them, were obliged to lay down their arms. It was in this way that, to use the happy expression of Sheridan, we "nibbled at the rind of France;" and in this way we wasted bit by bit the sinews of our military strength.

Immediately after this attempt the rebellion in Ireland broke out. The regular infantry in that kingdom was weak in numbers; there were some pretty good battalions of Fencibles; and the Yeomanry in arms were numerous and fierce; but the majority of the regiments of Irish Militia were not to be depended on. The want of discipline in this army was become notorious. Sir Ralph Abercromby, who had just succeeded to Lord Carhampton as Commander of the Forces, condemned in general orders (February, 1798) the disgraceful licentiousness of the troops. For this wise and honest attempt to check the abuses which dishonoured the service, this gallant veteran was immediately recalled by our government.

Some notion of the conduct of the troops in Ireland may be formed by the recollection that one regiment of heavy dragoons was broken up altogether; and that to render the stigma perpetual, its number has remained a blank in the army-list. Another regiment of horse ran away without striking a stroke in the action with the French at Castlebar, and had the credit of having galloped thirty miles without a halt. The

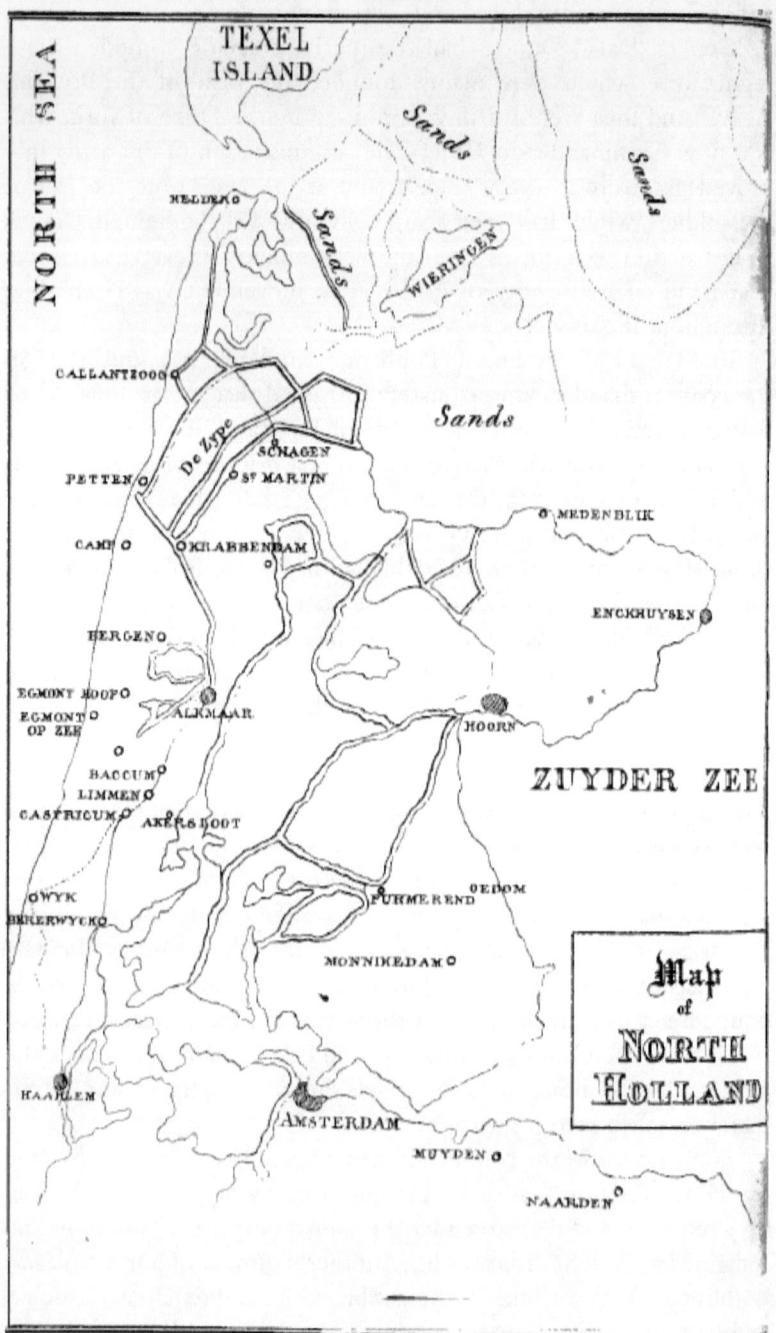

nature of the warfare, and the manner in which the first part of it was conducted, tended still further to injure the discipline of regiments and to demoralise both the men and officers.

In giving this cursory sketch of the British military service during the years which preceded 1799, my object has been to afford some insight into the average state of our army when the great enterprise of that year was undertaken. A treaty was concluded between the British Government and the Emperor of Russia in June; the former engaging to furnish 13,000 men, and the latter 17,000, with the object of expelling the French from the United Provinces. It was agreed that this allied army should be placed under the command of the Duke of York; and it was understood that the ulterior operations might not be confined to the Dutch territory, but might effect an important diversion in favour of the Allies on the Upper Rhine and in Switzerland. Both England and Russia were so thoroughly in earnest, that both contributed more than their respective quotas of troops. Each sent to the war more than 18,000 soldiers.

Narrative of the Campaign in North Holland, in 1799

The expedition under Sir Ralph Abercromby, which may be considered as the advanced guard of the Allied Army destined to act against the French in Holland and the Low Countries, left the shores of England on the 13th of August, 1799, escorted by a strong squadron of ships of war, commanded by Admiral Mitchell. The military force was composed of the

1st Guards		2 Battalions	Maj.-Gen. D'Oyley
Coldstream Ditto	}	2 Battalions	Maj.-Gen. Burrard
3rd Ditto			
2nd (Queen's) Reg.	1 "		⎫
27th "	1 "		
29th "	1 "		Major-Gen. Coote
85th "	1 "		⎭
1st (Royal)	1 "		⎫
25th "	1 "		
49th "	1 "		Maj.-Gen. Moore
79th "	1 "		
92nd "	1 "		⎭
23rd "	1 "		} Col. Macdonald
55th "	1 "		

with artillery, &c., fully 10,000 fighting men, and of a good quality.

The orders which our commanders had received were in some degree discretionary, A landing on the island of Goree was prescribed as the first object; and from thence it was proposed that the united force of British and Russian troops should penetrate into the heart of the Low Countries.

But the Helder was a point which the British Government had much at heart, for the sake of capturing the Dutch fleet in the Texel, and destroying the naval magazines at that station. Although our expedition put to sea at the most favourable season, such was the stormy and perverse character of that disastrous year, that the landing of the troops at the mouths of the Scheldt and the Meuse was found to be impracticable; nor was it till the 21st of August that our ships were able to approach the coast near the entrance of the Texel.

Preparations were made for landing on the following day, but in vain, for our fleet was again forced to sea by a gale of wind; nor was it till the 26th that it could return to the point which our commanders had in view, and the transports could be anchored near the shore. (It appears that Abercromby and Mitchell had agreed not to persevere in attempting to land at the Helder beyond the 26th.)

Although a heavy surf was still breaking on the beach, the debarkation of the troops began at daybreak on the 27th; several boats were swamped, and a few of our soldiers were drowned.

As our fleet had been descried by the enemy six days before, the Dutch General Daendels had gained time to collect five or six thousand of infantry, with some cavalry and artillery; and these he kept concealed among the sand-hills which skirt the shore. Immediately in front of that line of beach which the British had selected for their landing, these "Dunes" recede a little, but they close in and become bolder and more steep towards Callantzoog which lay upon our right; and here the enemy held the main body of his troops, ready to plunge upon our extreme flank if we should attempt to move forward towards the Helder town.

To the landing of the British soldiers, though it was rendered slow by the violence of the surf, no direct opposition was offered; but, as soon as six of our battalions (the brigades under Coote and Macdonald) were ashore and formed, and they began to move forward, they were assailed by a heavy fire, and a vigorous attack on their right flank.

✶✶✶✶✶✶

Sir J. Pulteney led them. He was thought to have pushed on rather too hastily, and too far, so as to have got his division engaged under disadvantages with the enemy's main body, and with cavalry and guns.

✶✶✶✶✶✶

Forced to change their front, and make head against the superior force of the enemy on the side of Callantzoog, our troops were at the same time cramped and confused by the narrowness of their ground; the strip of beach not allowing of a front of more than one battalion in that direction.

The enemy from the crests of the sand-dunes kept up a constant and destructive fire, while he was himself sheltered by their folds from the guns of the British shipping. None of our field artillery was yet landed, and for some hours our brave infantry, though reinforced by D'Oyley's brigade of guards, had to maintain a trying struggle; but they would not give ground; and they fought so hard that they fairly wore out the enemy.

★★★★★★

Some parts of Moore's brigade were on shore early; and when a good proportion had been landed and got into order, he advanced towards Helder town, from whence riflemen came out and skirmished with his advanced parties.

★★★★★★

Towards the evening the Dutch gave up the contest, and retreated some five or six miles to a position between the Alkmaar canal and the sea. The loss of the enemy in killed or wounded was probably small; but the disadvantages under which the invaders fought necessarily exposed the three brigades which were engaged to a serious loss of men; and a large proportion of the superior officers of the staff fell under the aim of the Dutch riflemen. Two lieut.-colonels and about fifty men were killed on the spot; and Lieut.-General Sir James Pulteney, five field officers, and nearly 400 others were wounded.

The debarkation of troops, guns, and supplies was completed without further difficulty; and Moore's and Burrard's brigades were prepared to move forward at daybreak on the 28th. Near the Helder Point stands the village of that name. It was at the time I am speaking of, partially fortified, having heavy batteries towards the sea, commanding the channel of the Texel and the deep water within it; but on the land side the works were imperfect and neglected.

In this place the enemy kept a motley garrison (to the amount of 1,800 or 2,000 men of one sort or other) up to the evening of the 27th; but, as soon as the issue of the fight on the beach was decided, they prepared to withdraw, spiked the guns in the batteries, and, when darkness fell, they retreated silently across the marshes and along the shores of the Zuyder Zee.

At the same time the Dutch squadron, which had been lying in the Texel channel, dropped inward as far as their draught of water would allow. In the morning of the 28th, Moore took possession of the Helder, with the naval arsenal and storehouses, well filled with ordnance of all descriptions; and the same evening there arrived from England two strong brigades of infantry (young troops); and these were quickly followed by the 11th Light Dragoons. But it was not till the morning of the 30th that Admiral Mitchell was able (as the Dutch had removed the buoys and landmarks) to lead his squadron through the shoals and narrows of the Texel channel, and to approach the enemy's fleet. A summons to hoist the Orange flag and surrender the ships to the *Stadtholder*, under the protection of England, speedily produced the desired effect.

Seven ships of the line, three of 50 guns, and several frigates were given up without firing a single shot; though their admiral vapoured, and declared that he and his officers were deserted by their cowardly crews, who refused to fight. (This was Story: the same man who deserted the brave DeWinter, and ran away from the Battle of Camperdown in 1707.) However this might be, here was the *English* object of the expedition achieved; the Dutch fleet, arsenal, and stores were in our possession. Happy would it have been if our ministers or generals had not set our army to the task of fighting its way to Amsterdam through the long defile of North Holland.

On the 1st of September, Sir Ralph Abercromby, leaving two battalions of the young troops at the Helder, for the protection and escort of stores and supplies, marched onward with about 12,000 men, and took up a very strong position, having its right at Petten on the German ocean, and its left at the Oude Sluys on the Zuyder Zee; with the cross canal of the Zuype along his front, and the great canal which leads from near the Helder to Alkmaar, passing through his centre. Before and behind his line stretched wide extents of low meadows and cultivated lands, well drained by wide and deep ditches communicating with various canals. At the salient angle of the position stands the village of Krabbendam; and here the high road from Amsterdam and Alkmaar, running alongside the great canal, entered the line occupied by the British.

Another road, from the side of Hoorn, entered near the village of St. Martin: and the great dyke which bounded the Zuype, and formed as it were the rampart of our defence, was also accessible here and there by means of minor dykes which abut upon it. The most important of these latter approaches was at a point between Krabbendam and Petten; and the defence of this part of the line was intrusted to the two brigades of guards. In the village of Krabbendam were posted the two battalions of the 20th regiment. Moore's brigade extended from thence to St. Martins, which village was held by Colonel Brent Spencer with the 40th regiment belonging to General Don's brigade.

The six battalions under Coote and Macdonald, and the 11th Light Dragoons were cantoned in rear of the centre, and at hand to support any part of the line which might be seriously attacked.

******

I have been thus diffuse in describing the position of the Zuype; because it has always appeared to me that the chief questions touching the conduct of the campaign hinged on this very important line of defence.

******

Sir Ralph Abercromby knew that the Duke of York and more British troops were following, and that a Russian Army was on the sea: therefore he waited quietly in the strong position he had taken up. The enemy knew as much, and were therefore eager to attack before the great mass of the Allies should be gathered and prepared to act. Large bodies both of French and Dutch troops had come up; and General Brune had taken the command of the Republican Army. He lost no time; he held the British troops cheap; nor was he deterred by the strength of the position they occupied. On came the enemy in three columns at break of day on the 10th of September. Their left led by Vandamme consisted entirely of French troops, and poured impetuously along the dyke, which I have mentioned as being defended by the English guards.

At the same time the centre of the Republicans, under Dumonceau, advanced with equal rapidity along the high road, and assailed the village of Krabbendam with headlong fury. Their right column, composed of Dutch troops and commanded by Daendels, attacked St. Martin's, but with less perseverance; and perhaps this was designed rather to draw our attention to that side, and weaken our defence at Krabbendam. Rushing forward without any cover, the column under Vandamme made their assault, and persevered in it with reckless bravery: but they had not a chance of success: they were mown down by the steady fire of Burrard's brigade of guards and his field pieces; and after suffering an enormous loss of men, they doggedly drew off to their previous quarters.

Nor was the attack on Krabbendam less marked by valour: the Republicans penetrated into the village, and in spite of the destructive fire from the houses, they fought hand to hand with our troops. But the 20th was a regiment that never would be beaten; and their commander, Colonel George Smyth, was an officer of first-rate ability. (This excellent officer died, unfortunately for our service just at the beginning of the Spanish war, before he had attained the rank of a general officer.) To him Sir Ralph Abercromby had, specially assigned the defence of this important post, and worthily did he discharge his trust. Although three-fourths of the two battalions of the 20th were volunteers recently received from the militia, they had already been imbued with the spirit of the old regiment; and so gallantly did they maintain their post, that there was no need of moving up the brigades in reserve to their support.

Dumonceau relinquished his attack and retreated; but Colonel Macdonald issuing from the lines quickened his movement, and increased his loss, capturing a gun, pontoons, and a good many men. Daendels, whose troops had been less compromised, drew off from before St. Martin with little loss; but the number of killed and wounded in the other two columns of the enemy was very great, probably more than a thousand men. On the side of the English only thirty-seven were killed; General Moore was slightly wounded, Colonel Smyth severely; six other officers of the 20th, and four of different regiments, with about 150 soldiers were likewise wounded.

This action of the 10th of September, was of much importance. It confirmed the confidence of the British troops in themselves and their commanders; and it proved how easily the position of the Zuype might be held by 12,000 or 14,000 men. On this day little had been done to strengthen it by artificial means; no heavy guns had been brought up, nor any redoubts constructed. Musketry and a few field-pieces had been found amply sufficient to render futile the most desperate assaults of the enemy. Though his attempt was rash, it was made with a reckless bravery which served only to swell the slaughter of his men.

Such was the posture of our affairs when the Duke of York arrived to assume the command of the Allied Army. He landed at the Helder on the evening of the 13th, and had the satisfaction of meeting there the first division of the Russian Army under their general-in-chief, D' Hermann. Reinforcements from England, light cavalry, artillery, and the young regiments recruited from the militia, continued to pour in daily. Within the week, the second division of Russians had arrived. Altogether, there was a great army, and all things looked smilingly, except the weather.

★★★★★★

About 18,000 British, and 12,000 Russians. Of the former about three-fifths might be accounted good troops, the rest raw militia-men, unacquainted with their officers. The 15th Light

Dragoons joined the army after the battle of the 15th September, and likewise 3,000 or 4,000 Russian infantry, with 300 Cossacks.

******

The duke's headquarters being fixed at Schagen Brug, the newcomers moved up in quick succession; and all the villages from the Helder to the Zuype were crowded with troops; the post of honour, on the right, being conceded to the Russians.

Whatever might have been the notions instilled into the British Government with respect to the political feelings of the Dutch, certainly there had appeared in North Holland nothing (except among the crews of their ships of war) to favour the idea that the people would assist us in restoring the House of Orange, The Dutch troops had fought against us with great bravery; nor, though they had been beaten, was the desertion from their ranks considerable. The farmers and others within our lines lounged about with their pipes in their mouths, as silent and sullen spectators of an unpleasant disturbance. They were willing enough to sell us their cattle, and let us their boats at good prices, but otherwise they appeared passive and gloomy.

The Hereditary Prince of Orange had arrived early; had hoisted his flag, had been joined by six or eight young men of family, who had made their escape from different provinces, and he was busying himself in endeavouring to form a regiment of his countrymen out of the deserters and prisoners. But it was sufficiently clear that, however odious the French domination might be in the provinces on the other side of the Zuyder Zee, there was little goodwill towards us in North Holland. If the Allies were to make their direct way to Amsterdam, it must be done by sheer fighting; and the enemy was every day receiving reinforcements, and fortifying his successive lines of defence.

Such being the state of things it was resolved at a Council of War (for all operations were to be directed by a Council of War) to move forward without delay, and make a general attack upon the enemy's position on the 19th of September. Now this position, immediately in our front, was very short, very strong, and held by above 20,000 men, of whom two-thirds were French. Their right, composed of the Dutch troops under Daendels, was strongly entrenched at Oudt Carspel, on the high causeway along which ran the great road to Alkmaar; their left was massed in and about the little town of Bergen, lying at the foot of the dunes (sandhills), and surrounded by thickets, enclosures, and woodlands.

Between Oudt Carspel and Bergen stretches an expanse of low meadows, reclaimed fen, intersected by numerous ditches, broad, deep, and full of water. Two or three small villages intervene, in which the French were strongly posted, with abundance of artillery, and the approaches rendered more difficult by abattis, palisades, &c. The dunes between Bergen and the sea present a formidable barrier of defence, from two to four miles wide, some hundreds of feet in height, and broken and twisted in the most irregular forms, like huge waves in an ocean stirred by tempests. Along their crests, and overhanging the road from Petten to Bergen, were posted the advanced guards and light detachments of the French, overlooking our lines, and flanking the route by which the Russians were to advance.

The object of the Allies was to arrive at Amsterdam; and the first step towards this object was the driving of the enemy from his position in our front. This was to be accomplished either by forcing our direct way through Bergen, Egmont, and Alkmaar; or by seizing Hoorn, which lay in advance of our left, and pushing forward from thence a powerful column, which should turn all the redoubts and works along the great canal, and thus enable the centre of the British to march straight upon Alkmaar, and there join the former column. In this case, the right of the Allied Army should have been held back, watching the left wing of the French, and ready to fall upon its flank and rear, if it should march from Bergen and Egmont to the relief of the divisions defending Alkmaar. By our following this second plan of operations it is probable that the enemy would have been obliged to fall back at once to the well-known position of Beverwyk.

It was the business of the Allies, therefore, either to bring the whole weight of their numerical superiority to bear upon the enemy in our fronts or to keep him occupied by demonstrations and false attacks, while a column strong enough to take care of itself, say 14,000 men, should march upon Hoorn, and from thence upon Alkmaar or Purmerend. But it was not to be forgotten that the movements of such a column from our left required a considerable time: for Hoorn was at the distance of fourteen or fifteen miles from our lines, and there were thirteen more from Hoorn to Alkmaar, while the latter town was scarcely eight miles from the front of our position. (Moore's strong brigade was nearer to Hoorn, having been sent on the 14th to occupy villages in front of our left.)

However, the Council of War resolved on the adoption of a plan which afforded our army neither the advantage of superior numbers, nor that of the time necessary for the effect of a movement on the side of Hoorn. It was determined that Sir Ralph Abercromby should be detached in that direction with about 10,000 British, but he was not to begin his march till dusk on the 18th, and at daybreak on the 19th, the Russians and the remainder of the British Army were to assault the positions of the enemy in their front. Our right was to march straight upon Bergen, our left along the high road to Alkmaar, and an intermediate column, which we may call our centre, was to move across the low meadows I have described, connecting the two former, and ready to support either the one or the other, as occasion might require. Some detachments were left at the principal posts in our lines with the artillery; and there marched forth (exclusive of Abercromby's column) nearly 20,000 men, to attack an army fully equal in numbers, and, as I have shown, very strongly posted.

Before the day broke, our right column poured impetuously forth. It consisted of twelve battalions of Russians, followed by Manners's brigade of English militiamen, and the 7th Light Dragoons. They were led by General D'Hermann, a brave and willing soldier, but possessing few of the higher qualities of a commander. Advancing along the road which runs at the foot of the sand-hills, the Russians pushed forward in one solid mass, overturning everything that stood in their way, storming the village of Schorel and other posts without a halt, regardless of the great loss of men they suffered, nor paying attention to the course taken by the enemies whom they dislodged.

On, on, on to Bergen! In this reckless fashion, D'Hermann forced his way, in a surprisingly short time, to the enemy's entrenchments, and the outskirts of the town; but the road behind him was strewed with his dead and wounded; the rear of his Russians were straggling after plunder in the villages; and his column arrived at its main object, jaded and in sad confusion. Still on, on! the fearless mass burst into the midst of the French, and for a few minutes they were masters of Bergen. If there had been a reserve, fresh and in good order, the battle was won. But there was nothing but the one mass of confused men. Such people were not to expect victory over the active and intelligent Frenchmen on their own ground. Besides the enemy's reserve in Bergen itself, all those who had been driven before the Russians, all who had been pushed out of the villages, had thrown themselves into the sand-hills, and were now swarming above the right flank and rear of D Hermann's entangled column.

Exposed to a tremendous fire crossing from every angle, the Russians were unable to do more; they fell into hopeless confusion; Generals D' Hermann and Tchitchagoff were made prisoners; and the mass rolled back along the road by which they had advanced. Still these Russians defended themselves desperately against their pursuers; and they reached and got through the village of Schorel, though it was already enveloped in flames by their own plunderers. Here the enemy was checked for some time by Manners's brigade, supported by successive detachments from General Dundas's column; and the Russians, whose ammunition was spent, were enabled to withdraw within the lines.

In the meantime David Dundas, with the centre column, which was intended to clear the low meadow country between the road to Bergen on its right, and that to Alkmaar on its left, advanced as soon as there was sufficient daylight to cross the wet ditches (by means of flying bridges) and attacked Walmenhuysen, a village occupied by the French with a considerable body of troops and many guns. (This column was composed of the two brigades of Guards and Prince William's brigade of militiamen supported by three battalions of Russians and two squadrons of the 11th Light Dragoons.) This post was carried in a very good style, the 1st Guards forcing it at one extremity, while Sedmoratzky, with three battalions of Russians, entered at the other. It soon, however, became necessary for General Dundas to detach a part of his troops to cover the left flank of D' Hermann's column; and two battalions to support and cover that under Sir Jas, Pulteney. Advancing with the remainder, Dundas made himself master of Schoreldam; and he maintained this post till the final retreat of the right column from Schorel, obliged him likewise to retire within the lines.

The third column under Sir James Pulteney, was composed of Coote's brigade, Don's four battalions of militiamen, and two squadrons of the 11th Light Dragoons. They advanced at daybreak along the high causeway leading to Alkmaar, flanked by the great canal on their right, and confined on the other side by a low stripe of mud and a broad wet ditch. Along the canal three gunboats, each carrying a 12-pound carronade, manned by seamen under the command of Sir Home Popham, kept pace with the head of the column. The posts occupied by the Dutch troops under Daendels at the head of the Lange Dyke, proved to be very strong, and their artillery swept the causeway and canal with destructive effect.

Owing to the nature of the ground it was very difficult for the British to extend their front, or to advance with rapidity. Their loss of men became considerable, and the Militia brigade (excepting the 40th Regiment under Brent Spencer) fell into much confusion. However, their straggling condition was observed by General Dundas, who had advanced more prosperously on their right, and he detached the 3rd Guards and another battalion to their help. A rush was made at the Dutch entrenchments; their batteries were carried; and their troops driven through Oudt Carspel and along the causeway to within a short distance of Alkmaar, But by this time the irremediable rout of the Russian column made it necessary for Sir James Pulteney to halt; and in the evening he received orders to retire immediately within the lines of the Zuype. He brought back a great many prisoners, but was obliged to leave the enemy's guns in the entrenchments he had carried.

The enemy had followed up the retreat of our troops with great activity and boldness, and the French now shewed themselves in such numbers opposite to the right of our position, and to the village of Krabbendam, that we began to feel apprehensions of their making attacks on the lines, which (under the actual circumstances) might be dangerous. A great part of our army was in sad confusion. Of the Russians there remained only three battalions under Sedmoratzky in a condition to fight. The rest of their troops had dispersed, officers as well as men, as soon as they got within their lines.

No attempt was made to supply them with ammunition, to keep a company together, or even to plant a sentinel. Some of the newly formed militia regiments of the English were in great disorder; a large proportion of their officers had fallen; and the men were panic-stricken by this result of their first encounter with an enemy. Pulteney's division was far in advance, and Abercromby's still further on the left. There remained little to trust to but our artillery and D'Oyley's brigade of Guards, which having been severely engaged, was arriving, much jaded, and with but little ammunition.

******

I cannot help recounting here an anecdote which serves to illustrate the unyielding spirit of the English soldier. As the shots of the French who were following our rear-guard came thicker and closer, the Duke of York grew uneasy about the post of Krabbendam, and he sent me off to find any of our troops which might have entered our lines near that point, and to direct them to return and occupy the village, Krabbendam touched the lines on the outer side; and through it ran the high road from Alkmaar to the Helder. The holding of this little place was essential to the security of our position; and nine days before the enemy had exposed himself to a great loss of men in desperate attempts to take it from Sir Ralph Abercromby.

But such was the discomfiture, and such the want of good handling of the troops during this retreat of the 19th September, that battalion after battalion passed through the village and entered the lines, without finding any general officer to give an order or a thought to the important object of keeping hold of Krabbendam.

I rode till, at a short distance within the lines, I found one of the battalions of the 1st Guards, under the command of Colonel Maitland, resting on their arms in column on the muddy road I delivered the duke's orders to the colonel, and begged he would not lose a moment in returning with me to Krabbendam, for the French were close at hand.

He told me that his battalion was tired out; that they had been hotly engaged many hours, had lost a large proportion of officers and men, and that their ammunition was nearly spent. I insisted, and urged the danger, and the fatal consequences which might ensue. Maitland (a brave officer, who was mortally wounded afterwards in the battle of the 6th October) still demurred. He assured me that his men were quite worn out; and he appeared to have lost the powers of his mind under fatigue of body and anxiety.

At this moment a grenadier, lifting his chin fixing the muzzle of the musket on which he was leaning, said in a loud and steady voice, "Give us some more cartridges, and we will see what can be done." The officers who were anxiously clustering about us at the head of the column, caught up the prompter's word. Maitland cried, "Shoulder arms!" They marched for Krabbendam; and I galloped to find and bring to them a supply of ammunition.

*****

However, means were found to make a show at the heads of the dykes, and the enemy's troops, after some skirmishing, contented themselves with having beaten us, and withdrew to their former positions.

It is necessary now to see what was done by the 10 or 11,000 British troops detached under the command of Sir Ralph Abercromby. In obedience to the orders of the Council of War, he collected his column, consisting of Moore's, Lord Chatham's, Lord Cavan's, and Macdonald's brigades; this last being doubled in number by the addition of one battalion of grenadiers and one of light infantry, taken from the strongest of the Militia regiments. Two squadrons of the 18th Light Dragoons accompanied this column. After six o' clock in the evening of the 18th of September, they began their march under a heavy rain, which continued all the night.

It had been expected that Sir Ralph should arrive at Hoorn by midnight; and that after giving his troops three or four hours' rest, he should prosecute his march on Alkmaar. If this design could have been carried out the positions of the enemy would have been turned: but even then, a sufficient time had not been allowed; for if Abercromby's column had appeared near Alkmaar at so early an hour as nine in the morning of the 19th, it would still have been too late to have decided the retreat of the French before they had routed the Russians at Bergen. But see what took place. Sir Ralph's 10,000 men, with their cannon, had to march in a pitch-dark night, and under torrents of rain, along one narrow paved causeway, flanked on both sides by low stripes of deep mud, which were confined only by broad ditches filled to the brim. We did not arrive at the gates of Hoorn till between three and four o clock in the morning, and then there was some delay in entering.

******

There happened this night one of those instances of unaccountable panic among brave troops which sometimes defeat in the strangest manner the plans of the best generals. In the present case it was attended by no mishap; but I feel far from sure, that if there had been 500 dashing fellows ready to rush recklessly out of the portals of Hoorn, they might not have dispersed our 11,000 men. The accident was this. At the head of our column marched a squadron of the 18th Light Dragoons under their young colonel, the gallant Charles Stewart (the late Marquis of Londonderry): they were followed by two six-pounders, and these by the 23rd and 55th Regiments, (hard-biting soldiers) who formed what was called the reserve, commanded by Colonel Macdonald.

When the advanced party arrived at the very gate of Hoorn, without being fired at or challenged, some staff officers (I being one) who had been sent to the front by Abercromby, knocked for admittance. No answer was returned; the knocking was repeated, and a loud hail to the gatekeeper was given.

In the meantime, the wearied infantry had grounded their arms, and stood leaning beneath the pelting rain, and more than half asleep, on their muskets. At length a sentinel was roused from his slumbers; he peeped over the gate, and dimly discerning a crowd of horsemen, he shouted an alarm: the guard waked up, and hastened noisily to draw more bolts and chains, while their drum was beaten to awaken the *burghers.*

Our officers cried loudly, "Open your gates, or they shall be blown down by our cannons!" and to enforce the effect of this threat, the dragoons were ordered to open to the right and left, so as to let the two guns be run up to the front.

Instead of giving the word of command quietly, the leading officer shouted, "Back, back, make way for the guns!"—"Back, back," was loudly repeated by the dragoon officers. Our jaded infantry were roused from their unconscious slumbers by the sudden clatter of the horses on the pavement, the rattling of the cannon wheels, and this unhappy cry of "back, back." In an instant the 23rd and 55th broke like a flock of sheep, plunging into the deep mud at the sides of the causeway, and dreaming for some minutes that they had been surprised and charged by a sortie of cavalry! The confusion was stopped in time; the Dutchmen opened their gates; and the reserve recovered their senses and their ranks. Heartily ashamed of themselves they were, for there were no braver fellows in our army.

★★★★★★

Our men had been under arms twelve hours: they were dead tired; nor could they have been fit to resume their march much before midday. But before midday the main body of the Allies was beaten out of the field. Sir Ralph Abercromby dispatched me at an early hour, to apprise the Duke of York of the state of affairs on the side of Hoorn; but though I was well mounted, and took short cuts across the marshes, I did not join His Royal Highness till the Russians were in full retreat, and Dundas was beginning to fall back. Another *aide-de-camp* was dispatched immediately to recall Abercromby personally, as his advice was required without delay; and to order that his column should retread their steps, and resume their quarters within the lines of the Zuype.

★★★★★★

It was the opinion of General Moore and others, that Abercromby's column ought to have been directed to profit by Pulteney's success, and to have co-operated with him in attacking Alkmaar, instead of being withdrawn to the lines.

★★★★★★

This disastrous day cost the British Army above 50 officers and 1,000 men; and the loss of the Russians was probably not less than 2,500; while on the other hand the enemy suffered much less in killed and wounded, though he left nearly 2,000 Dutch prisoners in our hands. Nor was this the worst. From this day there was a want of confidence and of cordiality between the Allies. D' Hermann, who remained a prisoner in the hands of the French, was probably a bad general, but he was a brave, zealous and straightforward fellow. His successor in the command of the Russians, General D' Essen, without possessing more military abilities, was false, intriguing, and ill-disposed towards the British. On the other hand, the Duke of York took up a violent contempt, as well as dislike, of the Russians. He ridiculed them at his table, and talked of them disparagingly, and too loudly.

After the battle, no change was adopted as to the general plan of the campaign. Preparations were made for another general attack on the positions of the enemy, who were daily receiving reinforcements. But the inclemency of the weather checked the duke's desire to advance; nor was it till the 2nd of October that our army marched forth again to try the fortune of another battle. This time it was determined to make the principal effort along the sea-shore, and the high sand-hills by which the shore is bounded. To Sir Ralph Abercromby was assigned this arduous service. His column was composed of Moore's brigade, D' Oyley's two battalions of the 1st Guards. Macdonald's reserve (four battalions), to which were attached 300 Russian *yägers*, Lord Cavan's brigade, nine squadrons under Lord Paget, and one troop of horse artillery, besides a few field-pieces. Sir Ralph was to make his way to Egmont-op-Zee, on, or rather in rear of, the enemy's extreme left.

The plan of operations was complicated; and considering that these involved and intricate movements were to be executed by raw troops, in a country where the communications were difficult and uncertain, it is not surprising that many blunders and disappointments ensued. The general scheme, however, appears to have been to advance in a sort of echelon from the right; our left (under Sir James Pulteney—12 battalions militia; 2 battalions Russians; 2 squadrons of 18th Dragoons; 7 gunboats) being refused, and only serving to menace the strong posts of the French on the high road to Alkmaar, so as to keep the enemy in check on that side. The Russians (who had been reinforced by the arrival of 3 or 4,000 more infantry and 200 Cossacks) were to move, as in the former action, along the road through Schorel, at the foot of the sandhills; but this time the English were (by a flanking movement from the right) to dislodge the enemy on the road, and to clear the way for our growling Allies.

General Dundas's column (Burrard's 2 battalions Guards; Coote's 4 battalions; Lord Chatham's 4 militia; 1 squadron 11th Dragoons), had multifarious duties assigned to it. It was (after opening the route for the Russians) to take care of both its own flanks; it was to attack Schoreldam; and it was, if it could, to maintain a communication across the wide chain of sandhills, with Colonel Macdonald, whose business it was to cover the flank of Sir Ralph Abercromby's column,—without losing sight of Sir J. Pulteney on the Alkmaar road and canal.

As the march of our right column under Abercromby was to be along the seashore, and it therefore depended on the state of the tide, the movement did not commence till after 6 a.m., when Macdonald started from Petten, drove back the French outposts, and cleared the first sandhills, Coote (though belonging to another column) followed him, and turning to the left over the sandhills, forced the enemy's parties on the Schorel road to retire, Abercromby's column pursued its course along the beach; and the Russians moved along their allotted route under the left flank of the hills.

The story of D' Essen's column may be very shortly told. They advanced doggedly, at first without meeting resistance, drove the enemy easily out of Schorel, and then forming between that village and Schorel dam (which was earned by Burrard's brigade), they there passed the rest of the day in interchanging cannon-shots with the French batteries at Bergen and in the meadows towards the Koe Dyck. Abercromby had reckoned on his protege. Colonel Macdonald, for the security of his left flank during the march along the beach.

The latter was to have hung on the seaward side of the sand-hills, clearing the flank, and at hand to receive support, if necessary. But Macdonald was a very wild warrior. On first entering the hills, he met with small parties, afterwards with larger, of the enemy; he got excited, followed them up, met with more, entangled himself in the waves of these great sand-downs (which are from two to four miles wide), had a battle to himself, and so completely lost sight of Sir Ralph's column which he did not rejoin till dark.

But the French were especially careful of the sandhills. There they were in great numbers, though such was the strange nature of the ground that their parties appeared to be scattered and ill-connected, as our people likewise were. The French were, however, more practised soldiers, and more alert and intelligent in turning to account every little wave on this great sand sea; and they not only furnished plenty of work for Coote and Macdonald, but they slipped between these brigades and Abercromby, and harassed the left flank of his column severely throughout his march. Having lost Macdonald, Sir Ralph was obliged to weaken and retard the march of his column by detaching the 25th and 79th regiments into the Dunes to protect the left of his main body while moving along the beach. General Moore found it necessary to direct this essential service in person.

Delayed by continual skirmishes, and more than once by serious conflicts, which obliged him to call up the Royals and 49th to his support, Moore fought his way (though he had been wounded early) till his weary troops arrived at the end of several horn's in front of a ridge of sand hills within two miles of Egmont. Here the enemy stood in great strength, and the beach was occupied by their cavalry and artillery. The left of Moore's brigade was much entangled in the broken ground; and had not been able to keep abreast with the 25th, which was on their right, and was toiling gallantly forward. On this regiment the French poured down from their position; their numbers were great, and their fire became destructive.

Three companies of the 92nd mounted hastily from the beach to the assistance of the 25th, but the storm of shot they encountered before they could recover breath or make good their footing, broke and scattered them. Moore was struck down by a ball through his face, and the 25th were overpowered. But the rest of the 92nd came up on their right, the other three regiments of the brigade closed as fast as they could upon the left, and after a desperate struggle, the French were driven back to the position from whence they had made this furious sally.

A dark October day was nearly spent. The progress of Abercromby's column had been extremely slow, regulated as it was of necessity by that of the brigade which was fighting its way in the sand hills. Of the rest of the army the general could see nothing, and heard but very seldom. Two battalions of the Guards, and four of the militia regiments were all the infantry in a condition to renew the contest, which remained at Sir Ralph's command; nor were there any troops in his rear on which he might fall back if repulsed.

******

The five battalions which Moore had commanded were spent

with fatigue, and they had suffered very severely; 44 officers and more than 600 of their men having been killed or wounded. Among the latter were the Marquis of Huntly and Alan Cameron, the colonels of the 93nd and 79th Highlanders.

★★★★★★

The French were strong in numbers and strongly posted. To have attacked them, situated as Abercromby was, would have been too desperate an experiment. Just as the day closed, the action apparently at an end, our light dragoons on the beach were dismounted to rest their horses, when suddenly down came two squadrons of *Chasseurs-à-Cheval*, at full speed, and were upon and among the Horse Artillery, who were in front of the column, before they were discovered. They hoped by this act of dashing gallantry to have carried off some of the guns; but luckily there was a group of ten or twelve officers chatting together close by (amongst them were Lord Paget, Colonel Erskine, and Sir Robert Wilson), and these, followed by half-a-dozen sergeants and others, who happened to be still on horseback, plunged at once into the midst of the French, and fought so furiously that the dragoons gained time to run together and mount, and then the thing was over. Most of the *chasseurs*, were killed or taken.

Immediately after this skirmish, the lost Macdonald rejoined Sir Ralph, with his four jaded and diminished battalions. In the hard service of this day's struggle, the loss had fallen most heavily on Moore's gallant brigade; he was himself severely wounded in two places, and the brave old Abercromby felt as though he had lost his right hand. (Sir Ralph had two horses killed under him in this day's fight.)

General Dundas executed the difficult part allotted to him in the complex manoeuvres of this day with great judgment and coolness, though thwarted and embarrassed by a variety of cross occurrences. One of his brigades (Burrard's 2nd of Guards) had got possession of Schoreldam, but as the Russians were not inclined to advance any further, Burrard could do no more than maintain the post he had won.

In the afternoon, therefore, there remained for the important object of dislodging the enemy from Bergen, and the Koe Dyck, only Coote's and Lord Chatham's brigades, instead of the whole of Dundas's division, and the 10,000 Russians under D' Essen. Coote's four battalions had a tedious and difficult work upon their hands, in fighting their way through the sandhills, at times in connection with Macdonald's people, but latterly with Lord Chatham's brigade of militia. David Dundas, taking these two in hand, when he found the Russians *would* not stir, manoeuvred the French out of the sand-hills up to Bergen in a very handsome and scientific style; and he finally took post on the ridge overhanging that town, though the enemy made some fierce sallies, in which they were repulsed by the 85th and the 27th Regiments.

Sir James Pulteney had little more to do than make a show on the enemy's right, and by appearing to threaten Oudt Carspel, to prevent their detaching troops to the assistance of those about Bergen. By daybreak on the 3rd, the Dutch under Daendels had evacuated Oudt Carspel, retreating on Alkmaar, from whence they soon afterwards pursued their march to unite with the French under Generals Brune and Vandamme, who withdrew slowly and sullenly from Egmont and Bergen. Our troops advanced so far as to take up positions beyond the Egmonts, Op-Zee, and Op-te-Hoof, and Alkmaar; and the headquarters were fixed in the latter place, a handsome and flourishing town.

The Allies claimed this as a victory; but in truth it was little more than a drawn battle, and its results were more injurious to us than to the enemy. We had lost 2,000 men, and the heaviest losses had fallen on our best regiments. Our enemies were neither broken nor discouraged, Brune fell back, because he had positions in his rear still stronger than those on which he had already fought and staggered us; and a reinforcement of 4,000 or 5,000 French were in full march to join him. He threw up works along the short and formidable line of Beverwyck, and he fortified Purmerend, on the east side of the Ye, inundating the country near it.

But the intervening country between Egmont and Beverwyck was still so strong, and afforded such great advantages to troops acting on the defensive, that Bruno was not at all disposed to give it up without a farther struggle. He continued, therefore, to occupy Limmen, Ackersloot, and other villages, with a large proportion of his army.

On the other hand, the Allies over-rated the advantage of occupying Alkmaar: they fancied that the French were beaten, and with thoughts intent on the celebrated position of Beverwyck, were anxious to arrive there, and to make their attack before the enemy could have time to complete and arm the works on which he was known to be employed.

★★★★★★

Yet our right wing under Abercromby, which was in front of Egmont, remained two days without connection with our left at Alkmaar. The Russians at length moved up, and occupied the intermediate villages.

✶✶✶✶✶✶

On Sunday, the 6th of October, therefore, our advanced posts on the right were ordered to move forward, to occupy some of the villages in front, and force the enemy's detachments to fall back upon the position where it was assumed that he would make his stand. Our army was to follow the next morning. But we had mistaken the intentions of our antagonists, as well as the numbers immediately in our front, and the strength of the ground. At first, the troops that were pushed forward met with but little difficulty in their task, and were allowed to occupy some of the villages and posts allotted to them after sharp skirmishing. But at an important point near Baccum, the advanced guard of the Russian column was checked by an unexpected and severe resistance.

Finding the enemy too strong for him, the commander sent back for reinforcements; regiment after regiment arrived, till seven Russian battalions were hotly engaged, and still they found the growing strength of the enemy overpowering them more and more. The French arriving rapidly, became the attacking instead of the defending party. Sir Ralph Abercromby, seeing how things were going, moved up to the support of the Russians; but the enemy's whole force was in motion. By degrees, the fighting, instead of being confined to Baccum, grew hot in every village and post along the line. The brigades of Dundas's division, as well as those under Abercromby, were drawn successively into severe action, and the Duke of York in Alkmaar was wondering what had fallen out, and what had become of his army.

Though the rain poured down in torrents, the musketry was incessant, *aide-de-camp* after aide-decamp was sent forth to make out what were the causes and objects of this off-hand engagement, and I was carried up and perched on the top of the tall steeple of Alkmaar, with a spying-glass, to try to ascertain for the duke what was the direction, and where were the main points of the fight. (I was crippled by a rheumatic seizure, having slept in a pool of water on the night of the 2nd, was unable to mount on horseback, and had been carried to Alkmaar in a boat.) But all was confusion, and in fact the troops were intermingled: they had been brought irregularly into action, without any definite plan on either side: engaging wherever they happened to meet with an enemy, and advancing or retreating in various directions as the one or the other party prove the stronger.

The country itself was extremely intricate, and the thick rain and the heavy smoke dwelling on the coppice-woods, and enclosures of the villages, made it impossible to distinguish anything clearly. This obstinate and bloody fighting ceased only with the day. At nightfall, the French drew back, and left our troops in possession of the line of posts for which we had unwittingly involved ourselves in this fierce and fruitless contest. The loss of the Allies was not less than 2,500 men, of whom about 700 were prisoners (General Hutchinson wounded; 3 lieut.-colonels killed; 2 taken); that of the enemy was heavier than it had been in the former battles, and between 400 and 500 of the French were taken. The only gleam of brilliancy through this dark thunderstorm, was a charge of five companies of the guards, under Colonel Clephane, into the village of Ackersloot, from which they drove two battalions of French,, killing many, and taking 200 prisoners.

In the last eighteen days, three stubborn and bloody battles had been fought. This action of the 6th October crushed every lingering hope of success. Our best troops were disheartened: our officers had lost all confidence; the Russians were angry, sullen, and scarcely to be counted as allies: again the line of posts, rather than position, in which our army was somewhat confusedly huddled, was by no means satisfactory; and we might now expect that the French, encouraged by the results of this last trial of strength, and reinforced by 4,000 or 5,000 troops from the interior of the Low Countries, would assume the offensive, and attack instead of standing on their defence.

As no reasonable hope could be entertained of our penetrating even as far as Haerlem, it became clearly preferable that the Allied troops should re-occupy their former strong position of the Zuype, rather than remain useless and exposed about Alkmaar; and if the retreat was necessary, the sooner it was carried into effect the better. The Council of War was unanimous in these opinions; and our jaded, drenched, and dispirited army was withdrawn in silence and unmolested within its former lines. The weather had continued, with few and brief intervals, to be dreadfully bad; torrents of rain, attended by storms of wind. The roads were become almost impassable; but as the enemy had not discerned, or at least had not molested our retreat, this circumstance became favourable to the Allies when they set themselves down as the defenders of a position.

It may, however, be easily conceived that the Allied forces under the command of H.R.H. the Duke of York were not in an enviable condition. Everybody was out of humour, and out of heart. Only three weeks before, there had marched forth from these same lines an army numbering 35,000 men, confident in their strength, and sanguine in their expectations of driving everything before them, at least as far as Beverwyck. In that position, indeed, the enemy was expected to offer a desperate resistance; but it was supposed that we should arrive there by the 24th of September, fresh and flushed with previous success. Nor did any man allow himself to doubt that such troops as those of Sir R. Abercromby's division had proved themselves to be, and with our new and "invincible" Allies, the Russians, we could fail to carry the line of Beverwyck; and then on such a day we were to be at Haerlem, and in so many more at Amsterdam.

Alas! what a change after three weeks of rain and untoward fighting! Here were the troops in their old lines, minus nearly 10,000 of the bravest men and officers, fatally convinced that they could not make their way forwards, though still numerous; pent up in a narrow corner of a dismal country, which afforded very insufficient quarters for the troops, and the great number of sick and wounded men; and of which the cattle were already eaten up. As to the mere question of defence against the French, there was little to be feared. The position of our army was extremely strong, particularly while the ditches along the front remained unfrozen; and we could command any quantity of ordnance from the Helder and the fleet for the arming of batteries; the only apprehension entertained sprung from our observing the gross negligence of the Russian sentinels and outposts on the right; and if the sharp Frenchmen had risked a dash in this quarter, during the long nights, the safety of the whole might have been compromised.

The news which arrived about this time tended to depress the minds of men still more. All the brilliant prospects of the war in Italy and Switzerland had been overclouded; the army of Korsakoff had been destroyed by Massena; and the wrecks of the conquering Souvaroff's had, though struggling desperately to the last, been forced back beyond the Upper Rhine. To our Russians, this disastrous intelligence afforded fresh food for discontent; they regarded their countrymen (and not without reason) as having been deserted and sacrificed by the Austrian Government; and the bitter fancy that they themselves had been deserted by the British on the 19th of September, became more deeply rooted in their minds.

The situation of our army was certainly dismal enough, aggravated as it was by the increasing severity of the season, which was already passing into a premature winter. There were reasons in abundance for the most serious consideration, and the most decided measures; but yet it is startling to think that the measure which was immediately adopted by generals still at the head of more than 25,000 men, was *Capitulation*. The allied forces had re-entered the lines of the Zuype on the 8th and 9th of October. By the 18th, a convention was signed, on the part of the Allies, by Major-General Knox (a very intelligent officer, to whom this duty was intrusted), after negotiations and *pourparlers* with General Brune, which consumed only three days.

******

From the French officers with whom we had intercourse during these few days, we heard of the arrival of Buonaparte from Egypt. The enthusiasm with which they announced this event was very remarkable. Though Napoleon had come alone, bringing nothing to France but the powers of his mind and the influence of his name, yet already did the French Armies hail his advent as the certain presage of victory.

******

The duke engaged to evacuate Holland entirely by the 30th of November; to restore the fortifications of the Helder, with all the guns, &c.; to abstain from cutting dykes, or making inundations; and to pledge himself that the British Government should send back to France 8,000 of the prisoners of war then in England.

Little more remains to be told of this gloomy story, except that the storms of that terrible year continued to be such that it was found barely possible to carry off the last of our troops before the time prescribed in the capitulation; and that in the meanwhile several transports and some ships of war were lost, and a great many of our soldiers and sailors were drowned. Sir James Pulteney remained to the last to see the terms of the treaty carried into effect. The Russians were quartered for the winter in Jersey and Guernsey, and our own troops were distributed in various quarters in England to recover their health, their spirits, and their discipline.

Observations and Inquiries

In reviewing the short campaign in North Holland, we have to consider it under two heads. 1st. That wherein the design and plans were interwoven with political objects; and 2nd, with relation only to the military conduct of the undertaking.

The expedition to Holland in 1799, was, if not conceived, yet principally managed, by Mr. Dundas, who was then the Secretary of State for War and Colonies. When it became certain that the Emperor Paul was determined to send his armies against the French, and that Austria would renew the war, the English Cabinet grew desirous of taking an active part, and employing troops as well as money. But as there were not within the kingdom more than 10 or 12,000 infantry (composing battalions of sufficient strength and discipline) which could be spared for foreign service, a resolution was taken to complete the skeleton regiments of the army (the unhappy remnants of war and yellow fever in the West Indies) by volunteers from the militia.

An Act of Parliament was passed for this purpose in the month of July; and during August the militiamen, allured by extravagant bounties, were drunk and rolling riotously into the ranks of various regiments of the line. Many thousands of stout fellows were obtained by this measure; but for the time they ceased to be well drilled orderly soldiers of our militia regiments, without becoming men on whom their new officers could rely for the regular service. So numerous were the volunteers that many regiments, which in August could hardly muster one or two hundred wasted old soldiers, found itself 2,000 strong; healthy, athletic young men, and well drilled, as far as mere drilling could go. But these men were hardly sobered from the riotous jollity of their volunteering; their minds were unsettled; to them their new officers and sergeants were utter strangers; everything was new and bewildering.

In this condition they were hurried down to the sea-side, packed into transports, and sent off in a tempestuous season to engage immediately with the French Armies in one of the most difficult countries in which war can be waged, These raw soldiers did not even bear the uniforms of the regiments whose colours they were expected to defend, and whose honour they were to uphold. There had not even been time enough to provide clothing for them. When the men were ranked in the 5th, or the 17th, or 35th, or others of these new swollen regiments, there they stood in the respective garbs of the various corps of militia from which they had been drawn. If only three months had been gained for them to know something of their officers and sergeants, and the ways of the regiment into which they had entered, the men would probably have done their duty well; but such was not the case, and one cannot be surprised that, with the exception of the 20th and the 40th regiments, these suddenly created battalions proved unfit to meet a brave and skilful enemy.

At the same time that our ministers adopted such a mode of forming an army for immediate service, they engaged the Russian Emperor to send 17,000 of his troops by sea to co-operate with us in an attack on the Low Countries. The crazy *Czar* was at this time at the highest pitch of his ardour for crushing French democracy. He was eager to send his Muscovites everywhere and anywhere, provided that other governments (and the English in particular) would bear a large share of the expenses necessary to bring his armies into conflict with those of France. Paul seems never to have doubted of the superiority of his rude soldiers over those of Western Europe. He expected his Russians to conquer, if they found the opportunity to fight, as a matter of course. And the wonderful success of his first four-and-twenty thousand men, who descended into Italy under Souvaroff, served to confirm and exaggerate this expectation.

******

Souvaroff was a leader quite out of and above the ordinary rules of military criticism. There might be some madness in him, or he might affect more than there was. His behaviour might be quoted as extravagant or even ridiculous; but he was a great captain, if his recklessness as to the lives of his soldiers be kept out of the question. He possessed the art of winning; and preserving the enthusiastic devotion of his soldiers. His energy was as inexhaustible as it was audacious. He taught his followers to trample, as he did himself, on every difficulty in their way. Obstacles only provoked him to strike out new resources; and wild and irregular as he was, he possessed in a remarkable degree that intuitive sagacity in the hour of battle which is one of the highest qualities of military genius.

******

In a mind ill-poised by nature, and thus excited by an overweening confidence, the disasters which subsequently fell upon the Russian Armies were likely to produce, and did produce a fearful revulsion. The utter defeat of Korsakoff, the consequent distresses of Souvaroff, and the disappointments and discontents of the army which joined the English in North Holland, fixed in the mind of Paul the madman's common persuasion that he was betrayed, insulted, and ill-treated by his Allies.

But to return to the British Ministry and Mr. Dundas's plan of campaign. The additional troops could not be obtained from the Militia, nor could the Russians be brought from the Baltic before September; but the war was hot in Italy, and on the Upper Rhine; and our Cabinet was anxious to be bearing a part. There seems to have been a magnetical attraction for English expeditions to Holland; and in 1799, the Prince of Orange and his mother (for the old *Stadtholder* was little better than a cypher) were full of a growing confidence as to a reaction of opinions among the Dutch, and as to their impatience of French control.

They believed that a large majority of the people were desirous that the former order of things, including their trade, should be revived; and the House of Orange flattered itself, that because the Dutch desired to see them again at the Hague, and the French removed from the country, they would rise in arms to bring these matters to bear. It is the old, incurable error of exiled potentates. There was undoubtedly in the Seven Provinces a party favourable to the restoration of the House of Orange, and a much larger proportion of the inhabitants desirous to get rid of the French, and to see the independence of their country re-established.

******

It may be doubted whether the Dutch would have taken arms in any part of the Union. If anywhere it would have been in the provinces of Groningen and Friesland. There was to be found the greatest strength of the Orange party; while that of the Independents lay in the great cities.

******

It was particularly in that peninsula which we chose for our campaign, that the dislike to the *Stadtholder* was the strongest, and the animosity to the French had been least excited. In North Holland the people were of the old republican character; and in 1799, they preferred the French as being republicans and as enemies of the House of Orange, to the English who hoisted the yellow flag, and circulated proclamations on behalf of the *Stadtholder*. We found scarcely a friend in the country: a very few Dutch gentlemen came into our army, but they made their way to us from distant quarters. It was fancied that the Batavian troops (as they were then called) would not fight; but we found to our cost that their battalions under Daendels fought as hard as the French under Brune and Vandamme.

Discouragement met us on every side; and after the unfortunate battle of the 19th of September (of which more hereafter), the game of the Allies was lost. It may be a doubtful question whether the erroneous choice of the line of operations (for fatally erroneous it was) ought to be charged altogether against the British Cabinet, or whether it might be partly ascribed to the British generals. But here it is necessary, and but just, to set down what was, and to whom was entrusted, the command of the Allied forces. The English Government having resolved to compose a great army, and to employ it in an invasion of the Low Countries, placed the supreme command, ostensibly, in the hands of the Duke of York.

There might be plausible motives for this appointment; it might obviate difficulties, and be satisfactory to the Emperor of Russia; it certainly was gratifying to George the Third; agreeable to the House of Orange, with whom the duke was intimately connected; and he was himself anxious to prove his zeal in the situation he held as Commander-in-Chief of the British Army. But the Cabinet (that is, Messrs. Pitt and Dundas) seem to have entertained strong misgivings of the fitness of their own appointment, for they clogged it with instructions that on every occasion of importance, His Royal Highness should convene a Council of War; and they prescribed that such Council should be composed of the duke, Lieut.-Generals Sir Ralph Abercromby, David Dundas, James Murray Pulteney, the Russian commander, and Major-General Lord Chatham. This nobleman was at the time a member of the British Cabinet, a very gentleman-like man, and a sensible man; but he was excessively indolent, and had no military experience whatever.

With this Council rested the decision on all questions of grave importance. To this Council, rather than to the Duke of York alone, should be ascribed whatever blame may be justly attached to the plans of operations, or of giving battle, the advance or retreat of the army, or finally of the capitulation. But much as I loved the duke personally, much as I felt many good and amiable qualities in his character, much as I owe to him of gratitude for long kindness to myself, I cannot but acknowledge that he was not qualified to be even the ostensible head of a great army on arduous service. At home, he administered the business of our military establishments sedulously, zealously, clearly, and impartially; but he possessed none of the higher qualities which influence the fate of a campaign, or turn the fortune of a battle.

He was of a cool courage; he would have stood all day to be shot at; but he had no active bravery. With a very fair understanding, he had little quickness of apprehension, still less of sagacity in penetrating designs, or forming large views; painstaking, yet devoid of resources, and easily disheartened by difficulties. Even his good nature and kind temper were injurious; for it too often happened that he could not bring himself to say No, when he ought to have said No, To these defects must be added habits of indulgence, and a looseness of talking, after dinner, about individuals, which made him enemies, and which in this unfortunate campaign probably excited, or inflamed the rancour of the Russian generals.

Of the lieutenant-generals who were associated to the control of our military operation, Sir Ralph Abercromby stood foremost. It ought to be unnecessary to speak in praise of such a man; but even in this book-making age, when we are overridden with biographical memoirs, there has appeared no biography of the good and gallant Abercromby. When Mr. Dundas selected him to lead, and sent him forward in command of what was the muscle and sinew of our army, there were but two faults to be found with the selection. The general was a little too old for hard service, and he was extremely near-sighted. Allowing for these defects of nature, Abercromby was a noble chieftain. Mild in manner, resolute in mind, frank, unassuming, just, inflexible in what he deemed to be right, valiant as the Cid, liberal and loyal as the prowest of black Edward's knights. An honest, fearless, straightforward man; and withal sagacious and well-skilled in his business as a soldier. As he looked out from under his thick, shaggy-eyebrows, he gave one the idea of a very good-natured lion, and he was respected and beloved by all who served under his command.

David Dundas was next in rank. He likewise was an aged man, but very different in manner and character from Abercromby, though he, too, was a brave, careful, and well-skilled soldier. General Dundas had raised himself into notice but a few years before this time, by having formed a system for the British Army (compiled and digested from the Prussian Code of Tactics), both for the infantry and cavalry. This work had been eagerly adopted by the Duke of York as Commander-in-Chief, and had become the universal manual in our service. The system was, in the main, good, and founded on right principles, though the book was ill-written, and led the large class of stupid officers into strange blunders.

★★★★★★

I remember one evening in the winter of 1804, during the Shorncliff camp, I was at Sir John Moore's lodgings at Sandgate; nobody there but General Dundas, Moore, and myself: the two generals talking, naturally at that time, on military matters. Dundas had his feet on the fender, and was cowering over the fire. Says Moore, "That book of yours, general, has done a great deal of good, and would be of great value if it were not for those damned eighteen manoeuvres,"—"Why,—ay," says Sir David, slowly, "ay, people don't understand what was meant.

Blockheads don't understand!"

******

But a uniform system had been grievously needed, for no two regiments, before these regulations were promulgated, moved in unison. Dundas was a tall, spare man, crabbed and austere; dry in his looks and demeanour. He had made his way from a poor condition (he told me himself that he walked from Edinburgh to London, to enter himself as a "Fireworker" in the artillery); and there were peculiarities in his habits and style, which excited some ridicule amongst young officers. But though it appeared a little out of fashion, there was "much care and valour in that *Scotchman*."

The third of our lieutenant-generals was Sir James Murray Pulteney, and a very odd man he was. In point of natural abilities, he was of a high rank. He had seen a great deal of the world, as well as of military service; he had read much and variously, and possessed a great fund of knowledge, and considerable science. Remarkably good-tempered, cool, unpretending, utterly indifferent to danger or to hardships—what was it that hindered him from becoming a commander of the first order? Just this: Sir James was dreamy, and he liked better to amuse his mind with doubts and varied trials of a problem, than to end it by a decision.

His view of a subject was, nine times out of ten, right; but he had no confidence in his own opinion, and he lazily surrendered his better judgment on matters which demanded action. Pulteney had awkward manners; received officers uncouthly; did not know, or seem to care, how to put them at their ease; and till one came to know him in intimacy, as I did a few years afterwards, the kindness of his nature, the extent of his knowledge, and the largeness of his views remained hidden under a grotesque and somewhat repulsive exterior.

******

On the day of landing in Holland, Sir James was shot through one of his arms. He walked away to the surgeon, chuckling and mumbling (as was his wont), "Well, now I have been shot through both legs and both arms." And mightily amused he appeared to be, at having thus made up the *parti quarré*.

******

Such were the British members of the Duke of York's Council. Of the Russian commanders little could be known. D'Hermann was made prisoner within a week; and his successor, D'Essen, held himself as much aloof as possible from the duke's Council and society.

It requires no ghost to tell the reader that this was not the wisest way of providing for the command of 40,000 men, transported in this stormy season into an enemy's country, which was known to be particularly strong in defensive positions, and where they would have to grapple with the seasoned soldiers and practised officers of France.

We may suppose that the foremost object in selecting the Helder as a point of attack was the capture of the Dutch fleet, and the destruction of their stores. Well, this was effected by Sir Ralph Abercromby's successful lauding, and secured by his action of the 10th of September. The easy defeat of the enemy, on the latter day, proved that the position of the Zuype Sluys could be held against any force the enemy could collect, particularly if redoubts were constructed, and armed with heavy guns, which, however, was not the case when Abercromby was attacked on the 10th of September. Then comes the question, whether it would not have been wise to fortify this position; and leaving therein a couple of thousand of old soldiers (say Coote's brigade), marines and seamen from the fleet, 7,000 or 8,000 of the militia regiments, and a Russian brigade, to have crossed the Zuyder Zee with the remainder of the army, and taken our line of operations on the Yssel.

We were completely masters of the sea, and had at our command large naval means. We could have transported to the neighbourhood of Zwoll 10,000 or 12,000 British troops, and as many Russians. (It was still in the power of the British Government to have reinforced this army with a large body of cavalry, and at least one brigade of infantry from England.) We had reason to expect that we should receive in that quarter the friendly assistance of the inhabitants. This line of operations threatened either Arnhem, or Utrecht and Amsterdam. The alarm in this last city would have been increased by the approach of our flotilla. The French could not have remained about Alkmaar, and have engaged in attacks on the strong line of the Zuype Sluys, while the most important places in the Netherlands were exposed to danger.

If they did remain there, so much the better for us; our main army would have had an easy game before them, assuming that the object of the expedition was to distress the enemy, to alarm him for the safety of the Low Countries generally, and to work a diversion in favour of the Allies on the Upper Rhine. (There had been a serious insurrection against the French the year before, on the Lower Rhine and the Maes.) If the French abandoned North Holland, and marched to cover Amsterdam and Utrecht, then the British troops left in the Zuype might have been brought across to rejoin the main army, leaving only 3,000 men or so to fortify, and (in co-operation with our fleet) to secure the Helder Point.

In this case we might have had 35,000 soldiers on the Yssel (and these soldiers who had not yet been cowed or checked) with friendly provinces around us, and Hanover at our back. The game would have been very different from that which was attempted: it had a larger scope, and must have carried a larger influence. Whether it would have been attended with decisive success may fairly be doubted, after the disasters which the Allies brought on themselves in Switzerland; but on these one could not calculate; nor could our army have been easily reduced to the sad necessity of a capitulation.

This scheme is one of the alternatives which have always suggested themselves to my mind as preferable to the attempt to penetrate by the road of Alkmaar and Haerlem to Amsterdam; and as it was mixed up with political considerations of great importance at that time, I speak of it as one which might have been suggested, or ought to have been weighed, by the British Government.

But to turn in the second place to an inquiry into what was done, and into what might have been done, by the commanders of the army from the time it was assembled within the lines of the Zuype.

The most unaccountable mistake, the great military blunder (which drew after it all the subsequent misfortunes), was the plan of attack upon the 19th of September. A resolution having been taken to bring the enemy to battle, our best general and 10,000 or 12,000 of our best troops were detached to Hoorn late in the evening of the 18th; and before daybreak in the morning the rest of the Allies commenced their attack on the enemy in their front. Abercromby's column never fired a shot, or saw, or attracted the notice of the enemy; while the Russians and General Dundas's division were beaten back into their lines before midday.

It was clearly intended that Abercromby should march straight from Hoorn to Alkmaar, while the rest of the forces were engaging and pressing the enemy along his front; and if sufficient time had been allowed, the results of the manoeuvre, turning the enemy in rear of his right, and throwing him up into a heap on the one road on his left, might have been brilliant. But the calculations were fatally erroneous. The line of Hoorn was probably the easiest, although the longest, way of approaching Alkmaar: it turned the enemy's actual position; and there would have been no danger in sending 20,000 men by that route instead of 12,000. The French were not in force sufficient to put our lines in any peril. What occurred when Abercromby arrived at the gates of Hoorn, proved how completely the enemy was taken by surprise on that side, and how little he was prepared to offer a strong resistance on the road from thence to Alkmaar.

✶✶✶✶✶✶

We found in Hoorn little more of military means than the *burgher* guard. The town councillors and the *commandant* were asleep in their beds, and the sentinels were asleep at the gates.

✶✶✶✶✶✶

The movements of the army should have been regulated by the progress of the left column; and have been confined to engaging and menacing the different points of the enemy's positions, till it was certain that Abercromby was in march from Hoorn, and gaining a line which compromised the safety of the French Army. If our antagonists had drawn off a large part of their troops from Bergen and the Koe Dyk to make head against this unexpected attack on their right, the Russians and General Dundas would have easily beaten their left. The strength of the enemy's position consisted not only in the difficulty of approach to each point separately, but in the shortness of their line altogether. By advancing from the side of Hoorn, we should have forced him to extend, and thereby weaken his position. On neither flank could he have remained strong enough to resist our superior masses; and if he had been forced and followed up on either extremity, he would have found a retreat very difficult.

It may be objected, that as Abercromby's wearied troops did not arrive at Hoorn at the hour designed, and would not have been able to resume their march before 11 or 12 o' clock on the 19th, the army would not have had sufficient daylight before them to advance, and fight, and win, and follow up a victory. This may be true, but why, when it was known that this unfortunate delay in the movement of the left column had taken place, why not defer the battle till the next day? Why leave the French all the advantages which their short and compact position afforded to their inferior numbers, and attack them there without our left hand, and that hand a more efficient one than the right?

If we had gained a decided victory on the 19th of September, we might have advanced at once to the front of the Beverwyk position. The Allies 30,000 strong and full of confidence: the enemy at that time not more than 20,000, disordered by defeat, and having as yet no defensive works constructed or armed along that important line.

The battle at Beverwyck might have been fought by the 23rd of September; and our army might have got out of the narrow and difficult province of North Holland before the day (October 2nd) when they had to struggle through the doubtful and disheartening Battle of Egmont.

Before we quit altogether the subject of our military operations in 1799, it may be worthwhile to give some farther consideration to the landing of Sir Ralph Abercromby's troops on the 27th of August. It is the first instance in modern times in which an invading army has successfully effected a landing in the face of an enemy prepared to receive the attack, and having at hand field-artillery and cavalry, as well as a considerable force of regular infantry. That such an operation is fraught with difficulty and danger no military man will doubt, although in the present instance, as well as in that upon the coast of Egypt in 1801, the venture was crowned with success.

On both of these occasions the leading division of the troops made good their footing; and were able to cover the debarkation of the rest of the forces, with the artillery, stores, and all that was required to render these armies efficient for farther service. But this problem, attempted as yet by the British only, became one of the deepest interest when, in the years 1803, 4, and 5, Napoleon was preparing his gigantic means, and maturing his plans for the subjugation of England.

The subject altogether is one which demands a separate and extended inquiry: it is one which ought to be studied not only by our military men, but by naval officers also, and even by the statesmen of England. On this problem of debarking a large army in the face of opposing troops there has hung in our own time the fate of London, if not that of Great Britain: and though such a state of circumstances and chances may never rise again, at least on so vast a scale as that which the genius of Napoleon had dared to contemplate, still the question must be one of great importance to Britain in time of war, I repeat, therefore, that it is worth our while to pay some attention to this instance of the landing of our army in North Holland in 1799.

The season was stormy: the coast was shoal and dangerous. On the other hand, we had the undisputed mastery at sea; nor were we cramped as to time, otherwise than by the weather and the state of the tide. Vice-Admiral Mitchell with a strong squadron of frigates and small two-deckers drawing little water was able to anchor near enough to the shore to protect the transports, and throw a storm of shot upon the beach, while the boats, heavy with soldiers, were rowing to their landing place. (Admiral Duncan was in the offing with the heavier men-of-war.) But the only boats were those of the men-of-war, ill calculated for such a service, and incapable of conveying more than 3,000 men at a time. To the officers of our navy this kind of operation was entirely new; nor did they understand the details, or feel the importance of arrangement on which military order and military success must greatly depend.

Thus, parts of regiments were conveyed to the shore, while parts were left behind. Battalions were intermixed; and companies had to find their proper places after they had landed, and were under the fire of the enemy. The soldiers had to wade and scramble out of the surf as well as they could, and look out for their comrades, and run to their stations in the line which was growing slowly into shape along the beach. Fortunately General Daendels chose to keep his men sheltered from the fire of the ships, and to cling to the strong post he had taken near Callantsoog. If he had rushed headlong on the flank of our first division of troops during the confusion of landing, he might have inflicted a great loss on the British, and perhaps routed these leading brigades.

There was time enough to have done the work before the guards could get ashore: and it was long before the rest of Abercromby's little army were able to land. It is true that the Dutch might have lost a good many men from the fire of our ships, but it was their business to be quick in their rush; and to have mingled their superior numbers so completely with the British soldiers, that the men-of-war would not have ventured to direct their shots against the confused mass of friends and foes. But Daendels either did not see the chance, or he felt his troops unequal to such a trial. He allowed our forces to land and form without hinderance: fought a merely soldier's fight., though gallantly, in the strong post he had chosen; and was at length beaten out of it by the growing numbers and unyielding bravery of his assailants.

But Abercromby had seen with alarm the confusion and danger which attended the debarkation of his 10,000 soldiers; and it was probably the impression made upon his mind on this occasion which led him to form and mature that admirable plan by which, eighteen months afterwards, his army was landed on the shores of Aboukir in complete order of battle.

Military Preparations 1800

After our evacuation of Holland in November 1799, General Brune received orders to march immediately with the greater part of his army to the Lower Loire, where the insurgent Chouans were growing too strong for the republican forces. It was a severe march in so inclement a season; but the circumstances were urgent, and Brune arrived at Angers by the 20th of January, 1800.

The Chouans, elated by some considerable successes, were indulging hopes that the Russians, now quartered in our Channel Islands, were coming, backed by a British Army, to their support. (They had overrun large districts, and had taken Mans and other towns; nay, in October, the Chouans had surprised the great city of Nantes, and they were masters of it for several hours). No movement, however, was made by the Allies; the royalist chiefs in La Vendée treated with Bonaparte; and Brune acting with great promptitude and vigour, crushed the insurgents of Brittany so effectually, that the last of their bands laid down their arms before the end of February.

It may be doubted whether it was desirable that a warfare of so low and cruel a character as that which had been waged by these Chouans should have been prolonged. They appear as a degenerate class when compared with the noble people of La Vendée; yet it is not improbable that if these wild bands of Brittany had been able to make head a few months longer, the smothered fire in Poitou would have again blazed out, and a wide-spread insurrection would have crippled the power of the French republic for aggressive purposes. If such might have been the case, the failure of the Duke of York's army to retain such a hold on the Low Countries, as would have kept Brune and his troops employed in that quarter, must be regarded as fatal in its effects on the issue of the war.

★★★★★★

Brune has been censured by some of his countrymen for granting any terms of capitulation to the Allied Army. If he had not, the results would have proved very dangerous to the Consular

Government. Nor could he have forced the lines of the Zuype, unless through the grossest negligence on the part of the Russians, or the treachery of their commander. Napoleon was contented with Brune's campaign, and made him a marshal for it.

******

The prompt destruction of the Chouans, afforded to Bonaparte the time and the means he required for the formation of that army, with which he crossed the Alps and overthrew the Austrians at Marengo.

The British troops which returned from Holland were quartered for the winter chiefly in the south and east of England. Many of the regiments were very sickly; and a few months of rest and good management were requisite to restore the efficiency of all, and particularly to improve the discipline of those corps which had received large proportions of militiamen. It was a dismal winter in this country. There had been two successive years of the worst weather imaginable. The harvest of 1709, had been miserably deficient; and the distress throughout the kingdom was terrible. There appeared no symptoms of a renewal on our part of offensive warfare; yet as early as December, 1799, there was a great project under the consideration of our government.

This plan had been conceived and submitted to our war minister by General Sir Charles Stuart, who had taken Minorca in 1798, and was at this time commander of the forces in the Mediterranean. He asked that 15,000 men might be sent from England; the least efficient of which should be placed in garrison at Gibraltar and Minorca, and should set at liberty the old regiments which were stationed there. He might thus have formed an efficient and seasoned army, with which he proposed to act against the enemy, on the coast between Toulon and Genoa; while the exiled General De Willot, a man of talent and energy, undertook to raise an insurrection in the neighbourhood of Marseilles,

It will be remembered that when, in December, 1799, Napoleon Bonaparte became the ruler of France, under the title of First Consul, he had found the armies of the republic greatly reduced in numbers. That army in particular, which still held possession of Genoa and the Western Riviera, was dispirited by its late defeats, and was languishing under severe privations and mortal diseases. It mustered in the gross about 38,000 men, including a dismal proportion of sick. (The officers, sergeants, and drummers are included in the French returns. Deducting these, there would remain about 34,000 rank and file.) It stretched along the coast of the Mediterranean, from the banks of the Var to beyond Genoa. Not only had the French to maintain possession of this great city and its extensive line of outworks, but they had also to defend the various passes of the Appenines to the Maritime Alps, along a line of more than 160 miles.

To secure the passage of the Var, and the mountain roads which lead from Piedmont upon Oneglia and Savona, was an object of importance scarcely inferior to that of making good the defence of Genoa. On the northern side of the Appenines, from Coni to Piacenza, there lay more than 80,000 Austrians, well supplied and ready to commence hostilities with the opening spring, exclusive of nearly 20,000 men who formed the garrisons of fortresses in Lombardy and Piedmont. To the commander of this Imperial Army, the foremost object ought to have been, that of crushing the enemy's troops in the Genoese territory before they could be reinforced.

The First Consul was prepared to meet the Austrians in Germany with equal numbers; but he felt great difficulties with regard to his Italian Army, weak as it was, devoid of resources, and exposed to be overpowered by a very superior enemy. It was then that Bonaparte formed his gigantic plan of crossing the Alps with 60,000 men, by routes which were considered impassable for cannon. But time was required to collect and equip such an army; and the more because the greatest art and caution were indispensable to elude observation, and baffle suspicion as to his design. In the meantime, it was to be feared that his 38,000 men, who were scattered from Nice to Genoa, and who believed themselves to be abandoned by their government, might fail to oppose to the Austrians, such a resistance as should afford time for the arrival of the chief consul's army in Italy.

******

The story of this army as given by French writers deserves attention, and affords a lesson to military men. In January, 1800, it still mustered more than 50,000 men including officers and Serjeants. Ten thousand recruits joined them before March. Yet so great was the mortality in the hospitals, and no unexampled the amount of desertions (many officers being included under the latter head), that when Massena arrived there remained only 38,000 men. Of these a great proportion were sick and they were in urgent want of clothes, shoes, money, and supplies of every kind (see *Thiébault: Soldier of Napoleon*: Volumes 1 & 2 by Paul Thiébault which are personal accounts of the Revolutionary

Wars and conflicts of the French First Empire; Leonaur 2014.) The right wing of the French (their headquarters being in Genoa) extended from Porta Fino to Savona; and it could bring about 11,000 rank and file into the field, after providing scantily for the forts and posts which it was necessary to maintain.

The left wing, under the immediate command of General Suchet, held the Maritime Alps, and the line of coast from Oneglia to the Var. It was less sickly than the troops on the right; and it could probably have produced as many fighting men in the field as the former, exclusive of between 3,000 to 4,000, who were detached to guard the Mont Genèvre and the Mont Cenis. But Suchet had to maintain a precarious communication from Oneglia, with Soult's division which lay about Savona; and he had to make strong provision for the passes on the side of Coni and Mondovi, where the Austrians were in considerable force.

★★★★★★

Bonaparte, therefore, selected Massena, as the fittest of his lieutenants to revive the confidence of the troops, and to maintain a desperate struggle to the last for the city of Genoa, and the passes of the mountains. Well did Massena fulfil the objects of his great commander; but it would not be difficult to shew, that if Sir Charles Stuart's plan had been promptly and vigorously carried into execution, the campaign would probably have been attended with results very different from those which actually ensued.

It is not presumptuous to say, now that we know what British soldiers are capable of, that such a body of troops would have marred the glory of Massena's sorties, and have probably occasioned the surrender of the city a month earlier than it actually took place. The consequences of such a difference in time are beyond calculation. Old Melas would have had 20,000 more men in hand when Napoleon crossed the St. Bernard: the battles of Montebello and Marengo would have been fought (if fought at all) under very different chances, and "Flodden had been Bannockburn!"

Observe what Napoleon wrote at St. Helena, with regard to the army in Liguria:

> *La cavalerie, les charrois périrent de misère; les maladies contagieuses et la désertion désorganisèrent l'armée. Enfin le mal empira au point que des corps entiers. tambour battant, drapeau déployé, abandonnèrent leur position, et repassèrent le Var.* (See *Mémoires écrits à Ste. Helène,*

tome 1).

But to return to the dismal facts: our ministers having for the moment exhausted the military strength of the kingdom by the expedition to Holland, seemed to relapse into their old condition of not knowing what to do. Instead of anticipating events, they followed them, and followed them by movements so tardy, that these became useless. Though masters of the Mediterranean Sea, they were blind to the importance of aiding the operations of Austria on its northern shore.

It was very much a question of time. If the British Army had been collected, as Stuart required and hoped, before the end of March, it might have arrived on the enemy's coast at nearly the same time as when the Austrians opened their campaign. On the 5th and 6th of April, their columns, 50,000 or 60,000 strong, attacked the French posts in the passes of the Appenines, from the mountains to the eastward of Genoa, to those which rise on the west of Finale. Hard fighting and alternate successes protracted a series of conflicts, which lasted through fifteen days; and this space of time (precious to the designs of Napoleon) was gained to the French, before the superior numbers of the Austrians prevailed so far, after an enormous loss of men, as to force back the whole of the enemy's right wing within the lines of Genoa.

But for the argument I have in hand, it is of particular importance to observe what was done by the left wing of the French under General Suchet. He had moved rapidly up, with all his disposable troops to the mountains near Finale; and between the 6th and 12th of April, he was engaged in a series of hard and bloody actions with the right of the Austrian Army commanded by General Elsnitz. Suchet was finally worsted; his communications with Massena were lost, and he was obliged to fall back to a position near Albenga. There he held his ground till the beginning of May, when Melas, having shut up Massena within the walls of Genoa, came in person with a portion of his army to this quarter. Suchet was unable to withstand such superior forces. He was beaten from post to post, and finally driven across the Var, with a heavy loss of men.

******

General Melas appears to have been in person, at Nice, so late as the 18th of May. On that day, he hurried off with a part of his army, in consequence of the appearance of Napoleon's vanguard in the valley of Aosta. Melas left Elsnitz with 18,000 men to attempt to force the passage of the Var, in the face of

Suchet's batteries. Two attempts were made, and were repulsed with heavy loss, and Elsnitz then drew off with his diminished and disheartened troops to rejoin his commander in Alexandria. See what Lord William Bentinck, who was with Melas writes to Lord Grenville on the 15th of June:—

(Extract):—"I am sorry to say that General Elsnitz's corps, which was composed of the grenadiers and the finest regiments in the army, arrived in the most deplorable condition. That general had received orders to proceed by forced marches, and to effect a junction at any rate. His men had already suffered very much from want of provisions and other hardships. He was pursued in his retreat by General Suchet, who had with him about 7,000 men. There was an action at Ponte di Nava, in which the French failed; and it will appear hardly credible when I tell Your Lordship, that the Austrians lost in this retreat, from fatigue only, near 5,000 men."

Even after the Battle of Marengo was actually begun, Melas was so much alarmed at the approach of Suchet, that he detached 2,200 of his cavalry, whom he could very ill spare, to observe and retard the march of this hostile corps. Now, if 10,000 British had landed at Savona or Oneglia, even so late as the first week in June, Suchet must have desisted from his pursuit of Elsnitz, and Melas would have had a very superior force of cavalry in the field of Marengo.

★★★★★★

But Melas had carried away too large a part of the troops which had driven the French into Genoa. Imagining that Massena was completely crippled, and unequal to resume offensive movements, the Austrian commander left such a force to maintain the blockade as proved to be inadequate to the service. These troops were repeatedly beaten, and they suffered very great losses from the frequent and furious sorties of the republicans.

Now, if Stuart had landed near Nice or Ventimiglia during these operations, Suchet's corps must have been destroyed. It would have been unnecessary for Melas to march to the support of Elsnitz. The successes which Massena obtained over that portion of the Austrians, which was left under General Ott round Genoa, would have been prevented by the very superior numbers of the beleaguers. Genoa would probably have been taken a month earlier, and at all events the Austrians might have had 15,000 or 20,000 more men, and in better condition, in the field of Marengo.

But it is high time after this long digression, to return to the proper subject of my narrative, the actual employment of the British troops by the British Government. My object in digressing has been to show the importance of the plan proposed by Sir Charles Stuart, and the results which might have been reasonably expected from it This masterly design appears to have been approved and adopted in the first instance by Mr. Dundas; and early in February, Stuart invited General Moore, and others to serve under his command. But there had been much remissness during the winter, in restoring the discipline and efficiency of the regiments which had returned from Holland. But little exertion was made: precious time was lost; and when the month of March arrived, it was announced that only 10,000 men could be furnished, instead of the 15,000 which Stuart had required and expected.

And now the members of the Cabinet changed their minds, or Mr. Dundas was out-voted; it was notified to the general that he should have only 5,000 men from England for the Mediterranean service, and ministers determined to send the best of the troops which remained at their disposal to Portugal. Sir Charles Stuart was a man of high abilities, but of a hot temper and haughty bearing. He considered himself to have been deceived and unworthily treated; he threw up his command, and the services of one of the ablest of our (Generals were lost to the country. (Sir Charles Stuart was the youngest son of the celebrated Earl of Bute, and was father of the late Lord Stuart of Rothsay. He died in May, 1801.)

The transports, on board of which were embarked the 5,000 men under General Pigott, were kept lingering at their anchorage till the end of April, when they were at last ordered to sail for Minorca. In the meantime, the idea of sending troops to Portugal had been abandoned; and Sir Ralph Abercromby was invited to take the command of the army in the Mediterranean; but it was not till the 13th of May that he was dispatched in a frigate, accompanied by Generals Hutchinson and Moore. They arrived at Port Mahon on the 22nd of June; and there Sir Ralph found letters from Lord Keith, who commanded our fleet off Genoa, pressing the general most urgently to bring his troops without delay to that place. So effectual had been the preparations made by the Governor of Minorca, General Fox, that eight battalions, with artillery, &c., were embarked the next morning and sailed under Aborcromby's command for Genoa. But it was too late! Our ministers had wasted in doubts and idle crotchets the three months, within which the Austrians might have been effectually succoured. The Battle of Marengo had been fought; and when Sir Ralph arrived off Genoa, he found the city and port once more in the possession of the victorious French. The British fleet had sailed away to Leghorn; and to that port Abercromby repaired with his 5,000 or 6,000 men.

Here he was beset by the Queen of Naples, who was staying at Leghorn; attended not only by her own ministers, but likewise by Lord Nelson and Sir William Hamilton. By all was Sir Ralph importuned to bring his troops ashore and engage himself in the renewal of the war in Italy. The general's decision was taken immediately. He distrusted their view of affairs; he felt the deep responsibility of acting without instructions from the British Government; and he refused at once to commit his little army in the prosecution of schemes propounded by the Queen of Naples. Ordering Moore to return to Minorca with the troops, Sir Ralph sailed for Malta, to observe the state of the blockade of La Valetta, and satisfy himself as to the probabilities of reducing the enemy's garrison to surrender.

The people of Malta had risen against the French in the autumn of 1799, and English ships of war had immediately blockaded the port. While Nelson remained in the command of our fleet in that sea, he was boiling over with eagerness to accomplish the reduction of that important place. In a letter from him to the Governor of Minorca, begging for military assistance, there is this characteristic passage:

> God forbid that we should be obliged to give up the idea of taking La Valetta! Only the thought of it almost breaks my heart!(Lord Nelson to the General in Command at Minorca, November 12th, 1799.)

It was not, however, till March 1800, that two British regiments (the 30th and 89th) were sent to assist the Maltese in maintaining an effectual blockade of the fortress. Such was the state of affairs when Sir Ralph Abercromby visited the island. He stayed but a few days; and immediately on his return to Minorca, he despatched Major-General Pigott with two battalions of the 35th regiment to strengthen the investment of La Valetta; which fortress was surrendered by capitulation on the 5th of September following.

Upon Sir Ralph's arrival at Port Mahon, on the 3rd of August, he found a large accession to the strength of his army. More than 4,000 men had arrived from the English Channel, after having been present at certain "nibblings" on the enemy's coast, of which I will speak presently. But the general found, also, despatches from Lord Keith, forwarding solicitations from General Melas (backed by those of Lord William Bentinck), that the forces under Abercromby's command might be landed at Leghorn. There had appeared in several parts of Tuscany a strong disposition to rise in arms against the French; and it was considered by the Austrian general that a body of 10,000 British troops, supporting insurrectionary masses in the mountains between Florence and Bologna, would greatly improve the position which his army then occupied along the Mincio, from Peschiera to the Po.

✶✶✶✶✶✶

Although Abercromby, uninformed as to the views of his government, was unwilling to engage his army in an Italian campaign, the plan suggested by the Austrians was by no means unreasonable, nor was it unsafe for the British division. It was proposed to give us possession of the port and fortress of Leghorn. The Neapolitan Army, strong in numbers though bad in quality, was lying at Rome and ready to advance to Florence. The Austrians were in possession of Ancona. The Tuscan peasantry *did* rise in arms, and they were thoroughly in earnest.

In large bodies, under the general direction of an Austrian officer, they swarmed in the Apennines from the borders of Lucca to those of Arezzo. The French Army, now under the command of General Brune, was confronted by equal numbers of Austrians, who held the strong position of the Mincio. Between these chief actors the truce which had commenced with the capitulation of Alessandria, had been renewed from time to time; and in the autumn of 1800, the French growing uneasy at the prospect of affairs in Tuscany, took advantage of this suspension of arms with Austria. The right wing of Brune's army suddenly crossed the Apennines, and marched in three columns upon Leghorn, Florence, and Arezzo. Of the two first of these towns the French made themselves masters without firing a shot, for there were no troops to defend them; and in the port of Leghorn they captured about fifty sail of British merchant vessels. On the side of Arezzo, however, the third column encountered a desperate resistance; it suffered much loss, and was for a time discomfited. The Aretines and the men of the mountains fought hard, but they were finally subdued by the arrival of the other French division from Florence. Now, if the British had been in possession of Leghorn, which they had the means of strengthening so that it could not have been taken unless by a regular siege, it is sufficiently clear that the enemy could not have risked this irruption into Tuscany; the Neapolitan Army would have been brought up to Florence, threatening Bologna, and communicating with the Austrians on the Mincio.

General Brune's operations would have been paralysed. It is true that the fate of the war was decided at the close of the year by the victory of Hohenlinden: but one could not foresee that the Imperialists were to be utterly routed in Germany; and, therefore, I hold the opinion that the solicitations made by General Melas and Lord William Bentinck, in August 1800, were justly grounded and well considered.

✶✶✶✶✶✶

Sir Ralph, however, having no instructions from home, and distrusting the accounts received from Italy, resolved to wait for further orders. He merely despatched General Hope to the Austrian headquarters to communicate with Melas, and to furnish information as to the true state of affairs in that quarter.

In the meantime, Abercromby, seconded by the activity of General Moore, who enjoyed his fullest confidence, applied himself earnestly to improvements in the discipline and fitness for the field of the army which was now assembled under his orders in Minorca. There were no less than twenty-two battalions of infantry, mustering on an average about 650 rank and file each, with several companies of artillery; but of horsemen there were only about fifty of the 11th Light Dragoons. Thus wore away the month of August, when, just at its close, arrived Major-General Craddock, bringing despatches from England which called Sir Ralph Abercromby to service in another quarter.

Before I proceed to speak of the lamentable expedition to Cadiz, it may be worthwhile to look back and inquire what our ministers had been doing since the spring with those military means which they had refused to Sir Charles Stuart.

I have already mentioned that 5,000 of the soldiers which had been promised to him were withdrawn, under the plea that they were wanted to support the King of Portugal against a rumoured invasion of Spaniards. But it was very soon found that there was no intention on the part of Spain to invade the neighbouring kingdom; and before the end of June our government was at a loss to know what to do with the said 5,000 men, and twice as many more, who were by this time fit for service.

✶✶✶✶✶✶

Whenever our ministers found that they had a large body of troops at their disposal they shewed symptoms of *wanting to do something*; but they never were prepared beforehand, and they seldom looked to the main objects of the contest in which they were engaged. Over and over again they missed the proper time for acting vigorously, and mistook the scene on which the power of England might have been brought to bear with effect on the fortune of the way.

✶✶✶✶✶✶

La Vendée had been long pacified by the wise policy which Bonaparte had pursued, and by the crushing of the Chouans in the preceding February; yet, now Sir Edward Pellew was ordered to attack the forts in Quiberon Bay, and a division of our troops was sent to make an attempt on Belleisle. As soon as they had arrived and were able to reconnoitre that fortress, they found that Belleisle was a great deal too strong to be meddled with; the British sailed away unharming and unharmed; and most of the regiments proceeded under Colonel Lord Dalhousie, to Minorca.

The next experiment of our ministers was directed against Ferrol. There might be a better excuse for this attempt, because there were ships of war in the harbour, and a naval establishment of much importance. In its result, however, this essay proved as abortive as that at Belleisle, and in a certain degree it was worse, because it brought some discredit on the arms of England; the forces employed, both naval and military, were large. The troops, under the command of Sir James Murray Pulteney, landed near Ferrol, drove the Spaniards, after a sharp skirmish or two, within the walls, and occupied the heights which overlook the fortress.

That the place might have been carried by a *coup de main*, was the general opinion of our naval men on the spot, and such likewise was the opinion of many of the officers of the army. But Pulteney, or those about him, thought otherwise: he judged that Ferrol could not be taken without a regular siege, and such a loss of time as would enable the Armies of Spain to come to its relief.

✶✶✶✶✶✶

It ought to be recorded, in justice to Sir James Pulteney's memory, that Sir John Moore reconnoitred Ferrol from the same heights, in December 1804, and came to the same conclusion. At the latter period, the British Government had resumed the idea of striking at Ferrol, and capturing or destroying the strong squadron, which then lay ready for sea, in the harbour. Moore was sent in a frigate that be might judge on the spot of the probabilities of success. He landed with two or three officers of the navy, under the pretext of shooting; but, while upon the bill making his observations, he was descried by a Spanish outpost, and the general had a hard run for his life, before he could reach the boat. Sir John told me he saw enough to convince him that Ferrol could not be carried by a *coup de main*.

★★★★★★

The troops were reimbarked, and they sailed away from Ferrol, grumbling against their commander, and stung by the violent taunts of their naval brethren. Unhappy as these attempts had been, unfairly as our troops had been tried, they were yet doomed to encounter a disappointment on a larger scale. Sir James Pulteney, with augmented forces, was ordered to repair to the Bay of Gibraltar, and to that place of rendezvous was Abercromby directed with more than 10,000 men from Minorca. He arrived there on the 14th of September, but it was not till the 20th that Pulteney joined them, and the united fleets of transport anchored in Tetuan Bay. In the meantime, Sir Ralph had learned that the yellow fever, in its most fatal form, was raging in and about Cadiz, the place which he had secret orders to attack.

The general was disposed, in consequence, to suspend his operations against that unhappy town; to repair with his great army to the Tagus, and to wait there till fresh instructions could be received from England. The admiral however. Lord Keith, put a different interpretation on the orders which had been received from our government. He considered them to be peremptory, particularly as to an attack on the Caraccas, and the capture or destruction of the Spanish ships. Under these circumstances. Sir Ralph Abercromby acquiesced, though reluctantly, in the prosecution of the enterprise.

A week was consumed in watering the great armament at Tetuan, and then came contrary winds and calms which delayed its progress, so that it was late on the 4th of October (just the season of equinoctial gales) before the fleet anchored off Cadiz. A great force it was which menaced this city in the hour of its distress. The army under the command of the wise and gallant Abercromby, mustered nearly. 22,000 rank and file (exclusive of the sick), and filled more than 120 sail of troop ships and transports. There, too, rode a brave and powerful squadron of men-of-war, under the orders of Lord Keith.

Up to this time, the leaders of our expedition had obtained little or no intelligence as to the state of preparation in which the Spaniards might be found; it was only known that an attack upon Cadiz had been expected there for some time past. It was now ascertained from fishermen and others, that there were about 8,000 troops in the Isle of Leon, a brigade of infantry at St. Mary's, and one of cavalry at Rota; it was stated likewise, that the fever was raging with unabated fury; that the daily mortality, in the town of Cadiz alone, exceeded two hundred persons; that it prevailed in all the villages around, and was equally fatal among the troops.

There could be no reason to hope that the British Army, if it should be landed, could escape the effects of the pestilence. Still Abercromby felt, dragged thither as he was by the construction which Lord Keith chose to put upon the orders of our government, that the honour of his army was at stake; and he prepared his troops to disembark.

The brigade of guards, and the regiments under General Moore's immediate command (which were called "the Reserve"), received orders to take the lead, and effect the first landing near Rota. But this vanguard could not have much exceeded 4,000 men; and a considerable time must, at all events, have elapsed before they could have been joined by a second division. Sir Ralph, therefore, felt it incumbent upon him to obtain from the admiral a distinct and sufficient assurance, that the succeeding debarkations of his army, with its artillery and indispensable supplies, could be effected with certainty, and a constant communication with the fleet maintained. If the navy could afford him this guarantee, the general was ready to land; nor did lie feel any doubt of his being able to effect the main purpose of the expedition by the destruction of the Spanish arsenals; but his orders from home enjoined that he was to make the attack only *if he was satisfied that his army could be safely re-embarked.*

To this direct question. Lord Keith was found very reluctant to afford a direct answer. Forced, however, to come to the point, he admitted that the opinions of the naval officers who were best acquainted with the coast were not in favour of the undertaking; that if a south-west wind should set in, the fleet could not remain at its present anchorage; that communication with the army could not then be preserved; and that if the weather should become foul and blow hard, the transports would be in danger of being driven ashore. Though Abercromby had generously offered to share with Lord Keith the responsibility of making the attempt, or of abandoning it, the admiral would neither take upon himself to answer for the safe landing of the whole of the army, nor for its re-embarkation, nor for the safety of the transports; while at the same time, His Lordship carefully eluded the invitation to bear his share in the responsibility of abandoning the enterprise.

It would have been the extreme of rashness if Abercromby had persisted in attempting to land his brave army under such circumstances. Lord Keith continued coldly and cautiously to decline giving any assurance that the several divisions of the troops could be set on shore in succession; or, that if the whole could be disembarked, a communication between the army and the fleet could be secured. At the same time, His Lordship would not let slip a syllable which might imply an assent on his part to the relinquishment of the attempt upon the Spanish ships and arsenals. Thus, ungenerously treated by his colleague, Sir Ralph Abercromby was driven to the necessity of relying on his own judgment, and forced to take upon himself the responsibility of abandoning this ill-considered enterprise.

Three things are sufficiently evident with regard to this attempt on Cadiz, or rather on the Spanish fleet and arsenals. 1st. That the British ministers brought together a mass of twenty or twenty-five thousand soldiers for a great undertaking, without having informed themselves whether their landing could be safely made, and their re-embarkation be secured. 2ndly. That a very dangerous season of the year was chosen for these delicate operations, which are always attended with more or less of risk on an enemy's coast, and when time may run short.

******

It may be noted that the number of troops which were selected to make the first landing, could hardly have exceeded 4,500 men, including officers and sergeants. The general would of course have thrown ashore, to meet an expected enemy, as large a force as he could. It is pretty evident, therefore, that the boats of the fleet were sufficient only to carry the above number, which was less than one-fifth of the gross aggregate of the army. Ministers, if they had thought at all on the subject, must have expected that there would be Spanish troops to resist the landing; but they had made no provision of additional boats of light draught of water, or of a construction proper for the service. Four thousand men might have been beaten and sacrificed, before a second division of troops could have come to their support; when if 8,000 could have been set on shore at the same time, they might have been sufficient to make good their footing. The landing in Holland, in the preceding year, had been made under the like disadvantages, owing to the same neglect, or ignorance, of what such a service requires.

✶✶✶✶✶✶

3rdly. That Lord Keith might have informed himself as well (if he did not) with respect to the safety of the anchorage off the bay of Cadiz, while he was lying at Gibraltar, as when he brought the fleet of transports to that insecure station. Admiral Bickerton, and the other officers who knew the coast, were with him from the first, and His Lordship's conduct in persuading Abercromby to proceed in ignorance of the real liabilities was as inexcusable as his personal evasions were ungenerous.

However, here was an end of this grand expedition; and the armies which had been brought together from the east and the west again parted company. Nearly one half of the regiments, composed mainly of soldiers enlisted for service in Europe only, repaired under the command of Sir James Pulteney, to Lisbon; while the rest, under Abercromby, proceeded up the Mediterranean, Sir Ralph was already in possession of the views of the British Government with regard to Egypt. He touched at Gibraltar, Minorca, and Malta, for the sake of exchanging some few of his battalions for others, and of obtaining, as far as the means of those garrisons could afford them, supplies of ammunition, and of hospital and commissariat stores. At Malta, indeed, he remained some weeks, completing the preparations of his army, expecting further instructions, as well as reinforcements, including cavalry, from England, and endeavouring to obtain information as to the strength and circumstances of the enemy whom he was about to assail.

The considerations which determined the British Government to attempt the expulsion of the French from Egypt, were of the greatest weight; insomuch, that we cannot but wonder when we come to view the insufficiency of the means employed, and the slackness manifested in strengthening our army for this service.

From the time when Napoleon Bonaparte succeeded in establishing the dominion of France upon the Nile, England had looked with jealousy, and some apprehension, to the danger which might eventually threaten our possessions in India, if a powerful and enterprising enemy should remain in the possession of Egypt. Very different was our position in Hindostan at the commencement of the present century, from that which we now enjoy—the fierce Mahrattas stood in unbroken strength—a mere rumour of invasion, either by Sikhs or by Affghans, struck deep alarm into our council at Calcutta. To the southward an arduous and costly campaign had been but recently concluded by the conquest of Mysore; nor were tranquillity and undisputed government established as yet in the provinces, which now form parts of the Presidency of Madras.

In Europe another consideration failed not to excite some apprehension in the minds of British statesmen. If the French should retain a long and undisputed possession of Egypt, it was but too probable that they might acquire a dangerous influence at Constantinople. Still stronger were the grounds for uneasiness when Paul, the hot-brained *Czar*, broke wrath fully from his alliance with England, and appeared likely to accept the preferred friendship of Napoleon Bonaparte. Such a union might have been based on mutual guarantees, of the Danubian provinces to Russia, and of Egypt to France.

But there was yet another and a more urgent motive for desiring to expel the French from Egypt, and to press forward the attempt without loss of time. England had lost all her Allies; and she was at the close of 1800, exposed to the hostility of every naval power in Europe. Napoleon was suddenly making the greatest efforts to equip the fleets of France, and Spain, and Holland. Calculating on our being obliged to keep a strong fleet in the Baltic, to make head against the Northern Powers, he was sanguine and strong in the hope that he should acquire a naval superiority in the Mediterranean. At the same time, he forced us to provide largely for the defence of our own shores, by preparations which threatened descents on England and on Ireland.

The British people had come to desire peace, and to feel that a peace was necessary. Our ministers, while acquiescing reluctantly in this conviction, were anxious that they should be in a position to negotiate on strong and advantageous grounds. The greatest difficulty they foresaw was that presented by the chief consul's known determination to maintain the possession of Egypt. To remove the French from thence had become the great and most pressing object of British policy. In the giving and taking, in the balance of the *status quo*, Egypt would be the most important point in a negotiation for peace. Yet scarcely a year had elapsed since the Cabinet of London had refused to ratify a treaty, by which General Kleber, then commander-in-chief of the French Armies in that country, had engaged to give up the fortresses, and evacuate Egypt altogether.

★★★★★★

It is not to be denied that Sir Sidney Smith, with a characteristic confidence, had opened and concluded the Treaty of El Arish, without having received any powers to negotiate, either from the British Government, or from our ambassador at Constantinople. Yet as his proceedings, however irregular, had been successful, and had secured a result of great importance to England; we wonder at first sight at the refusal of our ministers to confirm the convention. Yet it is to be recollected that in December, 1799, the plan suggested by Sir Charles Stewart was in the contemplation of our Cabinet; and that Bonaparte scarcely steadied in his place of power, was labouring with difficulty to collect troops in sufficient numbers to make head against the lately-victorious Austrians. To have brought to Toulon at this crisis an army of French veterans, would have been no less than a betrayal of our ally, and the destruction of the views which wore then entertained by our government.

******

It is true that the relative positions of France and England had been greatly altered in the interval, France had now no enemy to combat but England; and England was now without an ally, save that crumbling image of Ottoman greatness which still stood, though tottering, at Constantinople. It was under these circumstances that the British Government resolved on attempting, in conjunction with such aid as the Turks could or would afford, to expel the French from Egypt. We had wasted the whole of the year 1800, though we had 25,000 soldiers ready for service, and fleets which ruled on every sea. We had failed to assist the Austrians, or to save Genoa. We had retired with discredit from before Ferrol and Cadiz; and now, at the eleventh hour, our ministers sent Abercromby with 15,000 men to invade a country, of which all the fortresses and harbours were in the possession of a French Army, mustering not less than 28,000 veteran soldiers.

It had happened unfortunately that despatches from General Kleber, and letters from the officers of his army to their friends in France, had been taken at sea by an English cruiser. Both the official and the private letters were couched in the most desponding tone, and conveyed so gloomy and fallacious a view of the condition of the French Army that our ministers readily gave credence to accounts which gratified their wishes, and encouraged their hopes. Under this delusion, and without searching farther as to the facts, they framed the expedition to Egypt, believing that there remained for its defence not more than 15,000 or 16,000 sickly and discontented troops.

Campaign in Egypt in 1801

The British Army was ready to sail from Malta early in December, 1800, but it was detained by adverse winds till the 20th, when the first division got under weigh and steered for the coast of Caramania. The second division put to sea on the following day.

Before he quitted Malta, Sir Ralph Abercromby had sketched out a general plan of operations, admitting an alternative which he might be compelled by circumstances to adopt. To gain possession of Alexandria was his first and preferable object. The best information he had been able to collect represented the French garrison to be insufficient in numbers for the defence of the extensive fortifications; and the works themselves had been, it was stated, neglected, and were incomplete. (Such proved in the sequel to have been really the case. It was not till after the landing of the British, that the French exerted themselves to repair and strengthen the outworks of Alexandria.)

If Alexandria could be taken, its importance was hardly to be overrated. It afforded the only harbour on the coast of Egypt. The French Army in that country would be at once cut off from the chance of receiving succour from France. To the English it would present a secure base for their further operations, and a certain line of communication with Malta and England. On the other hand, it was feared that as the port of Alexandria had been very loosely watched for some time past, the enemy might have recently obtained supplies and reinforcements by sea. It was also asserted with confidence that the stormy weather, which prevailed usually from November till April, must render the landing of an army on the open coast of Egypt a very hazardous enterprise.

Then, if it should be found impracticable to effect a landing in the neighbourhood of Alexandria, the only alternative would be to disembark the troops in the roadstead of Damietta, where there was some partial shelter for shipping, and where less opposition was to be expected from the enemy. If such should be the course which he might find himself obliged to take, Sir Ralph proposed to lead his army up the Nile; and making Damietta the base of his operations, to act against the French forces which occupied Cairo; while the Turks, who were understood to be assembling at Jaffa with the intention of advancing to Salahieh, should pursue their march towards the great city, in co-operation with the English, and in conformity with their movements.

******

It must be borne in mind that the general had been ordered on this expedition with very erroneous information as to the strength of the enemy's army in Egypt. Out ministers believed that in the whole of Egypt there did not remain more than 9,000 French troops, with 4,000 or 5,000 auxiliaries, Greeks and Copts.

******

Abercromby was willing to entertain good hopes of success in this direction, because he had been led to expect that a strong body of troops from India might be landed at Suez in the spring of 1801, and his own movement upon Cairo would facilitate their junction. Still the general preferred the attempt upon Alexandria, if the weather should allow his troops to make good their landing near that place, and yet preserve their communication with the shipping. Though the naval officers in general took an unfavourable view of these questions, Captain Hallowell, and one or two others who were well acquainted with the coast and with the climate, considered the chances of effecting a successful debarkation to be far from improbable.

It was with these varying impressions on his mind that Abercromby proceeded to the place which had been chosen for the assembling of all his troops; for the preparing of his soldiers for action; and for procuring horses and other means of which he was as yet destitute. His two divisions of infantry were reunited in the Bay of Marmorice, on the 2nd of January, 1801. This bay, or rather the Gulf of Makri, of which it forms a part, is situated on the southern face of Asia Minor; and here the general proposed to remain a short time, during which he might concert measures with the Turkish commanders, procure horses for the service of his artillery, as well as for the remounting of the dragoons who were expected from England, and hire vessels for their conveyance to the coast of Egypt.

Immediately after Sir Ralph's arrival at Marmorice, he despatched

General Moore on a mission to the *grand vizier*, who was at the head of a Turkish Army encamped near Jaffa. His first object was to obtain some knowledge of the real strength and efficiency of the Ottoman forces. In the next place Moore was to endeavour, if he should find the Turks to be equal to the enterprise, to concert measures with the *vizier*, and to bring him into an engagement for a plan of co-operation against Cairo; the British advancing from Damietta, and the Turks from Salahieh. This scheme was now proposed, because Sir Ralph had recently been led to entertain less sanguine hopes than before of succeeding in an attack with his small army on Alexandria.

Some late reports magnified the strength of this place. Others asserted, that no drinkable water was to be found along the shores on either side of the town. The naval men represented the probability that their ships might be blown off the coast after landing the troops: and the English officers, who were attendant on the Turkish Army, had found that the *grand vizier* would decline to attempt a diversion on the side of Cairo, unless the British should be sufficiently near to afford him support.

General Moore's business therefore was, in the main, to ascertain whether the force of our ally was really such as to render his co-operation effective in the projected march upon Cairo; to assure the *vizier* of our firm purpose to support him, and even to take the initiative in the movements against the French. He was at the same time to try to secure a supply of at least one thousand horses for our own dragoons; and the aid of some Turkish cavalry who might be attached to the British column. Every exertion was to be used to obtain good intelligence as to the strength and resources of the enemy; and if the proposed plan should be adopted by the Allies, then means should be devised to mislead the French and make them believe that the attack of the English would be directed against Alexandria.

Up to this time General Koehler, an able officer in the British service, had been employed as our military agent at the headquarters of the *grand vizier*; but upon Moore's arrival at Jaffa he found that Koehler had died a few days before. The loss of his influence and acquaintance with Turkish affairs, and particularly with the state of that army, was unfortunate; but Major Holloway and other officers of our engineers or artillery, who had been attached with about thirty gunners to General Koehler's mission, remained in the camp; and Moore was introduced to the *reis effendi*, and afterwards to the *vizier* himself. The conversations which ensued were carried on in the most friendly spirit, and the dull old chieftain gave an easy assent to Sir R. Abercromby's proposals; but he knew nothing of the numbers or means of the French, and little of his own.

Moore, however, ascertained that this nominal army consisted of some 14,000 or 15,000 men; one half of them being horsemen, and all thoroughly "Irregulars:" that they had a good many pieces of cannon; but a scanty supply of provisions for their men, and none for their horses, wherewith to undertake the march across the desert: that the plague was in the camp, and numbers of men were dying every day; but there was no exertion, no forethought, no intelligence. General Moore rejoined his commander on the 20th of January, bringing this account of our allies, and these impressions of their worthlessness. Sir Ralph saw at once, that it would be unsafe to engage his army in operations which might render it in a great measure dependent on a mass of semi-barbarians, ignorant of the rules of civilized warfare, and little able to take care even of themselves, he had received no intelligence of the troops expected from India, and he determined without hesitation to resume his former design of directing his attempt upon Alexandria.

A sort of council of war was summoned, at which certain officers of the navy as well as of the army were present General Abercromby informed them of his intentions, and explained his motives; but he desired, before the final resolution should be taken, to receive satisfactory information from the officers of the navy on the following points:

1st. Can the anchorage in the Bay of Aboukir be depended on for the fleet of transports? 2nd. Will the navy be able to put on shore not only the troops, but likewise the ammunition, provisions, and even the water necessary for the army during two or three weeks, as well as the ordnance which would be required for the siege of Alexandria?

To these questions Captain Hallowell and Sir Sidney Smith (as being the officers best acquainted with the coast) returned favourable answers. The former, more particularly, declared that he felt no doubt of its being in the power of the fleet, when anchored in the Bay of Aboukir, to land everything that would be required for the troops, and to convey further supplies by means of boats, which might move abreast of the army as it advanced.

The result of this conference was a determination to attempt a landing in the Bay of Aboukir. Yet Abercromby, and those in his confidence, had ere this found reason to apprehend that the strength of the enemy was far more formidable than he had been taught to expect; and that the French could bring into the field superior numbers of fighting men, with all the advantages of a veteran cavalry, and a well-appointed artillery. By this time the British Army had been joined by the dismounted dragoons of the 12th and 26th Regiments, Still it was necessary to remain at Marmorice, not only to procure horses for the cavalry and mules for the carriage of stores, but likewise to collect, from Rhodes and other places, vessels for the transport of these animals.

★★★★★★

It was but slowly that horses were procured from the interior of the country. However, at last about 400 were got for the dragoons, and a sufficient number to draw eight or ten field-pieces. Out of nearly 1,000 horses, which were sent by the *vizier* at General Moore's solicitation, three-fourths were rejected as utterly unserviceable.

★★★★★★

In the meanwhile, rehearsals were made of a landing in the face of an enemy; and this practice proved to have been of much advantage when the hour of performance came. An admirable paper of instructions,(see Appendix, A and B), to be observed in the actual debarkation of the troops, was drawn up by Sir Ralph Abercromby and Colonel Anstruther, in conjunction with the naval commanders, and a rigid adherence to these instructions was enjoined on the superior officers of both services. To this pre-arrangement, and to the excellence of the plan itself may be ascribed in a great measure the perfect order and the quick success with which the landing of the army was effected on the 8th of March.

During this unavoidable delay, two large French frigates escaped our cruisers, and carried into Alexandria 800 soldiers, besides artillery and military stores of which the garrison was in great need. At length, on the 18th of February, our army was ready to quit the Bay of Marmorice; but a foul wind detained the fleet till the 22nd, when the whole (about 180 vessels) made sail, and on the 1st of March the leading frigate got sight of the land near Alexandria. The weather was unsettled and squally; the sea rough, and unfit for any attempt to disembark. It seemed therefore desirable to keep our great armament out of the enemy's sight; but Lord Keith led on the fleet till our people could distinguish the colours of vessels in the harbour, and our wide array was fully exposed to the observation of the French.

After laying-to till dusk the fleet made sail to seaward, and on the next morning they entered the Bay of Aboukir. The signal was hoisted for the troops to prepare to land; and the chief command of the boats, and the direction of the debarkation, were confided to Captain Cochrane. The weather however continued to be boisterous and unfavourable; and, as landing was impracticable, Sir Ralphs taking with him General Moore and some officers of the staff, ran along the coast in a cutter, to examine the beach more closely. They saw that sandhills, which were generally of a trifling height, rose irregularly from the shore, sprinkled here and there with clumps of date or palm trees.

From distance to distance there were small groups of tents between the Castle of Aboukir and the mouth of Lake Maadieh. Some working parties appeared to be busy on the sandhills; and two or three of the enemy's gunboats were lying at anchor close to the shore. On the generals return in the afternoon, orders were issued for the reserve and the brigade of guards to be ready to step into the boats at four o' clock the next morning.

******

At this very moment, one of the enemy's armed vessels, coming out of Alexandria, ran through the lines of our fleet, and anchored with impunity under the Castle of Aboukir, in a position to rake the beach on which we had determined to attempt the landing! Lord Keith's only observation was, that he could not spare a vessel to go after her!

******

When sailing from Marmorice, Sir Ralph Abercromby had sent forward Major McKerras and Major Fletcher of the Engineers, in a gunboat, to reconnoitre the coast about the Bay of Aboukir; but it was now found that these officers had ventured too closely in, and had been cut off by a superior vessel. Major McKerras had been killed, and Fletcher, with the gunboat, taken. This loss of our two most experienced engineers proved in the sequel to have been a very unfortunate circumstance.

For three days there blew a gale of wind from the north-west which put any attempt to land out of the question. On the 7th of March the weather began to be more moderate, and Abercromby sent General Moore and Colonel Anstruther, the quartermaster-general, to examine the little Bay of Aboukir more closely, and to ascertain whether the enemy had thrown up any works since his visit on the 2nd. The space on which it would be necessary to make the landing, was found to be about a mile in extent. To the right (of the assailants) there rose a steep and high sandhill; the seaward face of which was partially flanked by the guns of the Castle of Aboukir.

The ground along the curve of the bay, rising in banks from the beach, appeared to be everywhere favourable to the enemy, as he could keep his troops concealed and sheltered though close to the water's edge. On the left the sandhills were broken, irregular, and dotted with clumps of trees. The picquets of the enemy stretched along the whole extent, and individuals, probably officers upon the watch, were pacing to and fro; but there were no signs of batteries or of new works.

The wind had shifted to the southward and the sea had abated. The general determined to make his landing the next morning; but as the infantry were all on board of the large troop-ships, which were anchored six or seven miles from the shore, much time was required and much arrangement necessary for the proper performance of the service.

★★★★★★

The "troop ships" then in use were for the most part old two-deckers, sixty-fours or fifties, without their lower deck guns. It was a badly arranged service, and equally disagreeable to the officers of the army and the navy, who were always quarrelling.

★★★★★★

In the evening of the 7th two of our lighter vessels of war changed their stations, and anchored as near to the shore as they could conveniently lie. One of these vessels served to mark the right of the intended attack; and alongside these two vessels all the boats, containing the leading division of the army, were ordered to assemble in the darkness of the night. It had been found that the boats altogether were capable of conveying a greater number of men than the guards and the reserve could muster. The 54th Regiment, belonging to Coote's brigade, was therefore added to those which had been held in readiness under the former order.

At the same time (the evening) the rest of the troops were removed from the large ships into others of a lighter draught of water, that they might be the more quickly landed in support of the first division, when the latter should be on shore, and the boats should be at liberty to return for a second debarkation.

At two in the morning of the memorable 8th of March, 1801, the troops, which had been chosen to strike the first blow upon the sands of Egypt, stepped into the boats. Soon after daylight nearly all had reached the vessels which had been placed as the rallying points; but much time was consumed in disentangling the boats, and arranging them according to the line of battle of the army, so that when they touched the beach each brigade, battalion, and company might be in its proper place. The reserve, led by Sir John Moore, Hildebrand Oakes, and Brent Spencer, formed the right; and their division of boats was under the immediate command of Captain Cochrane.

✶✶✶✶✶✶

Captain Cochrane had the command of the whole of the boats employed on this service. Under him Sir Sidney Smith had the particular charge of the launches which conveyed the artillery, and he afterwards commanded the seamen who were landed to assist the army.

✶✶✶✶✶✶

Alongside the vessel on the left were marshalled the two battalions of the Guards, under General Ludlow, and the detachment belonging to Coote's brigade. It was 8 o'clock, a.m., before the line of boats pulled on abreast, and in steady order, towards the shore, and till that time the enemy had lain in silence observing our movements; but as soon as our boats came within their reach, fifteen pieces of cannon opened upon them with round shot, though the enemy's fire was somewhat disturbed and confused by that of several English gunboats which had been thrown in advance of our line. So closely were our soldiers packed in the boats that they could not move, and indeed the strictest orders had been given that they should sit perfectly still.

The seamen pulled steadily onward, the pace of each boat being regulated by that on the extreme right. In this calm order on they came, till they were within reach of grape shot, and then the fire became terribly severe and destructive. Some boats were sunk, and many of our men were killed or wounded as they sat motionless and helpless under the storm of shot, to which both seamen and soldiers answered occasionally by loud hurrahs!

When still nearer, the musketry of the French was poured in, quick and sharp, and our men were falling fast; but at length the boats upon the right felt the ground. Out sprang our hard-tried soldiers, each man was in his place, and with Moore and Spencer at their head, the 23rd and 28th Regiments, and the four flank companies of the 40th, breasted the steep sandhill. (The 28th seems to have been kept back in support of the rush made by the others.) Without firing a shot, they rushed at one burst to the summit of the ridge, driving headlong before them two battalions of the enemy and capturing four pieces of field artillery. After reining in his men, that they might recover breath, Moore opened their fire upon the French who were retreating rapidly across a little patch of plain ground, and then again, he pushed forward, again driving the foe before him, till he occupied some rising ground which afforded a favourable position. There Moore halted till he could learn what had happened on his left.

That wing of the reserve which had been entrusted to the guidance of Brigadier Oakes, touched the beach a few minutes after their comrades, whose exploit has been just described. The 42nd Regiment was the first on shore, and the 58th a few minutes afterwards; the ground in their front was of a more gentle slope than that upon the right, and here the French stood prepared, not with infantry only, but with some troops of cavalry. The enemy attacked at once, but the admirable order in which the 42nd had been landed, enabled them to repulse the assault by their heavy fire; and as the French drew back, Oakes, leading on this regiment, followed by the 58th, attacked in his turn, and driving the enemy over the sandhills, captured three of their guns.

Farther to the left the Coldstream and 3rd Guards ought, according to the plan prescribed, to have prolonged the line beyond Oakes' brigade, but the boats which carried them and the 54th Regiment fell into confusion. These battalions were consequently hurried into the shoal water, intermingled and disordered, and as their difficulty was observed by the enemy, the Guards were charged by the French cavalry before they could form their line. However, the attack was bravely repulsed, and General Ludlow soon got his brigade into its proper place—to the left of Oakes and the reserve.

******

In the severe service of this day the loss of the British was as follows; Army, 4 officers, 4 sergeants, and 94 rank and file killed: 1 officer, 1 sergeant, and 32 rank and file missing: 26 officers, 34 sergeants, and 455 men wounded. Navy, 2 officers and 49 seamen killed: 12 officers and 115 men wounded.

******

Here then was the problem, of landing 5,000 or 6,000 men in the face of an enemy prepared to meet them, satisfactorily solved. But the British had neither horsemen nor artillery on shore, and our gallant infantry were unable to follow up their victory and inflict a heavier loss on their beaten enemy. The behaviour of our troops in this arduous service was above all praise; the patience with which they bore the storm of shot while confined to their boats; the alacrity with which they leapt ashore and instantly formed their lines; these things were unparalleled, and are even more worthy of our remembrance than the gallantry with which our troops overthrew the French on every point, when the British foot was on the shore. Still it ought not to be forgotten that the storming of the steep sandhill on the right, by Moore's brigade, was long a theme of especial admiration in the army.

While the fight was going on, the boats returned to fetch the remainder of our infantry, and the whole of them were landed in the course of the afternoon, with some field pieces, and a few horses.

✶✶✶✶✶✶

The horses of the army had been embarked on board the vessels hired from the Greek islands. None of these kept up with our fleet, but they came straggling into Aboukir from the 10th to the 14th of March.

✶✶✶✶✶✶

In the evening the army moved forward some two or three miles, leaving a detachment to blockade the Castle of Aboukir.

✶✶✶✶✶✶

The *commandant* of this fort refused to admit, and even fired on a flag of truce which accompanied a summons to surrender. It was found necessary to land heavy guns from the fleet on the 13th, and to batter the old walls, but the castle was not surrendered till the 18th.

✶✶✶✶✶✶

Early on the morning of the 9th of March, General Moore and Colonel Anstruther, (quartermaster-general), went forth to reconnoitre, (escorted by the 92nd Regiment the Corsican Rangers, and a few dragoons, whose horses had arrived. They found the country to be of sand, the surface irregular, and in most parts sprinkled with palm and date trees. At the end of three or four miles, the two chiefs, who had pushed on so far with the dragoons only, fell in with a strong party of the enemy's cavalry, and were compelled to return. But they observed that about two miles in advance of the actual bivouac of our army, the ground was much narrowed between the sea and Lake Maadieh; and as it offered an advantageous position, the reserve was ordered to occupy it that evening. The next morning, the 10th, Moore again went out to renew and extend his observations; but he was soon met by the advanced guard of a large body of cavalry escorting French generals who were likewise engaged in reconnoitring. A skirmish ensued in which our Corsicans lost a few men.

During three days, the advance of the English was delayed by the difficulty which was found in landing provisions and ammunition: the wind was high and the surf dangerous. On the 12th, the army moved forward in (columns; and as they approached the screen formed by the enemy's horsemen, the latter retired gradually, till the British came in sight of some large bodies of the French infantry who appeared, at first, to be advancing as if to battle.(The enemy had been reinforced by the arrival, on the 10th of March, of four battalions and some squadrons of cavalry, from the upper country.)

Sir Ralph then gave the order to form lines, and so perfect had been the order preserved upon the march, though the columns had filed through trees and bushes, and amongst scattered ruins, that when they deployed there was scarcely any correction required. However, the enemy came no nearer, but his infantry was seen to occupy a range of heights bounding a comparative plain, on the opposite side of which stood the British. The distance between the two armies was about one mile and a half.

Both lay upon their arms during the night; but on our side, the 90th and 92nd Regiments were ordered out and placed under the temporary command of General Moore, who was specially charged with the duty of protecting our bivouac against a surprise. He divided the two battalions into six bodies, placed at intervals sufficient to cover the whole front of our army; and each of these bodies threw forward one third of its numbers, to form a connected and watchful chain, which was relieved at the end of each hour by one of the remaining thirds. Thus, passed the night in silence: the enemy was close, but he made no attack. Under the circumstances of our army, and the expectation that General Ménou would come down from Cairo, an immediate battle was earnestly desired by the British commander.

He determined that his army should move forward, and assail the heights on which the French were posted. At six a.m., on the 13th of March, the whole marched onward in three columns. That on the right consisted of the reserve, with a few horsemen, under Moore. The central column was composed of the brigades commanded by Craddock and Coote, the guards being kept a little behind them as a supporting body. On the left marched the three brigades, (Cavan's, Doyle's, and Stuart's) which in the order of battle were intended to form the second line. Somewhat in advance of the central column marched the 90th Regiment, and the left was led in like manner by the 92nd. (The 90th was followed by Craddock; the 92nd by Lord Cavan.)

Sir Ralph's plan was to turn the enemy's right, and to attack his position on that flank. However, as our columns approached, the French

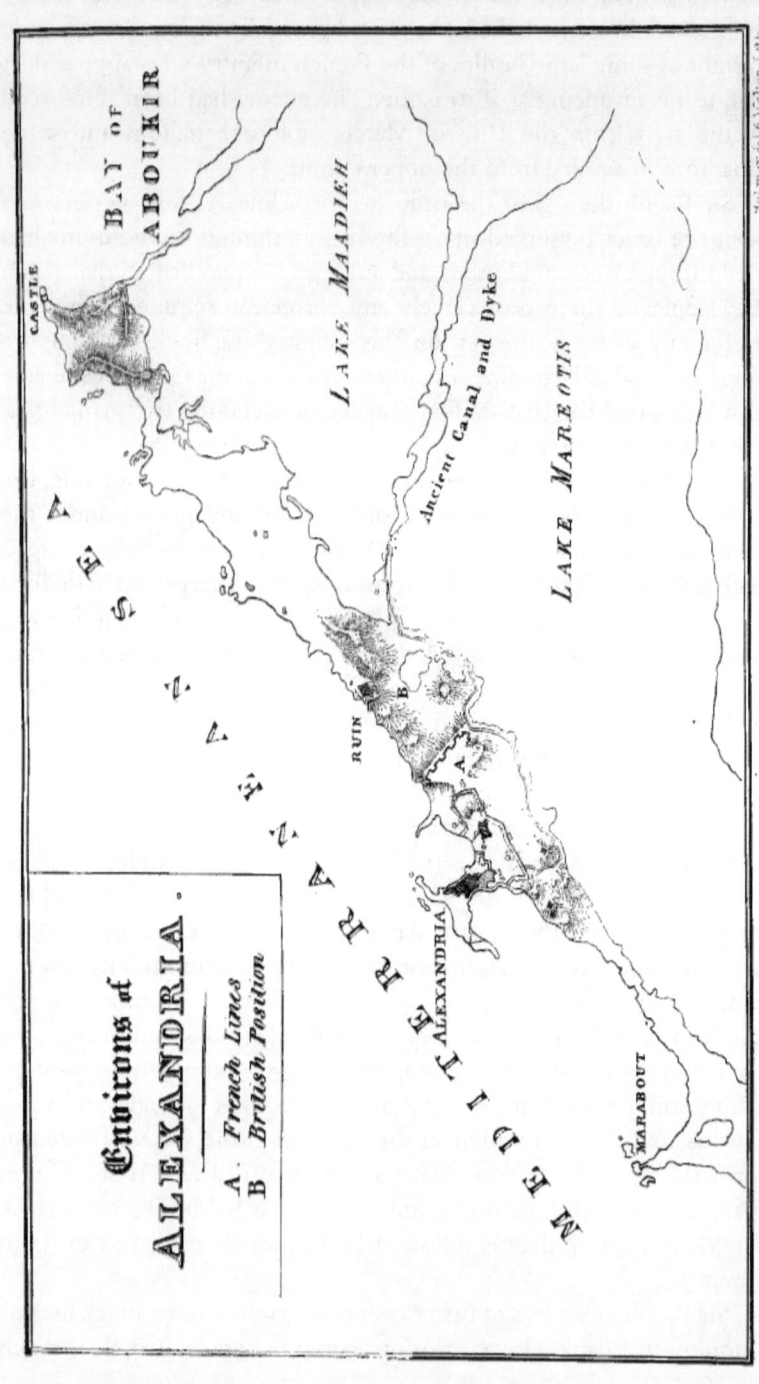

came down from their heights, while their guns opened on the British, and gathering rapidly to their right they felt with their cavalry, supported by masses of infantry, on the 90th and 92nd. These two regiments bore themselves nobly, repulsing their fierce assailants and maintaining their ground, though they suffered very severely before the columns which they headed could deploy and render them effectual support.

★★★★★★

The 90th (under Rowland Hill) was particularly distinguished. The French cavalry, led by Latour Manbourg, who was wounded, charged desperately on this regiment; and some of them were bayoneted in the ranks of the 90th.

The 92nd suffered equally from the grape shot of the French guns, and the musketry of a large body of infantry.

★★★★★★

The action now became more general; Craddock and Coote advancing rapidly in line, while Moore's reserve remained in column, and covered the right flank of our army. Forced back by the fire and onward movement of the British, the French drew off in haste, under the protection of their artillery which played with severe effect upon our troops; but these good soldiers never lost their order; their movements were executed with the regularity of a field-day at home. At length, the reserve arrived at a large mass of ruined buildings, standing on a rising ground and overlooking a plain, across which the French were retreating hurriedly. Moore observed that he had somewhat outmarched the left of the army, and that if our troops should continue to advance over the plain, they would come under the range of heavy guns planted on the fortified heights beyond it.

He, therefore, halted his people, and Craddock, whose brigade was next to the reserve, did the same, expecting that when the left came up, the whole would be halted to breathe the men and to gain time for reconnoitring the position of the enemy, which appeared to be formidable. But the brigades upon the left pursued their march without stopping; and the right wing then conformed of course to the movements Thus the whole advanced to the middle of the plain where they became exposed to a heavy cannonade from the French batteries on the heights in front. Here our troops were ordered to halt, and Abercromby called Generals Hutchinson and Moore to a consultation.

It was resolved that the plan which Sir Ralph had entertained from the first should be pursued: that the right of the enemy's position should be turned and assaulted, and that at the same time the left of the French should be attacked in front. With this view, Hutchinson was directed to lead forward the three brigades of the second line, and marching over the dried mud along the borders of the Lake Mareotis till he should have gained the enemy's flank, to array his battalions and storm the heights upon that side.

Moore was ordered to wait till Hutchinson had reached his ground and was opening his attack. Then the reserve was to push rapidly along the sea shore, supported by the brigade of Guards, and to fall upon the left of the French line.

Coote and Craddock, with 800 dragoons in their rear (one-half of whom were without horses), were to remain stationary, ready to support either of the wings, or to repel any sortie of the enemy. But Hutchinson had a considerable distance to traverse, some difficulties of ground, and some little opposition to overcome; and when he arrived on the ground from which his attack was to be made, he found the enemy's position to be so strong that he determined to send a report of his observations to Sir R. Abercromby, and to wait for his further instructions.

******

Dillon's regiment distinguished itself by carrying a redoubt with the bayonet; and the handful of men composing the 44th, likewise carried with the bayonet a bridge which the French attempted to defend.

The heights were defended by a powerful artillery, and if carried, they again appeared to lie under the heavy guns of the French forts, nor had our troops any tools for entrenching themselves.

******

The commander-in-chief despatched the Adjutant-General Hope to examine the ground, and judge of circumstances, and he soon afterwards followed in person; but while these things were going on, some hours passed away, during which our army was exposed to a continual cannonade and suffered heavy losses. The French had recovered their spirits and repaired their first disorder. They reinforced their left, which was to have been attacked by the reserve: and Sir Ralph at length relinquished his intention of forcing the enemy to a decisive battle. Our brave troops were withdrawn from the plain; and with feelings of bitter disappointment, but in perfect order, they retired to the position on which Moore had proposed to halt in the morning.

The loss of officers and men had been very great. Including all ranks, 1,300 had fallen in this unprofitable, though honourable conflict.

******

It is not improbable that the failure of the intended attack, and the great loss sustained by our troops on the 13th of March, were owing in some measure to physical defects under which both Abercromby and Hutchinson laboured. The eyesight of both the one and the other was extremely imperfect.

******

The British Army now took up the position between the sea and Lake Maadieh, in which was fought a few days later, the memorable battle of the 21st of March. The ground was elevated and pretty strong upon the right, where stood the remains of ancient buildings, overlooking the beach and in advance of the rest of the army. Here lay the reserve under Moore and Oakes. Separated by a little valley from this projecting flank, there rose a large sandhill which was occupied by the Guards and by Coote's brigade. The position on the left, where Craddock was posted with four battalions, was naturally weak, having an open plain in front and the dry bed of the Lake Mareotis; but it was somewhat retired, and partially covered on its right by the sandhill on which Coote's brigade was posted.

Altogether our position was *en échelon* from the right. Lord Cavan, Doyle, Stuart, and the dragoons, formed a second line. To strengthen the front, and more particularly the left of our army, working parties were set to throw up redoubts and *flèches*; and orders were given for the landing of heavy cannon with the intention of arming these works. From being the assailants, the British were suddenly assuming a defensive posture. After the action of the 13th, our officers were allowed to land their light baggage; for nearly a week they had no other clothes than what they carried on their backs. Good water had been found by digging (at the suggestion of Sir Sidney Smith), wherever date trees were growing; but there was much distress amongst the troops from a want of fuel; the fresh-cut trees proving of little use for this purpose.

In the meantime, the general was unable to gain any trustworthy intelligence. No deserters came in; and the Arabs told lies. All that Abercromby knew was, that the French had fought him on the 13th with 5,000 or 6,000 men; that the position they occupied in his front, at the distance of a mile and a half, was strong, and defended by a force of artillery greatly superior to his own. That if he could succeed in carrying it, there still remained the siege of Alexandria to be undertaken, with the prospect of having another army, from Cairo and Upper Egypt, upon his flank and rear. He knew also that nearly two thousand of his brave soldiers had already died in battle, or had been disabled by wounds. Our prospects began to wear a gloomy colouring. There were rumours, though uncertain, of the approach of Ménou with an army from Cairo; and Abercromby felt poignantly that he had been sent on this great enterprise with deceptive information and insufficient numbers.

An unfortunate affair of cavalry, which occurred on the 18th of March, had helped to vex the spirit both of the general and the army, A small body of the enemy's horsemen were observed in the afternoon, to be reconnoitring the left of our position. In the rear of that flank, lay our two regiments of dragoons, portions of which had just received their Turkish horses. General Finch was absent at the time; and Colonel Archdall of the 12th, impatient of affront, hastily mounted some 80 or 100 men, and galloped forth to drive away the enemy. He was met gallantly by the French hussars, and the two parties charged through each other. Before the British could rein in their half-broken steeds, and turn back upon their adversaries, they came under the fire of a company of grenadiers who were lying in ambush behind some ruins, for the express purpose of supporting their own horsemen.

Many of our men and horses fell; and before the party could get into order, the hussars had rallied, and were upon them from the other side. It was with difficulty that our dispersed dragoons made good their flight to the lines, leaving about thirty prisoners, and several dead, Archdall, whose rash gallantry had provoked this skirmish, lost an arm. On the other hand, the Castle of Aboukir was surrendered on the 18th of March, and the Queens Regiment rejoined the army.

On the 20th of March, Sir Ralph confided to the few whose opinions he valued, the resolution he had taken to make one more attempt to carry the position occupied by the French, though he was still uncertain whether the forts Crétin and Caffarelli, might not completely command it with their guns; or whether, on the other hand, the capture of these forts might not be facilitated by our gaining possession of the first line of heights. It was the general's plan to bring up his heavy artillery and entrenching tools as speedily as possible; as soon as they arrived, to push forward his guns in the night-time; and, when at daybreak they opened their fire upon the French lines, to assault at the same time both the flanks of the enemy.

If the attempt should fail; Sir Ralph proposed that his army should retire to its present position, and should hold this, strengthened as it would be by the heavy guns, while other lines of works farther to the rear should be rapidly formed and armed. On these in succession the troops should fall back; till their re-embarkation might be covered by the last of the lines of redoubts, the Castle of Aboukir, and the fire of the fleet.

Such were the dismal prospects which presented themselves at this time to the mind of the brave old Abercromby; but from such difficulties and dangers the British Army was happily delivered by the rash presumption of the enemy. On the very day when the general disclosed his plans to those who enjoyed his entire confidence, Ménou had entered Alexandria with nearly 6,000 of his best troops; which, added to those who lay in front of the British Army, gave the French general a force of about eleven thousand veteran soldiers disposable for battle, he determined on attacking the invaders without delay.

Up to this time the only change which had been made in the position of our army was, that Lord Cavan's brigade had been placed somewhat *en potence*, so as to cover the left of the British line from any attack which might be made by the enemy from the isthmus between the Lakes Maadieh and Mareotis, (the latter being partially practicable for troops). Generals Stuart, Doyle, and Finch remained with seven battalions, and the dismounted dragoons, as a second line. Along the front of the army (which lay *en échelon* from the right), several slight works had been hastily thrown up and were armed with the field pieces, and with two iron 24-pounders which had just arrived.

One of these redoubts, open to the rear, was formed somewhat in advance of the great ruins (called by the French "*le Camp des Romains*,") where lay the regiments of the reserve. From this work, a flanking though distant fire might be poured along the front of the height on which the guards were encamped: while two batteries in the centre commanded the plain in their own front, and flanked that of Craddock's brigade upon the left. The latter was further protected by a pretty large redoubt, and two redans.

During the night of the 20th of March, all remained as quiet as usual; and Moore, who happened to be the general-officer of the day, was just giving the order for withdrawing the picquets at daybreak, when some musketry was heard on the extreme left of the line. Moore's impression at the moment was, that it was only a false alarm; but he was riding to ascertain the cause, when a rattling fire burst out upon the right.

"This is the true attack," cried the general, and he spurred back to his own corps. The picquets were all falling back before the rapid approach of the enemy's columns, which could be dimly discerned through the darkness. But the British troops were already under arms, and repairing to their allotted posts. (It was a standing order that every regiment should be formed and at its post, an hour before daybreak.) When Moore arrived at the redoubt on the right, he found the 28th Regiment, under Colonel Edward Paget, already hotly engaged, though hardly able to see their assailants, the smoke and flashes rendering the darkness of the hour still more perplexing. The shouts of the French soldiers, and the rattling of their drums, were heard above the volleying musketry.

The effects of their fire were felt both from the front and from the sea-side. Paget was struck down by a shot in the neck. Moore's horse was wounded, and the general was for some time on foot. But his plan for the defence of "the Roman Camp" had been concerted beforehand with Brigadier Oakes, who now brought up one wing of the 42nd to cover the left flank of the 28th Regiment The ruins were manned by the 58th Regiment, whose fire was poured upon the beach to the right of the redoubt. Moore despatched orders that the 23rd and the flank companies of the 40th should support the 58th, and that the remaining wing of the 42nd should join that which was already in front.

Let us now turn to the plan of attack, by which the French proposed to drive the leopards into the sea. The division commanded by General Lanusse, an experienced and valiant leader, was to surprise and carry by assault the Roman Camp, following up its defenders without respite, and gaining ground so as to fall upon the right flank and rear of the British centre, while cavalry should pursue and complete the dispersion of our right wing. (General Lanusse's division consisted of Silly's and Valentin's brigades, strengthened by companies of grenadiers drawn from other regiments. Altogether about 3,000 men.) On the right of Lanusse, but a little retired, marched the division of General Rampon. It was his task to attack the British centre, as soon as Lanusse should have obtained any advantage.

Rampon again was to be supported on his right by Regnier, who was at the head of the strongest division of the French Army (nearly 3,500 infantry). This general was to give the signal for battle by despatching, before daybreak, 100 of the Dromedary corps, supported by

300 dragoons, who were to make a feigned attack on the extreme left of the English posts. In effect they surprised the redan on the isthmus, making our soldiers at that outpost prisoners; and it was the fire of this party which was first heard by our officers, and excited for a short time a belief that the French were directing their attack against our left flank.

But this demonstration was only to serve as a signal for the advance of Lanusse; and Regnier's real part was to occupy the attention of the left wing of the British; to deter them from moving to support their right; and finally to co-operate with Rampon in forcing our centre. There the French hoped, that the whole of their army, wheeling round to their right, would drive the British, in a heap, and in helpless confusion, to the waters of Lake Maadieh.

This plan of attack bears the marks of a grand conception, and shows nothing of the incapacity with which Ménou has been charged. It might have succeeded against inferior infantry, and the French had been used to deal with the Austrian soldiers, such as they were in 1796 and 1797. But the column under Lanusse was not of strength sufficient for the task assigned to it. The enemy well knew that the height crowned by the Roman ruins was the strongest post in the British line, though they did not know that it was manned by our best troops under our best officers.

We have left the 28th Regiment hotly engaged in their redoubt; the 58th in the ruins supported by the 23rd, and the flank companies of the 40th; and one wing of the 42nd just arriving, followed by the other half of the battalion, to cover the left flank of the 28th, At this moment, a close column of the French was discerned through the twilight, pushing on in silence, and already in rear of the 42nd. General Moore ran to the right wing of this regiment, faced it about, and charging instantly upon the enemy drove them headlong into the ruins, where they were met by the 23rd and 40th, and the whole of them were killed or taken.

Leading back the men of the 42nd, and rejoining the other companies, Moore encountered another body of French, These were driven back after a short conflict, but the general received a shot in his leg, and the regiment pursuing its advantage hastily, was charged and overthrown by a desperate onset of the enemy's cavalry. Though broken, the Highlanders, as they regained their legs, plied their muskets individually and so coolly, that they struck down many men and horses, while the 40th from the ruins poured a destructive fire on the flank of the enemy's squadrons.

The French, however, led by Generals Roize and Boussart, still galloped furiously onwards. Their ranks were disordered while plunging among the camp kitchens and tents of our reserve, and hardly had they extricated themselves from these difficulties, when they were met by General John Stuart with his foreign brigade; and destructive volleys completed the overthrow, we might almost say the destruction, of this great body of French cavalry. Stuart then moved up to the front, and bore an arduous and highly honourable part in the final overthrow of Lanusse's column in this quarter.

The fight still raged around the posts occupied by the 28th and 58th Regiments. The former had occasionally been engaged at the same time to their front and to their rear. Their ammunition and that of their assailants, was exhausted; the French and the 28th pelted each other with stones; but the fierce energy of the republicans was relaxing, though they would not retreat; two of their generals had fallen, and their loss of men had been enormous.

✶✶✶✶✶✶

Our field-pieces were useless likewise, for more than an hour, from the total failure of ammunition. On the other hand, since the morning light had enabled our gun vessels, which were anchored along the shore, to distinguish friends from foes, their fire had driven the French from the beach, and forced them to confine their attack to the landward side of our redoubt.

✶✶✶✶✶✶

When the British received at length a supply of ammunition, and their field-pieces re-opened their fire, the enemy drew sullenly off from the field of slaughter.

But I have spoken as yet, only of the desperate assaults which were made by the division under Lanusse, and by the French cavalry upon our right: it is high time to describe the movements of the enemy in other quarters. As soon as he saw that Lanusse was hotly engaged, and just as the day was breaking, General Rampon attacked the centre of our position, occupied by the English guards. Driving in our skirmishers, he first attempted to assault the front, but the volleys which he received were so well directed and deadly, that after a bloody contest he drew back, and manoeuvring to his right, he endeavoured to turn the left flank of the Guards. But here again, the enemy failed to make any impression. General Ludlow threw back some companies of the 3rd Regiment to receive the attack, while a part of Coote's brigade met the French column in front. Completely baffled and disheartened, General Rampon drew off his division after suffering a considerable loss.

While these conflicts were going on. General Regnier, with the strongest portion of the French Army under his command, remained almost motionless. The left of the British Army was in his fronts and the left was much the weakest part of our position; yet Regnier, after detaching a part of his division to the aid of Rampon, kept back his main body, without engaging further than in a cannonade, till the division of Lanusse and the cavalry had been nearly destroyed, and Rampon had been defeated. The battle had begun about 4 o' clock In the morning; soon after nine the French retreated to their former position on the heights.

Thus, ended the battle of the 21st of March, 1801. It was a fair trial of strength and valour between the soldiers of England and France, and great valour was shown on both sides; in numbers they were nearly equal. The French were older soldiers, more practised in their business, and familiar with victory. The British had some advantage in their position, though this advantage was impaired by the darkness of the hour at which the enemy made his attack. Had it not been for the provident order that every battalion should be under arms and at its post an hour before daybreak, some part or other of our line might have been taken by surprise; but all were on the alert, and the cool intrepidity of the 28th and 58th Regiments baffled the furious and protracted assault of the confidant republicans. Never were the discipline and determined valour of the British infantry more signally displayed than on the shores of Egypt.

★★★★★★

The losses of the British in that hard-fought battle, were 11 officers and 233 men killed, and about 1,160 wounded, amongst whom we have to reckon General Moore, Brigadiers Oakes and Hope, and Sir Sidney Smith. The loss of the enemy was very great, more than 1,000 of their men were buried by our soldiers, and about 900 (of whom 700 were wounded) were made prisoners. Two pieces of cannon and a standard, bearing the glorious inscription of Lodi and other victories in Italy, were captured Generals Lanusse, Roize, and Baudot were among the slain. Silly, Boussart, and other officers of high rank were wounded It seems probable that the total loss of the French was more than 3,000 men.

★★★★★★

At the time when the French cavalry broke through the 42nd Highlanders, Sir Ralph Abercromby was caught in the storm of charging horsemen. For a moment he was in the hands of one of the dragoons, whose thrust the old general had parried, still receiving a severe contusion from, the hilt of the sword; but the Frenchman was shot by a soldier of the 42nd, and Sir Ralph was enabled to extricate himself from the confusion. Till the defeat of the French Army was accomplished, the noble veteran concealed from everyone that he had received a ball in his thigh early in the action; but when his victory was no longer doubtful, the general allowed the wound to be examined.

Exhausted by pain and loss of blood, he was borne to the beach, and conveyed to Lord Keith's ship, and there he died in the night of the 28th of March. I have elsewhere sketched the striking lines of Abercromby's character. Wherever he had served, and his had been a long career, he had been respected and beloved. There was an absence of selfishness in Abercromby, a liberality of feeling, and an independence of spirit which entitled him to the highest respect as a gentleman; while his justice, his intrepidity, and experience assured to him, as a commander, the attachment and confidence of his troops. To fall in the moment of victory, and to know when dying that his victory was complete, was what the gallant veteran himself would have desired; but on the officers and soldiers who had toiled, and bled, and conquered under his leading, the tidings of his death fell like a chilling cloud.

With their grief for Abercromby there came mingled a painful doubt and apprehension as to the future. The command of the army devolved on the senior major-general, Hutchinson, and Hutchinson was hardly known by any but the officers of the staff, and by those imperfectly. His manners, his reserved habits, and his personal appearance, had created a prejudice against him, and his only recommendation was that he had accompanied Abercromby as a friend and volunteer to Holland in 1799; that Sir Ralph was believed to have set a high value on his opinion, and had asked and obtained his appointment as second in command on the Egyptian expedition.

But whatever might be the temper of the army, there was work to be done which admitted of no delay. There remained a powerful garrison in Alexandria, though Ménou had already detached 1,200 infantry and 300 horsemen to Ramanieh, with the object of maintaining the command of the Nile, and of securing his communications with Cairo. It was notorious that large reinforcements from France were expected by the enemy. The French troops at Cairo, strengthened by those which had been recalled from Upper Egypt, were considered to be more than a match for the disorderly mass of Turks under the *grand vizier*, and of the British forces from India, whose co-operation had been promised to our generals, no tidings whatever had been received.

Immediately after the death of Abercromby, General Hutchinson set himself sedulously to the work of fortifying the front of the British position. Ammunition and heavy guns had by this time been brought up in abundance, and strong redoubts, with connecting lines, were rapidly completed. The first object of the English commander was to isolate Alexandria, and to render effectual a blockade of that extensive place and its numerous garrison by a comparatively small body of troops. He saw that if he could effect this purpose, he might carry a part of his little army to the Lower Nile, gain possession of Rosetta, and perhaps of Ramanieh, and thus secure the resources of a fertile country, till the arrival of reinforcements from England might enable him to act against the enemy on a larger scale.

But with the view of isolating Alexandria more completely, and cutting its garrison off from all communication with Cairo, unless by the long and difficult circuit of the desert, Hutchinson determined on letting the waters of the sea into the vast basin of mud and sand, which had been in former days the bed of the Lake Mareotis. The level of this ancient basin was considerably lower than that of the Lake of Aboukir (or Maadieh), which communicated with the Mediterranean; and it was separated from the latter lake only by a narrow strip of earth, little more than sufficient to uphold the masonry of the canal, which parting from the Nile at Ramanieh, brought the water of the great river to the people of Alexandria.

On the 12th and 13th of April, this isthmus was cut through by the British, and the salt waters poured impetuously through the opening. In a short time, a little sea was formed, the area of which was estimated at more than twelve hundred square miles, and by the beginning of May the waters attained their natural level. Numerous gun boats, British and Turkish, passed into this new field of action, and while they secured a communication between our line and the Arabs to the westward, they confined and rendered difficult that which the beleaguered garrison had hitherto enjoyed.

While these works were in progress, and the British position was growing stronger day by day, Hutchinson was detaching successive bodies of troops toward Rosetta. The first of these columns, commanded by Colonel Brent Spencer, consisted of little more than 1,000

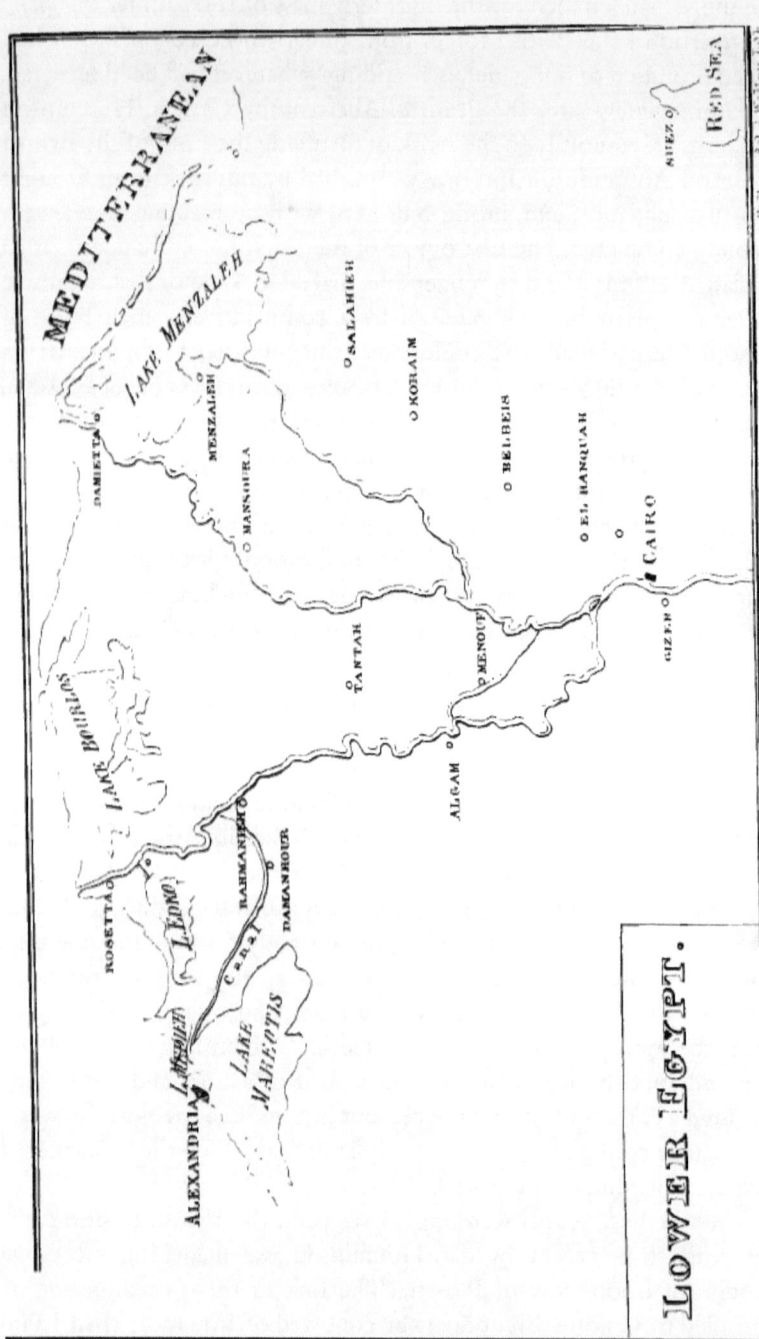

British infantry; but it was accompanied by about 4,000 Turks, who had arrived at Aboukir by sea, after the battle of the 21st of March. As they drew near to Rosetta, the French evacuated that town, crossing over to the right bank of the Nile, but leaving between 200 and 300 men to defend the fort of St. Julien, which was situated at the mouth of the river and commanded its principal channel. To reduce this place, which was of great importance with a view to our obtaining a naval superiority on the Nile, Spencer detached the Queen's Regiment under Lord Dalhousie, and the greater part of the Turks, while the fort was attacked at the same time by the allied flotilla and some ships of war.

With the remainder of his corps, Spencer took up a strong position at El Hamed, where he was joined by the Royal, 18th, and 90th Regiments; and where he lay watching the French, who were now collecting troops from various quarters at El Aft, a few miles higher up the river. Fort St. Julien was defended gallantly, but it was obliged to surrender on the 19th of April, and a strong division of English gunboats, under Captain Stevenson, together with a Turkish flotilla, ascended the Nile and came into co-operation with the army which was assembling at El Hamed,

As soon as the re-creation of the Lake Mareotis had deprived General Ménou of the power of acting against us offensively, otherwise than by assaulting the fortified front of the British position, Hutchinson despatched Generals Craddock and Doyle with six more battalions to El Hamed; and he followed in person, after committing to General Eyre Coote the command of that moiety of the army which was intended to make good the blockade of Alexandria. But it is curious to observe, when such mighty interests were at stake, and both France and England were sensible of their urgent importance, how small was the military force which our generals could command at the crisis of the contest for Egypt.

It is true that in the actions which had been fought, more than 3,000 of our soldiers had been killed or wounded; but four months had passed since the expedition had sailed from Malta, and, with the exception of the dismounted dragoons, who joined in Caramania, no troops had arrived from England to repair the losses or improve the means of our army. At the end of April, General Coote was left to confine Ménou within the walls of Alexandria with barely 6,000 infantry, (of whom 1,600 were foreigners,) 200 horsemen, and 250 gunners.

The column which was assembled at El Hamed and with which General Hutchinson proposed to act against the French upon the Nile, mustered do more than 4,300 infantry, 300 dragoons, and about 100 artillerymen; but of horses to drag our few fieldpieces there was a perplexing deficiency.

★★★★★★

The weakness of what were called "regiments," may be shown by stating that, to make up these 4,300 rank and file, there were at El Hamed twelve of such regiments, and four companies of the 40th.

★★★★★★

A Turkish corps of nearly equal numbers was ready to accompany or follow the British column; but the total want of military order amongst these allies of ours, and the pretensions of the *capitan pacha*, who commanded them, occasioned frequent embarrassments.

The enemy had now gathered in strength on the left bank of the river, and held a position at El Aft, between El Hamed and Ramanieh. It appeared to be the intention of the French general to give battle; and Hutchinson resolved to afford him the opportunity. Having considered the advantages of acting upon both the banks of the Nile, and thus enabling the flotilla of gunboats, English and Turkish, to ascend the stream and co-operate with the army, our commander detached the 89th Regiment and twenty dragoons across the river.

Twelve hundred Albanians were sent over at the same time; and the whole were placed under the command of Colonel Richard Stewart. His instructions were to cling to the right bank of the Nile, driving away any parties of the enemy which might otherwise molest and impede the flotilla; and to co-operate with the main body of the army as opportunities might present themselves.

On the 5th of May, Hutchinson commenced his march towards El Aft; but on that and the following day he made very short journeys, because the Turks professed that they expected the immediate arrival of some thousands of their cavalry; and the general felt that in horsemen, as well as in artillery, his little army was very inferior to that of the French. While upon his march he was overtaken, on the 7th, by this desired body of cavalry; and it was found to consist of about six hundred wild Syrians, on horseback, indeed, but without any sort of discipline. However, the French commander was not disposed to risk an action at El Aft, and he drew off in the night of the 6th of May, directing his retreat on Ramanieh.

The force which had been drawn together by the enemy, and which was under the command of Generals Lagrange, Valentin, and Morand, was composed of three demi-brigades of infantry and two regiments of cavalry detached from Alexandria, and of troops which had been withdrawn from Rosetta and other posts. It was not doubted that so strong and so important a position as that of Ramanieh would be stoutly defended by a corps which mustered nearly 4,300 veteran soldiers, including 800 good cavalry, and a very superior artillery.

As the enemy retreated from El Aft the British and Turkish columns followed on his track. Early on the 9th of May, they drew near to the French position, and Hutchinson prepared for the expected battle. At his desire the main body of the Turks advanced slowly along the bank of the Nile, their wild horsemen galloping forward and skirmishing far in front. But the British troops were held apart; and leaving a wide interval between themselves and their allies, they moved across the open country to the right, sending out their dragoons and some sharpshooters to feel for the enemy in the village of Daoud, which lies scattered on both the banks of the Great Canal.

On the opposite side of the Nile, Colonel Stewart had moved onward, keeping his little column nearly abreast of the main army; and, though Lagrange threw two or three hundred men across the river to dispute the occupation of a village which faced the harbour of Ramanieh, Stewart was able, after a short skirmish, to establish his people behind the bank of the Nile. The river is here so narrow that even musketry told with effect on the mouth of the little port, in which a large number of *djermes*, including several gun-vessels, were lying at anchor. By-and-bye Captain Stevenson's flotilla worked its way up the stream and engaged the French batteries; while heavy cannon were landed on the right bank to arm those which Stewart's men were set to construct, and which were completed during the night of the 9th.

But the importance of this position of Ramanieh must be explained. It is here that the road from Cairo is divided into two branches; one of which pursues its course down the river to Rosetta while the other, bearing to the westward, forms the only road of communication with Alexandria. From Ramanieh, likewise, the Grand Canal, which had conveyed to the same town the waters of the Nile, takes its departure; and the port, formed by some islands in the river, served as the *entrepôt* for military as well as commercial purposes between Cairo and the coast. Here too was a small fort, and something of an entrenched camp. Moreover, it was a matter of no light consideration, that if we could obtain a stronghold of Ramanieh, we should not only deprive our enemy of the advantages of its position, but we should acquire the command of the resources of a fertile country for the supply of the British troops at Aboukir, as well as of those in the valley of the Nile.

When these things are considered, it appears unaccountable that General Lagrange should have made so very feeble an attempt to hold his ground. The 9th of May passed off in cannonades and slight skirmishes. There were indeed some showy evolutions performed by the French cavalry, but they ended in nothing. On the other hand, Hutchinson relied confidently on the effect that must be produced by Stewart's batteries, when they should be able to open their fire, aa the certain means of driving the enemy's troops from the bank of the Nile; but he was apprehensive that, when dislodged, they might direct their retreat upon Alexandria, and that Coote's position might be thus endangered.

The general, therefore, manoeuvred to his right as far as he could venture to more without losing the power of affording succour to the Turks in case they should be charged by the French infantry. Towards the close of the day, indeed, such succour was suddenly required; and Doyle's brigade was detached in haste to check the enemy's attack on our allies. When a dark night closed in, our columns remained in a disjointed and somewhat confused position. The loss of the British in killed or wounded had been very trifling; but it was expected that sharper service would attend the coming day, and long before the dawn our troops were arrayed in order of battle.

By the first gleam of lights however, a white flag was seen to be floating on the fort of Ramanieh; and the first sounds which were heard came from the guns of our flotilla playing, far up the Nile, on the rear of the retreating enemy. Lagrange had evacuated Ramanieh in the deep silence of the night; and he was marching with the utmost rapidity in the direction of Cairo. His sick and wounded were left in the little fort under the protection of an officer and a few men who surrendered without resistance; and the number of prisoners made on this day was swelled by an odd accident.

******

On this same 10th of May there arrived at Aboukir the first reinforcement from England. The 1st battalion of the 27th Regiment and detachments for others. Altogether nearly 1,200 men.

******

An *aide-de-camp*, bringing despatches from Ménou and escorted by fifty dragoons, had made his way through the desert, and had arrived to within a short distance of Ramanieh, imagining that the English Army was still far distant. Attacked in the early morning by a body of Arabs, who shot the *aide-de-camp* and three or four of his men, the party were growing suspicious and apprehensive, when suddenly they fell in with about thirty of our 12th Light Dragoons going out to water their horses. Without any attempt at resistance or escape the French surrendered.

We were now masters of the important position of Ramanieh: and now came the question, what further course was to be pursued towards the expulsion of the French from Egypt? When Hutchinson set forward from El Hamed he had flattered himself that, with the aid of the Turks, he might be able to prosecute his march to Cairo; and he was the more anxious to take this course because there were vague reports that the long expected army from India had arrived at Suez. Besides the five or six thousand Turks who accompanied his column, he knew that the tumultuary host under the *grand vizier* was advancing from Salahieh across the Eastern Desert: and Hutchinson was also in secret negotiation with the Mamelukes in Upper Egypt.

★★★★★★

The strength of the Mamelukes had been very much weakened since the time when they valiantly but vainly resisted the invasion of Bonaparte; and they were divided by the feuds which had arisen between the two most powerful of their *beys*, Mourad and Ibrahim. After the Battle of Heliopolis in the spring of 1800, the former of these chieftains made his submission to General Kleber, and having vowed fidelity and engaged to pay a small tribute, Mourad had been allowed to settle with his followers in the desert between the Nile and the Red Sea. On the other hand, Ibrahim and some of the minor *beys* roamed about the eastward desert, preserving their independence; distrusting the Turks, yet acting cautiously in co-operation with the *grand vizier* against the French. Kleber and his successors appear to have kept up a constant communication with Mourad Bey, and to have relied on his fidelity to their standards up to the time of his death, which occurred while Hutchinson was on his march. Osman Bey, who succeeded to Mourad's authority, joined the British at Terraneh on the 29th of May, with about 1,200 superb horsemen.

The truth probably is, that both Mourad and Osman, who had felt the effect of the French arms, were waiting to see which of the two Christian armies might prove the stronger before they committed themselves by joining either: and in the mean time they made separate professions of friendship to each of the belligerents. The Mamelukes distrusted the Turkish chieftains more than the Christians, and this made them reluctant to join the British, while the *capitan pacha* was in our company.

✶✶✶✶✶✶

But the progress of our army had been slow; the heat of the season was making itself felt severely, and the British soldiers were growing sickly. No confirmation of the rumour that the Indian Army had reached the shores of Egypt met Hutchinson at Ramanieh, and he hesitated. He doubted whether it would be prudent to pursue his march up the Nile further than might be necessary to deter Lagrange from taking up a new position, where he might retain the power of crossing the Delta and falling on the flank of the *grand vizier*. Our general even despatched an officer to this chieftain, recommending that he should retire to Salahieh and remain there for the present; but the Ottoman *grandee* having set his wild army in motion was unable to stop it. The Turks had been told that they were to march Cairo, and take it, and make a great booty; and onward they continued to roll.

Hence arose new difficulties, and considerations which outweighed the objections that Hutchinson had recently entertained against the advance of his column. He felt particularly the importance of reaching a point upon the Nile, from whence he might be able, by a rapid march across the Delta, to gain possession of Belbeis. Our general feared that Belliard, who was in command at Cairo, would issue forth as soon as he should be strengthened by the arrival of Lagrange's division, and would crush the disorderly multitude of Ottomans.

✶✶✶✶✶✶

The rapidity with which Lagrange performed this march was surprising. In spite of the *sirocco* wind and the excessive heat, this column arrived at Cairo in the night of the 13th of May; the distance between Ramanieh and the capital being more than 80 miles.

✶✶✶✶✶✶

At Belbeis the British would be in a position to prevent such a disaster; and there was another consideration which rendered the possession of that town an object of further importance. It was in that neighbourhood only that a sufficient supply of camels could be procured for the service of the Indian Army which was expected to arrive at Suez.

Hutchinson took finally the resolution to march onward. But when he announced his intention to his principal officers, a storm of opposition, swelling almost into a mutinous cabal, arose in the camp. The opinions of the leading dissentients were made public with indecent passion. To attempt to march to Cairo with so small a force, and daring the hot season, must be attended with the destruction of the troops. There were no magazines or hospitals—the plague was around them—even if they should reach Cairo, they had no means of besieging the citadel; and their numbers were utterly inadequate to cope with the united divisions of Belliard and Lagrange.

The dissentients insisted on the necessity of pursuing that policy which Hutchinson himself had entertained for some days, that of leading back the British column to Aboukir, tearing only a strong detachment at Ramanieh. But it seems probable, that the opponents of the commander-in-chief did not openly avow what was in all likelihood the secret motive of their opposition, their personal dislike and their want of confidence in him. At this time the general had no man of rank near him, with whom he had been on terms of intimacy, or in whom he had been accustomed to confide. Moore was the officer on whose judgment he usually relied; but Moore had been confined since the battle of the 21st of March, by the effects of his wound, and he had not yet rejoined the army.

★★★★★★

In truth this cabal had become little less than a mutiny on the part of officers holding the highest ranks under General Hutchinson. They had written to both Coote and Moore, inviting their concurrence in a plan which tended virtually, if not absolutely to deprive Hutchinson of the command of the army; and their mad project was defeated mainly by the stern and uncompromising answer which they received from Moore.

★★★★★★

It may not be superfluous, and it may serve to throw some light on this stormy crisis, if I sketch the character of the British commander. John Hely Hutchinson, brother of Lord Donoughmore, was at this time about forty-four years of age, but he appeared to be much older. Harsh features jaundiced by ill-health, extreme short-sightedness, a stooping body, a slouching gait, and an utter neglect of his dress, presented in him a figure at variance with every idea that one forms of a soldier. Shunning general society, abstracted, reserved, slovenly, and indolent, with ungracious manners, and a violent temper, the general was little calculated to gain the confidence, or win the affections of those who had fallen suddenly under his command.

Yet was Hutchinson a man of no ordinary mark. He was a good scholar; he had read much and profitably; his understanding was strong, his information extensive. Nor had he neglected to study the theory of his profession. On military subjects his views were large; and his personal bravery was unquestioned.

Having fully satisfied himself that the course which he had finally resolved to pursue was the fittest and the best under the actual circumstances, General Hutchinson no longer doubted. He disregarded the remonstrances by which he was assailed, and he persisted in his determination to advance. He ordered two more of the regiments at Aboukir to join his column on the Nile; and with them was to come that staunch and trustworthy soldier, Hildebrand Oakes, whose wound was now nearly healed.

On the 11th of May, the army resumed its march to the southward; and early the next morning intelligence reached the general that there had arrived at Suez, not the Indian expedition, but a single man-of-war bearing Admiral Blankett's flag, and bringing only two companies of the 86th Regiment, and a few artillerymen. From Cairo also, there came certain information that General Belliard had marched out with the greater part of his troops to meet and attack the *grand vizier*. Hutchinson immediately dispatched officers to this chieftain, intreating him to avoid an action, and to fall back deliberately as the French advanced. It was clear that the enemy would not venture to push on to any great distance from Cairo, now that the allied forces on the Nile were drawing near to the capital.

On the 14th, our main column arrived at Shabour, on the left bank of the great river; while Colonel Stewart, advancing along the canal of Menouf, fell in with a number of boats laden with ordnance and military supplies, escorted by one hundred and fifty French soldiers. They were on their way from Cairo to Ramanieh, (the guns and stores being intended for the fortification of that place), and they were in ignorance of Lagrange's unexpected retreat. After a sharp skirmish with the Turks and Arabs, by whom they were first assailed, these people laid down their arms on the arrival and summons of the British commander.

The march of our main army was retarded by the prevalence of a fierce *sirocco* wind, which enfeebled the troops, and prevented the flotilla from making way against the current of the Nile, and Hutchinson did not arrive at Algam till the 11th of May. The *capitan pacha* halted and pitched his tents about a league in rear of the British camp. Early the next morning, there came spurring in Arab after Arab with the strange intelligence, that a considerable body of French troops had appeared in the desert to our right and rear. Two officers, escorted by the Arabs, were instantly despatched to reconnoitre; and they were followed by General Doyle with 250 dragoons, while his own brigade of infantry was ordered to march, with two guns, to his support.

At the end of about seven miles within the desert, the enemy was descried, massed and prepared for defence. It was evident that the French were much too strong for our dragoons; and our infantry was far behind. The enemy might retire, and take his route through the desert, either for Cairo or Alexandria, with little risk of being pursued. In this dilemma, a stratagem suggested by Major (afterwards Sir Robert) Wilson, was adopted with success. Galloping forwards and waving a white handkerchief, he summoned the French commander to capitulate, "as the allied army was at hand." This overture was indignantly and fiercely rejected by Colonel Cavalier; but it was observed that his soldiers appeared to be unsteady, pressing forward and listening with an eager interest for the result of the parley.

Scarcely had Wilson rejoined General Doyle, when he was overtaken by a French officer, requesting him to return. The conference was resumed, and was of short duration. The conditions proposed by the French commander were accepted by Doyle, and gladly ratified by Hutchinson. It was no trifling an advantage to have weakened the enemy by the capture of so large a detachment of his best troops.

★★★★★★

There had been no engagement between the armies (excepting the alight skirmishes near Ramanieh) since the battle of the 2lst of March. Yet in this interval, no less than 1,540 of the French were made prisoners; *viz.*, at Rosetta, 260; at Ramanieh, 160; on the canal of Menouf, 150; Colonel Cavalier's detachment, 570; and about 400, who were captured at sea while endeavouring to escape from Damietta and El Esbeh.

★★★★★★

Five hundred and seventy men, including officers, laid down their arms at the British headquarters, on condition that they should be sent to France, and their private property be respected. This corps, commanded by Colonel Cavalier, had been sent out of Alexandria, with 550 camels, to collect supplies for the garrison. It was composed of two or three troops of dragoons, some companies of infantry, one hundred and twenty of the Dromedary corps, (the picked men of the army,) and one light gun. They had hoped to gather a sufficiency of provisions and forage in the valleys about Damanhour; but in this hope they were disappointed. The villages were deserted; no ripe grain could be found. Colonel Cavalier then took the resolution of pushing on to Cairo, where the supplies of which Alexandria was in need might be procured.

With this view he entered the desert and marched rapidly along its eastern border. Supposing the English Army to be still at Ramanieh, and prevented from gaining better intelligence by the Arab horsemen who hovered about his column, the French commander pursued his course till he imagined that he had passed beyond the danger of encountering the Allies. He then turned towards the valley of the Nile, along which he intended to prosecute his march to Cairo; but on the 17th of May, Cavalier was disagreeably surprised by the sudden appearance of the British dragoons.

It seems clear that after the battle of the 21st of March, the French soldiery had lost their wonted confidence. There had been bitter feuds among the superior officers of their army; and a cabal, headed by General Regnier, was carrying on a dangerous opposition to the policy and measures of Ménou. These dissensions spread widely through the troops; but as long as they held the hope of crowning their former glories by the destruction of the British Army, they fought with all the valour and activity which had distinguished these veterans in the campaigns of Italy. But the results of the actions near Alexandria had discouraged them. The French, who were made prisoners, frankly told their captors that they had never before experienced such hard fighting. They imagined the British to be much stronger in numbers than they really were; and a despair of success in Egypt, and an anxious desire to return to France, gained ground in all the ranks of the army. A great proportion both of officers and men were ripe for capitulations, by which they might be restored to their native country.

Colonel Cavalier's detachments laid down their arms on the 17th of May; and before the evening closed, they were on board of *djermes*, and wending their way towards Rosetta. Nor was this auspicious day to end without further and more exciting encouragement to the growing hopes of the British commander. Tidings, the more welcome because they were wholly unexpected, arrived from the camp of the *grand vizier*. General Belliard, with four or five thousand infantry, nearly a thousand cavalry, and twenty-four pieces of cannon, had met the Turks, and had effected nothing! Instead of routing the disorderly host of Moslems, which Hutchinson had anticipated with dread, the French commander had turned back and retreated rapidly to Cairo, after a protracted cannonade and some sharp skirmishing.

It has been already mentioned that the *vizier* had been unable to control his headstrong bands. They had pushed onward rapidly, without any regard to the slow progress of the British up the Nile, and by the 15th of May, their foremost horsemen were within a day's march of Cairo. On that day, Belliard went forth with between 5,000 and 6,000 soldiers, and a powerful artillery. He hoped to surprise the Ottomans on their march, and to destroy, or at least disable, their army before the English should draw so near as to imperil the garrison of Cairo. If he should not succeed, his movement was to be called "a reconnaissance," but if he should effect his purpose it would be hailed as a grand stroke of strategy.

At daybreak on the 16th, Belliard fell in with the van of the Turkish host, far in advance of its main body. The French attacked at once, but keeping all their infantry in squares, on account of the great number of the Turkish horse, they suffered some loss from the fire of guns pointed by the handful of English artillerymen. As the French advanced, pouring in a brisk fire from their field-pieces, the Ottoman foot fell back, but their cavalry spreading to the right and left, kept caracoling round, and threatening the flanks and rear of the assailant.

In this way six or seven hours were spent without any effectual stroke, and though the *vizier* had arrived with the rest of his forces, the Turks pursued the same wary course of action. Belliard's troops were fatigued, and he became apprehensive that the cloud of horsemen, whom he saw far away to his right and rear, might push on to the gates of Cairo and excite an insurrection of the populace in that great city. Despairing of being able to force the Turks into a decisive engagement, the French general determined to retrace his steps, he retreated with great celerity, but in such good order that his pursuers could make no impression on his columns; and on the next day Belliard re-entered Cairo.

The apprehensions which had hitherto weighed on the mind of Hutchinson were now dispelled. There was no longer any doubt or difficulty as to seeming a communication, and perhaps some concert, between his army and that of the *grand vizier*. Knowing that Admiral Blankett's ship had reached Suez, our general naturally hoped from day to day that he should receive tidings of the arrival at the same port of the long-expected army from India. A march of a few days might bring this army, supposed to be 8,000 strong, into communication with the left flank of the Turkish troops, while Hutchinson should connect the movements of his column with their right. But great numbers of camels were deemed to be indispensable for the passage of the Indian Army across the desert. The general, therefore, despatched officers to Belbeis to purchase these animals and forward them to Suez.

At the same time, he sent Major Montresor to the latter place, with instructions to expedite the arrangements, necessary for the march of the troops arriving from India; and to concert with their commander a general plan of co-operation. In order to afford time for the completion of these measures, Hutchinson determined to remain several days at Al Gam, which is situated near the confluence of the Menouf branch with the great western stream of the Nile. From hence he corresponded with the *vizier*, and he succeeded in persuading this chieftain to move to his right, and thereby to put his army in more ready connection with the British column, instead of risking any partial attempt upon Cairo. The Ottoman troops accordingly encamped about Ben er Hasset and Ber Shoum, and Colonel Stewart's detachment, reinforced by the 30th Regiment, took up an intermediate position, which secured a communication between our headquarters and those of the *vizier*.

It was not till the 1st of June that Hutchinson resumed his march, and he proceeded with the more caution because he had now received intelligence that the Indian expedition had been unable to make its way up the Red Sea; the fleet had been dispersed, and the ships were dropping a few at a time into the Bay of Cosseir. All hope of the early co-operation of this army was thus extinguished, but the 200 men who had arrived at Suez in the admiral's ship, were invited to cross the desert and join Colonel Stewart; while the main body of the British force was strengthened by the arrival of Brigadier Oakes with the 28th and 42nd Regiments, 120 gunners, and 60 dragoons.

There had, however, arisen fresh causes for uneasiness: Admiral Gantheaume's squadron, (see Appendix D), bringing a large body of French troops, was known to be on the coast to the westward of Alexandria, and one of his *corvettes* had actually entered that port. Coote's division of our army was so much reduced by ophthalmia and other diseases, that there remained scarcely 4,000 rank and file capable of defending the lines. Nor was Hutchinson's own column less sickly; nearly 1,000 of his men had been sent down the Nile to hospitals in the rear, and for several days his troops were suffering much from a scarcity of provisions. The grumblings and remonstrances of the *frondeurs* were again heard in the camp, and the march was resumed under gloomy forebodings.

However, as the British column advanced, it came, on the 3rd of June, into communication with Osman Bey at the head 1,200 Mamelukes, a brilliant body of horsemen, far superior in every respect to the best of the Turks. But Osman looked on the *capitan pacha* with deep mistrust and aversion; nor would he bring his people into close connection with the allied column. He treated personally with Hutchinson, and his Mamelukes moved abreast of the British division, but at a distance of four or five miles to the right, so that, in case of treachery, they could plunge at once into the desert and disappear. But the time was not yet come when the Turkish commanders might safely, and with a prospect of success, allow a symptom to appear of the hatred which their government bore to the Beys, and the designs which were contemplated for their destruction. The *capitan pacha* received the Mameluke chiefs with all the courtesy and dissimulation in which the Orientals are masters of art; and the British officers imagined that he was sincere.

Within a few days General Hutchinson was relieved from his worst apprehensions, by the intelligence that Gantheaume, after having brought his squadron to anchor on the coast (about 150 leagues to the westward of Alexandria), had suddenly cut his cables and disappeared. In the meanwhile, the combined armies continuing to advance, though slowly, towards Cairo, and on the 15th of June, Hutchinson despatched to General Belliard an invitation to capitulate. This overture was at once rejected with that air of confident defiance, which French officers in a dilemma rarely fail to assume.

But by the 21st of June the allied troops had gathered closely round the capital of Egypt. On the right bank of the Nile, the *grand vizier* and Colonel Stewart were threatening to assault the wide-extended walls of Cairo; while Hutchinson and the *capitan pacha* had invested Gizeh on the left bank, and were throwing up batteries which might bear upon the bridge that connected this town with the greater city. On this side the outposts of the enemy had been driven in with ease, and chiefly by the Mamelukes, who distinguished themselves by their impetuous valour.

Within the beleaguered city councils of war were called by General Belliard. The chief engineer declared the enormous extent of the old walls to be indefensible against such numbers as it was imagined that the allies could muster, and though Lagrange and one or two others went through the form of protesting against a capitulation, yet on the morning of the 22nd of June, a French officer appeared at our outposts, with a request that an English general might be appointed to enter into a conference as to terms, and that hostilities might in the meanwhile be suspended.

******

The journal of this chief engineer officer, Brigadier D' Hautpoul, is annexed to General Regnier's *Memoirs of the Campaigns in Egypt*, and forms the most trustworthy and valuable part of the book.

******

Readily accepting this invitation, Hutchinson empowered Brigadier John Hope to meet the negotiators on the part of the enemy and to settle the terms for the surrender of Cairo. (General Moore, and Hope, the adjutant-general, had rejoined the army only two days before.) An armistice of forty-eight hours was granted, and during this time the only difficulty which occurred was that of keeping the thoughtless and insubordinate soldiers of the *vizier* from committing themselves by rash attempts to make their way into the city. The terms of capitulation were very promptly arranged, for both parties had the same object in view.

With the great majority of the French, the prevalent desire was that of returning to France; and Hutchinson well knew that the British ministers aimed above all things at the expulsion of the enemy's forces from Egypt before the conditions of peace between England and the Consular Government should come under serious discussion. The Turks indeed may have felt that they were disappointed in their hopes of vengeance and plunder, but their chieftains consented to sign the capitulation, though the terms appeared to be more than usually favourable to the enemy. (See Appendix E.) Yet there was prudence and sound policy in granting these terms; the numbers of the French within the walls of Cairo were found to be even greater than had been apprehended.

Of one description or another, of military men there were nearly 13,000, exclusive of civilians, and women and children. Though there were many in the hospitals, they could have brought more than 8,000 effective soldiers into the field, besides having several hundreds of invalids who were able to do duty in garrison. On the other hand, the English general could have barely mustered 4,000 rank and file for battle on the left bank of the river. It was not till the 10th of July that the French evacuated Cairo, passing over to Gizeh, where they remained till the morning of the 15th, employed in embarking their sick, and women, and baggage, on the Nile.

★★★★★★

Let me not leave unnoticed an act at this time, which was highly honourable to the French, and which marked their devotion to the memory of their former commander, General Kleber. This distinguished chief had been assassinated by a fanatic in the preceding year. Though the army had been rent by dissensions, and the policy of Kleber had been strikingly opposed to that which was upheld by Napoleon, now holding unfettered sway at Paris, the troops insisted on carrying to France, and investing with all the honours in their power, the body of Kleber. His remains were embarked on the Nile under prolonged salutes from the guns of his countrymen, re-echoed by those of the British Army.

★★★★★★

During this interval the *vizier's* troops entered the great city, and were guilty of many acts of plunder and violence, particularly towards such of the inhabitants as were suspected of having been in any degree on friendly terms with the French. At this time both Hutchinson and Craddock were so seriously ill that the command of our troops devolved upon Moore. With him rested the arrangements for the march to Rosetta, and the personal direction of a very delicate and doubtful service. Here were 8,000 French soldiers in complete military array, carrying their arms and ammunition, their cavalry well mounted, their field-pieces fully horsed, to be escorted 200 miles by about 3,500 British, (500 of our men remained at Gizeh for the protection of the sick generals), the *capitan pacha's* division of Turks, and 200 or 300 Mamelukes. But the plan and its details, as framed by Moore, were admirable, and they were carried into effect with perfect success.

On the 15th of July the march began. First went the wild horsemen of Syria, followed by the more orderly foot-soldiers of the *capitan pacha*: next, but with a long interval, marched the French infantry with their guns, their cavalry moving abreast, but on the left flank and farther from the river. After another interval, came the British column led by Moore; and our dragoons and the detachment of Mamelukes formed a rear-guard. A great fleet of *djermes* carrying the sick, the baggage, &c., and escorted by our gun vessels, dropt slowly down the Nile, so as to keep up a constant communication with the French and English columns.

During a march of several days there arose not a difficulty or disagreement of any sort. Our late enemies were in high good humour and in the gayest spirits. At the halting places, the English and French would mingle in companionship, and laugh, and discuss as well as they could, their battles and their fortunes. After a short rest at Rosetta, to give time for the preparation of transports in the Bay of Aboukir, General Belliard's army, with all its followers, and even most of their horses, were embarked between the 31st of July and the 7th of August; and they were escorted by British men of war to the ports of France. In the capitulation of Cairo, a clause had been inserted, under which General Ménou and the garrison of Alexandria were empowered to avail themselves of the same favourable conditions; but Ménou doggedly refused to profit by this opening. It remained, therefore, for the British commander to conclude the labour of the campaign by the reduction of this city.

The strength and means of the British Army had by this time been very greatly augmented. In the first half of July there had arrived from England, or Minorca, eight battalions of infantry, besides 300 men of the guards, and the 22nd Dragoons (without horses). This gave to the general, now Sir John Hutchinson, a disposable force of 16,000 men; and he had certain advices of the arrival at Kenèh, on the Upper Nile, of about 5,000 of the Indian Army under David Baird. Whatever might be the operations necessary for the reduction of Alexandria, they could now be carried on without fear of interruption. The garrison might be strong, but there were no other French troops in Egypt.

Before I enter upon a narrative of this siege, it may not be superfluous to give some account of the expedition from India to which I have just now alluded. It had been planned upon a large scale. The 10th, 80th, 86th, and 88th Regiments, with three battalions of volunteer *sepoys*, and ample detachments of artillerymen, sailed from the ports of India. (They brought with them bullocks trained to drag the guns and ammunition carts.) They were to be joined on their passage by the 61st Regiment, a troop of the 8th Light Dragoons, and one of Horse Artillery from the Cape of Good Hope. The battalions were strong in numbers; and if the whole had arrived at their destination, this army would have mustered nearly 8,000 rank and file.

But the navigation of the Red Sea, always difficult, was almost unknown to the English in those days: the dangers were many and more were the apprehensions. Even before the fleet reached the straits of Bab-el-mandel it was partially dispersed; some of the smaller vessels were lost, and many of the transports, buffeted by the northerly winds, gave up the struggle and returned to India. Within the Red Sea the dispersion seems to have been complete; Admiral Blankett made his way to Suez, as we have seen, with his single ship of the line; but his commodore, Sir Home Popham, gathering several of the troop-ships around him, was unable to advance beyond the latitude of Cosseir. After beating about for several days, and picking up some more of the straggling transports, Sir Home anchored in the Bay of Cosseir on the 17th of May.

During the next three weeks there continued to drop in, by one or two at a time, a good many of the missing vessels; but it was not till the 21st of June that General Baird, baring procured camels from the Arabs, and having gathered together about 5,200 of his men, was able to commence his march across the desert from Cosseir to Kenèh. The heat was intense: along the line of march to the Nile few wells were met with, and those afforded but scanty supplies of water. On this account it was necessary that the troops should move in small bodies and on successive days. Notwithstanding every precaution, the suffering of the soldiers was severe; but it was observed that the British bore the trial better than the natives of India. Twelve of our men were stricken dead by the sun; and many of the horses and camels perished.

The march, estimated at about 130 miles, was performed by the different bodies of troops in twelve, fourteen, or fifteen days; and early in July, Baird (Montresor was the second in command, and that excellent officer Samuel Auchmuty the adjutant-general), had the satisfaction of seeing his little army re-assembled at Kenèh, on the Upper Nile. Immediate exertions were made to collect boats; but it was long before a sufficient number could be obtained; and the troops dropped down the river to Cairo in successive detachments. Having again collected his forces at the Grand City, Baird prosecuted his voyage down the Nile, in obedience to the orders of Hutchinson; and he took up his quarters at and near to Rosetta at the end of August.

This division of troops arrived in a high state of discipline; but the men were sickly in consequence of their having been so much exposed to the sun during the hot season; and of the 80th, 86th, and 88th Regiments large portions had been driven back to India. It had been expected by the British Ministers that their 8,000 men would have arrived at Suez early in April, in time to bear an important part in the war of Egypt. But the calculations of our government had been formed under too sanguine a view of the circumstances.

They had not made allowance for the difficulties of procuring and equipping proper vessels for the transport of so large an army; or for those which were to be expected on a voyage in seas which were little known. Thus, Baird, with but two-thirds of his army, only reached the field of action when the result of the campaign was no longer doubtful.

Of the French Army, which consisted of not less than 27,000 soldiers when Sir Ralph Abercromby landed in Egypt, there remained now only the garrison of Alexandria; numerous indeed, but disheartened and out of humour. General Ménou had seized, and driven to sea his second in command (Regnier), and some other officers whom he considered to be the leaders of the cabal against his authority; but much of the sour leaven remained in the mass, though its working was kept out of sight. As far, however, as declarations and outward show could go, it appeared to be the fixed determination of Ménou to defend this last stronghold of Egypt to the utmost extremity.

The French lines upon the heights opposite to the British position had been diligently strengthened, as well as the forts in the rear; and the power of heavy artillery which might be brought to bear on this side, as well as the natural difficulties of the ground, appeared to render an attack from the eastward impracticable, or at least too dangerous.

By the beginning of August Sir John Hutchinson had been brought down the Nile, and carried to the flag-ship in the Bay of Aboukir; but he was yet, for several days, too ill to assume the personal command of his army. On the 15th he arrived in the camp; and in the evening of the next day he detached about four thousand men, under General Eyre Coote, to commence operations against the western face of Alexandria, Embarking at night-fall these troops, escorted by gunboats, passed up the Lake Mareotis in the darkness, and they landed the next morning on the shore where the isthmus is widest, five or six miles to the westward of the city walls and opposite to the promontory which juts to the northward, and terminates close to some little islands, on one of which stood the fort of Marabout.

The landing was effected without apposition; but, as Hutchinson deemed it not improbable that Ménou might detach a part of his forces to fall upon Coote before he might be prepared for battle, a show of attack from the eastward was made early in the morning of the 17th.

There were two little hills in advance of the French lines: one, to which our officers had given the name of the "Green Hill," stood in front of the enemy's right; the other, called the "Knoll," was in advance of his left; and on each of these was a French outpost The British troops were drawn out as if for battle, and Moore was directed to lead the reserve against the last-mentioned height, while Craddock's brigade attacked the "Green Hill." Both these posts were occupied without difficulty; but the generals found that their men became exposed to a dangerous fire from the French batteries, and they withdrew their columns out of the range of shot.

Craddock, however, left a part of the 30th Regiment (about one hundred and eighty men) lying on the "Green Hill;" and the enemy, observing this detachment, fancied that they could cut it off. The 75th demi-brigade made a rapid sortie from their lines; but the gallant companies of the 30th, instead of shrinking back before twice their numbers, gathered together, and rushing on their assailants with the bayonet broke and chased them back, killing some and taking several prisoners.

In the meanwhile, General Coote had completed the landing of his division and of several field pieces. In the evening (17th of August) he advanced about two miles in the direction of Alexandria, and took up a strong position amongst ancient quarries, where the isthmus becomes very narrow. At the same time, he detached the 54th Regiment to blockade the little fort of Marabout, and to cover the formation of batteries against it. The reduction of this place was necessary, because its guns commanded the entrance into the old port of Alexandria, and it was of importance that our vessels of war should be enabled to come in and cooperate with the left of Coote's division, while the gunboats in Lake Mareotis acted on his right. (The shallowness of the old port allowed only vessels of a light draught of water to enter.)

At daybreak on the 19th, two twelve-pounders and two 8-inch howitzers opened their fire on the fort and tower of Marabout, and on three French gunboats lying under its walls. The latter were soon disposed of; two of the boats were sunk, and the third was forced to fly to Alexandria, But it was found that the masonry of Marabout was not to be breached by twelve-pounders. Heavier guns were required; and during the 19th and 20th of August two 24-pounders were dragged by men, with great labour, across the widest part of the isthmus.

A battery had been prepared for their reception at the extreme point, which is separated by a very narrow channel from the islet occupied by the fort of Marabout. At daybreak on the 21st the guns opened their fire; at noon the signal tower fell crashing to the ground; and before evening the whole fort was in ruins. Even then the gallant Frenchman, who held the command, surrendered with reluctance, having lost 25 out of his 195 soldiers.

Sloops of war and gun vessels now entered the harbour, and Coote prepared to move forward, and attack the enemy's troops in a position which they had taken up in advance of Alexandria; and which would have been extremely strong if both its flanks had not been exposed to a cannonade from our shipping on one side and the flotilla on the other. Still the French seemed disposed to fight on the short and strong ridge which they occupied, amongst scattered ruins, defended by seven pieces of heavy ordnance, and a large proportion of field-artillery.

On the evening of the 22nd, Coote marched to the attack in three columns, led by Lord Cavan, and Generals Ludlow and Finch. A screen of sharpshooters and fieldpieces covered their front. The flotilla on Lake Mareotis and the gun-vessels on the old port moved forward on both flanks. As our troops drew nigh the French fired heavily, but with no proportionate effect, while the shot from the vessels on either side crossed thickly, and partially raked the very narrow ridge on which the enemy's line was posted.

Its elevation, and the ruins of ancient tombs and temples, which afforded much shelter, saved his troops from heavy loss. But the British columns pressed steadily and sternly forward, and the French commander, General Eppler, gave up the contest. His troops retired in good order, checking his pursuers occasionally by a heavy fire; and he re-entered the lines of Alexandria after losing a good many men and his seven 18-pounders. In this affair only three of the British soldiers were killed, and forty wounded.

After the action had ceased Coote continued to advance; and he took up a new position so close to the works of Alexandria, as to be within a long range of the Fort des Bains. At the same time parties of seamen and others were employed on the toilsome task of dragging up heavy ordnance with which the fortifications might be battered; but this was a very laborious work among the quarries, and catacombs, and ruins of the ancient city, nor was it till the 25th that these heavy guns could be brought into their places.

In the meantime, Sir John Hutchinson despatched Colonel Brent Spencer with four battalions of British, a body of Albanians, and some Mamelukes, to strengthen Coote's division. They embarked on the Lake Mareotis before daylight on the 23rd, and in order to draw off the attention of the French, another feigned attack was made from the eastward. Scattered companies crawled silently up the heights in the dark till they were near the enemy's lines. Then at a signal from the rear, they opened a rattling fire along the extensive front. The scheme was successful; the French manned their works in haste, and kept up for a long time a tremendous but harmless cannonade from all their batteries.

Coote had now more than six thousand effective men under his command, and he lay close to the enemy's works; but his advanced position was attended with one serious inconvenience. No water was to be procured from the dry sand-rocks on which his troops were posted. The wells from which it was necessary to fetch it were nearly four miles to the rear. On the other hand, the occupation of the western isthmus by the British had finally cut off the supplies of sheep and other things which the Arabs, though they detested the French, had not till then ceased to bring to the garrison, and for which they were very amply paid by Ménou.

★★★★★★

It may not be amiss to mention, as it serves to mark one of the difficulties of this campaign in Egypt, that Hutchinson had found it impossible to procure sufficient forage even for his small proportion of cavalry. He had been obliged to send to Rosetta two regiments of dragoons, and all the camels and other beasts of burden in his camp.

★★★★★★

Near as Coote's position was to the Fort des Bains, there was still an outpost held by the enemy which was likely to embarrass our operations against that work. Early in the night of the 25th of August, the 1st battalion of the 20th Regiment, under that admirable officer Colonel George Smith, marched silently forth with unloaded muskets; they turned the left of the French redoubt, and rushing in with the bayonet they captured or killed the whole of its defenders (about one hundred men).

At the same time a picquet, opposite the left of our line, was surprised and dispersed with loss by a party of the 26th Dragoons, Irritated by the success of this exploit, a strong column of the enemy, issuing from the city under cover of a cannonade, attempted to drive the 20th from the post they had so gallantly mastered; but the attack was repelled with ease.

The posture of the French garrison had now become extremely irksome. The soldiers had lost all confidence; and though they still possessed magazines of grain, they had no other meat than horseflesh, and even that supply was scanty. The blockade both by land and sea was so close and stringent, that there remained no hope of relief. Their lines upon the eastern heights were so extensive, as to require the constant presence of two-thirds of their effective soldiers. If they abandoned any part, Hutchinson was ready to break in with 10,000 men.

On the west, Coote acting on a narrow front, was close to the forts which alone protected the city on that side; and he was busily employed in forming batteries and arming them with 24-poundors. General Ménou felt that his game was lost, and in the evening of the 26th of August, he sent out a flag of truce with a letter, in which he asked for a suspension of arms preparatory to a capitulation. On the 30th the terms which came under discussion were adjusted and signed; and on the 3rd of September, the British troops took possession of the lines and the outworks of Alexandria.

The terms of capitulation were nearly the same as those which had been granted to the garrison of Cairo. If Hutchinson had chosen to insist on harder conditions and an absolute surrender, the French could not have held out many days; but they would have fought desperately; and much blood might have been spilled for what was become merely a point of military vanity. The English general know that the war was at an end on the continent of Europe, and that negotiations for peace between our government and that of France were under discussion. That our armies should be known to hold undisputed possession of Egypt was an object of the highest importance, nor ought a day to be lost in conveying information of this fact to the British cabinet. Therefore, Sir John Hutchinson assented without hesitation to the proposal, that General Ménou, with all his troops and followers, should be embarked immediately in English transports and be landed in the ports of France.

Thus, ended the campaign of the British Army in Egypt; a campaign of which the importance can hardly be over-rated. Not only did the result remove the greatest difficulty in the way of peace, and dissipate the fears of England with regard to India, but the success which crowned our arms on the shores of Egypt had further consequences. It revived confidence and an honourable pride in our military service. The British nation, exulting in the proved valour and the triumphs of their army, felt once more that they might rely upon their officers and soldiers as securely as they had long relied upon their seamen. The high character of the British Army shone brightly forth after the clouds which had hung heavily over it.

The miserable warfare in America, the capitulations of Saratoga and York-town, and the more recent disasters of our troops in Flanders and in Holland, had fixed a deep distrust in the public mind of our military men.

It was believed that our commanders, nay even that our officers and soldiers were degenerate, and unequal to cope in battle with the conquerors of Italy and Germany. The trial which had now been made under great disadvantages first dispelled this prejudice. Our service regained its ancient standing in the estimation of the British people. Their confidence was kept alive by the brilliant little affair of Maida after the renewal of the war; and was confirmed, I trust irrevocably, by the great actions and victorious career of Wellington.

Appendix to the Campaign in Egypt, 1801

Appendix A

Instructions for the captains (of the navy) commanding divisions, on landing the troops.

When the troops are to be landed by the boats of the fleet, great care should be had that they are kept at a proper distance from each other, at least fifty feet; and when the situation of the place will admit of it, they are to dress or take their respective stations from the right; otherwise, from the centre or left, as may be convenient, or as shall be previously appointed.

On no account must the boats crowd upon each other, nor are they to break the line, either by getting too much ahead or astern.

No boats are to come into the first line except the flat boats, and the launches having the artillery on board, these last towed by cutters. The second line is to be composed of cutters only, to attend upon the flat boats, that they may afford immediate relief should any boat require it, in which case they are to proceed directly, without waiting for orders, to give the necessary aid. The third line is to be composed of the cutters that tow the launches; and the boats belonging to each ship will keep in the wake of their respective flat boats.

To distinguish the boats having on board the grenadier company of each regiment, they will carry the camp colours of that regiment, and the other boats are to form to the left, until the regiment is completed, taking care that the companies are embarked on board the boats in the order they should be in when landed; and the captains commanding the divisions will consult with the commanding officer of the troops, and fix on the best method to obtain this object without confusion.

When the troops are to land, a situation will be pointed out upon the shore, where either, the right or left will proceed to; if from the right the boats from the left must observe open order, that the right wing may not be too much crowded together; and the boats to the right will pay like attention, when the left is the point from which they are to form.

Upon no account must any flat boat be nearer to another than fifty feet, and this will afford sufficient space for the cutters and launches in the rear to land between the flat boats, agreeable to the regimental order of the troops they have on board.

The flat boats are always to drop their grapnel from their stern at a proper distance from the shore, that they may haul off the moment the troops are landed.

It may often be necessary that the flat boats should pull quick round into an opposite direction, either for retreat or any other cause, in which case it is of the utmost consequence that they should do so together, and in one direction. Strict attention must therefore be paid to the signal that will be made upon that occasion; and if no signal is made, they are always to pull to starboard.

The captains commanding the different divisions will repeat all the signals made by the commanding officer of the disembarkation; and each captain should have a rowing boat attending him, with a careful officer to carry his orders to the boats of his division.

In order that the flat boats may observe the signals as soon as made, a musket will be fired from the commanding officer's boat, which is to be repeated by the captains of the other divisions. Each boat having the signal flags on board, must be provided with stretchers, that the flags maybe seen, should the weather be calm; and all signals will be made at a flag staff, in the centre of the boat.

The officers commanding the boats must take particular care that none of the troops stand up, as on many occasions it may endanger the safety of the boat.

Each flat boat must be provided with four or five breakers, or small casks of water, that immediate relief may be given the troops upon their landing should they require it.

When the first landing is completed, the boats (when ordered) will proceed to those ships having ensigns at their fore-top-gallant-masthead; afterwards to those having their ensigns at the mizen, until all the troops are on shore.

When the second landing takes place, the captains will proceed with their division of boats to particular ships, that the regiments may be landed in a collective body; and this is to be observed until all the troops are on shore.

The launches that landed the artillery, will proceed to such ordnance ship as will be pointed out, to land the light artillery and stores. Should this service not be requisite, they will assist in disembarking the troops agreeable to the last instructions.

The captains of the different divisions will deliver copies of these and all other instructions to the lieutenants under their orders; and they will give others to the midshipmen commanding the flat boats.

No person belonging to the boats to quit them upon landing, unless by the particular order of the commanding officer of the division.

Dated on board His Majesty's ship *Ajax*, 24th January, 1801.

Appendix B

Extracts from the General Orders of the Army.

Marmorice, February 16th, 1801.

When the troops are ordered to land, the men are to be put into the flat boats as expeditiously as possible, but without hurry or disorder; they are to sit down in the boats, and in rowing to the shore the strictest silence is to be observed; the troops are positively ordered not to load till formed on the beach; the formation is to be effected as soon as possible, the men are to fall in, in line, opposite to where they land; nor is any individual or body of men, in conceiving themselves displaced, to attempt to regain their situation by closing to either flank, till ordered so to do by the general officer on whom they depend, or the senior officer present on the spot.

The troops are to land with sixty rounds of ammunition and two spare flints per man; the ammunition which cannot be contained in the pouches to be carefully put in the packs. Three days' bread, and three days' pork ready cooked, is to be carried by officers and men. The same quantity is to be landed for the troops; it is not, however, to be delivered out but carried in kegs, and put under charge of the quartermaster of each regiment, with a party sufficient for the purpose; each man will carry his canteen filled with water.

Three days' barley will be carried for the horses of the cavalry, and of the staff and field officers.

The staff and field officers must provide themselves with forage sacks previous to the fleet sailing from this.

The men will carry their entrenching tools, and the proportion of necessaries specified in the orders 15th August last, *viz.*: two shirts, one pair of shoes, two pair of socks or stockings, neatly made up in their packs or knapsacks; their camp kettles and blankets. Regiments having both blankets and great-coats, will leave the latter on board.

It is absolutely necessary that the officers should bring on shore in the first instance, such articles only as they can carry themselves. Officers' servants are not only on all occasions of service to be present under arms with the corps to which they belong; they are to carry no more than any other soldier, and are to mount all picquets and guards with their masters. The smallest number of batmen possible will be permitted; mounted officers alone are entitled to them.

The music, drummers, and men least fit for actual service, are to be selected for all regimental duties, not purely military; and officers commanding corps will be held strictly responsible for their being at all times, and every situation, in the most effective state.

A proportion of the general hospital staff must be attached in the first instance to each brigade, and will be allowed such orderlies as are absolutely necessary from the brigade. Regimental surgeons are to be allowed one orderly each, to carry the field case of instruments.

The spare arms, tents, and horse appointments of the dismounted cavalry, and every article of spare baggage, are to be left in charge of a careful non-commissioned officer on board of each ship.

Appendix C

RETURN OF THE ARMY UNDER SIR RALPH ABERCROMBY, ON THE MORNING OF THE 7TH OF MARCH, 1801.

	Rank and file present fit for duty.
Major-General Ludlow.	
Coldstream Guards	766
3rd do.	812
Major-General Coote.	
1st Regiment (Royals)	626
54th (2 Battalions)	974
92nd	529
Major-General Cradock.	
90th	727
8th	439
13th	561
18th	411
Major-General Lord Cavan.	
50th	477
79th	604
Brigadier Doyle.	
2nd (Queen's)	530
30th	412
44th	263
89th	378
Carried over	8509

Brought forward	8509
Brigadier Stuart.	
Stuart's Regiment	929
De Roll's do.	528
Dillon's do.	530
Reserve.—Major-General Moore, Brigadier Oakes.	
23rd	457
28th	587
42nd	754
58th	469
40th (Flank Companies)	250
Corsican Rangers	209
Staff Corps	82
Brigadier Finch.	
11th Light Dragoons (one troop)	53
12th do.	474
26th do.	369
Hompesch's Hussars	138
Artillerymen	627
	14,965

Appendix D.

The attempts made by this Admiral Ganthéaume to carry succour to his countrymen in Egypt present a series of mishaps which were not very creditable to the naval service of France. As soon as the chief consul had triumphantly imposed peace upon Austria, he applied himself earnestly to the object of strengthening his army in Egypt. Great exertions were made in all the ports of France with the view of obtaining, at least a temporary superiority in the Mediterranean. Elects, squadrons, fast-sailing frigates, all means of conveying troops and supplies by which the permanent possession of Egypt might be made sure; the first squadron which put to sea was that under the command of Ganthéaume.

He escaped out of Brest in a heavy gale of wind, towards the end of January, 1801, with seven sail of the line and two frigates, all picked ships, and having 3,000 or 4,000 soldiers on board. He passed Gibraltar, and hugged the shore of Africa; Lord Keith's fleet was at Marmorice. Sir John Warren, with four sail of the line, was in Port Mahon. One of Ganthéaume's frigates retarded the march of his squadron; he steered to the northward in order to protect her passage to Toulon; but catching a distant sight of Warren, who had come out with his four ships, the French admiral took alarm and ran with his whole squadron into

Toulon.

While Granthéaume was on his passage, two frigates (*Justice* and *Egyptienne*) sailed from Toulon with 400 troops, ordnance stores, &c., and got safe into Alexandria. Two others (*Regénérée* and *Africaine*) carrying 600 soldiers started from Rochefort. The former reached her destination, but the *Africaine* was taken near Gibraltar by the *Phoebe*, after an action in which two French generals and more than 200 of the troops, exclusive of a great proportion of the crew, were killed or wounded.

Granthéaume did not get clear of Toulon by the 22nd of March: his squadron refitted and strengthened by the addition of more frigates; it carried about 4,000 soldiers. Off Sardinia two of his large ships ran foul of each other; both were greatly damaged, and the admiral made the best of his way back to Toulon, re-entering that harbour on the 5th of April. On the 25th he put once more to sea, but before he had passed Sicily a malignant fever was raging in his crowded ships, and Granthéaume deemed it best to send back to Toulon three ships of the line with 2,000 sick soldiers. With the remainder he worked his way circuitously to Derna, a roadstead on the north coast of Africa, nearly 400 miles to the westward of Alexandria.

It had been imagined that troops might march from hence, over burning sands, and amidst tribes of wild Arabs. But the first attempt of the French boats to approach the shore was met by musket shots and unequivocal signs of hostility, While the admiral and the general were pausing and full of doubts, some sails were seen in the offing; Granthéaume fancied they must be English men-of-war; he cut his cables, and under crowded sail returned to Toulon.

In the meanwhile, the chief consul was making great exertions to collect eighteen or twenty sail of the line at Cadiz, which might run up the Mediterranean, take on board the French Army, which was lying in readiness about Brindisi and Otranto, and land it in Egypt. But this scheme was thwarted, retarded, and finally rendered vain by their two actions with Admiral Saumarez's squadron.

Appendix E.

Convention for the evacuation of Egypt by the French and auxiliary troops, under the command of the General of Division Belliard, concluded between Brigadier-General Hope on the part of the Commander-in-Chief of the British Army in Egypt; Osman Bey on the part of His Highness the Grand Vizier, and Isaac Bey on the part of His Highness the *Capitan Pacha*; the citizens Donzelot General of Brigade, Morand General of Brigade, and Tarayre Chief of Brigade, on the part of the General of Division Belliard, commanding a body of French and auxiliary troops.

The commissioners above named having met and conferred, after the exchange of their respective powers, have agreed upon the following articles:

Art. 1. The French forces of every description, and the auxiliary troops, under the command of the General of Division Belliard, shall evacuate the city of Cairo, the citadel, the forts of Boulac, Gizeh, and all that part of Egypt which they now occupy.

2. The French and auxiliary troops shall retire by land to Rosetta, proceeding by the left bank of the Nile, with their arms, baggage, field-artillery, and ammunition, to be there embarked and conveyed to the French ports of the Mediterranean, with their arms, artillery, baggage, and effects, at the expense of the allied powers. The embarkation of the said French and auxiliary troops shall take place as soon as possible, but at the latest within fifteen days from the date of the ratification of the present convention. It is also agreed, that the said troops shall be conveyed to the French ports above mentioned by the most direct and expeditious route,

3. From the date of the signature and ratification of the present convention, hostilities shall cease on both sides. The fort of ——, and the gate of the Pyramids, of the town of Gizeh, shall be delivered up to the allied army. The line of advanced posts of the armies respectively shall be fixed by commissioners named for this purpose, and the most positive orders shall be given that these shall not be encroached upon, in order to avoid all disputes; and if any shall arise, they are to be determined in an amicable manner.

4. Twelve days after the ratification of the present convention, the city of Cairo, the citadel, the forts and the town of Boulac, shall be evacuated by the French and auxiliary troops, who will retire to Ibrahim Bey, (?) the isle of Rhoda and its dependencies, the forts of Foucroy and Gizeh, from whence they shall depart as soon as possible, and at the latest in five days, to proceed to the points of embarkation. The generals commanding the British and Ottoman Armies consequently engage that means shall be furnished, at their charge, for conveying

the French and auxiliary troops as soon as possible from Gizeh.

5. The march and encampment of the French and auxiliary troops shall be regulated by the generals of the respective armies, or by the officers named by each party; but it is clearly understood, that, according to this article, the days of march and of encampment shall be fixed by the generals of the combined armies, and consequently the said French and auxiliary troops shall be accompanied on their march by English and Turkish commissaries, instructed to furnish the necessary provisions during the continuance of their route.

6. The baggage, ammunition, and other articles, transported by water, shall be escorted by French detachments, and by armed boats belonging to the allied powers.

7. The French and auxiliary troops shall be subsisted from the period of their departure from Gizeh to the time of their embarkation, conformably to the regulations of the French Army; and from the day of their embarkation to that of their landing in France, agreeably to the naval regulations of England.

8. The military and naval commanders of the British and Turkish forces shall provide vessels for conveying to the French ports of the Mediterranean the French and auxiliary troops, as well as all French and other persons employed in the service of the army. Everything relative to this point, as well as in regard to subsistence, shall be regulated by commissaries named for this purpose by the General of Division Belliard, and by the naval and military commanders-in-chief of the allied forces, as soon as the present convention shall be ratified. These commissioners shall proceed to Rosetta or Aboukir, in order to make every necessary preparation for the embarkation.

9. The allied powers shall provide four vessels (or more if possible) fitted for the conveyance of horses, water casks, and forage sufficient for the voyage.

10. The French and auxiliary troops will be provided with a sufficient convoy for their safe return to France. After the embarkation of the French troops, the allied powers pledge themselves, that to the period of their arrival on the continent of the French republic they shall not be molested; and on his part the General of Division Belliard, and the troops under his command, engage that no act of hostility shall be by them committed, during the said period, against the fleet or territories of His Britannic Majesty, of the Sublime Porte, or of their allies. The vessels employed in conveying and escorting the said

troops, or other French subjects, shall not touch at any other than a French port, except in cases of absolute necessity.

The commanders of the British, Ottoman, and French troops, enter reciprocally into the like engagements, during the period that the French troops remain in Egypt, from the ratification of the present convention to the moment of their embarkation. The General of Division Belliard, commanding the French and auxiliary troops, on the part of his government, engages that the vessels employed for their conveyance and protection shall not be detained in the French ports after the disembarkation of the troops; and that their commanders shall be at liberty to purchase at their own expense, the provisions which may be necessary for enabling them to return. General Belliard also engages on the part of his government, that the said vessels shall not be molested on their return to the ports of the allied powers, provided they do not attempt, or are made subservient to any military operation.

11. All the administrations, the members of the commission, of arts and sciences, and in short, every person attached to the French Army, shall enjoy the same advantages as the military. All the members of the said administration, and of the commission of arts and sciences, shall also carry with them not only the papers relative to their mission, but also their private papers, as well as all other articles which have reference thereto.

12. All inhabitants of Egypt, of whatever nation they may be, who wish to follow the French troops, shall be at liberty so to do; nor shall their families after their departure, be molested, or their goods confiscated,

13. No inhabitant of Egypt of whatever religion, who may wish to follow the French troops, shall suffer either in person or property, on account of the connection he may have entered into with the French during their continuance in Egypt, provided he conforms to the laws of the country.

14. The sick who cannot bear removal shall be placed in an hospital, and attended by French medical and other attendants until their recovery, when they shall be sent to France on the same conditions as the troops. The commanders of the allied armies engage to provide all the articles that may appear really necessary for this hospital; the advances to be made on this account shall be repaid by the French Government,

15. At the period when the towns and forts mentioned in the present convention shall be delivered up, commissaries shall be named for receiving the ordnance, ammunition, magazines, papers, archives, plans, and other public effects, which the French shall leave in possession of the allied powers.

16. A vessel shall be provided as soon as possible by the naval commanders of the allied powers, in order to convey to Toulon an officer and a commissioner, charged with the conveyance of the present convention to the French Government.

17. Every difficulty or dispute that may arise respecting the execution of the present convention, shall be determined in an amicable manner by commissioners named on each part.

18. Immediately after the ratification of the present convention, all the English or Ottoman prisoners at Cairo shall he set at liberty, and the commanders-in-chief of the allied powers shall, in like manner, release the French prisoners in their respective camps.

19. Officers of rank from the English Army, from His Highness the Supreme *Vizier*, and from His Highness the *Capitan Pacha*, shall be exchanged for a like number of French officers of equal rank, to serve as hostages for the execution of the present treaty. As soon as the French troops shall be landed in the ports of France, the hostages shall be reciprocally released.

20. The present convention shall be carried and communicated by a French officer to General Ménou, at Alexandria; and he shall be at liberty to accept it for the French and auxiliary forces (both naval and military) which may be with him at the above-mentioned place, provided his acceptance of it shall be notified to the general commanding the English troops before Alexandria, within ten days from the date of the communication being made to him.

21. The present convention shall be ratified by the commanders-in-chief of the respective armies within twenty-four hours after the signature thereof.

Signed in quadruplicate, at the place of conference between the two armies, the 17th of June, 1801, or of the siege of Saffar, 1216, or the 8th *Messidor*, 9th year of the French Republic.

(Signed)   J. Hope, Brigadier-General.
Osman Bey.
Isaac Bey.

Donzelot, *Général de Brigade.*
Tarayre, *Chef de Brigade.*

Approved and ratified the present convention at Cairo, the 9th *Messidor,* ninth year of the French Republic.

(Signed) Belliard, *Général de Division.*

Military Transactions in the Mediterranean, 1805–1810

INTRODUCTION

The doubtful peace which had been patched up at Amiens was of brief continuance. On the 27th of March, 1802, the definitive treaty of peace had been signed. On the 8th of March, 1803, a message from the king announced to the British Parliament that we must prepare for war.

At this time the military means of England were at a very low ebb. The old militia, which had been nine years under arms, had been disbanded, as well as the fencible regiments of cavalry and infantry. Of regular troops there were, including the Guards, nearly 40,000 foot and 12,000 horsemen scattered over Great Britain, Ireland, and the Channel Islands.

	Cavalry.	Infantry.
In Great Britain	8,800	19,500
Ireland	3,200	16,500
Channel Islands	——	3,700

(Exclusive of artillery.)

The strength of this infantry, however, was rather nominal than real. Many battalions of the line were mere skeletons, a large proportion of their scanty numbers consisting of worn-out men recently brought home from the East and West Indies. Several of these battalions could not have mustered 400 men each, including raw recruits. Most of the strong and efficient regiments were in Ireland, nor could they be spared from thence. Our cavalry, however, was pretty strong in numbers and of a good quality.

The first measure adopted by the British Government was to call out the militia; and as the officers and sergeants were nearly the same as in the regiments which had been embodied during the first period of the war, and a large proportion of the men likewise, a short time sufficed to restore this branch of the service to its former efficiency.

Militia, June 1st, 1803.
(Rank and File.)
Great Britain   40,270
Ireland   12,370

The Army of Reserve Bill (the boldest military measure that any British minister had ever ventured to propose) supplied within two months 22,200 recruits.

******

The act for levying the army of reserve was passed July 6th, 1803. By the 1st of September there had been raised 22,200 men; and before the 1st of May, 1804, 37,000, exclusive of about 8,500 who had died, or deserted, or were rejected. It is to be observed that the act was not successful in Ireland. Out of the 22,200 men as above stated, only 1,500 were furnished by Ireland.

******

A large proportion of these men volunteered for general service in regiments of the line. Our skeleton battalions were filled up; and their progress in discipline was rapid under officers and sergeants who had seen service. Camps of instruction were formed in Essex, Kent, and Sussex. Of these the most important was that stationed near Hythe (Shorncliffe Camp), where the 4th, 43rd, 52nd, and 95th (rifles), together with two strong regiments of militia, were placed under the command of Sir John Moore.

The 14th Light Dragoons and a large proportion of artillery were attached to this camp; of which I may speak more fully hereafter, because the new system of drill and movement which was here introduced by Moore became the model for our infantry, and laid the foundation of that superiority which it afterwards evinced in the arduous campaigns of the Spanish Peninsula. In the meantime, Napoleon Bonaparte had loudly proclaimed his determination to conquer peace in London—in other words, to subjugate Great Britain. To this task he applied himself with characteristic energy.

******

La guerre entre la France et la Grande Bretagne avait été, de 1792 à 1801, la lutte du principe démocratique centre le principe aristocratique.

Sans cesser d'avoir ce caractère, elle allait dévenir sous Napoléon, la lutte d'un élément contre un autre élément, avec bien plus de difficulté pour nous que pour les Anglais; car le continent entier, par haine de la révolution Française, par jalousie de notre puissance, devait haïr la France beaucoup plus que les neutres ne détestaient l'Angleterre. Avec son regard perçant le Premier Consul aperçut bientôt la portée de cette guerre, et il prit sa résolution sans hésiter. Il forma le projet de franchir le détroit de Calais avec une armée, et de terminer dans Londres même la rivalité des deux nations. On va le voir pendant trois années consécutives appliquant toutes ses facultés à cette prodigieuse entreprise, et demeurant calme, confiant, heureux même, tant il était plein d'espérance en présence d'une tentative qui devait le conduire ou à être le maître absolu du monde, ou à s'engloutir, lui, son armée, sa gloire, au fond de l'Océan.—Thiers' *Cons, et Emp. Livre 17.*

★★★★★★

Through the summer and autumn of 1803, every river and port from Ushant to the Texel, was ringing with the clink of hammers, and the din of multitudes employed in building the greatest flotilla that ever darkened the sea. Napoleon hoped at first that he should be able to make his attack at some time in the winter of 1803-4, and such were the exertions used that nearly one thousand of his vessels were collected at Boulogne before the end of December.

Without speaking in detail of the French Armies which lay in readiness to embark, or of the fleets which were in preparation to transport them to the shores of England, I cannot but touch on the enormous expenses which such an enterprise demanded. It was not merely the cost of building and fitting out the flotilla. Various establishments on a gigantic scale were found to be indispensable at and near Boulogne. Great basins too were to be excavated there, and at Etaples, Ambleteuse, and Wimereux for the reception of the vessels. Forts also were to be constructed and with great difficulty, *in the sea*, for the protection of the outer roadsteads. To prepare in time for this vast expenditure was Napoleon's first care in 1803; and one of the means he adopted for this chance of conquering England, was the sale of Louisiana to the United States of America for eighty millions of *francs*.

Thus, the passionate desire of Napoleon to plant his conquering eagles on the ruins of London has served to make the United States one of the mightiest nations of the earth!

Urgent affairs, however, called the chief consul to Paris, and engrossed his attention during several months. (The conspiracy of

Georges Cadoudal and Pichegru, followed by the execution of the Duke d'Enghien, and its consequences.) This afforded to the English more time; and our preparations for defence were carried on with much activity, if not with the happiest judgment. Batteries were multiplied along the coasts. One fortified camp was formed at Dover; two others near Chatham and Chelmsford: and large bodies of troops were quartered or encamped in Essex, Kent, and Sussex.

But the most remarkable feature of the time was the flame which burst forth and spread its light over the whole of Britain. It was not merely the flame of patriotism, or of indignation at the bare idea that England should lie at the proud feet of a conqueror; it appeared to be fed and rendered intense by a passionate hatred of Napoleon personally. There had suddenly blazed up in the breasts of millions a fierce, unenquiring, unappeasable detestation of the individual. The Prime Minister (Addington) called for bodies of volunteers to aid in defeating Bonaparte; and before the end of Autumn 1803, 342,000 men had enrolled themselves, were provided with arms, and were devoting their leisure hours to military exercises.

Still our preparations were only in their infancy; and if Napoleon could have crossed the Channel in the winter 1803-4, as he first designed, our means to meet his veteran troops would have been found utterly unfit for battle, though the determination of the British people not to be conquered, and the unyielding temper of our stout old king, would have prevailed, though after long suffering and incalculable losses.

In 1804, we were better prepared. Our regiments of the line were strong, and more fit for the field; our militia well disciplined, and the volunteer corps tolerably familiar with the use of arms.

******

Gross return of Forces in Great Britain, Sept., 1804:

Guards and regular Infantry	75,000
Regular Cavalry	12,000
Militia	80,000
Volunteers (including Yeomanry Cavalry)	343,000
Total	510,000

Exclusive of artillery, &c.

******

There had not, however, been any interruption during Napoleon's absence from the coast of the preparations for his great enterprise. These had become in the meanwhile more extensive, and were better matured; and before the end of July, 1804, the self-made emperor appeared at Boulogne to resume and prosecute his mighty undertaking.

★★★★★★

Napoléon avait résolû d'exécuter dans un bref délai sa grande entreprise. Il voulait franchir le déroit vers le mois de Julliet ou d'Août 1804; et si les incrédules qui ont douté de son projet pouvaient lire sa correspondance intime avec le Ministre de la Marine, la multitude infinie de ses ordres, la secrète confidence de ses espérances à l'Archichancelier Cambacérès, ils ne conserveraient aucune incertitude sur la réalité de cette résolution extraordinaire.—Thiers' *Cons, et Emp. Livre* 20.

★★★★★★

At this time there were encamped and ready for embarkation on board of the flotilla 110,000 soldiers of the finest description. They composed the three *corps d'Armée* commanded by Davoust, Soult, and Ney; an advanced guard of six or eight thousand picked grenadiers under Lasnes, the Imperial Guards, and four divisions of cavalry (chiefly dragoons). Four hundred pieces of field-artillery, and a battering train, were attached to this formidable army, which at first extended from Bruges to Montreuil; but was, later in the season, compressed within camps in the immediate vicinity of Boulogne, and the smaller basins which had been formed near to that town. But this was not all. From sixteen to eighteen thousand men under Augereau were assembled at Brest, and ready to step on board the ships of war at that port; and another *corps d'armée* of about the same strength was prepared to embark in the Dutch fleet which was lying in the Texel.

★★★★★★

This expedition, at Brest, was to be directed to Lough Swilly, or such other part of the north of Ireland as it could reach in safety. If it were foiled in that quarter, it was to push on for the coast of Scotland. Such was the first design; but it was changed when Napoleon decided finally on uniting all his squadrons in the narrow sea.

★★★★★★

Altogether there were 150,000 soldiers (the very soldiers who four months later were triumphant at Austerlitz) ready for the invasion of this kingdom.

It would far exceed the limits of an introductory chapter were I to enter into particulars as to the preparations and various plans of Napoleon, between the spring of 1803 and the autumn of 1805, or of the chances of his success or failure in crossing the Channel at different periods; neither can I enter into a detail of the measures adopted in Great Britain to resist the invasion with which she was threatened. That the Emperor of the French was thoroughly in earnest can no longer be doubted. It is also pretty evident, that it was his design to land upon that part of the coast of England which lies nearest to Boulogne, that part which stretches from the cliffs of Dover to the borders of Sussex.

The landing of the enemy must have been made good in face of the numerous batteries which lined our shores, and of about eighteen strong battalions of infantry (two-thirds of them militia), and twenty squadrons of cavalry which lay close at hand. (The numbers of the infantry may be taken at fully 12,000 rank and file, the cavalry at about 2800 sabres. About fifty pieces of field-artillery would have been present.) But carriages and fish-carts would have brought several thousands from the rear within a very few hours; and of volunteers and yeomanry there would have been considerable numbers.

Sir David Dundas held the chief command in Kent and Sussex. It was his intention, if he should be beaten on the shore, to withdraw his troops, not in the direction of London, but throwing back his right and centre to retreat upon the entrenched camp at Dover. In that strong position he could have brought the enemy to bay, and gained time for the gathering of the strength of Britain around the metropolis.

******

During 1805, and 1804, I was employed on the staff of the Quartermaster-General's Department in Kent and Sussex; and in the latter year I was the senior officer, and had the good fortune to enjoy much of the confidence of Sir D. Dundas and Sir John Moore.

******

Or, if the general had found that Napoleon disregarded him, and was marching straight upon London, then Dundas would have sallied forth and pressed close upon the rear and right flank of the enemy's columns. The direct road from Canterbury and the passage of the Lower Medway were barred by the entrenched camp at Chatham. The French must have taken their routes by Maidstone, Tunbridge, &c., through a more difficult country, where their columns would have been delayed by the breaking up of the roads.

Sir James Pulteney commanded in Sussex; Sir James Craig in Essex. With the help of carriages the former would have reached the great chain of chalk hills before the enemy; or he might have brought 10,000 men to bear on their left flank while it was embarrassed by the difficulties of the way through the Weald of Kent: Craig would have crossed the Thames from Tilbury, or have hastened directly to London.

It would have been madness in the British to have risked a general battle in the field, even in such tempting positions as the chalk hills offer. Our troops were not then of a quality to meet and frustrate the manoeuvres of such an army as that which Napoleon would have led to the attack. We needed every advantage which numbers and position could afford. It was in London itself, or rather along the skirts of Greenwich, Southwark, and Lambeth, that it was our business to fight the great battle to the uttermost, day after day, and night after night; bringing to the relief of every post fresh combatants as they arrived in quick succession from all parts of the kingdom. What mattered the burning of some hundreds of houses, when compared with the mighty stake which was at issue! Our best reliance was upon the numbers and the enduring courage of Englishmen; upon the resolution of millions to vanquish tens of thousands.

★★★★★★

In taking this review of the great invasion with which we were threatened, I have purposely omitted all mention of the dangers which the enemy's flotilla would have had to encounter, if our navy had been able to assail it during its passage. I have assumed that Napoleon's latest and most masterly combination had been successfully accomplished; that his different squadrons had been brought together in the Channel, and that his fifty ships of the line were for some days masters of the narrow sea.

★★★★★★

May my readers pardon me for this discussion of what might have happened in days which have long passed! But it was the question which agitated the whole people of Great Britain, and engrossed the attention of her statesmen during two anxious years. During those years the British Army was growing into strength as to numbers, and efficiency as to discipline. At the close of 1804 there were in the United Kingdom nearly 105,000 rank and file of regular troops, including 16,000 cavalry, but exclusive of artillery.

★★★★★★

The administration of the army under the Duke of York was excellent. His Royal Highness was himself indefatigable, energetic, and just, and he had able assistants in his adjutant and quartermaster-generals, Harry Calvert and Robert Brownrigg.

★★★★★★

The apprehension of invasion continued through the winter of 1804, and with a greater cause to believe it close at hand; though by this time John Bull was beginning to be sick of hearing the oft-repeated cry that the wolf was coming, to grumble at not being invaded, and to be weary of his volunteer duties. Our statesmen, indeed, still viewed the position of affairs with much anxiety. Mr. Pitt, who was now again Prime Minister, gave his personal attention to measures of defence, and he adopted the expensive but effective plan of fortifying our southern and eastern coasts by towers, armed with heavy cannon and built at short distances.

However, a prospect of relief was beginning to dawn. The chance of a new war upon the Continent, which might call off Napoleon from his great design, was becoming every month more probable. For some time past there had been symptoms of ill-will and bickerings between Napoleon and the *Czar*, The timid policy of Austria began, though covertly, to incline towards an alliance with Russia. The British Government threw into the scale large promises of money; and at the beginning of 1805 our Cabinet felt themselves secure that both the imperial courts would send their armies into the field

It was in compliance with the desires and plans of Russia that Mr. Pitt prepared the expedition to the Mediterranean, of which the following narrative gives some account.

Military Transactions in 1805 and 1810

Early in the year 1805, the British Government resolved on sending to the Mediterranean some young battalions, which might form a sufficient garrison for Malta, and render the old regiments on that station (about 7,000 men) disposable for active service. There were at this time objects of importance in present view, and prospects opening into wider consequences.

The Emperor of Russia was connecting himself with England; and it appeared probable that Austria would soon come to ally herself with both in opposition to France. In the meantime, there had arisen apprehensions of an event, which might have been attended with a dangerous influence on British interest in the Mediterranean. A part of the kingdom of Naples was occupied by a French Army, which kept that state under subjection, and strong fears were entertained that our enemy would extend his views to Sicily, and oblige the helpless Court to admit French garrisons into the fortresses and harbour-towns of that important island.

This object might be effected either by open force, or attained by means of a treaty extorted from the wretched Government of Naples. The various contingences involved many questions of great nicety in politics; and on this account the British Cabinet resolved, though the number of troops to be sent out of England was small, to employ on this occasion an officer of high rank had tried judgment. They selected for the service Lieut.-General Sir James Craig, appointing him to the command of all our troops in the Mediterranean, except the garrison of Gibraltar. Four battalions of infantry (about 3,400 men); two more which were to be left at Gibraltar; 300 light dragoons (without their horses); and a large proportion of artillery composed this expedition.

Sir James Craig was a man who had made his way by varied and meritorious services to a high position in our army. He had improved a naturally quick and clear understanding by study, and he had a practical and intimate acquaintance with every branch of his profession. In person he was very shorty broad and muscular, a pocket Hercules, but with sharp neat features as if chiselled in ivory. Not popular, for he was hot, peremptory, and pompous: yet extremely beloved by those whom he allowed to live in intimacy with him; clever, generous to a fault, and a warm and unflinching friend to those he liked.

But at this time Sir James was broken in health, and it was only the hope that the climate of the Mediterranean might restore his strength which allowed of his being employed on active service. My friend James Campbell was appointed to be the adjutant-general, and I was placed at the head of the quartermaster-general's department. We were both entire strangers to Craig, and his manner to us at first was not engaging or conciliatory; but when he came to find we were disposed to do our duties actively and carefully, he warmed to us by degrees; and in the latter and more difficult times of his command I found Sir James Craig one of the kindest men I have ever had to transact business with; and one on whose just and honourable feelings I could always place an entire reliance.

Earl Camden was the Secretary of State for War and Colonies. His instructions, dated March 28th, 1805, directed our general to proceed to Malta:

> Unless in the progress of the voyage extraordinary circumstances should make it necessary to alter his course.
> It being of the utmost importance that Sicily should not fall into the hands of the French, the protection of that island was to be considered as the principal object of the expedition.

On his arrival at Malta the general was to be mainly guided by the advices he should receive from Hugh Elliot, our minister at Naples, who had instructions to attend particularly to two contingencies; the first, being that under which the co-operation of the British forces should be required by him, with the concurrence of the King of Naples; the second contingency was one in which our active interference might become necessary without such concurrence. In the former case the general was instructed to afford every assistance to secure Sicily for the king.

But in the second case, if the government of Naples should be brought to shut its ports against British ships, or if the French should attack the island, or be certainly known to be preparing forces for such an invasion, then Sir James Craig was to use his utmost exertions, in concert with Lord Nelson, for the defence of Sicily against the enemy. Such was the substance of the general's public instructions; but they were accompanied by others marked "most secret." By the latter Sir James Craig's attention was called to two further cases;

"First, that of an attack being made by the French upon Naples, and his being called upon by Mr. Elliot, *or the Russian commander*, to assist in defending the Neapolitan dominions. Secondly, the case of the French force being driven from Naples by the Russian Army, or withdrawn with a view to counteract the movements of the armies which may be acting against France in the north of Italy."

Lord Camden says:

> In either case, if you should receive any application from Mr. Elliot, or from the Austrian or Russian Commanders, previously to your receiving further instructions from me, and it should appear to your judgment that by co-operating with your force on the continent of Italy, you can materially contribute to the safety of the dominions of the King of Naples, and forward the objects of the campaign which may there be opened. His Majesty authorises you to concert with the general of his allies as to the most effectual manner of promoting that important end; and if it appears to you that this object can be most effectually promoted by joining your force with that of the Emperor of Russia, you are to put yourself under the command of General Lacy, &c.
>
> But, although His Majesty feels the most anxious desire to cooperate with his allies, as far as his limited force in the Mediterranean will enable him, yet there are other objects to which the force which you command may be advantageously disposable; which makes it important that it should not be engaged in such distant operations as may prevent you from being able to withdraw it under certain circumstances, and to detach it upon other services.

These "other services" were explained, in a supplemental despatch, to be the occupation of Alexandria, if the French should turn their views to the East; or the protection of Sardinia, if that island should appear to be in danger.

The different and unconnected objects to which Sir James Craigs attention was thus directed, afford us ample evidence that the views of our Cabinet were based on no principle, or sound plan of operations. Yet these were not all: a subsequent despatch, (June 8th, 1805—secret and confidential), instructed the general to gather information from General Fox, the Lieut.-Governor of Gibraltar, with respect to Minorca, and the feasibility of capturing that island. As the amount of disposable forces which Sir James might have at his command after his arrival at Malta could not exceed six or seven thousand men, it was evident that if anyone of these multifarious instructions was carried into effect, there would remain no means of attending to the others.

******

Although the despatch, which will be found in the Appendix (Viscount Castlereagh to General Fox, *most secret*, 19th July, 1805), bore relation exclusively to Gibraltar, and had no influence over the movements of Sir James Craig's army, yet the subject and intelligence it conveys are so curious, and shew so strongly the opinion which was entertained of the Spanish Government at that time, that I cannot refrain from inserting it. See Appendix A. (The original letter is in my possession).

******

Our troops were embarked before the end of March, but it was not till the 19th April, that we put to sea, in company with a fleet of several hundred ships bound to the East and West Indies and America, convoyed by many men-of-war. It was a noble sight! But we soon parted from the great body of the fleet, and pursued our own course under the protection of the queen and the dragon. Our passage across the Bay of Biscay was rough, but only two of the transports parted company; and on the eighth day we made Cape Finisterre, where we fell in with a frigate, sent from the Tagus to give warning to all British ships that the enemy's fleet from Toulon had come through the straits of Gibraltar.

But Admiral Sir John Orde, though he had dispatched this intelligence to our minister at Lisbon, had omitted altogether to state what he proposed to do, or where his squadron was likely to be found. In consequence of this alarm, we kept close along the coast of Portugal; and having received further and unsatisfactory reports, our general, and Admiral Knight who commanded the convoy, came, though reluctantly, to the resolution of running into the Tagus for present security.

Although self-preservation imposed this measure, it was on political grounds highly objectionable. The Court of Portugal was preserving with great difficulty its humble neutrality: it felt that Napoleon was seeking occasion to pick a quarrel; and the presence of an English Army in the port of Lisbon might but too probably afford the pretext he desired. Every possible precaution therefore was taken by the general to mark his respect for the neutrality of Portugal Not a man or officer was allowed to go on shore during the few days we remained under the walls of Lisbon; nor would Sir James Craig himself pay his respects to the prince regent.

But at the same time the apprehension that the enemy's fleet might enter the Tagus, rendered some precautions necessary, and the commanding engineer and I were sent to reconnoitre the forts. Our troops were in a trap; and it was clear that if the French appeared, and the Portuguese refused to protect us, we could be saved only by some desperate enterprise. Sir James Craig resolved, if such a necessity should arise, to surprise or storm Fort St Julian with his 5,000 men. (This fort commands the main channel of the Tagus below Lisbon.) Secret arrangements were made to have all the boats and troops in constant readiness, and a plan of assault was drawn out. Happily, we were not driven to this extremity: certain accounts arrived that the enemy's fleet had gone from Cadiz, and was not in our neighbourhood.

On the 10th of May we again put to sea, and the next evening we found Lord Nelson's squadron lying-to off Cape St. Vincent. The great admiral had just arrived from Gibraltar bay; he waited only to have a conversation with Sir James Craig and Admiral Knight; and he then bore up with his ten sail of the line to search for the enemy in the West Indies.

★★★★★★

The energy with which Nelson pursued the superior fleet of the enemy to the West Indies, and chased them out of the West Indies, appeared to us in those days to be admirable, evincing the highest judgment, as well as decision of purpose. Yet we know now that our great admiral was, in fact, following the plan chalked out for him by Napoleon. To lead our squadron on wild-goose chases to the Caribbean or other distant seas, in search of French fleets, which were sent purposely to tempt but to evade pursuit, and to return and unite in the British Channel, was the most masterly feature of the emperor's combinations for the conquest of England.

★★★★★★

We anchored at Gibraltar on the 13th; and the next day a brig-of-war arrived with orders that the expedition should remain where it was, in expectation of events. It was now known in England that the enemy's fleet, with troops on board, had steered for the West Indies;

and if they had remained there, we probably should have proceeded to the same quarter. Our stay at Gibraltar was protracted till the end of June; and circumstances made it uneasy. The Spaniards at Carthagena were getting six sail of the line ready for sea: Admiral Bickerton felt it necessary to take all his line-of-battle ships (four) to watch that port; and our fleet of transports was left in the roadstead of Gibraltar without better protection than a brig-of-war and two or three gunboats. There were no quarters for our troops on shore; and as the rock was in quarantine on account of the fatal fever which had lately carried off a great proportion of the garrison and inhabitants, scarcely any fresh provisions could be obtained, even from Barbary.

However indolent the Spaniards may be, the helplessness of our crowded transports could not fail to attract their attention; and they quickly fitted some forty heavy gun and mortar boats to pound us at our anchorage. Fire rafts also were in preparation; and these overt signs of hostility determined Sir James to send the transports out of the bay, and to keep them cruising between the east side of the rock and the Barbary shore, while the general and his staff remained at Gibraltar.

At length, on the 22nd June, orders arrived from England for our departure; and a few days afterwards Sir Richard Bickerton returned with his squadron to see us in safety past Carthagena. Gladly did we renew our voyage: our men were in high health; the weather was beautiful as we sailed along the shores of Africa, under convoy (after parting from the admiral) of the *Lively, Sea-Horse, Ambuscade*, and *Merlin*: and we anchored in the hot port of La Valetta on the 18th of July. The health of Sir James Craig, which had appeared to be very precarious while we were at Gibraltar, improved rapidly during this latter part of our voyage; and at Malta he seemed to recover all his strength and spirits. From his first landing he set to work indefatigably, inspecting regiments and departments every morning at 4 o'clock writing despatches and transacting business all day, giving great dinners every evening, and receiving the officers of his army with a profuse hospitality.

The Russian troops, which were at this time stationed in Corfu and the neighbouring islands, amounted to about 15,000 regulars and 2000 wild Suliotes. They were under the immediate command of Lieut.-General D'Anrep, a good officer and a sensible man; but he was secretly subordinate to old General Lacy, who was residing at Naples under the pretext of bad health, but prepared by the orders of his sovereign to take the chief command of both Russians and English, whenever the time might come for their being put in motion. Lacy was a curious example of the way in which the great powers of the Continent were accustomed to select their generals for even the most important commands.

He *had been*, no doubt, a brave and meritorious officer: but he was now between seventy and eighty years of age, and he shewed no trace of ever having been a man of talent or information. The son of an Irishman, and brought up in an Irish convent, he spoke the English language (though he had never visited the shores of Erin) with the strongest brogue I ever heard, and with peculiarities that I had never met with except in the Teagues of our old comedies.

At the councils of war held at Naples six months afterwards, he used to bring his nightcap in his pocket, put it on and go to sleep while others discussed the business. But the old gentleman was simple, kind-hearted, and (to use his own phrase) "always for fighting." His high rank in the Russian Army was clearly the motive for employing him, as it placed him above any English or Neapolitan commander; and his emperor had attached to Lacy, as chief of his staff, a certain General Oppermann, who was to suggest everything, and really direct everything. This was a clever fellow, but he seemed to be an intriguer, and he left an impression on one's mind of his being not too honest.

Hugh Elliot (brother of the first Lord Minto) was at this time our Minister at Naples. He was a man of no common talent and address; agreeable, subtle, and bold; of long experience in diplomacy, but apt, as clever men in that profession too often are, to be over-refined in his schemes, and to entangle himself in curious webs of his own weaving. His judgment was not equal to the acuteness of his observation; and his temper made him presumptuously sanguine at one moment, and unreasonably desponding at another. Elliot was in high favour with the queen, who managed everything at Naples; but his penetration and knowledge of the world were frequently foiled by the dark dexterity and unprincipled manoeuvres of that bold bad woman.

On Sir James Craig's arrival at Malta, he found that the governor, Sir Alexander Ball, had been for some time in communication with Mr. Elliot, and that the latter had received official enquiries from General Lacy, so early as the 10th of May, with regard to the number of British troops which would be ready to co-operate with the Russians on the continent of Italy, and as to the shipping which could be engaged at Malta and fitted at the expense of England for the transporting of the Imperial troops from Corfu. These questions it was not in Mr. Elliot's power to answer, for he had received no instructions from England touching such arrangements. But in the meantime, Napoleon, after having assumed the iron crown of Italy, had found that the Court of Naples was hesitating and endeavouring to avoid the recognition of his new title.

With his customary abruptness he addressed the Neapolitan envoys at Milan in the roughest and most imperious language, (Mr. Elliot to Sir Alex. Ball, 17th June, 1805), declaring that if the recognition of his title as King of Italy were not sent to Bologna before he should arrive in that city, he would take possession of Naples and strip King Ferdinand of all his territories. The affrighted court immediately communicated their dispatches to the English minister and the Russian general: and the latter declared without hesitation that there were no military means in readiness for the support of His Sicilian Majesty; adding his advice that, in order to avoid a commencement of hostilities, the king should submit to the necessity of circumstances.

At this time a French Army of 14,000 or 15,000 men under the command of General St. Cyr was occupying the provinces of Naples bordering on the Adriatic. They were ready to gather for action at the first signal from the emperor, and a few days would have brought them from La Puglia to the capital, where there were no means of resistance. The Neapolitan troops, always of a bad quality were reduced to insignificance in point of numbers: eight or nine thousand spiritless men, under the leading of wretched officers, were the utmost that could have been collected to oppose the veterans of France. King Ferdinand laid his humble recognition at the feet of Napoleon; and St. Cyr's troops remained quietly in their cantonments, consuming at their leisure the resources of the submissive kingdom.

The tenor of the information obtained by Sir James Craig on his arrival at Malta, the gathering of the Austrian armies with a view to operations in the north of Italy, and the expected arrival of 10,000 more Russian troops at Corfu, determined the general to lose no time in hiring and fitting out a great number of vessels as transports for our Allies, while he prepared his own division of British for embarkation. He despatched a vessel to Naples, and received on her return letters from Mr. Elliot, which apprised him that the Emperor Alexander had put an end to his negotiations with France; that Russian Armies were marching to the support of Austria, and that the forces of the latter empire were assembling in great numbers in the Tyrol and Venetian States.

But these letters afforded no information as to the plans of the Allied powers, nor any knowledge of the intentions of England or the wishes of Austria. With regard to Naples, Mr. Elliot, (to Sir James Craig, 4th August, 1805), mentioned that Napoleon was continuing to menace that government; that General d'Hédouville was expected to arrive from Paris with powers to exact a more absolute submission, and probably to require the cession of the principal fortresses. At the same time Mr. Elliot had learned, through Count Kaunitz, the Austrian Ambassador at Naples, that the count had been made the medium of conveying to the queen, Caroline, Napoleon's threat that if she did not retire immediately to the Austrian dominions, he would send an armament from Toulon to take possession of Naples. This threat was evidently designed to work on Her Majesty's nerves; but Queen Caroline's nerves were much stronger than her principles. However, the very menace of sending forth a squadron from Toulon, at a time when we had no line-of-battle ships in that quarter, was well calculated to make the English cautious in their movements.

Nearly at the same time as the receipt of these advices from Naples, the officer whom Sir James Craig had despatched to Corfu on his first arrival, returned. The information which he brought confirmed the fact that there were barely 10,000 Russians disposable for offensive operations; but General d'Anrep professed to expect from day to day the arrival of 12,000 more from the Black Sea; and he announced in his letters that he should embark with between twenty and twenty-five thousand troops for Naples. Our general was informed, however, at the same time that though the Russian commanders in general were courteous in their communications, there prevailed among the inferior officers, and even the soldiers, a strong feeling of ill-will to the British. (General d'Anrep was believed to share in this dislike.)

In his despatch of the 16th August to Lord Camden, Craig attributes this aversion to the arts exercised by the French during the peace, when great numbers of Russians were visitors at Paris: but there can be little doubt that it took its origin in the circumstances of our unhappy campaign in North Holland in the autumn of 1799.

It is worthy of note that though the British Ministry had collected a considerable body of troops at Malta, and had pointed out all sorts of active operations to their commander, they had neglected to provide any adequate supplies of ammunition. (Sir James Craig to Earl Camden, August 16th, 1805.) Sir James Craig found the ordnance magazines at Malta to be miserably deficient in powder and flints (in case of a protracted campaign), and he was obliged to urge the Secretary of State to send out an immediate supply, asking at the same time for a regiment of cavalry. The latter demand obtained no attention; though for service in Italy, or even for the defence of Sicily, cavalry were much needed.

But when Sir James Craig addressed his despatch of the 16th August to Lord Camden, he had received General Lacy's plan of a proposed campaign, drawn out by his superintendent Oppermann, and dated Naples, 3rd August. (General Lacy to Sir James Craig.) This plan is a military curiosity, and is deserving of record. It must be borne in mind that the Russians, whether they were to produce 25,000 men or only half that number, were to start from Corfu—the English, 7,000 were to proceed from Malta. The Imperial commander says:

> Now, my Russians shall come round to the bay of Naples; land there, and push forward some twenty or twenty-four miles, so as to cover the Terra di Lavoro and the capital against the enemy, who are quartered to the amount of 13,000 or 14,000 men in the provinces of Bari and Otranto. At the same time, you. General Craig, shall land with your 7,000 English on the coast to the southward of Taranto. You will, of course, draw all the attention of the enemy upon you, but he will not dare to march and attack you for fear of being cut off by me and my Russians; and so they will retreat; and then you and I will join and follow them up!

And this was the way in which the Moscovites formed plans of campaign in the year 1805! It needed but a few words of answer from Sir James Craig to demonstrate the utter absurdity of such a scheme; and when old Lacy received the reply, he laughed and said *sotto voce* to Mr. Elliot, "I thought it would never do!" It was plain enough that Oppermann's object was to monopolise all the resources of the capital and the richest provinces for the Russians; and to leave the English to take their chance; and a miserable chance it would have been. If the plan of a double landing (objectionable as it was in a military point of view) had been made in good faith, the parts of the performers should have been reversed: the passage from Corfu to Taranto was very short; that from Malta to Naples was straight and easy. But there was treachery, as well as professional ignorance, in the proposition.

On the receipt of Sir James Craig's answer, (Sir James Craig to Visct, Castlereagh, Sept, 27th), in the reasoning whereof honest old Lacy fully concurred, General Oppermann was obliged to acquiesce in the proposal that the Allied forces should proceed together to one point of disembarkation; and the immediate neighbourhood of Naples was determined on.

The want of mules and horses for the artillery and baggage was foreseen with anxiety by Craig, as well as the insufficiency of his cavalry; he used every exertion, but he procured very few animals from Sicily and Sardinia. The transports prepared for the Russian troops were sent to Corfu, and the bay of Agosta was chosen as the place where the two armaments should unite; but their invasion of Naples was to await the commencement of war by the Austrians. In the meantime, however, news came that five or six thousand French had arrived to reinforce St. Cyr; and fears were excited that he would anticipate the movements of the Allies, and would occupy Naples and its neighbourhood with his army, which was now supposed to amount to 20,000 men.

At the same moment the Neapolitan Government signed the secret convention with Russia which had been long prepared; but still Lacy waited for the actual commencement of hostilities on the part of Austria, before he should bring his troops to Italy. Of this ruinous delay Mr. Elliot complains bitterly in a letter to Craig, dated the 21st Sept.: he says that St. Cyr has received his reinforcements, and is in a condition to seize on Naples in a few days, while the Allied forces could not arrive in less than six weeks; and would even then be incapable of moving from the want of horses and mules. At the same time the French set afloat a report, which served to increase the alarm, that the combined fleets of France and Spain had sailed from Cadiz, with troops on board destined for the invasion of the Two Sicilies. And though King Ferdinand had ratified his treaty with Russia on the 11th Sept., on the 21st his affrighted Ministers were despatching to Paris an humble offer to observe a perfect neutrality, if Napoleon would be pleased to withdraw his forces from the kingdom of Naples.

It appears most strange that neither these ministers, nor their general the Count de Damas (who though he was of little worth as a military commander, was a Frenchman of some quickness and knowledge of the world), nor the Russians should have seen that Napoleon must be anxious to disembarrass himself of Naples, as soon as war with Austria should be inevitable, and that St. Cyr's army must be recalled to the north of Italy on the firing of the first shot.

M. Alquier, the French Minister of Naples, and General St. Cyr, were well aware that the Russians at Corfu, and the English at Malta, were in readiness to embark. So long as the French troops were kept together in La Paglia, commanding the roads through the Abruzzi, their retreat towards Upper Italy was secure; but if St. Cyr had marched to Naples, and had been delayed, or had got into any entanglement on that side, he might have lost the opportunity of drawing off, and of leading his 20,000 men to the Adige.

Napoleon perhaps knew that the Neapolitan Court had signed a treaty with Russia; but at least he was well aware of their hostile disposition and treacherous nature. He had exacted a treaty of neutrality between the French empire and the Kingdom of Naples, from the Marquis de Gallo at Paris; and he instructed M. Alquier to force the wretched King Ferdinand to accept and ratify it, at the moment when the fears of the Court were excited to the utmost pitch by the manoeuvre of sending reinforcements to St. Cyr, and the reports of the sailing of fleets from Cadiz.

With a cowardice which could be equalled only by the treachery of this action, the Neapolitan Government delivered a formal ratification of the treaty to M. Alquier, (General Lacy to Sir James Craig, Oct. 1805); and Mr. Elliot to the same, 16th Oct.; and at the same moment placed in the hands of the Russian minister a written declaration that this convention with France had been extorted from them by threats; that they were resolved not to adhere to it, and that they called on the Russians and English to fulfil their engagement to repair to Naples, as though no such transaction with the French Government had taken place. In communicating this grave intelligence to Sir James Craig, the Russian General made no comment whatever; expressed no doubt or hesitation as to the propriety of landing in the kingdom; but simply directed that the fleets should sail, and that when united they should make the best of their way to the bay of Naples. At the same time General Lacy mentioned, that immediately on the ratification of the convention between Napoleon and King Ferdinand, St. Cyr's army had broken up from their cantonments, and were in full march through the Abruzzi for Upper Italy.

In the perfidious transaction which I have just related the chief actors were Queen Caroline and M. de Tatitscheff, the *Czar's* minister at Naples. It was concealed as much as possible from Mr. Elliot; that gentleman had been no party to the proceedings, and he learnt them officially only after the consummation. He likewise, in writing to Sir J. Craig on the 16th Oct., confined himself to a dry communication of what had been done by the government of Naples. In his own mind Elliot felt as strongly as Craig did, when the latter received these despatches, that the conduct of the court had been equally foolish and perfidious.

The evacuation of the territory by the French, the relief from the burden and domination of their troops, and the security of breathing-time afforded by the treaty of neutrality, were all that Naples had at first professed to seek, and all that she could desire except revenge—"For revenge" (to use the beautiful language of Mr. Hallam) "she threw away the pearl of great price." Dealing perfidiously both with enemies and friends, regardless of her subjects, and blind to the true interests of her husband's crown. Queen Caroline provoked and richly merited the fate which was impending. Only four days after she and the Russian minister had summoned the allied troops to Naples, in contempt of the faith she had pledged one fortnight before, the capitulation of Ulm was signed, and the principal Army of Austria was in captivity.

The feelings of Sir James Craig, when he received in the last days of October, the letters of General Lacy and Mr. Elliot, deserve to be recorded in his own words; and I have given in the Appendix, his separate despatch on this subject. (Sir James Craig to Visct. Castlereagh, 9th Dec. 1805. See Appendix B.) He viewed the convention of the Neapolitan court with Napoleon as pusillanimous and unnecessary; but he considered their secret protest and disavowal as an act of such disgraceful perfidy, as would have justified him in withdrawing his troops, and refusing to enter the dominions of Naples, if he had not been already committed by his having placed himself under General Lacy's command. The orders to sail were come, the Russians were actually at sea, and their safety might be compromised if the English refused to act. Craig, therefore, with deep reluctance embarked his Englishmen, and put to sea on the 3rd of November.

Our force consisted of 300 Light Dragoons, without horses, nearly 500 artillerymen, and 4,670 British, and about 1,900 foreign infantry. Our fleet joined the Russians, under Admiral Greig and General d'Anrep, off Cape Passaro. But the weather proved unfavourable; we were tacking ten days within sight of Malta; weathered the west end of Sicily with difficulty; and at last anchored in the bay of Naples, on the 20th of November. According to the orders of General Lacy, the Russian troops (about 13,000 men, including 1,500 **Suliotes**) were disembarked close to the capital; the English at Castellamare, from whence they proceeded to cantonments in the neighbouring villages.

The first intelligence which met our general on his landing, was that of the surrender of Mack's army at Ulm, and the consequent retreat of the Archduke Charles from Upper Italy. But this disastrous news was carefully concealed from the public and from the troops.

Our quarters were sufficiently convenient, the people civil and compliant; but Sir James Craig was struck from the first with the utter indifference with which the Neapolitans, both in the town and country, appeared to regard the arrival of the allies. It seemed that they cared not a jot whether we came or not; and that their comparison between us and the French was probably much akin to that of the Turkish *pacha*, when he spoke of a dog and a hog.

Our first cares and greatest exertions were used to procure mules and horses; of the latter, Mr. Elliot had already managed to collect a couple of hundred for our dragoons; and as fast as the means of carrying our baggage were afforded to us by the feeble government, we prepared our brigades to march towards the frontier.

******

Craig had issued strict orders for the purpose of regulating and limiting the baggage of his army. The commanding officer of one of our regiments managed, however, to smuggle several dozens of choice Madeira, for his own use, into one of the waggons. The general found it out, seized the wine on the march and turned it over to the use of our hospital.

******

The first of our columns moved forward on the 9th of December, and were followed in succession by the rest of the British troops, along the high road through Capua, towards Mola di Gaeta.

In framing his scheme for the occupation of a line along the northern frontier, General Lacy had determined that the 7,000 Neapolitans, under the Count de Damas, should occupy the mountains of the Abruzzi, having in their rear the fortress of Pescara (in which a large depot of artillery and stores had been rashly accumulated); that the Russians should hold the centre of the line with their headquarters at Sulmona; and that the British should form the left wing, occupying Sessa, and other towns and villages, on the southern side of the Lower Garigliano; with an advanced corps (the Corsican Rangers under Colonel Lowe) in the defiles of Itri and Fondi. The winter was remarkably severe; and it is a curious fact that more than one *Russian* was frozen to death in the kingdom of Naples!

The strong fortress of Gaeta, on our extreme left, was held by a Neapolitan garrison, commanded by one of the princes of Hesse Philipstadt, and in his hands it was safe. Sir James Craig, in his anxiety to secure a hold upon the sea, and ignorant as yet of the prince's character, made some overtures to his highness, with a view of introducing a portion of the British troops into the garrison; but the proposal was very roughly rejected by the brave, though eccentric German.

In ordinary times our position would not have been bad; the screen of our 30,000 men would have availed to cover the assembling and the forming of a second army, and of the popular masses which the worn out government pretended and attempted to excite. The Russians, too, always professed to be expecting the arrival of large reinforcements from the Black Sea. But in the meantime, our 20,000 fighting troops (Russians and English) were thrown out of action; they were null and of no effect, for the general purposes of the Coalition. Unnecessarily injuriously late as the movements of the troops had been, still, if General Lacy had given orders on the 16th October (when he knew that the neutrality of Naples was secured), that both d'Anrep and Craig should have proceeded direct to Venice or Trieste, the issue of that great campaign of Austerlitz might have been different.

Massena could not have pressed close on the Archduke Charles, as he did, with his whole army; a large part of it at least must have turned upon us, and the archduke might then either have struck back and crushed the divided enemy, or have united his forces with those of the two emperors in Moravia.

But to return from what might have been done to what was actually done. We were placed on the defensive, with no enemy (except the garrison of Ancona) nearer to us than the Po. Our fate was to be decided by what might turn out in Austria.

In the meantime, it may be worthwhile to record that it was not till long after our arrival in Naples, that intelligence was received there of the Battle of Trafalgar, fought on the 21st of October. A rumour of such an event first arose in the capital, after a private letter had been received there by a brother of the Spanish Admiral Gravina; but the results were glanced at very obscurely.

The queen alone believed at once that Nelson was killed. "If he had fought and survived," said she, "I am sure he would have written to me or have despatched the news," Fully seven weeks elapsed before the certain intelligence of this great victory reached from Gibraltar to Naples. No British squadron came to the coasts of Italy; and with one ship of the line (the *Excellent*, of 74 guns), three or four frigates, and a small force of Russian ships, we hardly felt ourselves secure, that attacks on Naples or Sicily, might not be ventured upon by the men-of-war which the enemy still possessed in Toulon.

One of the many embarrassing circumstances in our position was the want of intelligence; there were no packets to the Mediterranean in those days; and after the first disasters of the Austrians, the communication with England through Germany was cut off. We obtained no certain knowledge of events; all we learnt came through the bulletins of Napoleon, or such garbled and doubtful versions as the Court of Naples or the Russian minister allowed us to receive. Though Sir James Craig had been instructed to consider the operations of the Anglo-Russian forces in Lower Italy, as mainly designed to assist the operations of the Austrians on the Adige, we had never been put into communication with Vienna, or with the Archduke Charles.

Everything came filtered through the suspicious channels of Russian diplomacy. It would seem, that while St. Cyr's army remained in the kingdom of Naples, the Austrians approved of our, I mean the 20,000 Russians and English, acting in that distant quarter; as they probably hoped that ire should engross the attention of this portion of the French forces, and so far give relief to the archduke's flank. But when, after *a most unaccountable delay*; Prince Charles came to be informed of the real state of affairs at Naples, he wrote on the 22nd of November, to General Lacy urging him to sail immediately with all his forces, to land at Venice, and throw himself on the rear of Massena's army.

This despatch, (Sir James Craig to Viscount Castlereagh, Dec. 14th, 1805), however, did not arrive (or at least it was not imparted to Craig) before the 13th of December, when the allied troops were already spread along the frontier, and the time for useful action in that quarter had passed away. It is not to be disguised, that there were many circumstances in the conduct of the Russians at this period calculated to excite a belief that they were playing falsely with their allies, Austrians as well as English.

From among other things, I may select one instance of a very suspicious complexion; M. de Tatitscheff (after the notable intrigue I have related, when the King of Naples signed the convention of neutrality with France, and at the same moment furnished M. de Tatitscheff with a formal disavowal) wrote an account of this transaction to the *Czar's* ambassador, who was then at Potsdam, but he made use of a cypher which the latter was, or pretended to be, unable to make out; and by this means Austria was kept in ignorance of a most important event at the very crisis of her fate.

The French bulletins brought to Naples after the middle of December the astounding news of the Battle of Austerlitz, and of the armistice to which the Emperor of Austria had been reduced to submit;

but no instructions came to General Lacy or M. de Tatitscheff, nor any certain information as to a suspension of arms generally between France and Russia. (Sir James Craig to Viscount Castlereagh, Dec. 31st, 1805.) It was known, however, that French forces were already moving towards Bologna, and that Napoleon, relieved from all hinderance on the side of Austria, had publicly declared his resolution to drive the Bourbon dynasty from Naples, and take possession of the kingdom.

The position of our little, ill-connected army ("joined, not matched"), now became extremely critical. We could look for no help from without, nor for any diversion in our favour. We were almost destitute of cavalry; so few were the horses provided by the Neapolitan Government, that we had been obliged to leave a considerable part of our field guns at Castellamare. The Russian infantry, though they had encountered no fatigues, were so sickly, that they could scarcely have produced more than 8,000 regular firelocks in the field. (General Lacy himself told us that every one of his battalions had more sick than the whole of the British division.) The Neapolitans had swelled their numbers only by raw recruits, who were sure to set the example of flight on the firing of the first shot; and this motley army of allies, each distrustful of the others, was scattered across Italy from Pescara to Gaeta.

That there was no time to be lost in taking a decision as to our attempting, or not, to defend the frontier, became still more evident a very few days after the first alarm, when intelligence arrived that French columns (the same to the same, January 2nd, 1806) were already on their march from the Lower Po and La Romagna, to the amount of between thirty and thirty-five thousand men. Sir James Craig had been from the first clearly of opinion, that the idea of defending these extensive frontiers, with such means as the allies possessed, was vain and dangerous; that we must be defeated, and that both the Russians and the English might be cut off from their transports, and unable to effect their re-embarkation; but he declared that if General Lacy should determine on maintaining his position, the British would not abandon him, but would uphold the honour of the allied arms to the last extremity.

In the meantime, the court of Naples was tossed to and fro by fear and rage: they shewed themselves, as they always did, as presumptuous as they were helpless. The queen insisted on defending the advanced positions; and her friend M. de Tatitscheff, pronounced an opinion that the Russian troops ought to wait for direct instructions from their emperor. But fortunately, General Lacy and Oppermann were just at this crisis returning from a military examination of the frontier: they had found it to be much less strong than they had expected, and they hesitated not to concur with Craig in the opinion that the allied troops ought to fall back before the enemy came near, and while such movements could be made without disorder.

An official declaration of the sentiments entertained by both the Russian and English commanders as to the necessity of this measure was signed by them and presented to King Ferdinand, and His Majesty was invited to issue corresponding orders to his own forces. The Court alternately stormed, and upbraided, and entreated; but the military necessity was manifest to all men of cool judgment, and the retreat of the army was ordered.

Next came the question where the retreat should stop. (Sir James Craig to Viscount Castlereagh, Feb. 11th, 1806.) Craig had always in his mind the original instructions he had received to secure Sicily (Appendix C); but he could not venture to avow this object to the Neapolitans or the Russians; neither could he hint at another apprehension, that our imperial allies, having no resources in their ships, nor money, nor credit, would in case of a protracted warfare pillage the country for their own subsistence, and thus convert the peasantry into enemies!

Sir James, therefore, was desirous to embark at once, when the weather should be favourable, and not run the risk of having to perform this difficult operation in the face of an enemy. On the other hand, the Russians, who had brought us into the scrape, seemed to be completely at a loss as to what they might or ought to do. They did not dare to take a decisive course without having direct orders from their emperor. He had sent them into the kingdom of Naples, and his pleasure only could release them. Queen Caroline of course worked with all her machinery to fortify the wavering councils of the Russian generals, and Sir James Craig still declared that though he entirely disapproved, as a military man, of the proposed attempt to resist the great armies which were now at the enemy's command, he would share the fate of the general under whose orders he had been placed.

At a council of war held at Naples on the 4th of January, it was resolved, in conformity with a plan proposed by General Opperman, that the allied armies should retire on the advance of the French to the mountains of the Principato, and defend the two Calabrias. The only dissentients were Sir James Craig and Brigadier Campbell Major-General Stuart and I concurred with the Russians; and I have not a doubt now that I was wrong in my opinion. But I was a young man eager for active service, and ignorant of the important objects which were involved in securing Sicily from the French before it was too late. However, our resolutions were but an idle waste of time.

When they were communicated to the court, the answer was not simply dissentient: it was a storm of invectives against the plan and its proposers. The queen would hear of nothing short of a desperate resistance, which might cover the capital to the last extremity: and old Lacy, who was now alive to the dangers of his position, was reduced to the utmost perplexity. From this he was happily relieved on the 7th of January, by the arrival of a letter from the Emperor Alexander (dated as far back as the 7th of December), directing the general to take immediate steps for the safety of his Russian troops, and to embark them for Corfu.

No time was lost; the columns were put in motion; the English for Castellamare, and the Russians for Naples. Our division began its embarkation on the 14th of January, and sailed on the 19th. On the 22nd the British troops under Sir James Craig were anchored in the harbour of Messina.

Here begins a new chapter in the history of our proceedings in the Mediterranean. Nine months had passed since our departure from England, and we had at last reached the place which had been originally our main object.

But our position at Messina was singular. We anchored under the guns of the fortress, in our transports crowded with troops, as the friends and allies of the King of Sicily. But the King of Sicily (or rather those who guided the old man) was at the moment furiously exasperated against us; nor was there any immediate probability of his assenting to our landing in the island.

The Governor of Messina, without being a clever man, was a cunning old Tuscan who had seen a good deal of the world, and knew somewhat of England and Englishmen. He was very civil; allowed us just what he could not refuse to allies; threw every impediment in our way that he could without giving open offence; and soon taught us to see that Governor Guillichini was very much afraid that the landing of an English Army at Messina might deprive him of the profits of his government without rendering him compensation. During four long weeks did our transports lie in the harbour of Messina, without leave for either man or officer to go ashore (save and except Major-General Stuart and myself).

The patched-up health of Sir James Craig had broken down under the anxieties of the late events, and he remained on board his ship in a very precarious state, but still preserving a clear mind and the resolution to fulfil his difficult duties. (Sir James Craig to Viscount Castlereagh, Feb. 11th, 1806. Appendix D.)

His task had become more arduous because Mr. Elliot, either seduced by the Court of Naples, or possessed by some vain fancy that he could baffle the French by diplomacy, had protested against our repairing to the ports of Sicily, and had even undertaken for the queen the management of a negotiation with the approaching enemy. It was in vain that Craig insisted on the evident fact that the weak and unprincipled court held nothing at its command, wherewith it might redeem itself from the vengeance of Napoleon, save only the admission of French garrisons into Sicily, and the exclusion of English ships from all their ports; that the bad faith and selfishness of the Neapolitan Government were become notorious; and that if the British armament returned to Malta, it would probably be unable to retrace its steps, or to receive a summons for assistance, till after the enemy should have got possession of Messina and Syracuse.

Mr. Elliot persisted obstinately in his wild scheme of negotiation: but Sir James Craig took on himself the responsibility of acting in opposition to our minister's remonstrances; and with a wise and bold foresight he had brought his 7,000 men to the harbour of Messina. A very few days sufficed to disperse the fine dreams of Mr. Elliot and Queen Caroline. The French marched on, refusing sternly to listen to any overtures from a government which was doomed to extinction. King Ferdinand took refuge in affright on board his only line-of-battle ship, with such of his property as could be gathered in the tumult and confusion of the moment; and his troops abandoning the Abruzzi crossed La Puglia by forced marches and sought shelter in the mountains of Calabria.

Now came the *palinodia*; now came expressions of pleasure that Sir James Craig had not quitted Messina; and though the court were still reluctant to give us possession of the citadel, they ordered Guillichini to afford us all those accommodations which we had long needed, but which had been hitherto withheld. The fugitive monarch sailed for Palermo; and as soon as his arrival there was known, Sir John Stuart was despatched by Craig to offer compliments and so forth, and to solicit permission that the British troops might be landed for the better security of Sicily, and might be intrusted with the defence of the fortresses of Messina and Milazzo, the points most immediately exposed to attack from the enemy.

★★★★★★

It ought to be recorded that during all these movements, from our first sailing from Malta, there had never been an English squadron in these seas. One 74 specially appropriated by Lord Nelson to the King of Naples' service, and three frigates as convoy for our large fleet of transports, formed our only naval protection: though the enemy had still several men-of-war in Toulon and Carthagena.

★★★★★★

When Ferdinand hurried away from Naples, his more venturous queen remained; still boiling with rage against the allies, and particularly the English, (whom she seized every occasion of stigmatizing by the most insane abuse), and wildly cherishing the fancy that she might yet gain time, arrest the march of the enemy, and save her capital by other sacrifices. She despatched the Duke di San Teodoro to Rome with powers to offer to the French general the possession of Gaeta, provided he would halt on the north side of the Garigliano, and there await the result of her further negotiations with Napoleon at Paris. (Brigadier Campbell to Sir James Craig, Feb. 1, 1806. Campbell had been left at Naples to watch and report.) Joseph Bonaparte received the offer with coldness; his advanced guard was already at Terracina, but his artillery was not yet brought up, nor were his columns connected and ready to enter the kingdom.

He knew also that the English had halted at Messina, and that little chance remained of his being enabled by negotiation to gain possession of Sicily. Joseph therefore dismissed San Teodoro with a brief intimation that he would grant an armistice of forty days, provided his troops were put in immediate possession of the fortress of Capua. Now Capua is within one day's march of Naples, and Queen Caroline did not care to trust herself to such near neighbourhood. At the same time, she received from General Acton, the king's particular friend, who had accompanied Ferdinand to Palermo, a letter of reproachful remonstrance on account of the intemperate and vindictive language she had notoriously held regarding the English, their only remaining allies and the only hopes of their salvation. She began to waver, but still returned to her negotiations.

San Teodoro was again despatched to Joseph Bonaparte's headquarters, while Cardinal Ruffo was on his way to Paris. Thus, did the wretched woman cling to her intrigues through alternate days of nervous hope and deep despair, till the will of Napoleon was notified, not to her but to his brother. The mandate admitted of no mistake. An unconditional surrender of the whole kingdom was all that was demanded. (Brigadier Campbell's *Journal*.) The French troops crossed the frontier on the 9th of February: on the 11th the queen embarked, and sailed for Palermo. The regiments of guards accompanied her; but the troops of the line had already marched towards Calabria, and the hereditary prince, attended by the Count de Damas, now hastened to the same quarter.

In the great city of Naples there was no sort of commotion during these events; the people of all classes seemed to be completely passive or indifferent. On the one hand they disliked and despised their old government; on the other, they had no friendly feeling towards the French.

On the day when the queen departed, and the functions of government were abdicated, the courts of law were open, and business was carried on as though there were nothing the matter. The interregnum was very short: the French columns pushed forward without a halt; received the surrender of Capua without firing a shot; and took unopposed possession of Naples and its castles. The fortress of Gaeta alone rejected the summons of the invaders, and opened its guns on some troops which made an audacious attempt upon an outwork.

During these occurrences our troops remained on shipboard, religiously respecting the sovereignty of King Ferdinand at Messina, though the people of that town and its neighbourhood took care that we should not be ignorant of their eager desire for our landing. At length when all the false hopes which the court had raised to mislead itself had been completely dissipated, the tardy invitation came to Sir James Craig to disembark, and a reluctant authority to occupy the citadel of Messina. The British troops were landed on the 17th February, and every exertion was immediately made to put the fortress into a condition to resist the enemy.

It may not be amiss to record what became of our Russian Allies, because Sir James Craig had been originally placed under the orders of their general-in-chief. When the resolution to embark the two armies and evacuate the kingdom of Naples was finally determined, Lacy, in taking a last leave of the English chief, had communicated to him the emperor's commands that he (Lacy) should conduct his 10,000 or 12,000 men to Corfu; and after leaving strong garrisons in the Seven Islands, should repair with the surplus to Odessa as soon as the season permitted it.

✶✶✶✶✶✶

When our Imperial Allies came to embark, they discovered that they had no provisions for their voyage to Corfu nor money to buy any. They held indeed an order of credit from Petersburgh for £40,000; but no banker at Naples would cash it. They could not have escaped, if Sir James Craig had not run the risk of supplying them with biscuit, and lending them £25,000.

✶✶✶✶✶✶

Nothing was said regarding Sicily; but the Russians sailing from Naples after us, passed and spoke our armament while anchored in the harbour of Messina. General Lacy proceeded to fulfil his orders; and the troops which he left at Corfu were found, in the next year, acting in a way not very consistent with a unity of views and interests in confederate nations.

Before I lose sight of the Russians altogether, I will make some few remarks on the troops in whose companionship we had been engaged. I had seen something of a Russian Army in 1799; but I found that even six years had made a surprising difference, at least in the appearance of their soldiers. Those who served with us in Holland were exactly the stiff, hard, wooden machines which we have reason to figure to ourselves as the Russians of the seven years' war. Their dress and equipments seemed to have remained unaltered; they waddled slowly forward to the *tap-tap* of their monotonous drums; and if they were beaten they waddled slowly back again, without appearing in either case to feel a sense of danger, or of the expediency of taking ultra *tap-tap* steps to better their condition.

But I must do their troops, in 1805, the justice to say that in appearance at least, and in movements at a review, they had made a surprising progress; they were now well armed and equipped, and had very much the outward character of good German soldiers. They were regular and firm in their movements, but they were still slow; and their regimental officers appeared to be very deficient in intelligence and activity. Even some of their major-generals were little better than semi-barbarians, ignorant, sensual, selfish, and perhaps venal.

The Suliotes whom they brought with them, for the eventual benefit of Italy in case of an active campaign, were the wildest of the mountain clans of Albania, Their very gait told their tale: it was the noiseless creeping of a cat in search of prey: their long steps gave forth no sound; their eyes, though lighted by no passion, were incessantly moving, and marking all things before and behind and on every side. A sort of coarse shirt belted round their waist, with a capote of the skins of sheep or goats formed their dress: and a long gun and a stout knife their arms. They could have done little harm to the French, but they would have been deadly protectors to the Italians.

In most respects I believe that the Russian infantry is now-a-days, (1854), but little different from those who came to Naples in 1805; and brave as the soldiers may be, I cannot regard their armies as very formidable out of their own country, or in a protracted campaign. Their hospitals and commissariat were and are deplorably bad: they are always in want of money, nor ever have they credit. Without the means of raising money, and without good hospitals and an effective commissariat, a great army cannot long keep the field.

But to return to our own concerns. We are on shore; we have possession of the citadel, as well as of the town of Messina, and are pushing our posts right and left along the coasts. We find the people generally enthusiastic in their welcome of the English; the priests and monks (reverend folks of great weight) among the foremost; the nobles glad to have anybody to protect them, but somewhat jealous lest the wealth of the English should cast them into the shade. When we first landed, we were taught to look with a suspicious eye on the few merchants of the place: they, we were told, were secretly attached to the French. Now these were the cleverest and best educated people of Messina; and I came to know some of them well.

They certainly were thoroughly disaffected to the Neapolitan Government, than which (particularly as it bore on Sicily) there could hardly be a worse. They desired the coming of the French, not from any affection to Frenchmen or to Napoleon, but because they longed for better laws, and relief from capricious tyranny. They believed also that the immense power of France would ensure to them protection and a durable government; and at first, they considered the English only as birds of passage, there today, but likely to fly before the storm tomorrow. As time wore on and the British force increased, and our determination and power to defend Sicily became more manifest, while at the same time we checked the arbitrary oppression of the government, these men gradually warmed to us, and would have become most heartily ours, if we had taken the island to ourselves.

But a little time had elapsed after our landing before the hereditary prince and Monsieur de Damas (the former the nominal, the latter the real commander of the forces sent by Queen Caroline to defend the Calabrias when she left Naples) came flying to the Straits of

Messina, and were brought across by our transports. These illustrious personages had taken post with sonic 6,000 or 7,000 regular troops (*Neapolitan* troops) near Campo Tenese or Lagonegro, and had been told to expect, and possibly did foolishly expect, that the "patriotic" people of the Calabrias would rush to arms and join them in a mass. As it turned out the Calabrese did not stir; but the French came; in no great numbers indeed, but sufficient for the purpose. At the first fire the Neapolitan troops dispelled in all directions, and the prince fled as fast as he could towards Sicily.

Which ran away first is uncertain; but this is sure, that out of the 7,000 fugitives of all ranks, we did not find on the shore near Reggio above one thousand (and those chiefly dragoons) to be transported across the straits. The French followed the chase gaily and rapidly, and by the 24th of March their posts and picquets were lining the straits of Messina.

M. le Comte de Damas, the commander-in-chief of the ex-army of the ex-government of Naples, had been one of the foremost in the favour of Queen Caroline, but he was disliked by the people, and secretly even by the courtiers. He was a French emigrant, who had belonged formerly to the *coterie* which surrounded the unfortunate Marie Antoinette; a man of pretension and address, but not of abilities; gallant and gay in the proud alcoves of royalty, but without resources or judgment in difficulties. When he crossed to Sicily as a fugitive general, without the credit even of having made fight for half an hour, he found no one to shew him countenance; no attempt on the part of his royal patroness to screen him. M. de Damas was civilly thanked for his past services, and dismissed from his employments.

This was the signal for the reinstatement of old General (Sir John) Acton in the open favour of the king; and therewith the re-establishment of a certain degree of British influence in the court. Acton was now far advanced in age; neither much enlightened nor energetic; but he was a well-intentioned man, and as straightforward as one could expect a man to be who had been trained in the old courts of Italy. He had always possessed a great power over the mind of the king, though he had often occasion to feel that he was liable to be sacrificed at any moment by the cowardice and selfish love of ease which mainly guided the actions of his royal master.

And here let me say, to give the devil her due, that the public have been unjust in ascribing *all* the crimes and follies of the Neapolitan Court to Queen Caroline; for though Ferdinand did not equal her in talents or in courage, he was quite her match in falsehood and aptitude for treachery. If he had been a mere noble of Naples with a plenty of game to shoot, plenty of good things to eat and drink, and a few toadeaters and buffoons on whom he could have played off his jokes, he would have passed through life with the credit of being a good-humoured comical fellow, and a capital sportsman;—there are such gentlemen in other countries besides Naples; but placed upon a throne, and tried by difficult times, his ignorance, narrow-mindedness, cowardice, and treacherous deceit, arose in dark relief from the cast.

When General Acton resumed an influence at Palermo, he soon found that the stormy projects of the queen and the intrigues of the people about her, were likely to perplex still farther the difficulty of affairs, and perhaps to unsettle the resolutions taken by the king.

******

It is but just to record that the Frenchman who was specially attached to her person (in the post of lover), Monsieur de St. Claire, was always considered to steer as clear of the queen's political manoeuvres as he possibly could.

******

He therefore prevailed on Ferdinand to pay a visit to Messina, attended by Acton himself and Mr. Elliot; the necessity of making immediate provision against invasion affording a plausible pretext. The queen and all her cabal were left at Palermo.

King Ferdinand was received by the Messinese with grand illuminations, and fireworks, and pageants; in all which things the Sicilians are proficient. The peasantry crowded into the town in their holiday attire to gaze at their sovereign for the first time: they applauded the fireworks with gay vociferation, but they raised no shout for their *Rè Ferdinando*. He was a queer mortal this tall gawky old king! On one of the days he spent at Messina, he happened to be on a battery, just as some large boats in the French service, laden with ordnance and stores, were trying to steal along the Calabrian coast to Reggio. Some of the Sicilian gunboats were firing at them, and the enemy, running field-pieces along the shore, were endeavouring by a return of shots to protect their vessels.

I chanced to be standing beside His Majesty: he was watching the skirmish on the opposite coast with childish eagerness; at every shot he laughed aloud, threw out his long bony limbs in strange gesticulations, and poured fourth volleys of buffoonery in the Lazzaroni dialect. It never seemed to occur to him that the people in the boats on both sides were his subjects; and that the shots might strike off their heads or legs. No, it was a sight he had never witnessed before, and he was himself in perfect safety.

Acton, and Elliot, and Craig, brought Ferdinand at this time to issue certain proclamations to facilitate the measures proposed by the English General for the defence of the island, and an order for the assembling of the Constitutional Militia; which proclamation and orders produced no effect whatever. But when Craig came to inquire into details, and to inform himself as to the means of defence, it appeared evident that the government possessed "*no* means of defence" (Sir James Craig to Viscount Castlereagh, Malta, April); that there were no magazines, no ammunition, no artillery; that even the important fortresses of Syracuse and Agosta were almost without garrisons, and entirely destitute of ordnance and stores, in case of attack. Of troops, there were nominally 8,000, really about 6,000 rank and file of all sorts (each bad of its sort), in and about Palermo. And here were we, 7,000 English and foreigners in our pay, undertaking to defend the great island of Sicily against Napoleon!

Among the many difficulties under which our sick general had to labour, the want of communication with England was not the least. Sir James Craig had received no fresh instructions under these altered circumstances, nor any sort of answer to his despatches to Lord Castlereagh. It was not till he had been compelled by extreme illness and exhaustion to resign his command and sail for England, that his successor received a despatch from Mr. Windham announcing the accession to office of the "Talents" Ministry; and conveying the king's full approbation of Sir James' proceedings up to the 14th Dec. 1805, the date of the latest letter which had reached England when Windham wrote (3rd March, 1806).

The Whig Cabinet urged, more strongly than their predecessors, the paramount importance of securing Sicily; and they directed Lord Collingwood to detach a squadron for the express purpose of protecting this island and co-operating with our army. Poor Craig had not the satisfaction of knowing that his conduct under very nice and trying circumstances had been approved by our government before he arrived in England. Worn down to extremity, he resigned the command of his army to Major-General Stuart, and sailed with but little prospect of surviving the passage to England. He did, however, rally on the voyage, and he recovered so much of health as to exercise afterwards the high duties of Governor-General of Canada. (Sir James

Craig died in January, 1812.)

Before Sir James Craig quitted the army, he ordered the 81st regiment from Malta to strengthen us; and we were all busily at work in quartering our troops, acquiring a knowledge of the country, providing stores, and constructing works for the defence of the straits. The town of Milazzo on the northern coast, some four-and-twenty miles from Messina, was occupied about the middle of March. The natural strength of this little peninsula, and its roadstead (though it has no harbour), rendered it a post of importance; and it facilitated our communication with the interior, with Palermo, and with the open sea. Three or four line-of-battle ships under Sir Sidney Smith (the hero of Acre) arrived at Palermo in consequence of the late orders given to Lord Collingwood; and our prospects began to brighten.

As we extended our acquaintance with the neighbouring country, we found everywhere good will, an evident affection to the English name, and a strong desire that we should remain, and take the lead in the country. They did not mince the matter: they avowed their detestation of the Neapolitans, but they would do anything for the English. We began to form a little flotilla for the better defence of the narrow seas: the mariners of Sicily and the Lipari islands (the latter the better hands) flocked in as volunteers for the service; but when they found General Stuart proposing that his boats should carry the Neapolitan flag, the men declined. "Up with your own flag!" they cried, "*Viva il Rè Giorgio! ma pél Rè Ferdinando, no, no!*"

Stuart found it necessary to give way: the British Jack was hoisted, and our boats were manned in two days, I had the direction of this appendage to our army, which was much increased in 1809, when Captain Reade of the 27th regiment was placed in the immediate command. Two or three artillerymen were put into every gunboat, and four or five soldiers in each of the long fast rowing boats called *scampavias*. This flotilla afterwards did good service; and even in its very early days I had the pleasure of seeing some of the boats manned by these Sicilians and Lipariotes, who are lightly called cowards, lay vessels, of superior bulk and carrying French soldiers, on board, and capture them, and bring them away, in the sight of both armies. "*Viva il Rè Giorgio,*" worked wonders.

Though I propose to give hereafter a more full account of Sicily, as it was not till afterwards that I enjoyed opportunities of visiting almost every part of the island, still it may not be amiss to take a view of our situation at this time, comparing it with that held by our formidable enemy on the opposite continent.

The general form of Sicily is that of a huge triangle; the worst form, therefore, for defence, inasmuch as it presents the greatest extent of coast in proportion to its area. Of small bays and roadsteads, and open beaches where troops may be landed in fine weather, there is an abundance; but there are few good harbours: indeed, we might confine the list to Messina, Trapani, Siracusa and Agosta. These are all defended by pretty good fortresses; but at the time of which I write, Messina only was in the hands of the English; the other three were miserably manned, and deficient in everything necessary to sustain a siege.

There were no roads in the island; at least nothing more than a few miles for the airings of the nobility out of Palermo, Catania, Messina, and one or two other large towns. Goods of all sorts were conveyed to or from any distance in the interior on the backs of mules. The tracks worn by the strings of these animals were extremely bad, particularly in the mountain districts, and communications were consequently slow. The sea indeed was open to us; and boats and boatmen were plentiful. Though the rugged neighbourhood of Messina produces no corn or cattle, we soon attracted ample supplies from Catania and the southern coasts; and wine was but too abundant and too cheap. For ammunition, guns, and salt provisions we had to depend at first on Malta, Our numbers were not great, but we were active; and though the promises and proclamations of King Ferdinand failed to produce any effect, we soon established ourselves strongly and comfortably.

As no militia made their appearance, though the people were evidently well disposed to give us aid. Sir John Stuart solicited and obtained permission from the court to raise a corps of 500 men who were to be officered chiefly by young nobles, and to form a battalion for service in Sicily enjoying British pay, and wearing the British uniform. This invitation brought in men pretty quickly; but luckily very few officers. Most of the latter retired in a short time from so troublesome an occupation, and their places were filled up by officers taken from the Corsican Rangers and other foreign corps. So here we were in May 1806 with nearly 7,500 men, our left wing fortified at Milazzo; and with outposts on our right stretching towards Taormina; an active little flotilla scouring the straits, and a few vessels of war at and near Messina.

On the other side of the narrow channel, General Reynier had established himself with a strong division of French troops in Lower Calabria; and he was using every exertion to bring heavy guns and stores, from Salerno on the one side and Taranto on the other, to arm the coasts opposite to Sicily. But these weighty supplies could be conveyed only by boats stealing along the shore; and their passage was precarious and difficult on account of the English cruisers, even before they had to encounter our flotilla. Sometimes, however, their cautious vessels evaded our vigilance; the Castle of Scilla was armed; and batteries began to appear along the coast as far as Reggio. (Nearly all their heavy guns were brought by boats from Taranto to Cotrone; and thence were dragged across the isthmus to Tropes or to Palmi.)

In the letters of Paul Louis Courier amusing accounts will be found of the high-mightiness and self-sufficiency of Reynier at this time: he is depicted as assuming all the consequential airs of a viceroy of the two Calabrias; looking to Sicily as a future prey, and to the English as a little knot of impudent fellows who would be scattered by the mere whiff and wind of his fell sword. General Reynier, however, was an able officer, and had good troops under him. In the upper province was General Verdier with another division, but a good deal dispersed, and already embroiled with the mountaineers who were growing angry and taking to their arms. (See letters of Paul Louis Courier.)

Some 10,000 or 12,000 men were at and near to Naples (where Joseph Bonaparte had established his court), and one division was occupied in blockading the garrison of Gaeta, and holding the communications with their troops in the Abruzzi and La Puglia. Altogether there were about 30,000 effective French soldiers in the kingdom of Naples; and the people of the provinces in general were quiet; though robberies were becoming more frequent, and there were rumours of the gathering of bands in Calabria. These Calabrese (I mean the mountaineers) are a savage and difficult race to deal with. Amongst them are always some who are, or who have been, *banditti*; and these fellows live undisguised among their fellow peasants, and tell their tales of adventure, and become objects of sympathy if pursued, and of admiration if successful.

If the mendicant friars come at any time, from political or religious motives, to set their influence to work, the Calabrese are prompt to gather in armed companies and to do their bidding. They are ready enough to rob and ravage and murder; they will massacre the stragglers or even cut off small outposts of an enemy; sometimes they will defend themselves pretty obstinately in a strong mountain village ("Castello"); but they never have shewn courage when attacked by regular troops, nor perseverance in keeping together and sustaining a warfare in their mountains. No reliance can be placed on their promises or their intelligence; and their leaders are generally the most worthless scoundrels and the most savage ruffians of their respective bands.

At first the French despised these fellows; but they soon found that their couriers were intercepted, officers were murdered, negligent parties through the country surprised, and they came to dread the Calabrese more than the evil justified. (See P. L. Courier.)

The Court of Palermo, and the queen in particular, had emissaries soon in every province; sparing no pains to stimulate the friars, and the leaders of bands to gather the mountaineers and assail the French. The English Admiral, who had arrived with a small squadron to protect Sicily, was just the man that Queen Caroline desired for the furtherance of her designs. Sir Sidney Smith entered at once into her wild schemes of raising the Calabrese; and without the slightest communication with Sir John Stuart, our naval commander was invested with unlimited authority on the land (the southern provinces of Naples) as well as on the sea.

Sir Sidney was an enthusiast, always panting for distinction; restlessly active, but desultory in his views; extravagantly vain; daring, quick-sighted, and fertile in those resources which befit a partisan leader; but he possessed no great depth of judgment, nor any fixity of purpose, save that of persuading mankind, as he was fully persuaded himself, that Sidney Smith was the most brilliant of *chevaliers*. (Let me not in exposing this brave man's foibles omit to add that he was kind-tempered, generous, and as agreeable as a man can be supposed to be who is always talking of himself.)

The coming of the admiral, and the energy of his first proceedings soon produced a wide effect; arms and ammunition were conveyed into the mountains of Calabria; the smaller detachments of the enemy were driven from the shores; and some of the strongest points were armed and occupied by the insurgents and parties of English marines and seamen. The admiral spread his ships and small craft along the coasts from Scylla to the bay of Naples; he took the island of Capri; threatened Salerno and Policastro; scattered through the interior his proclamations as "Commander-in-Chief on behalf of King Ferdinand," and the insurrection soon kindled throughout the Basilicata and the two Calabrias; though the bands acted in general with little concert or collective strength

Let us now turn our attention to the English troops cantoned about Messina, and little noticed either by the admiral or by the Court of Palermo.

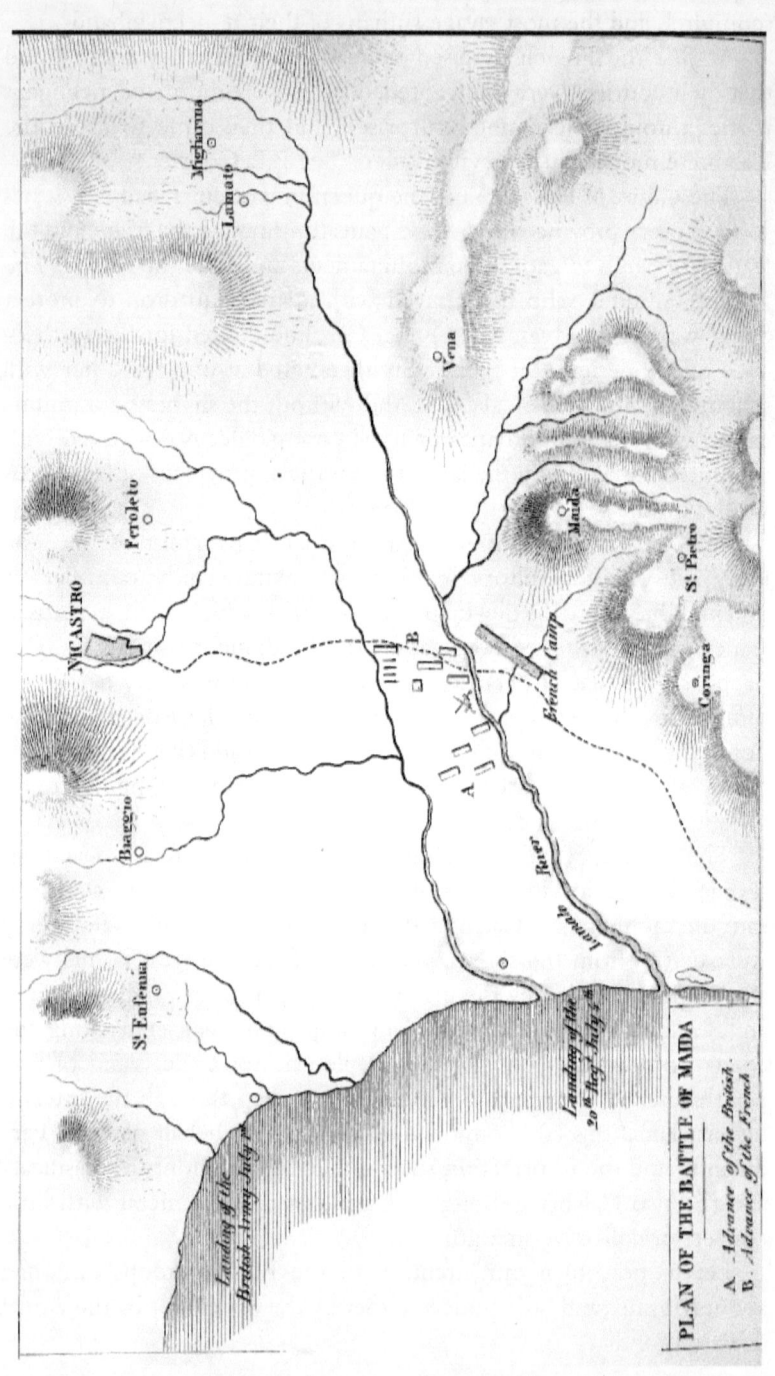

During the months of May and June 1806 the intelligence which we received from all parts of Calabria led us to the belief that the French had acted rashly in pushing their troops so far to the southward and that while they appeared to be threatening Sicily from Reggio and the neighbouring coast, they were really weak in numbers and exposed in their position. Their line of communication with Naples was of a dangerous extent; running through mountainous defiles, and across the beds of torrents: the bridges few, the roads very bad.

All the accounts furnished by our spies in Calabria, as well as those received directly from the Court of Palermo, tended to persuade us that the numbers of the enemy scattered over the Lower Province did not exceed 5,000 men under General Reynier; and that there might be nearly as many more in Upper Calabria and the Basilicata commanded by General Verdier; but the latter was understood to be fully occupied by risings of the mountain peasantry in such force that several of his detachments had been cut off; that his communications were interrupted; and even his headquarters at Cosenza threatened with an attack. It was therefore reasonable to infer that Verdier was not in a condition to afford assistance to General Reynier.

We knew likewise that Marshal Massena, with the main body of the French Army, was now engaged by the siege of Gaeta, where the wild-brained Prince of Hesse, was making an obstinate resistance.

★★★★★★

This Prince of Hesse Philipstadt was the best of the Neapolitan generals. Though drunken, and eccentric to the very verge of insanity, he was faithful, active, and brave even to rashness; nor was he deficient in acuteness. While his eye was on them his men did their duty, for they were more afraid of him than of an enemy; and his occasional buffoonery made him a favourite with the soldiers of the South.

★★★★★★

In Lower Calabria, though the risings of the peasantry had not become so formidable as in the Upper Province, the detestation of the French was described to us as being general (except in the large towns); and already there were many little bands, styling themselves *Masse* (though they proved to be in reality little better than knots of brigands), assembling in the mountains, and harassing the small outposts and the communications of Reynier's division. What these "*Masse*" really were, we did not understand at that time so well as we did afterwards, and they shall be described more particularly in a future page.

Taking this view of our enemy's force and position, and having at our disposal a fleet of good transports and the complete command of the seas on both sides of Calabria, it did not appear to be a very rash undertaking to strike a sudden blow at Reynier's little army, believing as we did that, even if he abandoned all his posts, he could not meet us with equal numbers in the field. Sicily was to be considered as a great fortress, of which our troops formed the garrison: a sudden attack on the advanced division of the enemy was an operation similar to a sortie. If we should be worsted, we had little doubt of our being able to re-embark and return to our island.

An undecided combat would be more injurious to the enemy than to ourselves, for the Calabrians would gather against him from every side, while utter ruin seemed to await the French if they should be completely beaten in a fair fight. But weighing the question on both sides, we came to believe that if we could make good our landing with 5,000 men in the Gulf of St. Eufemia, Reynier would find it necessary to retreat to Catanzaro; that the insurrection of both the provinces would then become general, and that Massena would be obliged to abandon the siege of Gaeta,

Our troops were at that time cantoned within narrow bounds—most of them in Messina and Milazzo; the rest in the neighbouring villages. They were ready to step on board the transports, and as the vessels were fully victualled, there was no necessity for any preparation as to provisions. Sir John Stuart having taken the resolution to make the attack, the secret was well kept; it was known only to his Military Secretary (Captain de Sade) and myself; for at that time I acted not only as quartermaster-general, but had the temporary superintendence of the adjutant-general's department during the absence of Brigadier James Campbell.

We had not the means of transporting many horses; a few for the staff and commanding officers of regiments; 16 of the 20th Light Dragoons, and horses for three field-pieces, together with mules for a few mountain-guns and the camp-kettles of battalions, were all we could manage to convey. So, at the same instant one afternoon we laid the transports alongside the quays to ship our guns and horses; and we despatched orders to the several corps which were chosen for the service to march in the night and embark at daybreak.

The troops selected for this expedition were the Light Infantry Brigade under Lieut.-Colonel Kempt, composed of the Light Companies of the 20th, 27th 35th, 39th, 44th, 58th, 61st, 81st, and Watteville's Regiment; about 120 men ("Flankers") of the 35th, and between two and three hundred of the Corsican Rangers, mustering altogether about 1,000 effective rank and file.

★★★★★★

"Flankers." These were soldiers taken from the battalion companies in each regiment, and placed under the command of picked officers. They were trained to act as sharpshooters; were not told off in line with their battalions (except at reviews, parades, &c.) and in the field were kept in rear of the flanks of their respective battalions or brigades, ready to act either to front or flank as occasion might require. This was a plan of Sir James Craig's, and introduced at Malta in 1805. It was discontinued when Sir John Moore took the command of the army.

★★★★★★

The grenadier battalion and 1st battalion of the 27th regiment under Brigadier-General Cole. The 2nd battalion of the 78th, and the 1st of the 81st regiment under Brigadier-General Acland; and the 1st battalion of the 58th, and the regiment De Watteville (Swiss), under Colonel Oswald. The battalion companies of the 20th regiment under their excellent Colonel, Robert Ross, were embarked, but were left as a detachment to threaten Reggio and Scilla, and to prevent or delay the assembling of the enemy's forces, by alarming him at various points along the coast. Colonel Ross's orders were to follow the fleet as soon as he might consider these purposes accomplished.

We sailed without delay under convoy of the *Apollo* frigate and two other vessels of war, and anchored in the Bay of St. Eufemia, on the evening of the 30th of June. There was a small picquet of French troops on the shore, which retired immediately into the woods; and two armed Calabrese, rowing off to our ships, assured us that there were very few of the enemy in that neighbourhood. Orders were immediately issued for the landing of our troops at daylight; but as a heavy transport which carried Colonel Kempt and most of his light infantry had not arrived, Colonel Oswald was appointed to lead the debarkation with seven flank companies and the Corsican Rangers. No enemy appeared on the beach; and the boats, after having landed this first division near a tower called the Bastione di Malta, returned for a second cargo.

As the latter approached the shore, Oswald moved forward in the direction of St. Eufemia (a village standing about a mile from the point of debarkation), pushing his scouring parties through the trees and wild underwood which spread along their front and on the right. His advanced people had proceeded but a little way, when they were assailed by a brisk fire from the thickets, and a company of the Corsican Rangers were charged and driven in by a superior body of the enemy, who was in his turn checked and forced back by the advance of our grenadiers. The enemy retired skirmishing through the wood, till Colonel Oswald seeing that the second landing of our troops was effected, pushed rapidly forward and charged the enemy on both flanks with so happy a combination as not only to put him to rout, but to make about eighty men and two captains, prisoners, besides a good many who were left dead. It was remarkable that a sergeant of light infantry was the only man hurt on our side.

The enemy proved to have been three or four hundred Poles, with a few French, collected hastily by Colonel Grabinski on the appearance of the English fleet They suffered severely from his temerity, and his want of judgment in risking a contest in the wood, after having missed the true opportunity of doing us mischief while our troops were struggling through the surf.

In the course of the next morning, July 1st, all the troops were landed, with six guns, and ten mountain pieces which were to be carried on the backs of mules. The engineers were set to work to form lines of defence with sand-bags round the old tower near which we landed, with a view to protect our re-embarkation in case of disaster. In the meantime, the main body of our troops advanced inland, to St. Eufemia, and San Biaggio, and some as far as the little town of Nicastro.

The country hereabouts is tangled with olive-grounds, and thick brushwood of so great an extent and so intricate a nature as to afford no secure positions for such a small army as ours. But the necessity we were under of landing our horses and mules, as well as provisions, reserve-ammunition, &c., prevented our leaving this neighbourhood during the 2nd and 3rd of July, for a heavy surf prevailed upon the beach and rendered the business slow and dangerous.

During these two days we were joined by about 200 straggling Calabrese, provided for the most part with firearms; but they were ruffians of the lowest description.

On the morning of the 3rd we received positive information that General Reynier had pitched his camp, or rather his bivouac, near the shallow River Lamato and below San Pietro di Maida: that he had a considerable number of troops with him, but was waiting for the arrival of those who had been quartered at Reggio and other distant parts. The accounts of his actual strength were contradictory; some rating it at 6,000 men, while others asserted that it did not exceed 3,000.

In the afternoon of this day Sir John Stuart, attended by some staff officers, and taking a company of grenadiers as an escort, reconnoitred the enemy's position from a rising ground directly opposite, which commanded a tolerable view of the plains of Maida. The French camp appeared to be very strong to its front, and on its right; but it seemed (as we afterwards found it) liable to be turned upon its left.

The general likewise reconnoitred the outskirts of the extensive woods of St. Eufemia, and gave orders for the posting of the troops so as to be prepared for the march of the next morning, as well as for security during the night It was a singular circumstance that at the very time when Sir John Stuart was examining the French position, General Reynier, escorted by forty *chasseurs à cheval*, was within the edges of the same wood, engaged in a reconnaissance of the British positions. The two commanders crossed each other's track more than once, and missed meeting only by a few minutes.

In consequence of the observations made this evening, an order was issued for the march of the troops at daylight on the morning of the 4th, with the declared purpose of attacking the enemy's camp. Four companies of Watteville's regiment under that good Swiss officer, Major Fischer, with a detachment of artillery men, and three out of our six fieldpieces, were left to secure the tower and our entrenchments on the beach.

As soon as the day dawned we commenced our march, with 4,795 rank and file, a great majority of whom had never seen an enemy. The 27th was the only battalion of old soldier's: the flank companies of the 20th, 27th, 35th, and 61st also were hard-biting fellows of long standing; but the 58th, 78th, and 81st were young regiments, and the six companies of Watteville's regiment were partly Swiss, partly enlisted prisoners or deserters; and as fate would have it there lay in Reynier's camp a Swiss battalion, commanded by a cousin and namesake of our worthy Louis de Watteville. The object of our advance was to gain the left of the French position which was clearly their weak point; for to say the truth we gave little heed to the reports which stated the enemy to be stronger in numbers than ourselves. Our course, therefore, ran along the shingly shore and some marshy pastures which bordered it: our progress was slow and there was a considerable difficulty in bringing on even our three field guns.

The Calabrian sun arose in its full strength of July, and our men began to be jaded, before they reached the open ground near the mouth of the Lamato. (Particularly the grenadiers, who had come from Nicastro and had been marching all night.) A detachment of the enemy's light cavalry retired as we drew near; and just as our two columns opened into the lower part of the plain of Maida, we descried the French Army filing by its right from the position in which it had bivouacked on the high ground and descending into the upper portion of the same plain. Still this movement did not serve to decide the question whether Reynier meant to fight or to retire. If the latter were his intention, this was the best manoeuvre; for he thus came into the direct road to Catanzaro, and even on a shorter line than our own to Nicastro: nor could we see enough of his columns to form a judgment as to his numbers.

But looking, as the French general must have looked, at the chances of the approaching conflict, everything appeared in his favour. His army had the advantage in numbers as well as in the seasoning and experience of war; he had 300 cavalry, we had none. The point which he occupied gave him the choice of a retreat, if a retreat could be necessary, either to the eastern coasts, or the Upper Provinces; and if he should defeat the English, and what Frenchman in that army doubted it! we should be forced to retread our harassed way through the shingle and the marsh, while one of his columns might hasten along the hard road and anticipate us at the tower.

But we, fortunately, entertained none of these views. We saw the enemy drawing off from the strong grounds, and as our own troops disentangled themselves in succession from the marshes and coppices, they were formed in order for battle, and advanced in the direction to which the movement of the French appeared to point The shallow stream of the Lamato, bordered with thickets, ran upon our right; the plain, gradually widening, was in our front; and on the left there extended broken and irregular patches of coarse grass and bushes and coppice-wood. Our advance was made in an *échelon* of brigades, the right, Kempt's (later General Sir James Kempt, G.CB.), Light Infantry, taking the lead.

Next came Acland's brigade; then Cole's; and Oswald with his thirteen companies (58th and Watteville's) followed in rear of the centre as a reserve.

For some time we saw nothing of the enemy, excepting their cavalry, which manoeuvred across our front, raising a great dust which served to screen their infantry, and three pieces of horse-artillery whose fire did little injury, and was returned with interest by our own three guns under Lieut.-Colonel Lemoine and Captain Pym. As our right drew nigh to the steep and woody bank on the left side of the Lamato, where the French huts were standing, Colonel Kempt detached the Corsican Rangers across the stream to scour the thickets and secure him from ambuscades on his flank, sending at the same time the light company of the 20th as a support.

Scarcely had the Corsicans entered the wood when they were met by a brisk fire, followed by the headlong charge of about 200 French, and were driven in such confusion upon the 20th that this company was hard put to it to keep its ground; its Captain, McLean, was killed, and if the men had not been of sterling stuff the company must have been broken. The fire for some minutes was very sharp, and the parties, were close to each other; but Kempt instantly detached Major Robertson across the stream with the flankers of the 35th, and matters were speedily righted. The French retreated in confusion; the Corsicans rallied and pursued them, and the men of the 20th and 35th rejoined the right of their brigade.

While this skirmish was going on, our little army was advancing very gradually up the plain, but as yet nothing was distinguishable beyond the thick dust of the French cavalry, who made repeated feints of charging on one or other of our brigades. The extreme heat of the morning also produced a sort of mirage in the low grounds, which served further to perplex our sight, and we still inclined to the belief that Reynier was retiring up the valley, and covering his march by the display of his horsemen, and by the little ambuscade on the hill. Suddenly, however, the enemy's cavalry moved rapidly away beyond the front of our extreme left; and as their dust cleared off, we saw the French infantry formed for attack and marching rapidly upon us.

We saw at the same time that the enemy outnumbered us considerably; their formation as well as ours was oblique, the enemy's left and our right being each in advance. Their 1^r *Legère* (three battalions) led on by General Compère, and supported by a regiment of Poles, advanced in line upon the brigade of British Light Infantry; which likewise continued to move onward, A crashing fire of musketry soon opened on both sides, but it was too hot to last at so short a distance, and the fire of the English was so deadly, that General Compère spurred to the front of his men, and shouting "*En avant, en avant!*" he led them to the charge with the bayonet. As they drew nigh, their ranks disordered by the fatal fire of the British, Kempt gave the word, and his 800 light infantry (for we must not reckon the Corsican Rangers for much in this part of the day's work), pressed eagerly forward to close with their antagonists.

But the two lines were not parallel; the light companies of the 20th and 35th encountered the extreme left of the French, but the rest of the enemy's brigade broke before their bayonets crossed. They had, however, come too close to escape; it was a headlong rout; General Compère fell badly wounded within our ranks, and his superb brigade (I may use the term, for never did I see a finer, or more soldierlike body of men), were utterly dispersed with a fearful slaughter, which was continued over a long extent of plain, and the lower falls of the hill of Maida.

On the right, but farther back as if *en échelon* of the 1^r *Legère*, the 42nd regiment of the French was advancing more deliberately towards Aclands brigade; but the sudden overthrow of the battalions on their left, and the rapid pursuit of our light infantry stopped their advance, and seemed to alarm them for the safety of their flank. After some firing, in which they were well supported by their artillery, the 42nd retreated a considerable distance, and then formed again in such a position, as either to support Reynier's right wing, or to cover his left and rear, in case of Kempt's Light Brigade turning upon them instead of pursuing the fugitives. Acland pressed forward with the 78th and 81st (both young regiments), but being threatened by the enemy's cavalry, his men got into some disorder, and suffered loss while attempting to form squares under the French guns.

In the meanwhile, General Cole's brigade (seven companies of grenadiers and eight of the 27th Regiment), had been brought to a stand by the superior numbers of the enemy's right wing. (23 *Legère*, 3me battalions; Swiss 1 battalion.) Besides the musketry on their front, these brave soldiers were galled by numbers of sharpshooters scattered through the low clumps of brushwood on their left, and were perplexed by the stubble in which they stood, having been set on fire by the enemy's shells. But they bore themselves gallantly; the left wing of the 27th was thrown back to answer the fire of the *tirailleurs*, and to receive any charge which might be made by the enemy's cavalry; and Oswald's reserve moving up, to fill the gap which now existed between Cole and Acland, the balance was pretty well restored.

Yet we found great difficulty in bringing up the necessary supplies of musket ammunition; the enemy's troops were well posted and fresher than our men; the heat was tremendous; and the result of the day seemed yet far from certain, when as I was riding along the rear of Cole's brigade, anxiously watching the French sharpshooters, who were stealing farther and farther round his left, and were backed by their horsemen, one of my assistants came galloping to me from the beach, with the welcome tidings that the 20th Regiment had landed, and was coming through the brushwood at double quick time. I rode instantly to meet them, and explained to Ross how matters stood.

He caught the spirit of the affair in an instant, pressed onward, drove the swarm of sharpshooters before him; gave the French cavalry such a volley, as sent them off in confusion to the rear; and passing beyond the left of Cole's brigade, wheeled the 20th to their right, and opened a shattering fire on the enemy's battalions. The effect was decisive; Reynier was completely taken by surprise at the apparition of this fresh assailant; he made but a short and feeble effort to maintain his ground; but he drew off his troops skilfully, falling back on his 42nd Regiment, and covering his retreat by sharpshooters and by his *chasseurs à cheval* and horse-artillery.

If we had then a couple of hundred of good cavalry, we might probably have destroyed the enemy's army; but we could do little more with our jaded infantry. Our columns continued to advance upon the enemy till he abandoned the plain of Maida, and retreated rapidly up the valley (beneath the town of that name) through which runs the road to Catanzaro.

When the left wing of General Reynier's army had been routed in the early part of the fight, a great proportion of the fugitives had fled across the Lamato, and over the hills on the lower fall of which their troops had been bivouacked. In this direction they were pursued by Kempt and his gallant brigade, who allowed them no time to recover their communications with the rest of their army. But in following the French thus dispersed and streaming along the slopes of the hill of Maida, our light infantry likewise were drawn to a considerable distance beyond the rest of the British troops, and could bear no part in the later struggle of the day. Kempt's forward position, however, overhanging the valley, made it the more necessary for Reynier to accelerate his retreat, since a retreat in this direction had become unavoidable.

The rapid movement of his column was watched, and followed for some time on a parallel line by our Light Brigade, but Colonel Kempt kept his men well together, anxious to recover his communications with our main body, and to receive orders from Sir John Stuart

But where was Sir John Stuart? and what great part did he play in this brilliant action? In truth he seemed to be rather a spectator than a person much, or *the* person *most*, interested in the result of the conflict. He formed no plan; declared no intention, and scarcely did he trouble himself to give an order. Perfectly regardless of personal danger, he was cantering about, indulging himself in little pleasantries, as was his wont; and he launched forth with particular glee when a Sicilian marquis, whom he had brought with him as an extra *aide-de-camp*, betook himself to shelter from fire behind a haystack.

But after the charge of Kempt's light infantry, and the utter rout of the French left wing, a change came over the spirit of Sir John Stuart. Still he dawdled about, breaking into passionate exclamations, "Begad, I never saw anything so glorious as this! There was nothing in Egypt to equal it! It's the finest thing I ever witnessed." From that moment he was an altered man, and full of visions of coming greatness. As I found that I could get no orders from him, I made it my business to go round to the leaders of our several brigades, to give them what information I could, and try to supply their wants.

The action, though sharp, had not been of long duration, and by mid-day our soldiers were resting on their arms, gasping with heat and thirst, and watching through the dust, with disappointed eyes, the rapid retreat of the French column. Our ammunition was nearly spent; there was no water for the men, save on the right, and every step we might make in advance led us farther away from our supplies of every sort. Reference was made to Sir John Stuart, and he then gave orders that the army, except the Light Infantry Brigade, which was, as we have seen, far away on the hills of Maida, should return to the beach for repose, and food, and supplies of ammunition.

When we returned to the beach, we found that Sir Sidney Smith had arrived during the action, and his flag-ship was anchored abreast of our bivouac. He came ashore to compliment the general (though there was no great love between them), and as he pressed Sir John to sleep on board the *Pompée*, the general, taking me and his *aides-de-camp*, went off in the evening. But in the meantime, we were amused with an *alerte* attended by laughable circumstances. A permission had been given, that the men of each brigade in turn might refresh themselves by bathing in the sea, the rest lying by their arms.

While the grenadiers and Enniskillens were in the water, a staff officer came galloping in from the front, crying aloud that the enemy's cavalry were coming down! In a moment the troops sprang to their arms and formed; and Cole's brawny brigade rushing out of the sea, and throwing their belts over their shoulders, grasped their muskets and drew up in line, without attempting to assume an article of clothing. The alarm was utterly groundless; a great dust and an imperfect view of a herd of scampering buffaloes, had conjured up a vision of French *chasseurs* in this noodle of an officer, one of my assistants.

The admiral paid Sir John Stuart every honour, and shewed us great hospitality; but he was so good as to tell us that he had expected we should be defeated, and had determined to run the *Apollo* frigate ashore, with her broadside to the beach, in order to cover our flight. He treated us as was his usual custom, to the whole history of the siege of Acre, not omitting that remarkable circumstance, that when there happened a short intermission of fire during several weeks, everybody jumped up in consternation, exclaiming, "What can be the matter!" The two chiefs held little or no conversation on ulterior measures, but Sir Sidney closed the evening by taking one of the many shawls with which his cabin was hung, and instructing Sir John in the art of wreathing it, and putting on the turban after the fashion of the most refined Turkish ladies.

At daybreak next morning we relanded; and our columns marched to the little town of Maida, situate on a high hill above the plain. Here Sir John Stuart set himself seriously down on the 5th of July to write his despatches to England, referring all persons and all business to me. In the meantime, Colonel Kempt had advanced some distance along the hills, and detached the light company of the 20th to follow the track of the enemy, and gather information. (Capt. Colbourne, who later became General Lord Seaton, had taken the command of this company in consequence of Captain McLean's death.)

It pressed forward, expecting that our army was advancing in the same direction, and it overtook the rear of the French column, which was marching in great confusion, but discovering to his mortification, at the end of the second day, that he was entirely without support, Capt. Colbourne found it necessary to fall back on his battalion. During forty-eight hours our troops remained kicking their heels and eating grapes about Maida, while the general was absorbed in his compositions. He issued a general order of compliments and thanks, but he could not finish his despatch to the Secretary of State to his mind, nor could he give his consideration to the farther movements of the army.

At length in the evening of the 7th, he resolved to go back to Sicily, and Colonel Oswald's brigade was pushed in advance on the road to

Monteleone. The rest of the troops followed the next morning, and I recollect being much amused while we were passing through a wood of mulberry trees, and picking the fruit for breakfast, at bearing a private of the 27th chaunting in a sarcastic tone,

> The King of France with thirty thousand men
> Marched up the hill, and then marched down again.

The small body of Polish troops, which had left for the protection of his hospitals and magazines at Monteleone, surrendered without resistance; and we here captured a great number of sick and followers, as well as provisions, forage, &c. At Monteleone, Sir John Stuart again applied himself to the important business of writing his despatches. The *aide-de-camp* who was to bear them had been held in constant readiness for four days, and so had the brig which was to convey them to England; but the hero of Maida was still unable to tell his story or round his phrases completely to his satisfaction; and in fact the letter which was published in the London *Gazette* was not finished till we reached the straits of Messina, a fortnight after the battle.

Let us now look back to the action itself, and to the movements which were made, and those which might have been made. The behaviour of our troops was remarkably good, and excepting a momentary confusion in Acland's two young regiments for which the soldiers were less to be blamed than the commanding officers of the two battalions, nothing went amiss. The men were cool and ready, and their fire was deadly. Colonel Haviland Smith commanding the 27th, and Colonel O'Callaghan commanding the grenadiers, and their brigadier, Lowry Cole, who afterwards won an abundance of laurels in the great campaigns in Spain, shewed themselves to be worthy leaders of such gallant corps; but the most brilliant parts on this little stage were acted by Colonels Kempt and Ross (Robert Boas of Ross Trevor, afterwards killed when in command of our little army near Baltimore; and General Sir James Kempt, G.C.B.): to them the glory of the fight at Maida is chiefly due.

But it was a *lucky* battle in every respect, not neglecting to remember the smallness of our loss, engaged as we were in a fair plain with a superior force of Napoleon's old soldiers.

✶✶✶✶✶✶

Capt. Maclean, 3 sergeants and 41 men killed; Majors Paulettt Hammell, and David Stuart, 7 other officers, 8 sergeants, and 263 men wounded. On the other side the number of the

French slain on the field was extraordinarily great. More than 500 of their bodies were buried; three-fourths of them belonging to the 1st Légère.

******

We had about 5,300 men in the fields the enemy considerably more than 6,000; I have unfortunately lost the French returns of their strength, which fell into my hands, and were in my possession many years. Including the Poles at Monteleone and other places, but exclusive of the troops left at Scilla and Reggio, Reynier had under his command 7,300 men; and I believe he had in the action about 6,300, including nearly 300 cavalry, an arm in which we were entirely deficient The French ought to have beaten us; and General Reynier certainly handled his troops and opened the action in a masterly manner. But they were too confident; and when General Compère's brigade, rushing at our light infantry, encountered a murderous fire which shattered his centre, and an eagerness to meet him with the bayonet which his troops had probably never experienced before, a panic seized them, and his three battalions fled in utter confusion when it was too late to escape the slaughter, carrying away their 2nd line of Poles in their flight.

This early overthrow of Reynier's left wing put an end to his hope of destroying us, but still left him a fair chance of making it a drawn battle on his right, and of maintaining a hold on the country. This prospect again was frustrated by the happy accident of the landing of our 20th Regiment, and their rapid and unexpected attack on the right of the French line. Reynier then, beaten back in the direction which his left wing had taken in its flight, made his retreat at once by the road towards Catanzaro, It was in many respects the most favourable line for him to cover his disheartened column by his cavalry and guns; he had less to fear from the insurgent Calabrese, and if the English should follow, every hour led them farther from their ships and their means of supply.

We might perhaps have pursued our beaten enemy a little more actively than we did. The 20th Regiment was fresh, and might have been pushed forward to support the light infantry; and by pressing on the rear of the French, more prisoners might have been taken in the next twenty-four hours. But Reynier marched rapidly, and kept his soldiers pretty well together; nor could we have destroyed his army without bringing up all our troops, and forcing him to another battle. The first object of the English was secured; we were now sure of clearing Lower Calabria of the enemy, and our communication was open, by Nicastro, with the insurgents in the Upper Provinces. It remains to be considered whether the victory we had obtained might not have been turned to better account, and made the groundwork of important operations.

In any case, we ought to have occupied the hut-camp of the French after the battle instead of returning to the beach. While provisions and ammunition were coming to us from the shipping, Oswald's brigade might have been detached to capture the enemy's stores and hospitals at Monteleone, and to organise the insurrection, which would have effectually isolated the French garrisons in Reggio and Scilla. Nicastro might have been occupied by the four companies of Watteville's regiment which had been left at St. Eufemia, and patrols from thence would have been sufficient to rouse all the mountaineers between Cosenza and Catanzaro.

But though General Verdier was blockaded in the upper province, and Reynier's disheartened troops were for the moment powerless, still it seems to me doubtful whether we could have done much good by marching by the direct road through Upper Calabria with our whole force, although this force might have been considerably increased by our bringing, as we then might, 200 or 300 of the 20th Light Dragoons and perhaps as many Neapolitan cavalry from Sicily, and the rest of the 35th Regiment, 500 good soldiers. (Four battalions of infantry, 2,400 strong, arrived at Messina from England just after the battle.)

The nature of the country, and the want of means of transport would have rendered our march slow; and though we might have cut off detachments, and injured our enemy a good deal, I think that his main bodies would have made good their retreat on Naples, though after much suffering. But there was a larger field of operation open to our commanders by sea and land; and here it becomes necessary to take a review of the positions and circumstances in which the French forces were placed in southern Italy.

When the victory of Austerlitz, and the signature of preliminaries with Austria and Russia, set Napoleon at liberty to wreak his vengeance on the perfidious Court of Naples, he lost no time. Within a week the conqueror proclaimed that the Bourbon Dynasty had ceased to reign at Naples. He ordered Marshal Massena to assemble a large army on the Lower Po: and to march without delay through the Roman States. His numbers were announced aa 40,000 men; but it is pretty certain that little more than 30,000 crossed the Neapolitan frontier.

Formidable as such a force might be while connected, it was not sufficient for the occupation of a kingdom nearly 300 miles long, in great part mountainous, its communications difficult, and presenting on three sides an immense extent of sea-coast exposed to the insults of the English squadrons. The vast and turbulent population of a capital open to attacks from the sea, required the constant presence of a strong body of French troops; and the important fortress of Gaeta, where the Prince of Hesse commanded, bade defiance to the enemy, though all the other fortified places of the kingdom had surrendered without resistance. (Except the little fort of Civitella del Tronto.)

At first the French (after making an unsuccessful dash at an outwork) contented themselves with a blockade of Gaeta on its land front only, for its communication with the sea remained perfectly free up to the time of its surrender. But when Reynier had overcome Calabria, and affairs appeared to be quiet and secure in the capital, Massena in person undertook the siege of Gaeta. It was a difficult operation on account of the narrowness of the front of attack, and the hardness of the bare rock along which the besiegers had to labour. On the other hand, as their front was narrow and their flanks secure, they did not require a large army to support their works.

The Neapolitan garrison was composed probably of the same description of troops as those who fled in the field at the first fire of an enemy; but they had here at their head a German prince who knew them well, ruled them with a rod of steel, and by his familiar buffoonery, and his daring example, mastered their fears, their affection, and their admiration. The Prince of Hesse put one in mind of the wild captains of free corps in the days of the Mansfeldts and Christian of Brunswick. He appeared half crazy; he was dissolute and regardless of rules; but he was unsparingly active and unconquerably brave. Under his command the defence of Gaeta was protracted for months; and the losses and sufferings of the French had been great before the English made their sortie from Sicily. But the fortress was by this time reduced to difficulties.

Now if our admiral had sailed immediately after the action at Maida, and our general had sent with the squadron a thousand of our soldiers and the news of our victory, it is more than probable that Gaeta would not have been taken that year. And if Sir John Stuart, after making sure of Monteleone, and leaving Oswald to sweep the Lower Province, had re-embarked on board his transports, and proceeded along the coast to threaten Policastro and Salerno, the French must have hurried out of the Calabrias and the Basilicata to gather round the capital. What in fact was the course they followed? General Verdier, harassed by the insurgents, alarmed at the intelligence of an English landing, and fearful of being cut off, abandoned Cosenza, and led his diminished and disheartened troops by forced marches at hundred miles to the northward; while Reynier encumbered by the numbers of his wounded men, and anxious to repair the spirit and order of his beaten army, lingered several days at Catanzaro.

At length finding that Verdier had gone off, and that the insurgents were growing every day more numerous and more daring, Reynier resumed his retreat with dismal prospects. His short line by Cosenza being cut off, he was forced to follow the windings of the sea-coast. At Cotrone he left his sick and wounded, (where they were captured a few days afterwards by a little expedition from Messina), and every incumbrance; and with less than 4,000 men he pushed onward with extreme rapidity. At Strongoli, and again at Coregliano, the Calabrese had the boldness to resist his march; but both villages were carried by storm and burned, and a fearful slaughter was made of the inhabitants; and on the 4th of August General Reynier arrived with the wrecks of his little army at Cassano. There at length he halted, knowing reinforcements from Naples were at hand, and finding that the English had not followed up their enterprise,

Gaeta had fallen, and Massena was coming in person with 6,000 men to rally the remains of Verdier's and Reynier's divisions, and to put down the insurrection in Upper Calabria, The game was over, because Gaeta had fallen; and my belief is that if our admiral and our general, instead of talking on the evening of the 4th of July of the siege of Acre, and Turkish ladies and Greek girls, had concerted and acted immediately on a vigorous plan of operations, the results might have marked our victory at Maida as a feat productive of an important change in the great war of European nations.

It was not till the 18th of July that Gaeta was surrendered to the French, in consequence of the Prince of Hesse having been very severely wounded. If Sir Sidney Smith had arrived there by the 14th or 15th, he would have been in time to save the fortress; and he had ten or eleven days in hand for this short passage. It is hardly possible that calms should have retarded ships of war so long a time, even in a Neapolitan July.

To turn next to what the British general might have done. Before quitting Monteleone he might have summoned 600 of the Neapolitan dragoons, and 4,000 of their infantry to take his place in that position. His call would have been answered with the greatest alacrity. Although the British troops with which our commander would have re-embarked would have been now reduced to less than 3,000 men, the show of transports would have been as great as before: and so completely were the communications of the French generals cut off by the insurrection around them, that they could not have known what number of soldiers the fleet was carrying.

A threat therefore of landing near Policastro and occupying the strong positions on the only high road (which runs within a very few miles of that Gulf) would have had the effect of turning Reynier's line of retreat. Instead of finding rest and safety at Cassano, he would have been forced to pursue his weary way, harassed by the Calabrese, along the coast of the Adriatic towards Taranto or La Puglia; while Verdier, with little more than a thousand men, must have continued his flight to Salerno.

Now, still assuming that Gaeta had been saved, the prospect would have been darkening apace over the French in Naples. Sir John Stuart's next appearance might have been at Capri, or better still at Ischia, which he might have taken with as much ease at this time as he afterwards did in 1809. The capital would have been in a ferment: the strength of the English expedition, and the extent of the insurrection would have been exaggerated; all the hot passions of the south would have been at work. The distant detachments of the French, necessary though they were to control the provinces and levy supplies, must have been called in for the security of the capital and the rich Terra di Lavoro.

Then the Abruzzi, the Basilicata, the Principato, would have followed the example of Calabria; the revolt would have become universal; and it would have been the more formidable, since the prestige of French invincibility had been destroyed at Maida. And what under such circumstances, would Marshal Massena have done? Could he have ventured to persist in the siege of Gaeta with a British squadron in the bay, and a thousand British soldiers added to the garrison? Could he risk all on this hazard, when his communication with Naples by sea was cut off, and that by land must now require detachments for its security? So long as Massena's army was detained before Gaeta, its influence over the public mind at Naples was inconsiderable; and if he raised the siege of Gaeta and marched to the neighbourhood of the capital, assuredly he would have effectually controlled the populace, and might have bidden defiance to the landing of the British; but he could not have removed their squadron from the bay, nor their troops from the islands; and while we were there, no ease could be felt by King Joseph.

The French Army would have been pinned down to that vicinity, and though they might have kept outposts as far as Sessa and Benevento, and Salerno, they could not have prevented the insurgents from blockading their garrisons in the Abruzzi and La Puglia; nor the English from insulting and alarming the French posts from Salerno to Gaeta. We had the means too of heightening the uneasiness of the enemy, by the show of our receiving successive reinforcements; for, in fact, the British Army numbered 13,000 men before the end of August, and three months later, between 17,000 and 18,000.

But it will be asked, what substantial good was to be produced by our threats? What influence could they have had on the fortunes of the war? Would not French reinforcements have poured in from the north of Italy to frustrate our puny attempts on Naples? Now it did so happen at that time, though we knew it not, that considerable reinforcement, could not have been spared to Massena. Our commanders were ignorant of the state of political affairs; they knew indeed that Russia was again at war with France; but they did not know that Prussia, and even Spain, were on the eve of breaking into open hostility. Successes in Italy, and the spreading of revolts against the French might have had a great effect on the councils of Austria, particularly a few months later, when Napoleon withdrew his army to the Vistula after the sanguinary battles of Pultusk and Golymin, or retired from the destructive conflict of Eylau.

But this long speculation on what might have been made to result from the defeat of the French at Maida, rests on this postulate, the relief of Gaeta; and to this object neither Sir Sidney Smith nor Sir John Stuart chose to apply themselves. The admiral had no mind to go to a place where he would have been only on an equality with the Prince of Hesse, Sir Sidney had run headlong into the snares of Queen Caroline at Palermo; had been loaded with flattery; had vowed himself her champion, and had received from her a commission as "Commander-in-Chief by sea and land *in the Calabrias.*" He was in close correspondence with all the scoundrels who called themselves "*Capitani delle Masse,*" and his ships were thronged with brigands seeking arms and ammunition, which were employed more frequently in murdering and plundering the peaceful inhabitants of towns than in resisting the French.

On the other hand, Sir John Stuart was extremely jealous of Sir Sidney's favour and his pretensions to command; and consequently, was anxious for an early separation. The two chiefs parted therefore without, a word of consultation, but with mutual compliments and confirmed aversion. The admiral drawling along the Calabrian coast, and helping the insurgents to attack the few isolated towns and castles from which some unfortunate French soldiers had been unable to escape; and the general hastening through the Lower Province to exhibit his laurels in Sicily.

After gathering in the detachments which Reynier had left in Tropea and Reggio, there remained only the rock-castle of Scilla, with a gallant little governor, who was determined to give us all the trouble he could.

※※※※※※

After parting from Stuart, Sir Sidney Smith, instead of hastening to Gaeta, and without saying a word on the subject to the general, sailed to the southward and made a dash at Scilla. He was beaten off, and he then disappeared altogether!

※※※※※※

We plied him sharply from 12-pounders and howitzer batteries, and the practice of our artillery was excellent; but we could make no impression on the solid old walls. After losing a few days, during which the greater part of our troops passed over to Messina, we were obliged to bring up 24-pounders and open a breaching battery at a very short distance. The castle then surrendered.

Viewing our expedition in the light of a sortie from Sicily, nothing could have been more successful. The enemy had been driven out of Lower Calabria: he had been defeated in fair fight under such circumstances as reversed the previous belief of the Italians and Sicilians, and taught them to consider the British soldiers to be superior to the French. This in itself was no trifling gain. All the stores and guns and boats which our enemy had been collecting with a view to his establishment in Calabria, and for the future invasion of Sicily, had fallen into our hands. Five hundred of the best of the enemy's troops had been slain in battle, and between two and three thousand more were prisoners.

These results had been obtained with little loss of life on our part; and a confidence had revived in our officers and soldiers which increased in an immeasurable degree the moral strength of our little army. But before we reached the straits of Messina the fatal effects of exposure to the pestilential air, which prevails during summer and autumn on the shores of St. Eufemia, began to appear amongst our troops; and every regiment that had been employed on the expedition suffered severely from intermittent fevers for several months.

Sir John Stuart's command of the army was gilded by fortune; but it was of short continuance. When he returned to the straits of Messina, he found there General Fox, sent by the Whig Government to assume the chief command in the Mediterranean, and bringing intelligence that large bodies of troops were following, and moreover, Lieutenant-General Sir John Moore. To have an officer of superior rank appointed to the command in chief was no more than Stuart had expected, and he would have been well content, dazzled as he was by his sudden glory, to have served as second to General Fox: but the coming of Moore, who was senior in rank and far superior in reputation, was a bitter pill, which the recent conqueror could not stomach.

He made up his mind to return to England; but in the meantime, General Fox did all that was in his power to soothe his disappointment and uphold his temporary importance. Stuart was invested with the command of the troops in Calabria, where two or three of our battalions were left, reinforced by Neapolitan cavalry and some of their best infantry under Baron Acton, the brother of the minister, and in everything that was to be done on that side of the straits. General Fox solicited the opinion and endeavoured to meet the wishes of Stuart. The 78th regiment was despatched in transports, escorted by the *Amphion* frigate, commanded by that admirable officer, William Hoste, to attack Cotrone. Cotrone and other places on the eastern coast were taken, and considerable numbers of wounded and sick Frenchmen were made prisoners.

A few days afterwards, the 58th and 81st regiments, under Brigadier Acland's orders, were sent by sea to threaten the coasts near Salerno, and communicate with Colonel Lowe, who held possession of Capri with five companies of his Corsicans and a few artillerymen. But Gaeta had fallen in the meantime; the Neapolitan who succeeded the Prince of Hesse in the command of the fortress surrendered it instantly. Massena's army was set at liberty to cover Naples, and re-open the communications with the wrecks of Reynier's and Verdier's divisions.

******

The French returned to Cosenza as early as the middle of August. P. L. Courier gives us sketches of their modes of proceeding, and those of the Calabrese in letters dated Scigliano, 21st August, and Mileto, 10th September.

******

The opportunity of doing more had been lost; and the British forces were again concentrated in the north-eastern angle of Sicily, with British detachments in and about Scilla and Reggio; and Baron Acton with his Neapolitans at Monteleone, supporting the bands of Calabrese insurgents.

Sir John Moore arrived at Messina in the beginning of August, and took his place ostensibly as second in command of our army. He enjoyed General Fox's entire confidence; and as the latter was infirm in health and incapable of much exertion, it was clearly the intention of the British Government that the active command of our troops should be entrusted to Moore, whose reputation stood higher than that of any other officer in the service. Shortly after Sir John's arrival he proposed to visit the coast of Naples up to Capri, that he might obtain a personal acquaintance with the state of affairs, and some knowledge of the localities. The *Apollo* frigate was placed at his disposal; and as I had an attack of malaria fever which made a change of air desirable, Moore took me with him.

The only circumstance which makes this cruise of a fortnight worthy of record is an anecdote touching Sir Sidney Smith. We fell in with his fine ship, the *Pompée*, of eighty-four guns, in the bay of Policastro, crippled and torn by shot. These shot had been received the day before from an old watch tower, on which one gun was mounted. The story told by the officers of the *Pompée* was this; Sir Sidney coasting along, as was his wont, having the *Hydra*, and another frigate in company, and looking out for brigands to receive his muskets and his orders, espied a French flag flying on this tower of ancient days. He simply gave orders that the ships should run in and drive the enemy out of their little fortress by cannon shot; and these orders given, the admiral went quietly to his cabin to write his letters.

The *Pompée* drew near and opened her fire; the one gun then responded; the broadsides of the man-of-war were returned for half an hour by this solitary but unerring gun; at length the captain found it necessary to interrupt the admiral's correspondence by informing him that Lieut. Slessor, and a midshipman, and several men were killed, many more wounded, and the ship seriously damaged. Sir Sidney looked surprised, but gave orders that the boats should be lowered, and the marines sent ashore to reduce these obstinate Frenchmen.

As soon as the boats touched the beach, some thirty Corsicans ran from the tower to meet them, waving a white handkerchief, and telling the officer that they had been longing to desert to the British, but as the ship fired at them instead of inviting them to surrender, they had no choice but to use their gun to the best of their ability. We went on our way, leaving the *Pompée's* crew employed in repairing her damages, and in burying the poor fellows whose lives had been thus idly thrown away. Moore viewed the coasts, gathered information from the *commandant* of Capri, and ordered Acland with his two battalions back to Messina.

As soon as Gaeta had surrendered, columns of French troops marched rapidly into the Principato; and the broken divisions of Reynier and Verdier having concentrated in Upper Calabria, they began to resume offensive movements. The disorderly bands of mountaineers who had drawn together in large masses, were scattered by the first advance of the French battalions, and a panic spread like wildfire even through the lower province. Instead of being prompted by the rumour of an advancing enemy to unite their bands and occupy the passes, or rally on the Neapolitans at Monteleone, the captains of the *Masse* seized the moment of confusion to set off in all directions to plunder the towns and villages, confident in their numbers and in the arms lavished on them by the British admiral; confident, I say, that they might now indulge their lust for plunder and outrage without resistance on the part of their unhappy fellow-countrymen.

I might quote proofs from many documents in my possession, but the following extract from an official report made by a staff officer (now Sir Richard Church) dated August 28th, will be sufficient to shew what these people were whom Queen Caroline cherished as the props of her crown, and whom Sir Sidney Smith was proud to reckon under his command.

> I found the town (Nicastro) in the most dreadful state of confusion and dismay from a massacre and pillage by the *Masse*. Half an hour previous to my arrival, *two* of the inhabitants had been murdered in the streets; and the *syndic*, governor, and many others had been repeatedly fired at. From these circumstances, and at the urgent solicitations of the inhabitants, I conceived it my most particular duty to remain, and if possible, restore order.
> During the whole day parties continued to arrive until they amounted to above eleven hundred: they were immediately supplied with rations of every description. Towards evening they suddenly attacked the house of Don Giuseppe Nicotera, with the avowed intention of massacring their whole family

and pillaging the house.

I am happy to state before they had found any of the family or carried away anything of consequence, I arrived at the house, and from the steady conduct of the detachment of cavalry, as also by making use of threats and persuasion, I succeeded in forcing them out of the house, and immediately ordered their chiefs out of the town to take post towards Scigliano, with which order the greatest part complied; a number still remained, and I thought it necessary to patrol the whole of the night. (See also in the Appendix a letter from Sir J. Stuart himself to General Fox, dated Palmi, 26th August.)

Together with the chief command of the army, the appointment of Ambassador to the Court of Palermo had been conferred on General Fox by his brother, who was desirous that, under the circumstances of the island, there should be a unity of power in British hands. It was now become necessary that the general should present himself to their Sicilian Majesties, and he made over the command of the army *pro tempore* to Sir John Moore. Stuart immediately applied for and obtained leave to retire to Malta, until he could find an opportunity of returning to England. These two men had served together in Egypt, and a mutual dislike was the result of their acquaintance. Every quality in Moore was real, solid, and unbending. In Stuart all was flighty and superficial, though there was a good deal of original cleverness.

The former was penetrating, reflecting, and, though his manner was singularly agreeable to those whom he liked, to those whom he did not hold in esteem his bearing was severe; while Stuart was vain, frivolous, and sarcastic. It may be remembered that in the battle of the 21st March, 1801, near Alexandria, the desperate onset of the French burst fall upon the reserve of the British Army under Moore's command.

The 42nd Regiment was broken by the headlong charge of the enemy's cavalry, and the 28th and 58th only maintained their posts by dint of the most obstinate and valiant exertions against superior numbers. In rear of the reserve was Stuart with three foreign regiments: he brought them up gallantly to the rescue; and the enemy, already shattered and wavering amidst the unflinching gallantry of Moore's battalions, was overpowered by this second line.

A very large share of the honour of that day's victory was justly awarded to General Moore; but Stuart always fancied himself aggrieved, and he cherished the belief that he and his foreigners won the battle of Alexandria. Moore, therefore, was the man of whom he was particularly jealous, and with whom he could not bear to serve. However, these two generals had an amicable interview before Sir John Stuart embarked for Malta, and I give this extract from a letter which Moore wrote at the time (Sept. 5th, 1806), to General Fox, both as it regards Stuart, and still more Sir Sidney Smith and the state of Calabria.

> I have had a long conversation with Sir J. Stuart: he was particularly reasonable, and I really believe that he expressed nothing but what he thought at the moment. I do not, however, expect that he will ever for any continuance, be very consistent on the subject of the Calabrias. Amongst the enclosures you will find a letter from Sir Sidney Smith, with a copy of the letter which I mentioned to you I had seen when on board the *Pompée*.
>
> It is with his usual impudence that he pretends to hope that my progress along shore has in any respect led me to think with him, when he knows how strongly I have expressed the reverse. The knowledge I acquired in my tour leads me to regret that he has, as he says, neglected other business in order to attend to the affairs of the inhabitants on the coast; for amongst them I think he has only been active in mischief. Sir Sidney may perhaps have painted in his imagination a people brave and hardy, intelligent and capable of defending their mountains against an enemy. But they must be animated and united by some common sentiment that is praiseworthy. They must not be the dastardly dregs of the Calabrese, led by assassins to plunder and murder every person who is decent and respectable in the country.

In the beginning of September, the French began to push their patrols towards Monteleone, and they made a show of attacking Baron Acton. As the latter found that he could not place the least reliance on the Calabrese, and the English would not advance from the straits, he gave way before the first demonstration of the enemy, and fell back to the towns upon the coast, where the British still held the Castle of Scilla, and a few other posts of observation. The French, however, would not yet venture to take their quarters in the lower extremity of Calabria, close to an English Army nearly twice as strong as that which had recently taught them so severe a lesson.

They had no magazines or heavy guns, and Reynier, who was again in the chief command, was content to fix his headquarters at Mileto, pushing outposts towards Palmi. Being unmolested by the British, he employed his leisure in dispersing the bands of Calabrese, executing a great many who fell into his hands, and reducing the country as far as it was occupied by his troops, into a still subjection.

Thus the armies on both sides remained for some months (excepting that Baron Acton's Neapolitans were recalled to Palermo in November, leaving only a garrison in the Castle of Reggio); our own improving its means of defence, and placing garrisons in Catania, Agosta, and Syracuse; while the French were waiting for reinforcements and ordnance, preparatory to the siege of Scilla, and the re-occupation of the whole coast of Lower Calabria. In the latter part of August, General Fox received advice that preliminaries of peace between France and Russia had been actually signed at Paris; nor was it till nearly two months afterwards that he learnt from Corfu that the Emperor Alexander had refused to ratify the treaty, and that war was likely to be renewed.

During this interval, therefore, our general conceived that England was standing alone and unsupported in her resistance to Napoleon, and that there was no object to be answered by diversions or attempts upon the continent. But before December, 4,000 very fine infantry joined his army from England, despatched apparently by our government, for the purpose of rendering the British forces in Sicily equal to undertake active operations; and though no direct instructions arrived, some preparations were made in anticipation of expected orders; our transports were kept in constant readiness, and four or five thousand of our best troops, under General Edward Paget, were hutted on the beach at Milazzo. Our army at this time mustered more than 17,000 men, (See Appendix), but we were lamentably deficient in cavalry.

As the political schemes of the Court of Palermo, and in some measures our own military plans were influenced by the turns and chances of the great struggle between the armies of France and Russia, it may be convenient here to take a brief review of the course of war in the north of Europe. In the middle of October, 1806, the Prussian monarchy had been shattered to fragments by the Battle of Jena and its immediate results. The activity and unchecked success with which Napoleon followed up his victory were unparalleled in the history of modern warfare. In less than a mouth he was master of the wide countries, and many of the strongest fortresses, between the Elbe and the Oder. His victorious columns poured on to the eastward; and the Russian Army which was marching to the support of the King of Prussia, encountered the leading divisions of the French at a short distance from the Vistula.

The Moscovites were by no means prepared to arrest the mighty force of the enemy. They retreated in order to unite themselves with their columns arriving from the rear; and the French entered the capital of Poland on the 28th of November. Napoleon, who had remained some time in Berlin, rejoined his army at Warsaw about the middle of December, and resumed offensive operations a few days afterwards. The Russian Armies were now collected, and strong in numbers and confidence. A series of obstinate and bloody conflicts took place between the 23rd and 27th of December; there was a fearful loss of men on both sides; and the rigour of the season was alike injurious to the invaders and their opponents.

While the Russians retired towards the Niemen, the French drew back to Warsaw and the borders of the Vistula; and both parties were glad for a time to find rest in winter-quarters. However, the ministers of the *Czar* at foreign courts seized on these specious circumstances, and they trumpeted forth in the south and west of Europe that Napoleon's mighty army had been repulsed, nay, defeated at Pultusk, and the foremost to believe the tale were the infatuated sovereigns and Court of Palermo.

Even before these accounts arrived, on the bare knowledge of the fact that the Emperor Alexander had refused to ratify the preliminaries of peace, the Sicilian Government became clamorous for an attack upon the enemy. Sir John Acton had been, before this time, wormed out of his post as Prime Minister, by the intrigues of Queen Caroline and her faction. The Marquis di Circello was at the head of the government; and all the schemes of his royal mistress were in full activity. Most urgently and importantly did she press our minister at Palermo, and our General at Messina, to engage at once in an attack on the French at Naples; or if not on Naples itself, at least on the Calabrias; and Circello insisted the more vehemently, "because," said he, (Mr. A'Court to General Fox, Dec. 13th, 1806) "a balanced state of the struggle in Poland may induce the two emperors to agree upon a peace, for their allies as well as themselves, on the basis of *uti-possidetis*." (Mr. Drummond to the same, Dec. 18th.)

Just at this moment Mr. Drummond arrived from England to take his post as the British minister at Palermo, and bringing the latest instructions from the Cabinet of St. James's. He wrote immediately to General Fox, describing the fever in which he found the Sicilian Court, and their impatience for an expedition. But Mr. Drummond, at the same time, considering this to be a question which ought to be decided by the opinion and on the responsibility of the English commander, begged to be made acquainted with General Fox's sentiments, and his views of the subject.

Now General Fox, and still more strongly Sir John Moore, were averse from engaging in any expedition without orders from home; and they were particularly disinclined to commit their troops or connect themselves with the projects of Her Sicilian Majesty, They were fully convinced that she was not only rash, but that she was utterly false, if not treacherous. They were resolved to keep a firm hold of Sicily; and not to risk the British Army in enterprises of doubtful success without authority from their own government. It was determined therefore that Sir John Moore should repair to Palermo; that he should explain to Mr. Drummond very fully the views and opinions of the generals on the actual state of affairs; and try at least to fix the judgment of our minister, if he could not succeed in satisfying the Sicilian Court.

Sir John's interview with the ambassador was apparently productive of all the effect which had been hoped: Mr. Drummond, (Rt, Hon. W. Drummond to General Fox, Jan, 2nd, 1807), declared himself to be completely convinced that the generals were right in their opinion, that the time was not fit for an invasion of Naples; and he inveighed loudly against the queen's party, the actual ministers, their ruinous policy, and their anti-English feelings.

Such continued to be the opinions of Mr. Drummond till after Sir Sidney Smith had been removed from Palermo, by his being ordered to proceed with Admiral Duckworth to the Dardanelles; and the ambassador's letters during that interval not only shew his concurrence with our military commanders, but they mark in the strongest characters his opinions of the queen and her cabal, including most particularly Sir Sidney Smith, who was at that time the cherished confidant and first favourite of Her Majesty. (See Appendix K for Mr. Drummond's letters of the 23rd and 27th Jan.)

That Caroline detested the English there can be no doubt; that she urged the Emperor of Russia, as Mr. Drummond states, to send to Sicily a large army which might set aside the British influence, is highly probable; but that so early as January, 1807, the queen could be endeavouring to open secret negotiations with Napoleon, almost staggers belief. Yet the fact that she was engaged in such an attempt, through the medium of the Spanish Court, appeared to be afterwards confirmed by advices which General Fox received from Spain by way of Gibraltar. The queen had only one bait to offer to Napoleon; only one condition which could tempt the great conqueror to incline his ear to this degraded woman.

This only bait was Sicily, with its fortresses and harbours, and the sacrifice of the English Army.

Give me back, sire, my beloved Naples, and I will not only be your most faithful vassal henceforth and for ever, but I will betray into your hands the fortified ports of Sicily with their English garrisons!

However, if such overtures were made, they were of no effect. The British Army remained tranquil on the eastern coast from Syracuse to Milazzo; our generals on very bad terms with the Court of Palermo, and thwarted and impeded by the Neapolitan authorities, as much as the latter dared to let their ill-will appear. But these annoyances became more sensible when our ambassador, within a month after the departure of Sir Sidney Smith, whom he detested, suddenly renounced all his former opinions, adopted the views and policy of Circello, and threw the weight of his official character into the scale in favour of the court and in opposition to Generals Fox and Moore.

In the meantime, orders had been received which very materially changed and impaired our military position. Before the close of January, despatches arrived from England, conveying to General Fox the information that our government proposed to act offensively against Turkey, if the Porte should not at once accept the terms which were to be dictated by our ambassador; that an English squadron was to appear immediately before Constantinople; and that 5,000 troops were to be held in readiness at Messina to proceed directly to Alexandria, in case the Turks should reject our terms and resist our squadron. These surprising orders appear to have been connected in the minds of the British Cabinet with the war in Poland; and it becomes necessary to resume, but briefly, our notice of the war between France and Russia.

So early as August 1806, two months before the commencement of hostilities with Russia, Napoleon had despatched General Sebastiani as his ambassador to the Porte. Foreseeing the likelihood of a severe struggle when the *Czar* should come to the support of the Prussian monarch, the French emperor instructed his military diplomatist to prepare the minds of the Turks, and animate them to throw off the weight of Russian ascendancy. He was to point out the happy opportunity, which would be afforded by a war between Napoleon and Alexander, of recovering the ancient dominion of the *Sultan* over Moldavia and Wallachia; and to dispel their dread of the Russian arms by the promise of ample support, and the assurance of an intimate and perpetual alliance with France.

Sebastiani performed his part ably and successfully. The sluggish Turks began in September to shew towards Russia symptoms of restiveness; nor were they moved by the advice or remonstrances of the English ambassador, who saw and strove to check the growth of French influence. Under such circumstances the game of Russia clearly was to soothe, to gain time, to avoid any measures which might provoke the Turks into actual hostilities, at a moment when it was of vital importance that all the forces of the *Czar* should be concentrated in Poland. Instead of this, without an attempt to conciliate, or turn to account the national inertness of the Mussulmen, the Russians adopted the most irritating measures.

As soon as they found a firm opposition at the Porte, they marched 40,000 men into Moldavia. An army of this strength might have turned the tide of war on the Vistula or the Narew, where the *Czar* was about to encounter the veteran armies of France with inferior numbers. But Alexander bore not in mind the old maxim of the Romans, to deal with one enemy at a time, and to wait for the prosperous issue of one contest before engaging in another. Napoleon was coming to the attack with 130,000 troops inured to war, and familiar with victory. At this moment the *Czar* detached 40,000 of his soldiers to Turkey, and moreover he kept a considerable force fighting with the Persians in Georgia!

However, the confidence of the Russians in their strength was not without misgivings; and they pressed the Cabinet of London to make diversions in their favour by sea and land. It was impossible at that season of the year for England to send fleets or armies to the Baltic; nor were operations at the mouths of the Elbe or the Weser practicable since the downfall of Prussia; but the south of Europe was open to us. And here it is necessary to advert to an important part of Napoleon's combinations for the conduct of his campaign. Having wrung from the reluctant Court of Austria the full possession of Dalmatia, and seized upon Ragusa; he was forming in that quarter a large army under Marmont, destined to cross the Northern Provinces of Turkey, and act in conjunction with the Mussulmen against the south of Russia.

******

There had been a good deal of fighting in the preceding spring for the possession of the Bocche di Cattaro; but the French had in the end expelled the Russians, and reduced the Montenegrins to subjection.

******

In Upper Italy there remained but few French troops: in the kingdom of Naples hardly more than twenty-five thousand, including Neapolitans, scattered through its wide extent. It was an object of the highest importance to arrest the movement of Marmont's army: it was the most effectual diversion England could make for the relief of her Russian ally. If our government had sent to Sicily in November seven or eight thousand of the infantry, and a couple of thousand of the dragoons who were idle at home, we should have been strong enough for the purpose. The landing of twenty or twenty-four thousand British troops in the north of Italy, or even at Leghorn, would have compelled Marmont to detach a large proportion of his army to meet our invasion.

I speak not here of the chances which presented themselves of successes in Italy, nor of the effect which such successes would have had on the still wavering councils of Austria, I speak only of the object which Russia had at heart, that of relieving her in some degree from the pressure of the war. Another mode appeared to be this: That twenty sail of the line, instead of seven, and with 10,000 troops on board, should have been despatched direct to Constantinople, and by the most energetic measures, coupled with the offer of the most liberal terms, have half awed half persuaded the Porte into an instant peace. (It appears from Lord Collingwood's correspondence, that the British Government ordered only *five* ships to the Dardanelles; Lord Collingwood took upon himself to add two more.)

This alternative might possibly have succeeded; and our 10,000 men and their transports were ready at Messina, But instead of affording a prompt support to our ally, by acting vigorously in either the one or other direction, our Cabinet came to the miserable determination of sending five or six men-of-war, without soldiers, to the Dardanelles; and 5,000 soldiers, without a fleet, to occupy the town of Alexandria! To make the matter worse, and our plans more objectionable, our allies, the Russians, were particularly jealous of England's supposed designs on Egypt, and were sure to view our seizing on Alexandria with a suspicions and angry eye.

★★★★★★

The Russian minister, M. d'Italinski, had come about this time to Malta. *Why* he came there was never declared. But Mr. Drummond says in a note to General Fox, "If you could order one of the transports to run over to Malta, I could obtain correct information from M. d'Italinski, concerning the state of negotiations with the Porte. It is a subject on which d'Italinski, would not enter fully with Sir J. Duckworth or perhaps with any person except myself. You are aware of the jealousy which exists, and that the Russians by no means wish us to interfere. They will be very sorry to see us in possession of Alexandria. Still d'Italinski would not withhold his opinions from me, because our habits of intimacy, with many important communications which we have mutually made to each other, have inspired both with confidence."

★★★★★★

Still the British Government, in a spirit of short-sighted and petty selfishness, gave orders that 5,000 men should be detached from their army in Sicily to seize and occupy the town of Alexandria; "not to conquer Egypt." It was clear that this measure could not draw off a single soldier from the French or Turkish Armies employed against the Russians, while it rendered the British Army too weak to enter on a serious enterprise on either side of Italy, and thus served to dispel any apprehensions which the enemy might have felt with regard to that country.

The state of Egypt was at this time unsettled and full of trouble. The *pacha*, Mehemet Ali, was silently weaving those plans by which he afterwards worked his way to an independent sovereignty. The Mamelukes, though much reduced in power, still held together, and kept their ground in the Upper Province. They watched the *pacha* with dread as well as jealousy; while in his breast were carefully hidden the designs for their destruction, which he at last accomplished by the deepest and most cruel treachery. Acts of open hostility indeed were occurring from time to time; but they were the character rather of those passing outbreaks of savage suspicion, which are common amongst the nations of the East, than of a declared and lasting war.

Both the Mamelukes and the *pacha* were objects of distrust to the Porte, and all the three were intriguing secretly, each against the other two. But the spirit of intrigue was not confined to Mussulmen; both the French and the English Consuls at Alexandria had been for a long time busily at work, and of course in opposite directions. And the latter gentleman bore so large a part in drawing the British expedition to Egypt, and in the measures, which brought disaster and disgrace on our arms, that I cannot avoid making some mention of his proceedings.

Major Missett, our consul-general, had resided some years in Egypt, and being a man of a busy and inquiring turn of mind, he had taken an active part in the politics, and had connected himself with one of the contending factions, of the country. Clever, vain, and impatient, he had long been engaged in schemes for re-establishing a British interest. He reckoned on the Arabs as sure supporters; he had carried on a secret correspondence with the *beys*, and thought he had secured the alliance of the Mamelukes.

But Major Missett was a cripple; he was unable to go forth from Alexandria and see things with his own eyes. He could only listen to the reports of his own emissaries or correspondents, but his sanguine nature prompted him to believe that a handful of British troops would suffice to extinguish the influence of France, and crush the rising power of Mehemet Ali. In this spirit our consul-general urged upon ministers the ease and importance of seizing on Alexandria, and in an evil hour they listened to his counsel.

The commanders of our expedition were specially instructed to consult Major Missett, and be guided by his experience of Egyptian affairs in all proceedings which were not purely military. But our government appears to have been left in ignorance of the fact, that the immediate neighbourhood of Alexandria afforded no supply of provisions; and equally so of the numbers and warlike character of the Albanian soldiers whom the *pacha* had been collecting and training with great diligence.

******

It seems strange that ministers should have been content to rest in ignorance of at least the physical resources of Alexandria, for hardly five years had passed since it was evacuated by a British Army, and there were many men within call who could have afforded them ample information on the subject.

******

It was lightly imagined not only that Alexandria could be taken without difficulty, but that the possession of this city would be of itself sufficient to render the British general the arbiter of Egyptian factions, and the virtual ruler to whom they would all turn their eyes for advice and guidance. Thus, the Secretary of State instructs General Fox:

"In choosing an officer to command this expedition, attention must be paid not only to his military talents, but to those qualities which may best suit him for a civil or political trust of considerable importance, which the service in which he is to be engaged must from its nature involve him. His interference in those party dissensions which generally agitate Egypt, or in those contests for power which are generally maintained amongst the *beys*, will probably be unavoidable; and the precise line, which it will be proper for him to take in the exercise of such interference would be difficult at this time to point out."

★★★★★★

Here is an instance of the cruel positions in which our commanders and governors are too often placed. They are engaged by the orders of their government in transactions of a doubtful issue. Their instructions are couched in general or ambiguous terms. Distinct explanations are avoided, and this because British ministers are afraid of being called to account in Parliament, if the consequences do not prove satisfactory.

★★★★★★

It was probably in consideration of his conciliatory temper, and his frank and engaging manners, that General McKenzie Fraser was selected for the command of the expedition to Alexandria. He was a fine specimen of an open, generous, honourable Highland chieftain. A man of very good plain sense, but one who had never studied the higher branches, either of politics or of military science. Everyone in the army loved McKenzie Fraser, but no one deemed him qualified for a separate and difficult command. If the special instructions of our Cabinet were interpreted so as to indicate Fraser as the properest person to play the part of mediator in Egypt, it became the more essential that his second in command should be an officer well qualified to lead the troops, and form just opinions on military questions. But unfortunately, the major-general who was appointed to this post was one who had been merely a brave, hardworking, regimental officer. As such he had been patronised by Sir John Moore; but on this ill-fated expedition he shewed how totally devoid he was of military talents. Fortunately for himself he expiated his blunders by dying gallantly in battle.

A body of troops, to the amount directed by the British Government, was prepared for embarkation early in February, 1807; and held in readiness to proceed as soon as advice should be received of the issue of our attempts at Constantinople.

★★★★★★

20th Light Dragoons, 70; Artillery, &c., 180; 31st Regiment, 35th *ditto*, (two battalions,) 78th *ditto*, 2nd battalion, 2,970; De Roll's regiment, *Chasseurs Britanniques*, Sicilian Volunteers, 2,030.

★★★★★★

The fleet of transports sailed from Messina on the 6th of March; and the enemy's troops in Calabria instantly fell back, apparently with the intention of concentrating their forces between the gulfs of St. Eufemia and Squilace; but having soon ascertained that the British expedition had proceeded to the eastward, the French not only returned to their former posts, but they pushed forward a body of troops with the hope of surprising Reggio. There, however, the Neapolitan General Tschudi had some pretty good regiments, and the enemy found it prudent to remain at a distance.

No smile of fortune cheered this unhappy expedition to Egypt. From its outset its prospects were crossed by untoward accidents. In the night after sailing from Messina, thirty-three sail of transports with the *Apollo* frigate parted company, and the general (on board the *Tigre* of 84 guns), with little more than 2,000 soldiers in sixteen transports arrived off Alexandria on the 16th of March. They anchored on the coast to the westward of the port; but though the Turkish garrison of that extensive town did not consist of more than 250 soldiers, the governor feared not to shut his gates against invaders who presented so paltry a show of strength. However, a letter from the British consul pressed General Fraser most urgently to land without loss of time, and risk a sudden stroke before the Albanians could arrive from Rosetta. He stated that the population of the town were in favour of the English; and that the governor was wavering between his dread of an insurrection, and the remaining influence of M. Drovetti, the French consul, who had despatched couriers to summon the Albanians to Alexandria.

Fraser was much puzzled. He felt that the force at his immediate command was insufficient to overcome resistance, if a stout resistance should be offered; and the heavy surf and scarcity of boats, made it difficult to carry ashore even the small number of troops which had arrived. However, he thought it his duty to make the trial; and in the evening of the 17th, a few hundreds of our men were landed by the exertions of that admirable seaman, Captain Hallowell. In the course of the next morning some more companies were brought ashore; but the total number of soldiers hardly exceeded 1,000, when the debarkation was arrested by the increasing violence of the surf.

Still urged by the importunities of Major Missett, Fraser moved towards the town in the evening of the 18th. Some old redoubts and lines from which the Turks fired upon our column from some old guns, were carried with very little loss or difficulty; and the British drew near to the gate of Pompey. But the gate was barricaded, and the Turkish soldiers plied their muskets from the walls.

No sign of outbreak amongst the inhabitants gave encouragement to our attempt; and the general determined prudently to march round the city, and occupy the isthmus between the lakes and the sea, placing troops in the old Castle of Aboukir, and on the cut between the lakes of Maadieh and Mareotis. Fraser thus barred the two narrow routes by which alone the Albanians could arrive from Rosetta or from Cairo; and he secured time for the arrival and landing of the rest of his little army. Early on the 20th, the Apollo, with most of the missing transports, anchored in the bay of Aboukir; Duckworth's fleet arrived from the Dardanelles; and in the course of that day the Turkish governor surrendered Alexandria by capitulation.

Here then was the specific object of the expedition accomplished; and here instantly began the difficulties of our general. Only two days after he had taken possession of Alexandria, he was astounded by an official representation from the consul-general, that the city was on the verge of famine; that there was barely enough of grain within the walls for the subsistence of the people during the next ten days; and that at the end of the ten days the native population must be starved, and the British garrison must be reduced to live upon the salt provisions brought by the transports. Major Missett stated that Alexandria was entirely dependent for food upon the country about Rosetta and Ramanieh; wheat and rice being imported from the former, and bullocks, sheep, and barley from the latter. He, therefore, urged and implored General Fraser to send forth troops without loss of time, and to seize and continue to hold the two places above-mentioned.

Now if Alexandria was thus entirely dependent on the upper country for the means of feeding its inhabitants from day to day, or week to week. Major Missett (who had resided there for years) must have been as fully cognisant of the fact, before he urged upon our government the expediency of sending an army to garrison the town, as he was after the army had arrived. Yet there are no traces of his having mentioned this dependence; and the consequent necessity of attacking, conquering, and continuing to hold two towns at the distance of thirty and forty miles from the British headquarters. The Secretary of State appears to have been completely ignorant of such a necessity, for his instructions are limited to "merely the capture of Alexandria;" and to this single point, therefore, were the orders confined which Fraser had received from the Commander of the Forces in Sicily.

✶✶✶✶✶✶

Experience proved, after all, that this necessity did not exist. We never got possession of either Ramanieh or Rosetta yet the British continued to hold Alexandria for six months; without the occurrence of any distress or difficulty about provisions. The fact was that Major Missett was indulging in grand schemes, and trying to draw his countrymen on to the conquest of Egypt.

✶✶✶✶✶✶

The poor general was sorely perplexed. He felt that his instructions did not authorize him to do more than occupy the city. The words "not to conquer Egypt," appeared to forbid his advancing into the country and engaging in hostilities. On the other hand, the consul-general, to whom he was specially ordered to have recourse for advice and information, and to whose long experience in Egyptian affairs there was no authority to oppose, called upon him in the strongest terms to send troops to Rosetta without a moment's pause, on pain of seeing the people of Alexandria plunged into all the horrors of famine. Major Missett represented at the same time that the defences of Rosetta were contemptible, and the Albanians a merely savage rabble, few in numbers and quite incapable of resisting a British brigade.

We cannot wonder at General Fraser's having given way to this official importunity, backed by such strong assertions. He ordered two battalions (the 31st Regiment and the *Chasseurs Britanniques*) accompanied by some field artillery, and commanded by Brigadier Robert Meade, to march directly upon Rosetta; but unfortunately, with this little detachment was also sent Fraser's second in command Major-General Wauchope. No opposition was encountered on the march; our troops reached and occupied the heights of Aboumandour, which overlook the town of Rosetta.

All was still; the walls appeared to stand without defenders, and the gates remained open. But no person came forth to meet the British; no information was received as to the state of affairs within the town; nothing was known of the numbers or temper of the Albanians, or of their means of resistance; there might be two, or two hundred, or two thousand of them. All was dark and silent, and doubtful. Yet then, without reconnoitring the place, or feeling his way, or making attempts to obtain intelligence, General Wauchope quietly led his ill-fated column into the narrow, gloomy, and intricate lanes of Rosetta. They were allowed to enter; and when thoroughly entangled and hemmed in by the lofty buildings, they were assailed by a storm of fire from every quarter, from the house-tops, and every cranny and opening in every house.

Our soldiers could make no return, for no enemy met their eyes. All that they could see were the quick flashes of the firearms; and our brave men fell fast and helpless under the death-shot. Wauchope was slain outright; Meade very badly wounded in the head; and an instant retreat beyond the gates became the only possible chance of saving the whole body from destruction. It is highly honourable to the character of the regiments which were suddenly involved in such a confusion of slaughter, that they preserved their order, made their retreat to the hills in a soldier-like manner, under Lieut.-Colonel Bruce, and even carried off their wounded. The Albanians rushed after them in pursuit, but were unable to do more than cut off a few unfortunate stragglers.

This ill-managed and disastrous affair was attended with the loss of four officers and 181 men killed, and nineteen officers and 263 men wounded. The shattered, but not disgraced, survivors of Meade's brigade were led back to Alexandria in the first days of April; and General Fraser began to feel very strongly, how insufficient was the number of troops at his disposal, if instead of merely forming the garrison of one town it was necessary that large detachments should be sent forth to occupy two others; and not only to occupy them, but to win them first from an enemy who, it was now too clear, was disposed and able to make a stout resistance.

But the delusion as to the necessity of possessing Rosetta still prevailed; it was again urged in the strongest manner by Major Missett, backed by the chief magistrate of Alexandria. An impending, immediate famine was dinned into the ears of General Fraser, and he (with the concurrence of the English admiral, who was now with a squadron on the coast) resolved to send a second and a stronger corps to reduce Rosetta.

The troops selected for this service amounted to 2,500 men, more than half of the numbers, which remained in Alexandria. (20th Light Dragoons, artillerymen, 35th Regiment—1st battalion, 78th Regiment—2nd battalion, battalion of Light Infantry, regiment De Roll, detachment of seamen.) They were placed under the command of Brigadier-Generals William Stewart and John Oswald; and they carried with them a large proportion of artillery and engineer's stores, which were now seen to be necessary for battering the walls of Rosetta. The march of an army in the sands of Egypt is slow work. On the 3rd of April, the British reached only the wells of Aboukir; the 4th was spent in landing heavy guns and stores, passing the cuts between the lakes and the sea, and pushing the advanced guard (about 500 men, commanded by Lieut.-Colonel Macleod) to the village of Edko; the main body arrived there the next day.

It was now found that the Albanians, besides holding the town of Rosetta, had a strong detachment posted at El Hamed, a village about five miles above Rosetta, and standing on the neck of land between the Nile and Lake Edko. General Stewart deemed it essential to seize and hold this position for the security of the right flank and rear of his little army, while it was engaged in the attack upon Rosetta. He, therefore, detached Macleod's corps against El Hamed, and the enemy's troops (chiefly cavalry) gave way after merely the show of a skirmish. On the 7th, Macleod was relieved by nearly 300 of Roll's regiment under Major Vogelsang, and the important post of El Hamed was intrusted to his keeping. With the rest of his troops Stewart advanced to Rosetta, driving in the enemy's skirmishers, and lodging his men securely in the sand-hills close to the walls.

Mortars and carronades were brought into play in the course of the next three or four days; but as the British force was insufficient to invest more than a small portion of the town-walls, the enemy made frequent sorties against our left, and they skirmished boldly, though with little or no effect. From the numerous loopholes in the walls, the Albanians kept up a constant fire of musketry; but our troops were well covered and suffered little loss.

On the other hand, the enemy seemed to regard our shot and shells with great indifference; they fired upon our flags of truce, and they hanged a poor Arab who had been induced by a large reward to carry a summons into the town. In this manner, ten or twelve unsatisfactory days wore away, enlivened only by a gallant and well managed exploit of a detachment of the 78th Regiment in the night of the 16th. Major Macdonnel, with 250 of his Highlanders, assisted by 40 seamen, crossed the river silently in the darkness; and having made a circuit, he completely surprised a body of Albanians in a battery, which had been particularly annoying to the right flank of our lines. He dispersed their soldiers, actually fired several rounds from their own cannon into the town, destroyed the battery, brought away the guns and camels, and recrossed the Nile with hardly any loss.

But it is time to advert to circumstances, or rather to the false information and false hopes, by which General Fraser had been misled, and Stewart was misguided. The consul (perhaps deceived by his correspondents, or by his own emissaries) had assured the general that the Mamelukes, evading the forces of the *pacha*, were in full march to unite with the British in this attack upon Rosetta. Stewart had set out with this expectation—he continued to cherish it: he persevered in the attack under this deception; and he looked anxiously from day to day for the arrival of these allies at El Hamed.

★★★★★★

The *beys* had without doubt been eager to encourage Major Missett's scheme of bringing a British Army to Alexandria. They were delighted to hear of its arrival, and promised all that our sanguine consul could desire. They trusted that the English invasion would oblige their enemy, Mehemet Ali, to move from Cairo to the coast, and thus leave the grand city exposed to their attacks. Cairo was their object. But the *pacha* was too strong, and proved himself too skilful and too rapid in his movements, to yield to the Mamelukes either time or opportunity to effect their purpose.

★★★★★★

At that point, however, instead of relief and support, he was destined to receive a fatal blow.

While the British batteries were firing in vain at the old walls of Rosetta on the west side of the Nile, the Albanians had been receiving reinforcements from Damietta and other places to the eastward. A considerable body of their cavalry had been observed to draw together on the right bank of the river opposite to El Hamed, where it will be remembered a detachment of 300 of our foreign troops was posted under Major Vogelsang. His business was to watch the isthmus between Lake Edko and the Nile, an extent of not less than two miles, or two and a half when the waters of the lake were low, as they were at this time. Athwart this neck of land there ran a *canal,* such as is in use in Egypt, but differing so materially from what we are accustomed to call a "canal," as to require some explanation.

The design of this water-course, as of very many others in Lower Egypt, is to receive and convey, for the purposes of irrigation, &c. the superabundant water of the Nile at the season of its periodical overflow. At other times of the year the bed of the watercourse is dry; but on either hand rises a great embankment, massive and high. In the present instance, the canal of El Hamed served to lead the overflowing waters of the river into Lake Edko; but its lofty dykes, beginning on the margin of the Nile, did not stretch completely across the isthmus. Between their western extremity and the lake in the dry season a sandy plain remained, about half a mile wide, which was practicable for horsemen.

As far as the line extended this double embankment afforded to our troops a tolerably strong front, particularly against cavalry; for there were only two roadways through the dykes; one nearly in the centre, opposite the village of El Hamed (which was in advance and was occupied by a company of our Swiss), and the other close upon the bank of the river. Both of these roads were held by Major Vogelsang's soldiers, with a gun on each. (De Roll's regiment had been originally Swiss: but from time to time it had been renewed and augmented with foreigners of various kinds—many of them prisoners or deserters.)

On the 19th of April the Turkish cavalry, which had gathered on the right bank of the Nile, crossed the river above El Hamed; and advancing from Dibeh they made an attempt on the left of Vogelsang's posts. The attack was feeble and was easily repelled. At the same time the garrison of Rosetta issued forth in greater numbers than usual against the left of General Stewart's lines: their assault was fierce, but it made no impression on the 35th regiment, whose steady fire drove them back with loss; and their retreat was quickened by the charging of our handful of dragoons. These offensive movements of the enemy rendered Stewart uneasy for his people at El Hamed.

On the same evening, the 19th, he detached the light companies of the 35th and De Roll's, under Captain Tarleton, to strengthen Vogelsang; instructing him to make an effort to oblige the Turkish horsemen to recross the Nile. Tarleton made this attempt at daybreak on the 20th, but he found the enemy far too strong for him, and he retired towards the canal. Before however he had cleared the plain, and brought his men into safety, he rashly divided the detachment under his orders; directing one hundred of De Roll's upon the village of El Hamed, while he marched with his own company to the post upon the Nile. This imprudence brought on the first catastrophe. The Turks galloped up with all their force, surrounded the detachment of De Roll's in the open ground; charged from every side, and cut most of them down, with little attempt at resistance on their part. A few escaped into the village.

This serious intelligence reached General Stewart by eleven o'clock, a.m. He instantly despatched Colonel Macleod (with two companies of the 78th, one of the 35th, a dozen dragoons, and a six-pounder) to take the command at El Hamed. In the evening he sent two more companies escorting provisions, ammunition, and tools. On the first arrival of Macleod's troops, the enemy's horse withdrew from the front of our line, and retired up the plain towards Dibeh; and so little did the colonel find cause for apprehension, that before nightfall he reported to headquarters that his position was perfectly secure.

He had posted Captain Tarleton with three companies of British, and his few dragoons, and a three-pounder at the western extremity of the dyke, to watch the plain towards Lake Edko; one company of De Roll's in the village of El Hamed; another with a gun, at the gap in the centre, under the orders of Major Mohr; and Major Vogelsang with the remainder of De Roll's, and three companies of British, and a six-pounder upon the border of the Nile on his left.

★★★★★★

The British seem to have been separated and intermixed with strange caprice. Thus, Tarleton had the grenadiers of the 78th, and two companies of the 35th, away on the right: while Vogelsang had one company of the 35th and two of the 78th at the extreme left.

★★★★★★

General Stewart, however, did not feel his mind at ease; and early in the night he visited Macleod's posts in person, and gave him final orders. The spirit of Stewart's instructions was this: if the enemy should attack the position, it is to be maintained stoutly while there appears a fair chance of success: but if the Turkish force should prove to be too strong, the British troops are to be drawn off from the left, and then from the centre; and both are to move under cover of the dyke and join Tarleton's detachment on the right.

On that side the whole force (still amounting to nearly 700 men) are to be kept in a mass, retreating along the shore of Lake Edko, holding on to that support, and pointing towards the rear of the army before Rosetta. (But Stewart himself found difficulty in returning to his camp. Already had a part of the Moslem horsemen come round the right of our position in the darkness: they were spreading over the plain in the rear; and the general owed his escape to the speed of his charger.)

The general had indeed, when he delivered these orders, made up his mind to relinquish the siege and retire to Alexandria, if he should not find that the Mamelukes were close at hand in the course of the following day. He was now fully aware how false had been the information of his Arab emissaries; and how very little chance remained of reducing Rosetta in the face of an enemy growing daily more numerous and more enterprising. It was his design that his main body retiring from Rosetta, and Macleod's corps from El Hamed, should converge, and unite on the north-eastern shore of Lake Edko; and from thence continue their retreat in one body to Alexandria, But the general had already lingered twenty-four hours too long.

In the night of the 20th a report was brought to Colonel Macleod that a fleet of *djerms* was coming down the Nile with troops; but he disbelieved or disregarded the story. Daylight undeceived him. More than eighty vessels were in sight; two of them square-rigged and carrying heavy guns. A messenger was despatched with the intelligence to Stewart, and the man reached headquarters: but this was the last intercourse. The Turkish horsemen were scouring the plain; no answer could be returned; no small reinforcement could be sent with safety.

The general took his decision instantly. He broke up his camp: packed his sick and wounded, and the best of his stores on camels; and he sent them off under escort of the remaining companies of the 78th and De Roll's; while he kept up a hot fire from his carronades and mortars, until the retreating column had gained some way to the rear. Then destroying his heavy guns, under the bold front presented by seven companies of "the brave 35th regiment," and three which remained of the light battalion, he formed his rear guard of these troops and some forty dragoons, and entrusted to Brigadier Oswald the arduous duty of drawing them off in face of the enemy, and of covering the retreat of the encumbered column which had preceded them.

The Albanians and the Turkish horse sallied forth from every gate: they surrounded Oswald and assailed him with great audacity; while many of their horsemen pressed forward to attack the other division of our little army. Here they were constantly repulsed by the 78th and De Roll's, who were formed in an oblong square around the loaded camels. On the 35th the fight fell more heavily, for the long firearms of the Albanians told upon their ranks: but the steady and well-supported fire of the battalion, the good service of our six-pounders, and the flanking fire of the light companies, baffled every attempt to disorder the retreat. Not a man was left in the enemy's hands.

By one p.m. both the columns arrived on the shores of Lake Edko;

and the Moslemin at length desisted from their attacks. But Stewart looked in vain along the lake for his detachment under Macleod: neither they nor signs of them appeared. It remains for me to relate what information was afterwards gathered of their disasters.

When Macleod observed the approach of the Turkish gunboats, he felt that his exposed post on the bank of the Nile could not be maintained. But instead of following the tenor of his instructions to draw off along the dyke to the right, and gain Lake Edko, be ordered Major Vogelsang to march with his four companies and the six-pounder to a sandhill about three-quarters of a mile in rear of the centre, and there take post, while the colonel rode away himself to the right, with the view of bringing Captain Tarleton's three companies to join Major Mohr's post in the centre; and as he passed the latter, he directed Mohr to withdraw the advanced company from the village of El Hamed.

All these movements appear to have been made in a hasty and disorderly manner. The brave soldiers under Tarleton were hurried down towards the gap; but before they could arrive, large bodies of the Moslem horse had galloped round, both on the right hand and on the left, and the Albanians had rushed into the abandoned village of El Hamed, and from thence had scrambled up the dykes and opened their fire on De Roll's people under Major Mohr. Macleod seems then to have halted Tarleton's three companies, and formed them as two sides of a triangle resting on the dyke, and presenting an angle to the plain, in apprehension of being charged by the cavalry. But our men were here exposed to a destructive fire from the Albanians in their rear, and had to struggle even for the crest of the dyke which had been taken as their support: a great number were here slain. (Colonel Macleod was one of those who fell.)

Mohr's foreigners were at the same time in sad confusion: and a hasty order being given by someone that the whole should fall back on Major Vogelsang's post on the sandhill, the attempt to fall into column was made with such precipitation that the companies became intermingled and fell into the greatest disorder. The fire of the Albanians thickened from the rear, the Turks charged furiously on both the flanks, and only five or six of the British succeeded in reaching the sandhill. But this post afforded no safety; it was good for nothing. It just served to prolong for a short time a hopeless resistance.

Here were 250 or 300 disheartened men, with a single gun, surrounded by several thousands of fierce fellows flushed with success. The rifles of the Albanians thinned our ranks, and the gun they had captured was brought up and opened on the square. On a sudden Vogelsang exclaimed "Cease firing, cease firing!" and he rushed out waving a white handkerchief; the firing ceased, and the Turkish horse instantly charged from every side, cut down the few who yet resisted, and made prisoners of the remainder.

This is a sickening story, and it is useless to conceal the fact that great censure fell at the time on the field officers employed at El Hamed; nor was it undeserved. To General Stewart no blame appears to be due, unless it be for having listened with too credulous an ear to the false reports of the Arabs, and having believed too long the tale of the coming of the Mamelukes. But his plan for the retreat of his detachment seems to have been judicious; and (although the sudden arrival of 6,000 foemen by water had not been foreseen) if the village of El Hamed, in advance of the canal and flanking its dykes, had been maintained obstinately, instead of its being relinquished without a shot, there appears no reason to doubt that five or six hundred brave men might have been brought together on the right, and marching in a square with their two guns, might have traversed the short space which lay between them and Lake Edko, in spite of the Turkish troops unprovided with field artillery. On the 20th and 21st of April 36 officers and 780 men were lost at El Hamed, and of these between four and five hundred were afterwards found to be prisoners, the great majority of them wounded.

It is but doing justice to Mehemet Ali to say, that he shewed much humanity, and even kindness, to the officers and men who had fallen into his hands; and this was, I believe, the first occasion on which a Turkish commander treated his captives as prisoners of war (according to the practice of civilized nations) instead of making them slaves. A few of our men indeed, had been hurried off in the first confusion by individuals who concealed them in the country, and held them as their own slaves, but even these were gradually redeemed by the *pacha*, and restored when the British evacuated Egypt,

To return to General Stewart. Despairing of the arrival even of fugitives from El Hamed, embarrassed by his wounded men, and still threatened by the Turkish horse, he pursued his retreat. He gathered in the detachments and stores which had been posted along his route, and arrived before Alexandria on the 24th of April. The troops had behaved uniformly well when directed by William Stewart himself, or by his able second, John Oswald, whose firmness and good judgment were conspicuous on every occasion. Without taking into account the unhappy detachments at El Hamed, the losses before Rosetta and during the retreat, amounted to eleven men killed, and eight officers and 161 men wounded. Such were the results of this second attempt to avert an imaginary famine from Alexandria.

General Fraser, however, was naturally thrown into great alarm. He had lost nearly one thousand of his soldiers, and the remainder were disheartened by defeats. He had scarcely 4,000 men of all sorts left to defend a very extensive line of ruinous or imperfect works, for which, the engineers reported at least 6,000 to be necessary; and there was now an enemy's army, flushed with success, within thirty miles of his position. Moreover, the general was still undeceived with respect to the means of feeding the population of Alexandria, but his fears on this score were speedily relieved.

Immediately after Stewart's return, it was discovered that there were large stores of rice in the town! and from this time, and thenceforward, the Arabs, invited by good prices, brought provisions constantly and plentifully to the markets of Alexandria. A reinforcement of 2,000 British troops, (21st and 62nd Regiments and detachments), under Major-General Sherbrooke, arrived speedily from Messina: and instead of Fraser's being attacked by Mehemet Ali, that chieftain despatched his *dragoman* (together with Captain Delancey, one of his prisoners), to hold towards the British General a friendly language, tending to overtures for an undisturbed evacuation of his country. So, matters rested till the September following, when the British troops were withdrawn from Alexandria, and the city was quietly restored to the *pacha*, in conformity with the treaty negotiated by Sir Arthur Paget at Constantinople.

We must now turn back to the main body of the British Army, which remained in Sicily, after the departure of the troops detached to Egypt in the first days of March, 1807. Exactly at the same time a letter was received from General Benigsen, with the Russian account of the Battles of Pultusk and Golymin. Marshal Massena had been summoned by Napoleon to Poland. French troops had, it was believed, marched from Naples to the north. The presumption of the Court of Palermo was raised to the highest pitch; and the time appeared to be propitious for an attempt on Italy; but by this unhappy detachment, the strength of the British Army had been reduced to 11,000 men.

Our generals were cautious: they were without orders from home; and they entertained the deepest distrust of the sovereigns at Palermo. Our minister at that court, Mr. Drummond, had by this time adopted a line of conduct the reverse of what he had previously pursued. He had been brought over, as I have already stated, to the queen's views by the flattery and attentions which she lavished on him from the moment that she lost her favourite, Sir Sidney Smith. Drummond now threw his official weight into the scale of the court; adopted all their prejudices against the barons and the municipal rights of Sicily, and he eagerly joined in importuning General Fox to engage in an expedition against Naples. (Mr. Drummond to General Fox, March 19th and April 16th; and the Marchese Circello to Drummond, March 23.)

The refusal of our generals (I use the word "generals," because the advice of Sir John Moore mainly guided the decisions of General Fox—General Fox to Mr. Drummond, April 2nd, 1807), were grounded on their ignorance of the intentions of His Majesty's Ministers; and the belief that their views were at present directed towards the Levant rather than to the shores of Italy; as well as on the conviction that the strength of King Ferdinand's army was grossly exaggerated, and that of the enemy in Naples as grossly underrated. The general says:

> No reliance can be placed on the troops of His Sicilian Majesty, organised and officered as they are at present; nor could the temporary appointment to their command of any individual (however great his own personal merit) counteract the general abuses of the system, the particular influence of the queen's faction, and the evils that would result from having every secret divulged, and every plan betrayed.

The letter goes on to shew, that after leaving garrisons in the fortresses, the number of British troops which could be landed in the kingdom of Naples must be greatly inferior to that which the French could bring into the field.

Thus, the British minister and the general went on bickering through several weeks, though Drummond so far recanted his first assertions as to admit that Ferdinand's army mustered altogether only 6,500 men; and that the enemy in Naples had 10,000 *French*, exclusive of Italians and foreigners. But an accident happened at this time which diminished still farther the British force in Sicily. A mutiny broke out at Malta in a regiment which had been levied for the English service by a Monsieur de Montjoye (under the assumed name of Count Froberg). Nearly a thousand foreigners, of all sorts, had been drawn together by the most criminal and disgraceful means. Inveigled, crimped, pressed, deceived. Most of them were Greeks or wild Albanians.

When brought to Malta, they were placed in a detached fort; confined there, and treated with a brutal severity. The savage men burst into a mad revolt; they seized the fort, hoisted Russian colours, and fired shot and shells upon La Valetta. It became necessary to storm the fort. The British regiments carried it by escalade; slew a great number of its defenders, and overpowered the rest, after they had made a desperate attempt to blow up the magazine of powder. But so great was the alarm created in Malta, that General Fox found it expedient to send an English battalion from Sicily to reinforce the garrison.

On the 28th of April, 1807, Mr. Drummond writes to General Fox:

> I suppose you have heard of the total change of ministers at home. How far this may operate with respect to our position here, I know not. I find the circumstance has given great pleasure to the Court of Palermo.

******

In this letter, Drummond takes a curious review of the principal nobles of Sicily. In explanation of some attempt which he professed to have made for the admission of Prince Belmonte into the Cabinet of Palermo, he writes:

"But who is there in the country, with the exception of Belmonte (of whom I could not think favourably, from the many reports I had heard), who could have been brought into the Government? Pantelleria is our avowed enemy. Cassaro is governed by Brissac; General Acton is hated by the whole country; Butera is shallow and without principles; Sambuca is too old; Trabea is a buffoon; Tomasi is a man of low birth, and with great knowledge is capable of playing any game, and therefore, if he could he useful, he might be dangerous."

******

This intelligence of the overthrow of the Whig Cabinet, and the restoration to power of a party which had opposed and censured the foreign as well as the domestic policy of their predecessors, cast additional doubts over the minds of our generals in Sicily. They looked for a prompt intimation of the views which the new ministers might entertain; and in the meantime, they held their disposable troops in readiness; but they refused to engage without orders in the wild plans which were now ripening in the Councils of Palermo. It was known there that the cautious Cabinet of Vienna had at length ventured to offer its mediation, not only as between France and Russia, but with the professed object of restoring the peace of Europe. It was fully believed that if Napoleon rejected this proposal, the Austrians would seize the advantage which the position of the belligerents in Poland presented, and would throw 100,000 men on the rear of the French Army.

The opportunity certainly was most tempting: but the nerves of the Aulic Council were not equal to so grand a stroke. The Russian Minister at Palermo, M. Tatitscheff, pressed, with an importunity and in a tone of complaint which were hardly decorous, though natural under the circumstances of his sovereign, (Mr. Drummond to General Fox, May 2nd, 1807), that the British troops from Sicily should be poured immediately into the kingdom of Naples: and the queen took the desperate resolution of invading Calabria even without the aid of the English. All the troops she could muster were despatched under the command of the Prince of Hesse to Reggio; while at this very time the people of Messina and the Val Demone, goaded by the exactions and oppressions of the Commissioners of Revenue, were deterred from insurrection against their government only by the presence of the British troops.

At the same moment also arrived the news of our disasters near Rosetta, and General Fox found it necessary to detach 2,000 more of his soldiers to Egypt. Yet still the court persisted. The Prince of Hesse was ordered to move forward. As he advanced, the enemy's detachments retired before him, clearly with the purpose of drawing him to a distance from the coast, till he reached Mileto. There he was attacked by the French in the morning of the 28th of May. His troops were routed, his guns were taken, and the unhappy prince escaped from the field with a few score of his dragoons. The *Masse* as usual kept aloof from the fight; and the behaviour of the Neapolitan troops was dastardly, with the exception of the Samnite regiment under General Nunziante, who held their pursuers at bay, got into the mountain, and made their retreat in pretty good order to Reggio.

The French, however, were not disposed to follow the chase to the Straits of Messina. There were the British ships and the British troops; and with a fair wind they might reach the bay of St. Eufemia in twenty-four hours, and repeat the lesson which had been taught at Maida. Meanwhile, deceived by the falling back of the enemy's outposts on the first advance of the Prince of Hesse, the court, and Mr. Drummond, and M. Tatitscheff were in ecstasies. They fancied that Calabria was re-conquered; and on the 29th of May the Russian diplomate writes imperiously to press for a decision on the part of "*ce commandant en chef des forces Britanniques.*" "*L'Empereur mon auguste maître avait prescrit à M. d'Alopeus d'insister auprès de votre gouvernement afin que les forces de terre et de mer Britanniques eussent ordre de soutenir les operations sur Naples.*" (Mr. Drummond to General Fox, May 30th.)

Now if the conquest of Naples had been a point essential for the general objects of the allied powers, it ought to have been undertaken three months earlier, before 7,000 of our men had been detached so unwisely and uselessly to Alexandria. The attempt might have been made in February with powerful means, and would probably have been crowned with success. But it seems to me doubtful whether success at Naples would have been of much service to the *Czar*, or have disconcerted the plans of Napoleon. It was in the north of Italy that our blow ought to have been struck; and for this great purpose the Cabinet of St. James's ought to have sent us additional troops in the winter.

The opportunity had been lost. Our army in Sicily, now reduced to less than nine thousand men, could hardly have sent forth so many as 5,000 (after providing for the citadel of Messina and the other fortresses); nor would it have been safe to detach even this small number to any considerable distance.

However, the change of ministers at home did produce a change of views with regard to military operations. Not very immediately however, for it was not till two months after Lord Castlereagh had succeeded Mr. Windham in the direction of the War Department, that he opened his views and addressed his instructions to General Fox, nor were these received till the end of June. They certainly evinced more judicious views with regard to military operations, than had been shewn by the preceding ministry. Lord Castlereagh's despatch is of so much importance, that I have given it in the Appendix (Lord Castlereagh to General Fox, May 21st, 1807.—Appendix M) but he wrote under impressions derived from false intelligence with regard to King Ferdinand's paltry forces; and in ignorance both of our having been obliged to detach 2,000 more men to Egypt, and of the dispersion of the Neapolitan troops in Calabria. The Secretary of State holds out no hopes of his sending reinforcements to the Mediterranean though he writes:—

> The strength and efficiency of the corps lately assembled under your orders, having been considerably reduced by the detach-

ment of the troops under the command of General Fraser, it is impossible not to feel how much the power of what remains in Sicily to undertake offensive operations has been impaired.

But Lord Castlereagh directs General Fox's immediate attention to an invasion of Naples in conjunction with King Ferdinand's army; and he imagines that the united forces might be made up, for this purpose, to 20,000 men. He recommends that British garrisons should be left in one or two of the strongest fortresses in Sicily to secure our re-entry into the island, and that General Fox should carry with him as large a proportion as possible of the Neapolitan troops, on account of "the jealousy which has appeared on more than one occasion with respect to our position in Sicily," or in plainer terms, to guard against treachery on the part of the court. His Lordship considers such an expedition under two points of view:

1st, as affording a chance of re-establishing our royal ally permanently in his kingdom of Naples: and 2ndly, as a military operation by which the French Army in the territory of Naples might be destroyed, and a diversion might be effected in favour of our northern allies, by our drawing on the south of Italy the forces which the enemy was assembling in the Frioul and Dalmatia. A discretionary latitude was, however, left by Lord Castlereagh to the British commander with respect to the time of action, to his information as to the strength of the enemy, and a due consideration of the military risk. (General Fox to Mr. Drummond, July 1st.)

These instructions, this knowledge of the views entertained by the Cabinet, could not have reached our general at a more unpropitious moment; but their views thereon and their decisions were communicated to Mr. Drummond without delay. Lord Castlereagh had supposed erroneously that the Neapolitan troops were open to the inspection, and at the orders of General Fox; and also, that their numbers were considerable. Neither the one nor other of these assumptions was the case. The strength of the British Army had been reduced far below Lord Castlereagh's estimate. But still as the wishes of our government were now signified, General Fox desires Mr. Drummond to ascertain whether His Sicilian Majesty will permit his troops to be inspected and mustered by the British commander; and will place them effectually under his orders during a conjoint expedition.

The unity of command would be indispensable. If these points be conceded, the court may be informed that General Fox will be ready to co-operate with a view to offensive operations, reserving to himself a discretion as to the time, manner, and expediency of acting. In point of fact there could not at this time have been collected for an expedition to Naples more than four or five thousand Neapolitans, and little more than that number of effective British soldiers. However, a permission having been obtained from the Court to inspect their troops. Sir John Moore was setting out for Palermo, when on the 10th of July General Fox received orders to resign the command of the army in the Mediterranean.

Moore, a man to whom every officer and soldier looked up with an entire confidence, now assumed the station which his military talents and his distinguished services had richly merited. But he came to the command of our diminished forces just when offensive enterprises on our part were rendered vain by the events of the war in Poland. As yet indeed the disasters of the Russian Armies were unknown in Sicily; and Sir John Moore proceeded to Palermo, in order to ascertain by personal inspection the real strength and condition of the Neapolitan troops; and at the same time to try if, by conciliatory explanations and arguments, he could bring the court to grant him, not the nominal, but the real command of their forces; with the power to reform abuses, remodel and improve their system, and render their regiments efficient for active service.

In the last letter addressed by Lord Castlereagh to General Fox, (14th June), after our losses and difficulties in Egypt had become known to the British Government, instructions had been conveyed for the evacuation of Alexandria. His lordship says:

> It is obvious, that there is no other alternative but to make an option between the evacuation of Egypt, or the abandonment of Sicily. It is impossible that both these objects can be effectually maintained; though both might be lost, as well as the army itself, by improvidently contending against the difficulties which the pursuit of the former object presents.

Before this time ministers, however, had despatched Sir Arthur Paget to Constantinople, to negotiate with the Turks, and if possible, to re-establish that peace which ought never to have been broken. To this Ambassador it appeared to be of great importance that the English should not quit possession of Alexandria while he was treating with the Porte; and in this opinion Lord Collingwood, who was now with his fleet in the Levant, entirely concurred. The admiral writes thus:

We are now the only respectable power in Egypt, the *pacha* fearing us, the *beys* courting us, and the Arabs manifesting their attachment most unequivocally. To shrink from it at this moment would be ruinous to the negotiation. (Lord Collingwood to Sir John Moore, July 19th, 1807.)

Moved by the strong representations of the ambassador and of our illustrious admiral, Sir John Moore determined to suspend the order for withdrawing the British troops from Egypt, though he felt very strongly that their absence crippled his army for offensive movements. At this time, we mustered in Sicily about 9,000 infantry, 400 artillerymen, and 200 dragoons: but so sickly was the season that out of these numbers nearly 1,400 men were in hospital.

The personal negotiations of our new commander at Palermo were received by both the king and queen with civility and a show of friendliness; but while they allowed him to review their troops, they evaded the chief and only important object, that of conceding to him the effectual control over their little army, and the power of rendering it serviceable either for an attempt on Naples, or for the defence of Sicily. (For these transactions, and for Sir J. Moore's view of Mr. Drummond's conduct, see the letters of the former of the 25th and 28th of July, and 19th September, in the Appendix, N. O. and P.)

But Moore's attention was now directed earnestly to the latter duty: for the defeat of the Russians at Friedland, and the armistice of Tilsit were by this time known at Palermo. He saw that England now remained single-handed to contend against the colossal power of Napoleon; that the shores of Calabria, and the Seven Islands, and the port of Toulon might be within a few months swarming with French troops; while Sicily was without organisation or national feeling. The people could not, the Court would not, adopt any effectual measures for its defence. Upon the vigilance of the British fleet and the energy of the British troops rested the only chance of resisting the powerful attacks which were now foreseen.

The peasantry of the island were warmly attached to the English; but they loathed their own government and were without arms or leaders. (A nominal militia had been enrolled some time before; but it was a name, and nothing more.) The monks detested the French; the nobles dreaded them; but the latter were men generally deficient in talents, energy and spirit. In the large towns there was much diversity of feeling; but for the greater part the more intelligent and active-minded citizens bore so deep a hatred to their Neapolitan sovereigns that they would have favoured a French invasion, and afforded their help to rid Sicily of the English, because the English did not rid them of their oppressors.

Before I speak of the measures contemplated by Sir John Moore for the defence of the island, it may not be deemed superfluous that I should give some account of its condition, such as it was in 1807. As quartermaster-general of the army it had been my duty to visit almost every part of Sicily; and to make myself acquainted with its resources, routes, and military positions. Of the statistical details I give an abstract in the Appendix; confining myself at present to the more important subjects of consideration.

Sicily, as I have before stated, may be regarded roughly as a vast triangle; though there is in fact a fourth, but short, face to the westward, from near Mazzara to the Cape of San Vito. The extent of the eastern side, from the Faro of Messina to the point below Cape Passaro, may be set down as nearly 120 miles, or 170 as one follows the routes along the coast. The southern, or south-western, front stretching from Cape Passaro to Mazzara may be reckoned at about 160 miles in a straight line; the western face at between 30 and 40; and the northern front may be accounted as little less than 170 miles; while if we follow the windings and indentations of the coast, the distance may be as much as 250.

Upon every side there are landing-places in abundance for large boats; but very few bays in which a fleet of ships of war could ride in security for a length of time. The gales rise suddenly, and the sea grows quickly dangerous; but storms are rare during the four months of summer. On the eastern coast, the ports of Messina, Agosta, and Syracuse are excellent for line-of-battle ships; and these places were in the hands of the English. The fortifications were respectable and in good condition. Trapani, at the western extremity of the island, was also a fortress; but it was garrisoned by Neapolitans, and its works were in a neglected state. The harbour was small, difficult of access, and of minor importance.

Palermo itself, a rich city with a population of 180,000 souls, stands near upon the shore of a fine bay, wherein line-of-battle ships have good anchorage, and safe in fair weather; but the bay lies open to the prevailing winds from the northward. The city was walled, but could not be considered as fortified; and the extensive shores of the bay were very imperfectly defended by some detached forts and a few sea batteries. The large gulf of San Vito, between Palermo and Trapani, but more particularly the immediate vicinity of the capital, were the points where a danger of attack was most to be apprehended from Toulon, or from Spain. The south side of Sicily was open almost everywhere to a landing in fair weather, and this was chiefly to be feared on the coast between Terranova and Girgenti.

The French were masters of both the shores of the Adriatic, and of the Seven Islands; and from thence a short run would bring them to this defenceless coast. But their passage would be still shorter to Catania; and on the smooth beach between that city and the little River Giarretta, a landing might easily be effected in the calm season. Still more nearly was the north-eastern angle of the island about to be threatened by the large army which the French might now collect without risk in Lower Calabria. In the narrowest part the width of the straits of Messina is less than two miles; at Reggio five or six.

If the danger of invasion had been confined to the latter quarter only, Sir John Moore's task would have been comparatively easy. The preparations and movements of the enemy could be observed; our ships of war and an armed flotilla were there to dispute the passage; and in the triangle of mountains comprehended within the citadel of Messina, the fortified peninsula of Milazzo, and the strong post of Taormina, our general might confidently hope to baffle a French Army very superior in numbers to his own. But what was he to do if, while lying with his five or six thousand British soldiers in this extremity of the island, and watching some twenty thousand on the opposite coast, he were to be startled suddenly by the intelligence that an enemy's army had landed on the southern coast, or had seized upon Palermo: it was in anticipation of such an event that Moore framed his plan of defence.

He looked to prolong the war, not only till the troops from Alexandria could arrive at Syracuse, but even till another army might come to his assistance from England. The fortresses of Messina, Agosta, and Syracuse, nay, even Milazzo, could not be taken without being regularly besieged. The French could be masters of the sea only for a moment: the harbours remained in English hands. Moore took the resolution, if the enemy landed in the south, to march to a particular point in the heart of Sicily, and to act from thence according to the movements and strength of the invaders.

On a huge hill in the centre of the island stands Castro Giovanni, on the site of the ancient Kuna. The situation of this town is very remarkable: the height on which it stands is so lofty, and its sides are so abrupt and precipitous, that one would term it an isolated mountain, did not the nature of (he soil, and the flatness of its top, degrade it into a gigantic hill It stands up from the centre of an elevated plain, which is itself encircled by a range of heights considerably inferior to the colossus which they surround at a distance. (The hill of Castro Giovanni is, however, connected with the mountains to the northward, but by a ridge of much inferior height.) On my first visit to this place I was seized with a fit of military enthusiasm; and in this strain I began my notes:

> Castro Giovanni is to a soldier a miracle of nature. Her hand has here formed a sort of entrenched camp which may he deemed impregnable. So lofty and spacious as to defy equally the effect of shot or shells. Commanding a view of every movement which an enemy could make upon any side. Abundantly supplied with fine water which gushes from every face of the rock, and from the very summit of the mountain. Girded in by a belt of precipitous cliffs totally insurmountable, except in a few spots where very little labour is required to render them equally so; with a fine plain of considerable extent upon the top: and such a quantity of good land on the under falls and at the base of the mountain, covered by the range of guns, as would suffice to feed a numerous garrison. Enjoying a salubrious air, and placed in the midst of a plentiful country.

Such was the place which Sir John Moore determined to make the stronghold of the British Army, and the base of his operations, if an invading enemy should elude our fleets. It was his intention to leave sufficient garrisons in the fortresses on the coast, and to march rapidly with the remainder of his troops, say 5,000 men, to Castro Giovanni, where he might hope to be joined very shortly by an equal number returning from Egypt. To the same stronghold he would have summoned whatever portions of the Neapolitan troops might still hold together, and particularly the cavalry. With ten or twelve thousand men our general could, from this grand position, have commanded the resources of the most fertile districts in Sicily.

The ports of Syracuse and Agosta were within five or six marches: a long time must pass before the French could assemble such armies, or collect such means as to reduce the fortresses, or venture to march into the interior; and if the British Government were serious in their determination to defend Sicily, they would have time enough to send out forces equal to encounter the enemy in the field, and squadrons

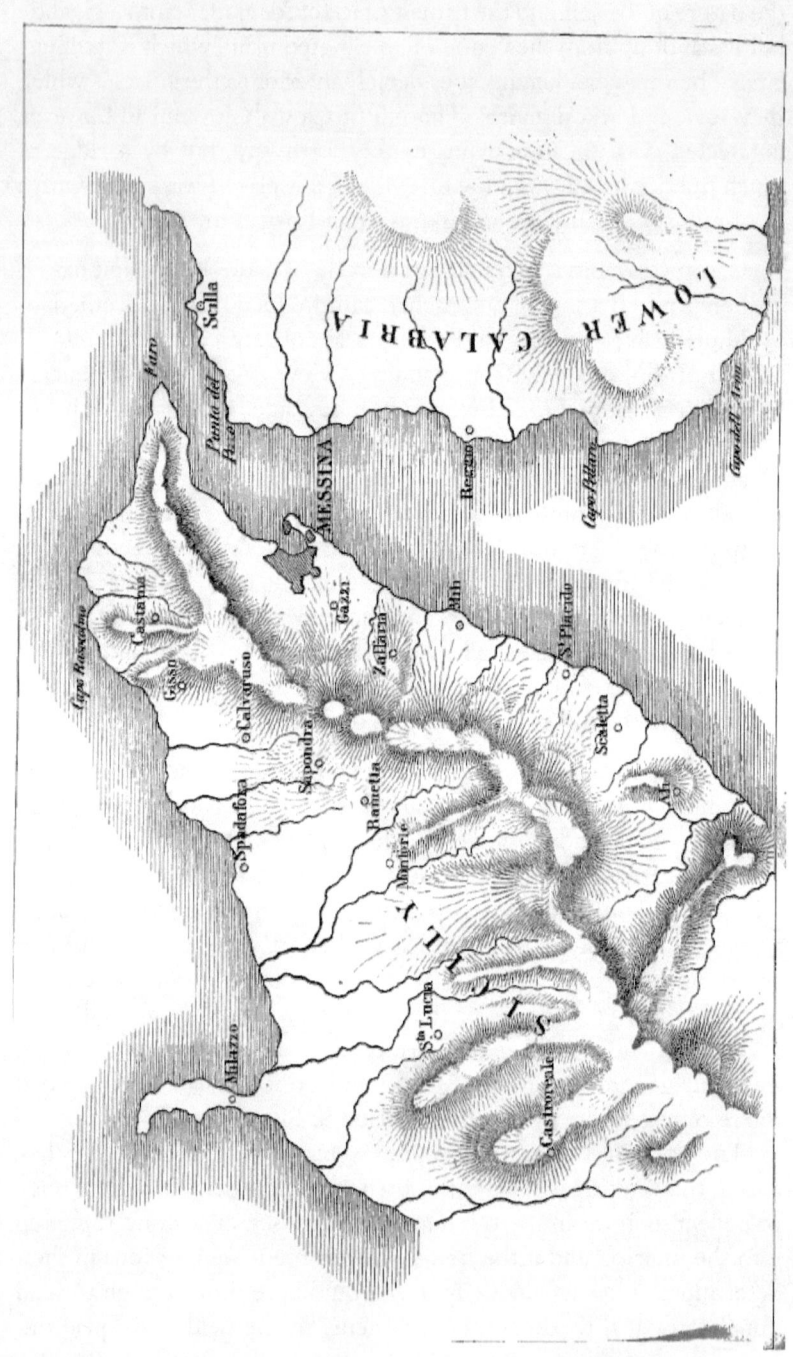

to blockade the coasts and prevent the arrival of reinforcements to the first invaders. Here was the groundwork of a great campaign to be undertaken for a great object, and with many circumstances which were strikingly favourable.

From the moment Sir John Moore returned from Palermo to his headquarters, he applied himself indefatigably to the task of preparing his troops for the sudden movement which might become necessary; and I annex, (Appendix Q), one of the general orders which he issued at this time as a specimen of the system which Moore pursued in the command of an army. Though few in numbers, and deficient in cavalry, the force under his orders was excellent in quality, and "confident against the world in arms."

But the peace of Tilsit, the ostensible alliance of Russia with France, and the humble submission of Austria, had left the mighty genius and the mighty strength of Napoleon so completely free from embarrassment, that it seemed as if he had only to say to his fleets and armies, "Go forth and seize on Sicily," and that his will must be done. Here were eight or ten thousand audacious Englishmen, within two miles of one of the great conqueror's vassal-kingdoms, pretending to resist his power! The 40,000 men whom Marmont had collected round the head of the Adriatic were now disposable; and besides the French vessels at Venice there was in that sea a squadron of Russian ships, which might be used for the conveyance of soldiers, and which Lord Collingwood was watching with great jealousy.

French men-of-war and a large body of troops were ready at Toulon and Genoa; and Spanish ships prepared to join them from Carthagena. Intercepted letters from Joseph Bonaparte spoke quietly, as upon a matter of ordinary business, of the number of French troops which would be required to garrison Sicily, (see Lord Collingwood's correspondence of September and October, 1807), nor could there be a doubt that within a month the enemy's forces would be swarming in Calabria,

At this moment of peril, when the chance of our being able to maintain our dangerous post appeared to be more doubtful than ever, when Moore was looking anxiously for reinforcements from England, a despatch arrived from Lord Castlereagh ordering the general to sail for Gibraltar (where he was to meet farther directions) with 7,500 of our best troops, as soon as the 5,000 men under Fraser should have arrived from Alexandria. The deep concern for the safety of Sicily, which had been a primary object of interest with successive administrations, seemed to have vanished like the impression of a dream. While our enemy was engaged elsewhere, and our army was strong, we were left unemployed: when Napoleon became free to act against us, and able to collect any amount of force for the enterprise, our ablest commander and the flower of our troops were suddenly withdrawn.

I will not pause here to criticise the conduct of military affairs while they were entrusted to the management of Lord Castlereagh. It will be no difficult matter hereafter to exhibit proofs that the measures of successive Cabinets from 1793, to 1811, when the great views and the victorious career of Wellington began to command deference and acquire authority, were vague, crude, and devoid alike of military and political sagacity. My present business is with their proceedings, I cannot call it policy, in the Mediterranean.

I am quite aware that in the Autumn of 1807, the knowledge which our ministers had acquired of the secret articles of the treaty of Tilsit, justified them in anticipating Napoleon at Copenhagen and Lisbon. The great law of self-preservation justified their seizure of the fleets of Denmark and Portugal. But Sicily was in imminent danger, and besides the objection to the withdrawal of troops from thence at such a moment, the length of the voyage to Lisbon, and the uncertainty of the passage of a fleet of transports, ought to have forbidden the idea of securing the Portuguese capital by troops detached from Messina.

In fact. Sir John Moore did not arrive at Gibraltar before the end of November, exactly at which time Junot, with a French Army, in a miserable condition, was drawing nigh to the capital of Portugal. (However, the object of the enemy's march had been frustrated, by the sailing of the Portuguese ships, with the royal family, for Brazil.) At Gibraltar the general received his further orders to proceed to Lisbon, where he was to be joined by General Spencer with 8,000 men from Ireland; and if he found the objects of the British Government attained, with respect to the Portuguese fleet, he was then not to return instantly for the defence of Sicily, but to go on with his troops to England! and to England he went.

General Fraser's troops, returning from Egypt, arrived at Messina before the end of September; and as the men made prisoners by Mehemet all had been liberated, this division proved to be stronger in numbers than had been expected. Sir John Moore sailed a few days afterwards, carrying with him the Guards, 20th, 35th (2nd batt), 52nd, 61st, 78th, and Watteville's regiments. There remained for the defence of Sicily about 6,000 British infantry, 270 dragoons, 400 artillerymen, &c. and 2,100 foreigners. But the unexpected departure of their general with so large a proportion of our best battalions, and the apparent indifference of the British Government as to the fate of Sicily, had cast a gloom over the spirits of those who were left to defend the island.

To the command of these troops Sir John Moore had appointed Major-General Sherbrooke, a man who had won reputation by his gallantry in India, but who was little known to the army at large, he had come to the Mediterranean the preceding year, and the brigade he commanded winced a little under the sharpness of his discipline, while they revenged themselves by comical stories of his rough sayings and impetuous temper. But Sherbrooke was no ordinary man; few officers could bare discharged with better judgment, none with more unwearied activity and zeal, the arduous duties which devolved upon him after Moore's departure.

He was an original. A short, square, hard, little man, with a countenance that told at once the determined fortitude of his nature. Without genius, without education, hot as pepper, and rough in his language, but with a warm heart and generous feelings; true, straightforward, scorning finesse and craft and meanness, and giving vent to his detestation with boiling eagerness, and in the plainest terms. As an officer, full of energy, rousing others to exertion, and indefatigable in his own person.

From the moment Sherbrooke assumed the command of our little army, he applied himself to the improvement of our means of defence. In Colonel Bryce, the chief engineer, he found an able assistant; forts and batteries were formed along the shore of the straits; roads of communication were opened; the fortresses were improved; the discipline of our troops was confirmed by the personal attention of the general, and the activity which prevailed in every quarter revived the spirits and the confidence of our officers. Nor was Sicily less cared for by the British admirals. While Collingwood himself watched the Adriatic, his worthy lieutenant, Thornborough, was in constant observation of the enemy's squadrons in Toulon and Carthagena; but Lord Collingwood's sense of the danger to which this noble island was left exposed was already strong, and he was fully alive to the vices, the follies, and the treacherous tendencies of the Court of Palermo.

It might be supposed that the long-practiced intriguers of that court would have found it no difficult matter to impose on so plain and downright a person as John Sherbrooke; that they could easily deceive and turn to their purposes a man who had never had to do with courts or politics. On the contrary, none of our successive commanders ever baffled them so completely! They could not comprehend a man who told them only what he wanted, and what he thought, without caring whether they were pleased or not. They were always imagining, and perplexing themselves by attempts to discover some hidden designs, or reserved opinions; while in Sherbrooke's nature there was neither concealment nor reserve.

But though the general found little difficulty in his communications with Palermo, he could not feel himself at ease with the Neapolitan authorities in Messina. None of their troops were amongst us; but there was the governor of the place, a cunning old rogue, who had seen much of the world, and leant towards its rascalities. Nauseously civil, and thoroughly false. Hating the English because they took the power of his position out of his hands; fearing the French; mistrusting his own court; and watching for any turn of the wheel which might be of advantage to Governor Guillichini.

Around him were some officials of the lowest description; and a swarm of spies in the pay of the court, who passed backwards and forwards between Calabria and Sicily, without a check or hindrance, many of them being as much in the service of the French as of Queen Caroline. But there was also in Messina an arsenal belonging to King Ferdinand, with guns and ordnance stores, and a division of gunboats; and this important establishment was under the orders of a Neapolitan colonel who was strongly suspected of being in the pay of the enemy. Of this man I shall have more to say by and bye.

Since the peace of Tilsit we had been looking for the arrival of French Armies in Calabria; but to our surprise their troops did not move forward and shew themselves on the coast of the lower province before the close of 1807. The plans of Napoleon were now dilating to so vast a magnitude, that the acquisition of Sicily sank into minor importance; or at least was to be postponed till mightier combinations were matured. The great army which had conquered Russia and dictated peace upon the Niemen, was still required in the North to enforce that peace; to set up the new Duchy of Warsaw, and overawe the Cabinet of Vienna; to drain what was left in Prussia of its remaining resources.

Another army was upon its march from Bayonne, destined to seize on Portugal and form the advanced guard of a greater expedition against Spain. Of the 40,000 men assembled under Marmont at the head of the Adriatic, a large part was now required to carry into effect the secret agreement of Napoleon and Alexander for the partition of Turkey. Albania, the Morea, the Seven Islands, were to be occupied by the French troops. Sometime therefore elapsed before reinforcements could be afforded to King Joseph; and without a great addition to his army, he could not venture to extend his troops to the extremity of Calabria, much less could he risk any attempt on Sicily. At the end of the year, however, the enemy was known to be gathering strength both in the upper and the lower province; General Reynier, who again commanded in the latter, pushed forward his outposts gradually, and before the close of January, 1808, the eagles of Napoleon appeared once more upon the shores opposite to Messina.

At this time the Castle of Reggio was occupied by a weak brigade of Neapolitans. It was contemptible as a fortress; and their government had done little or nothing to improve its defences, in the year and a half which had passed since the Battle of Maida restored it to their hands. Still it could not be taken (unless through treachery or cowardice), by an enemy unprovided with heavy artillery; and the French had none.

The Castle of Scilla, though a very small place, was of more importance. Perched on its peninsular rock it barred the passage of boats along the coast; and while it remained in our hands, the enemy was unable to form batteries, or hold their posts in security along the straits of Messina. Scilla had been occupied by the English from the time of its capture in 1806; and since our prospects had grown dark, much pains had been taken to render the little place as strong as its position would admit, and to provide for the eventual safety of the garrison. The castle was commanded on the land side by the rising slope of the mountains; and in the same direction shelter to sharpshooters was afforded, at a very short distance, by the stone houses of the town.

But the old masonry of the fort was not to be damaged unless by heavy guns; whilst its own artillery swept the beach, the town, and a considerable space around it. Sherbrooke entrusted the defence of Scilla to a man who was every inch a soldier, George Duncan Robertson, major of the 35th Regiment The garrison was composed of four companies detached from regiments in Messina, with a large proportion of artillerymen; and the engineer undertook to construct stairs from the sea, which bathed the promontory, up to the postern of the fort.

With admirable skill they cut steps in the living rock, and formed an easy communication (concealed and covered from an enemy's fire) from the water to the gate of the castle. Constant intercourse was thus secured, unless in stormy weather, between Scilla and the Faro point; and supplies could be thrown in when wanted, or wounded men removed. As we knew that Reynier had no heavy guns, we felt very little uneasiness when we saw his troops gathering in considerable numbers on the coast between Reggio and Scilla, and more particularly near the former town; but we were soon taught what it was to have allies.

On the 30th of January, 1808, in the early morning, General Sherbrooke and I were watching without glasses the movement of three or four of the enemy's battalions, among the gardens and orange orchards on the northerly skirts of Reggio. Presently we observed the four Neapolitan gunboats, which belonged to Messina, pulling across the straits. Sherbrooke's immediate inquiries at the arsenal were answered by the message that the boats bad been ordered over to cannonade those Frenchmen who were exposing themselves so close to the shore. And surely enough the vessels began to fire when they were still some two miles distant from the Calabrian coast.

This did not arouse our suspicions, for such was the common custom of the Neapolitans. But they continued to push on, and to draw near to the French, and such was by no means their custom. Sherbrooke's worst apprehensions were excited; "By ———," cried he, "they are going to desert! Run, run to Captain Handfield, and tell him to try to bring these d———d villains back."

Captain Handfield was the commander of the *Delight* brig-of-war, which was lying moored to the quay of Messina. I ran and found Handfield on deck. In an instant the mooring chain was cast off, every sail let fall; in a few minutes the *Delight* was stretching across the strait under a cloud of canvas. But the "villains" had by this time managed to run the gunboats ashore under a long line of stone walls lined by the French infantry. The latter were going through the form of firing volleys over the heads of the Neapolitan crews, and these again, after discharging their guns, hauled down their colours. By the time the *Delight* arrived near enough to use her carronades, the French soldiers were on board the gunboats.

The brig, owing to the eagerness of her commander to get hold of these vessels and drag them off, ran so close as to be exposed to a deadly fire of musketry from the walls and fences along the shore; poor Handfield, a most gallant and active young seaman, was killed, and two-thirds of his crew fell in a few minutes; the deck of the *Delight* was cleared, and she ran ashore. Then the French soldiers boarded, with the hopes of securing the guns of the English brig, as well as those of the Neapolitans.

But by this time, the *Bittern* sloop-of-war, which was cruising in the straits, had been attracted to the scene of action. Her commander, Captain Downes, stood in; and now began a second fight; the French striving to keep possession of the unfortunate brig; Downes endeavouring to drive them away, and either to get her afloat or destroy her. Short tacks and a heavy cannonade on the one side, a blaze of musketry and lighter guns on the other. But the soldiers on board the brig could not long withstand the shot of the sloop; and after losing many men they scrambled ashore. It was found impossible to float the poor *Delight*, and she was burned. But the French had secured the 24-pounders brought by the gunboats; and with these they were enabled to arm a battery against the old Castle of Reggio.

It was unnecessary to do more; the Neapolitan governor surrendered the next day. If he had stood a few shots, and held out till the next morning, we should have had a fight; for Sherbrooke had determined to land in the night and fall upon Reynier. The relief of Reggio would not have justified the risk; but the heavy guns were objects of vast importance under the circumstances in which we were placed. To recover or to destroy these 24-pounders was our general's aim. Without them the French could not reduce Scilla, nor could they bring their boats along the coast; and establish themselves upon the straits.

However, the mischief was done and was now irremediable, thanks to the treachery of the colonel-*commandant* of the Neapolitan arsenal.

★★★★★★

Sherbrooke repaired to the arsenal after witnessing the loss of the boats, and he apostrophised the *commandant* in nearly these words: "I don't know what your government will do with you. You are not under my command, luckily for you; for if you were, by G— I would try you by a drumhead court-martial, and hang you up within half-an-hour." And Sherbrooke would assuredly have done so.

★★★★★★

Nor did General Reynier lose any time after these means had been placed in his hands. On the 2nd of February he had taken possession of Reggio; by the 4th the serviceable guns from that castle, as well as the 24-pounders from the boats had been transported to Scilla, and brought under cover of the houses within breaching distance; other batteries were armed with howitzers and field-pieces, and the fire of the whole was concentrated upon the fort. Major Robertson and his little garrison defended their post with admirable intelligence and bravery; but the match was too unequal. The French made more than one effort to get round the foot of the rock, and cut off the means of retreat afforded to the English by the steps from the sea: but these attempts cost them dear; their detachments were driven back with heavy loss.

At length after the castle had been pounded during thirteen days, its guns dismounted, and the wall facing the town beaten into ruins, Robertson found it necessary to evacuate the post which he had defended so gallantly. Boats were collected silently in the night; all the wounded who could bear removal were carried off; and company after company descending the steps at the back of the rock embarked with little loss, the rearmost sections keeping up a fire upon the enemy. The brave garrison of Scilla rejoined their comrades at Messina on the 18th of February, leaving a mere ruin to be occupied by the enemy.

The coasting communication was now open to the French, open at least whenever their large boats could evade the vigilance of the English cruisers. But the enemy worked cautiously: his posts were established along the shore from Salerno to Scilla, and armed successively with heavy cannon. As opportunities offered, his little convoys, bringing guns and supplies, ran on from post to post till they reached their destinations.

In this way the French managed to establish themselves solidly on the straits of Messina within a few weeks, and to commence works under cover of which flotillas might be collected for the invasion of Sicily. On our side we laboured strenuously to render our line of coast as strong as we could; and our gun-vessels and armed boats were constantly on the alert to intercept and damage those of the enemy. From England we had advice of approaching reinforcements. This was good, but we were warned also that a general was on his way to supersede Sherbrooke; and this was now considered by the army to be a misfortune.

★★★★★★

Before we part from Sherbrooke, let me record one trait of his mode of administering justice, when martial law was in force in Messina. Our soldiers could seldom resist the constant temptation of cheap wine. In the wine-houses they were riotous and quarrelsome, and apt to treat the Sicilian customers very roughly. The consequence was, that several of our men were stabbed; but it happened very rarely that the stabber was seized on the spot, or could be identified. Every Sicilian carried a long knife; and it was become urgently necessary to stop the deadly use they were making of this weapon.

The general issued a proclamation denouncing death to anyone who should assassinate a British soldier; and most assuredly it was his intention to carry this menace into effect. One morning it was reported to Sherbrooke that a soldier had been killed over night, and that the assassin was taken on the spot. A drumhead court-martial was ordered to assemble immediately, and a gallows to be erected. But in the meantime, the general inquired personally into the circumstances. He found that the drunken soldier had assaulted a Sicilian who was sitting quietly in a wine-house; the latter, in his exasperation, had snatched up a stool, and dealt such a blow as to fracture the aggressor's skull. "Oh, oh!" said Sherbrooke, "this is quite another affair!"

Then turning to the trembling prisoner, he said, "You have killed one of my soldiers, my man; but you have killed him in hot blood, and in a fair fight which he provoked. You had a right to resist; and you did not use your knife; if you had, I would have hanged you. As it is, I set you free; and here is a piece of money to reward you for not having used your knife." This example was not lost upon the Messinese.

★★★★★★

At the end of April 1808, Sir John Stuart arrived at Messina, with higher rank and enlarged powers, to take the chief command on the theatre where his laurels had been won two years before. He brought as his second in command Lord Forbes, a very worthy and good-natured gentleman, who had seen no service but as a captain in the footguards. Troops also came to us in slow succession; but not such troops as had been carried away by Sir John Moore.

The return of Sir John Stuart, Count of Maida, was hailed with delight by the Court of Palermo; and they evinced at once a readiness to communicate cordially with him, which they had withheld from Moore and Sherbrooke.

★★★★★★

General Sherbrooke returned to England on being superseded in the command. He was afterwards at the head of one of Lord Wellington's division at Talavera, and in Portugal; and finally, Governor-General of Canada.

★★★★★★

They even sent some hundreds of their cavalry to the neighbourhood of Messina, and placed them under Stuart's orders; and the queen fondly hoped that she should prevail upon the count to risk a second attack upon the enemy's troops in Calabria. But scarcely had Sir John established himself in his command, when the scene and prospects of the war suddenly changed. The Spanish people had risen in their fury; and from every part of the Peninsula there came pouring in the news of insurrections, and the arming of the principal cities against the French. Cadiz and Carthagena were no longer points from which any danger to Sicily was to be apprehended. Before the end of July, Dupont's army had surrendered to the Spaniards, and Moncey's had been repulsed by the raw levies of Valencia.

The hasty ambition of Queen Caroline was inflamed, and she turned all her schemes for the moment to the object of getting one of her sons accepted as the Regent of Spain. As for the British Army in Sicily, our eyes were straining towards the great held which had opened to us thus surprisingly; and we almost forgot that the French forces in the kingdom of Naples were growing stronger, and that their footing in Calabria was becoming every day more solid, and more dangerous to Sicily.

On the other hand, the Russian fleet, which Lord Collingwood had been long watching with anxiety in the Adriatic, had by this time passed out of the Mediterranean. We were relieved both from the apprehension of Spanish ships doing the bidding of Napoleon from the westward, and of the Muscovites from the east.

There remained only a squadron of French men-of-war in Toulon, and this was carefully observed by Collingwood, who always attended with great interest to the protection of Sicily. He had been lying at Syracuse when the French were attacking Scilla; and foreseeing the probability at that time of the enemy's making an attempt upon the island, the admiral begged the Governor of Syracuse and its dependent district to inform him what were the Sicilian means of defence at his, the governor's, disposal to resist invaders. The answer was:

> Of all sorts of men on the military roll there are above 700, including artillery, invalids, and militia. But they are merely on the roll; for they are unarmed, undisciplined, and without any kind of pay. The only officers are two ensigns. (Lord Collingwood to Mr. Drummond, Feb. 6th, 1808).

Such was indeed the condition of Sicily on every side. From 1805, to 1813, the defence of Sicily was made good by the English fleet, the English Army, and the English money.

✶✶✶✶✶✶

"Why did you not keep Sicily at the peace?" asked a Prussian statesman of me in 1836, "Oh, why I suppose we had jealous neighbours," said I. "Well, and have you not jealous neighbours now?" was his reply.

✶✶✶✶✶✶

At the end of May Lord Collingwood quitted the waters of Sicily, in order to give his close attention to the more urgent concerns of Spain; and we were left nearly destitute of naval aid during several months. Our army, though increased in numbers, was in the summer of 1808, declining in what is called nowadays its morale. There was no longer the hearty good-will and energy of which it bore the stamp under Moore and Sherbrooke; and even the officers of high rank were anxious to leave us. Three of those who had commanded brigades at Maida, Cole, Acland, and Kempt, had before this time returned to England to seek employment in other fields and under other commanders. There grew up grumblings and scoffs amongst our officers; duties were neglected; and the vessel floated along mainly through the former *impetus remorum*.

On his part, Sir John Stuart was uneasy lest he should be ordered positively to transport his troops to Spain, a theatre on which he had no inclination to appear, (Lord Castlereagh to Sir John Stuart, July 29th; conditional); and he seemed for a time disposed to engage in some attempt on the coast of Italy. Pains were taken to ascertain the positions of the enemy's troops, and the condition of their fortresses. Transports were collected at Milazzo, ordnance embarked, and horse-ships fitted up. We learned that five of the French battalions had marched to Upper Italy, and King Joseph's guards for Spain. But our disposable force was small, and we had no ships of war to assist us; though there were many circumstances in the kingdom of Naples at that time to encourage us to make an attempt in that quarter. (The season had been sickly beyond example: in the two months of August and September, 200 of our men died of fevers, and there were 2,700 in the hospitals.)

Meanwhile we overlooked a change which was fraught with serious influence on our position and prospects. The quiet and unpopular Joseph Bonaparte; had been summoned by his mighty brother to Madrid, and in his stead the fiery and impetuous Murat was coming to fill the throne of Naples.

✶✶✶✶✶✶

Colletta in his *Storia di Napoli*, draws admirable portraits of King

Joseph and King Joachim. It was the atrocious conduct of his police which rendered the former odious to the Neapolitans.

******

On his head was to rest the crown of Sicily, if he could drive the British troops out of the island; and the practised and sanguine warrior was not likely to blench before the difficulties of the enterprise.

In the meantime, Sir John Stuart was desirous to keep up some show of offensive designs, and he resolved to increase the garrison of Capri. This little island had been held since 1806, by the Corsican Rangers under Colonel Lowe; and our general now detached the regiment of Malta to augment the garrison; swelling its numbers, but by no means improving its quality. The Corsicans, though there were some amongst them who were hardly to be trusted, were on the whole a brave and well-instructed body of men led by intelligent officers; but the Maltese were of an inferior caste; a few of their officers indeed were British, and their commander, Major Hammill, was a gallant soldier.

But it was an error to accumulate foreigners, and particularly untried and mistrusted men, at an outpost close to the headquarters of an enterprising enemy. Four companies of British with some twelve-pounders, would have made Capri secure; the 700 Maltese occasioned its loss. But in truth, Capri was fancied to be so strong, or rather so difficult of access, that it mattered little what description of soldiers were to make a show along the cliffs, or fire from behind rocks upon the landing-places. And our general was unwilling to detach any of his English infantry to a distance,

Murat had made his entry into Naples on the 6th of September; and on the 25th came his clever and beautiful queen, Caroline Bonaparte. Great rejoicings and festive displays succeeded the arrival of the new sovereigns; and while the thoughts of men in and about the capital were diverted by receptions, and balls, and illuminations, and fireworks, King Joachim was forming and maturing a plan for the surprise of Capri. The sight of that rocky island, as it met his view every morning from his palace windows, galled his audacious spirit. There flew the British flag; and through that point passed the secret correspondence of the Court of Palermo with Naples.

******

This correspondence, which had subsisted since 1806, through Capri and Ponza, was of a very mysterious and doubtful character. The Minister of Police at Naples had certainly been a party to it at one time; and the probability is, that this intercourse was of considerably more advantage to the French than to the queen, who was the directing correspondent at Palermo.

✶✶✶✶✶✶

Quietly and without drawing observation, Murat provided and armed his vessels; while he sent an able officer of engineers (probably the historian Colletta) to hang about Capri in a little fishing-boat, and to mark carefully where it might be possible to effect a landing. The commandant of the island, Colonel Lowe, was completely without suspicion of any design to attack him; and he felt the more secure because there was an English frigate of thirty-two guns cruising in the bay; and no one admitted the idea that Neapolitan small craft would ever venture to face the British pendant.

The small island of Capri is divided by nature into two parts, and the only communication between the two is by means of steps cut in the face of a precipice. On the western and south-western side, the volcanic rocks of Anacapri shoot up to a great height. The coast of this portion of the island is of the most rugged nature: heaps of wild rocks, tumbled together in confused masses, rise irregularly to cliffs of lava and rude terraces, connected by a steep slope with the top of the vast cliffs which overhang Capri "proper." Two narrow landing-places, and but two, are to be found amongst the rocks of Anacapri; and these can be approached by boats only in the calmest weather, for the coast is open to the full swell of the Mediterranean, and a tremendous surf breaks along the rocks when there rises any wind.

In Capri *proper* there are two or three landing-places, one in the petty, narrow port (as it is termed), immediately below the town; and another on a patch of beach, to the northward called the "Marina." Both of these were commanded and well watched, and the rest of the coast of Capri, though less forbidding and less exposed to storms than the other side. Of the island, was too rugged and dangerous for the landing of troops. The little town of Capri was surrounded by a thin wall, such as is used not uncommonly for merely fiscal purposes. Here Colonel Lowe had a few English artillerymen, and his own regiment of Corsican Rangers; but he had detached three companies, and the whole of the Maltese battalion to Anacapri.

Murat, (Colletta, *Storia di Napoli*), after receiving the report of his engineer, determined on making his attempt on the side of Anacapri, despite the rocks and the danger of the sea, and the greater advantage with which the British frigate might engage them in the more open waters. The king selected for his enterprise the flower of his little army; three thousand grenadiers, *chasseurs*, and *voltigeurs*; and he entrusted the command to the ablest of his generals, Lamarque. The show of attack was to be directed by the main bodies of the flotilla against the Marina and the port of Capri, but a few boats were to steal round, and if possible, throw their men ashore in the creeks, and on the rocks of Anacapri.

In the night of the 3rd of October, the French soldiers were embarked, and the expedition sailed, chiefly from Naples, but a smaller division went forth at the same time from Salerno. On the 4th Colonel Lowe found to his surprise that his island was menaced from every side by the enemy's vessels. There were gunboats, and armed *feluccas*, and two small brigs of war, and a *corvette*; and where was His Britannic Majesty's frigate, the *Ambuscade!* Instead of dashing at the enemy, or hanging upon their skirts, or even staying to observe their operations, and wait for opportunities, Captain D'Urban sailed away for Ponza, to apprise the Neapolitan squadron on that station and any English ships he might meet, of the attack on Capri, and to call them to the rescue.

★★★★★★

In the following year Murat's flotilla, having then a frigate of forty guns, a *corvette*, and two brigs, were attacked off Baia by Captain Staines in the *Cyane* (a much smaller ship than the *Ambuscade*), supported by one brig; and they were closely engaged, thrashed, and driven with heavy loss and disgrace into the very port of Naples.

★★★★★★

This hinderance to the enemy's design was thus unexpectedly removed; and the weather and the sea proved as favourable to their objects as they could have desired. They followed their plan without deviation: they cannonaded the landing-places in the lower portion of the island, while Lamarque himself, with Colletta, and some hundreds of *voltigeurs* and light infantry, pursued their way to Anacapri. Unobserved by the Maltese garrison, the leading boats crept silently into one of the little creeks I have mentioned, and threw some eighty or a hundred *voltigeurs* (with the general himself) upon the rocks. These men scrambled quietly, and still undetected, up the cliffs; and extending themselves widely, they concealed and sheltered themselves behind masses of rock, in order to cover the landing of their comrades.

At last the purblind Maltese found out that an enemy had landed, and they swarmed hastily to the edge of the terrace above, and fired at the rocks behind which the French lay ensconced, and from which the sharp-shooting of the latter told with effect on the exposed line of red-coats. While this was going on, four or five hundred more of the enemy had made good their landing; and these soon climbed the cliffs, and joined their adventurous general. Still it was not an easy matter to scale the rest of this rugged precipice in the face of an enemy: the position of the French was becoming critical; the sea was rising, and the approach of boats was interrupted by the surf.

Lamarque lay quiet during the rest of the day; and the night came to his rescue; for it proved fine and calm, and a brilliant moon exposed the Maltese sentinels, and watching-parties, to the shots of their enemies lying darkly among the rocks. While this sharpshooting was carried on, the French general formed the rest of his men in two loose columns, one on each extremity of the line he occupied; and both scrambled up, as rapidly as they could, to the rocky terrace above.

Appearing at once on the right and on the left, pouring in their volleys, and charging, with loud shouts and rattling drums, they encountered only one random fire from the dismayed Maltese, who fled in every direction. Major Hammill was killed, and the rout was complete. The French rested on their arms till day; but during the night there occurred an incident which is worth recording, because it shews what may be done by presence of mind and an enterprising spirit.

Three companies of the Corsican Rangers, under Captain Church, had been detached to Anacapri by Colonel Lowe. (Captain Church later Sir Richard Church; and, after the time of which I write, well known in high commands both in the army of Naples and that of Greece), When the French scaled the cliffs and routed the Maltese, these companies were separately occupied in watching paths away upon the flanks; nor do they appear to have been noticed by the enemy. Two of them indeed drew off through the rocks and effected their retreat unobserved. But the success of the French attack was painfully evident to Captain Church, who soon found that the line of retreat for his own company was intercepted.

But finding, also, that the dark uniforms and brown barrels of his Rangers had served to conceal them from notice, he formed a daring plan, and acted upon it with success. Having lain in silence till the moon went down, he then led his Corsicans amongst the rocks to the rear of the enemy's position on the terrace, so as to gain the line by which they had mounted from the sea. Turning here, he ascended the cliffs, and conducted his men through the left of the enemy's line.

When challenged by the French sentinels, the Corsicans officers answered that they had just landed from Naples; and that more of their men were below, trying to get ashore. (Murat had a regiment of Corsican sharp-shooters then in his service; and their countrymen well knew their numbers and designation.) They were allowed to pass, unmolested, through the slumbering enemy; and Church, making his way to the head of the steps down the precipice (which the French had not yet discovered), led his Rangers by that difficult, and in the darkness, very dangerous, passage to Capri, without the loss of a man.

When the sun rose, the enemy found that many, of the fugitive Maltese had taken refuge in their barracks, a rude building which was called a fort; and here they laid down their arms on being summoned. The French likewise discovered and occupied the steps in the cliff. The weather continued as favourable as possible for the assailants, nor did any men-of-war make their appearance. In the course of the 5th of October, the rest of the French troops made good their landing at the same dangerous and difficult little spot where General Lamarque had so boldly thrown himself on shore. Some field-artillery was likewise disembarked, with a small proportion of ammunition and provisions.

All these things had to be hoisted up the rugged cliffs; and, when they had reached the summit of Anacapri, to be lowered down the great precipice to the level of Capri *proper*. In the meanwhile, the French troops invested the town, and prepared batteries for the reception of their light guns. A summons to Colonel Lowe to capitulate, was answered by a refusal By the 7th, the batteries, armed with six or eight pounders, opened upon Capri: the shot went through the slight wall of the town without bringing it down; there was much of sharp-shooting on both sides; but on the morning of the 7th, English and Neapolitan vessels of war came in sight, and the enemy's flotilla took refuge in Castellamare and Naples.

The fire from the ships annoyed and interrupted the puny batteries of the French, and kept, open the communication between the town and the port. Here, then, was General Lamarque, with 3,000 picked troops, a very few field-pieces, and a scanty supply of ammunition, cut off from communication, and without the hope of succour or the means of retreat. He had to expect the arrival of English troops from Sicily; and the only chance of saving his division depended on his being able to reduce the town of Capri garrisoned by 700 men, before a relieving army could arrive. But his means of attack were very slender; his guns light; his supply of shot small. To make a breach was Lamarque's object; but even his eight-pounders sent their shot through the flimsy wall, making holes without shaking it; and he did not care to draw too near, because the English had four ship carronades, 32-pounders, though they did not venture to fire very often, because the carriages were rotten.

On the other hand. Colonel Lowe had managed to despatch a boat in the night of the fourth, which threaded its way through the French flotilla, and reached Messina. The town of Capri was a poor place to defend, but Lowe was sure that every effort would be made for his relief. Every effort *was* made, and without one hour's delay; but a fatality hung over the whole of these occurrences. The singularly calm weather which had enabled the enemy to land on Anacapri, singular in the season of the equinox, was suddenly followed by a succession of furious storms. The transports which were despatched by Sir John Stuart, as fast as each vessel could be got ready, and without waiting for convoy, were tossed about for ten days without being able to reach Capri.

✶✶✶✶✶✶

The first transport which, sailed, carried gunners, ordnance, engineers, officers, and tools; for which Colonel Lowe had written expressly. This vessel was not many leagues from Capri, when she met the tempest. The commanding officer was attacked by brain fever, brought on by extreme sea-sickness. He insisted on their putting back to Messina; and the master obeyed. If she had kept the sea, the island would have been saved.

✶✶✶✶✶✶

Some of them were driven back to Sicily; nor was it till the night of the 17th of October, that a single transport with 300 men arrived. But she came too late, a capitulation had been signed a few hours before. Colonel Lowe (besieged during seven days) finding his ammunition and provisions nearly exhausted, fearing that his advice-boat had been intercepted, and despairing of succour, had surrendered Capri, under condition of withdrawing his garrison to Sicily.

Success is held to justify military enterprises; but the rashness of Murat's attempt on Capri is hardly to be justified by the result. It was only by the combination of the most improbable circumstances that success was rendered possible; and a failure would have been attended with the loss of a large body of his best troops, whom the new king could ill have spared. Let us just recall these improbable circumstances. It was very improbable that a British frigate should quit her station, and allow an enemy's flotilla to act without molestation, how and where they chose.

It was very improbable at that season that the weather should continue so calm during three consecutive days as to admit of the landing of 3,000 men, with artillery and stores, in the rude opening in the rocks of Anacapri. It was improbable that a regiment wearing the British uniform should fail to defend a cliff of the most rugged description against an enemy inferior in numbers. Nor was it probable that during ten days it should have proved impracticable for English ships to make the passage from Sicily to Capri. However, King Joachim did succeed, and great was his exultation.

Great, also, was the effect which this startling blow produced in Sicily. A panic appeared to seize on all classes; and an impression of the superiority of the French arms, and of the new king's military talents, fastened its hold on the minds of men, and seriously weakened their confidence in the power of the English to protect them. Capri was in reality of little value: it merely afforded us the means of hearing what the enemy was doing in Italy; but it locked up one of our regiments, and there had been times when we could ill spare 700 men from Sicily. Still the loss of so strong a post threw discredit on our arms, and awakened a distrust of our foreign corps; while it removed from the eyes of the Neapolitans a perpetual memorandum of their impotence at sea, and excited in them a high confidence in the military skill and fortune of their new sovereign.

Murat, indeed, exerted himself to the utmost to become popular with all classes, (Colletta, *Storia di Napoli, lib. 7*); he undertook a revisal and reform of the laws; he broke up the inquisitorial and sanguinary system of police, which had rendered King Joseph particularly obnoxious; and he applied his attention earnestly to the discharge of the long arrears of pay which were due to his troops. In this last object Joachim succeeded but partially: he paid, indeed, a part of this heavy debt; and he bade his soldiers look to the spoils of Sicily for the remainder.

After the taking of Capri, Murat pushed his troops southwards in considerable numbers; and he used active exertions to draw more service from the natives of his dominions than his predecessor had done. About 4,000 picked Neapolitans were incorporated in his Guards and in French regiments; and two battalions, to which he gave the name of *Veliti*, were formed of young men of a higher class and more easy circumstances, who had been exposed in the troubled times to the persecution of the *Masse* and brigands of the provinces, and who were now inclined to take service and revenge. (It was not till the end of

1809, that Murat ventured to introduce the conscription; and from that measure we may date the beginning of his unpopularity.)

In the month of November, the returns of King Joachim's army shewed an aggregate force of between forty and fifty thousand men, of whom twenty-three thousand were French: and a large proportion of the best troops, particularly French regiments, were now gathering in the two Calabrias. At the same time Murat wisely revoked the decree of Joseph Bonaparte, which had long held these provinces under martial law, and which had kept them under a severe oppression, and in a state of constant irritation. All the notorious leaders of the plundering bands had fled into Sicily, and many hundreds of the Calabrese peasantry who had committed themselves by taking arms against the French had followed their example.

★★★★★★

Out of these starving fugitives the English general began, towards the close of the winter, to form a corps of sharpshooters under British officers. But Sir John Stuart would not admit any of the *Capimasse* (the fellows who had commanded the insurgents in their own country); nor any men who were suspected of having been concerned in murders or outrages. Still they were a wild set at the beginning: nor was it till after two or three of them had been hanged for plundering at Ischia, that they were brought under good control. Their numbers were afterwards much increased by recruits from Calabria, and they became in the succeeding years a useful corps.

★★★★★★

Whether Murat entertained at this time any serious design of attacking Sicily may be doubted; but he made the show of assailing us, and we could not forget that he was a venturous warrior. However, this representative of Napoleon must have been aware of the preparations for war in Austria, and of the probability that a large proportion of his best troops might be suddenly summoned to march northwards. In fact, this call came upon Murat before the end of December, and in the course of January, 1809, 4,000 infantry and 1,000 *chasseurs-à-cheval* (all French) had moved towards Verona.

★★★★★★

On the other hand, conscripts arrived from France to nearly the same amount as to numbers; but in the month of March the drain was renewed, and seven battalions of French and two of Swiss marched for Upper Italy. These troops were drawn from the Calabrias, where they had been, till March, thirteen or fourteen thousand of the enemy's best troops.

******

On the side of the English there was a want of early information, and a clashing between the conditional orders from our government at home, and the inclination of our general. The British Cabinet had been earnestly desirous that Sir John Stuart should lead or detach troops to act upon the coast of Catalonia in the autumn of 1808; and Lord Collingwood, who was attending anxiously to the course of affairs in that quarter, supported the views of our ministers by his own opinions and suggestions. But Stuart was still reluctant; and, unfortunately, the panic which seized on the Sicilians after the loss of Capri, afforded him very plausible grounds for the delay which he desired. Now the month of November was the crisis of the war in Catalonia.

The French in that quarter were neither, strong nor confident. St. Cyr, who had just been appointed to the command of their army, foresaw the difficulties which he was expected to surmount. His great objects were to relieve Barcelona, where provisions and powder were running short; and, to lay foundations for the reduction of Gerona. But to escort a vast convoy to Barcelona was no easy task; and St. Cyr found it necessary to commence operations by laying siege to the fort of Rosas. With the important aid of British seamen this place held out till the beginning of December; and during an entire month it would have been in the power of an English Army to have landed at Palamos or Arens del Mar, and have manned the defiles which led on Barcelona, even if the fame of their arrival had failed to raise the siege of Rosas.

******

Again, in June 1809, the landing on the coast of a British corps (of half the numbers whose time was idled away at Ischia), must have produced very important effects, while the immortal Alvarez was holding the French Army at bay under the walls of Gerona.

******

But it must be admitted that Sir J. Stuart could not in prudence have ventured to detach at that time more than five or six thousand men to so distant an object. And it must be added, that he had not a general officer above the rank of brigadier, to whom such a service could have been entrusted with confidence.

Before the French began to move towards the north of Italy, Rear-

Admiral Martin had been detached, with three line-of-battle ships to Palermo by Lord Collingwood, for the special purpose of aiding in the defence of Sicily; and we no longer looked to the sea with doubt and apprehension.

Though Murat had stamped his government with the impress of that prompt energy which appeared to be his own characteristic; though every preparation seemed to be in progress for an invasion of Sicily; though boats were built and collected, seafaring men enrolled, and columns of troops displayed upon the coasts, still there were good grounds for believing that there could be no real purpose of engaging the French Army in so serious an enterprise under the actual circumstances of Europe.

Early in December the Court of Palermo had received such advices from Vienna as left little doubt of the resolution to renew the war, at which the Imperial Cabinet had arrived; and in February Austrian, officers, duly accredited, passed Malta on their way to London. But in the meantime, as the panic, excited by the taking of Capri, had not subsided amongst the Sicilians two months afterwards, and the public feeling in all the towns was as bad as possible, Sir John Stuart was willing to try whether the king, or the barons, or the people, could be brought by British help and encouragement, to make any serious exertion for the defence of their island.

There had been a pompous scheme put forward by the Court early in 1808 for the levy of a volunteer army to the amount of 40,000 men. The real design of this project was to throw dust into the eyes of the British minister; and to buy the support of certain influential barons, by giving them local patronage and the means of jobbing. Of course, no volunteers made their appearance; and if they had, the government possessed neither the means of paying nor of arming them. At this time then Sir John Stuart wrung from the court, though with great difficulty, an order for embodying two battalions of these supposed volunteers, one at Agosta, the other at Milazzo. Each was to consist of about 500 men; and the English general undertook to pay them and to supply them with arms and accoutrements.

Now let us see the result of this experiment. Of the Agosta battalion not a single man was produced! But at Milazzo, by crimping and all sorts of discreditable means, 380 men were brought together. Such was their voluntary ardour that the officers found it necessary to place them immediately in confinement: and about ninety of them being locked into a house, they tore off the roof, and betook themselves to the mountains. A few days afterwards the colonel found it expedient to discharge the remainder of his "volunteers;" and thus ended the only attempt to form a national army for the defence of Sicily.

Thus, then wore away the winter; but in March, 1809, we knew with certainty that war between France and Austria was close at hand. Not only was a proportion of the enemy's best troops despatched to the north, but his batteries along the shores of Calabria were disarmed, and his gunboats and transport vessels were withdrawn to Naples. At the same time Count de la Tour, a general officer in the Imperial service, arrived in Sicily, commissioned to make known to the British commander the plans which Austria had in view, with regard to the war in Italy, and to solicit our active co-operation.

It was designed that the Archduke John should cross the Isonzo before the middle of April, and march rapidly upon the Adige: while a detachment embarking at the head of the Adriatic, under the protection of the British squadron in that quarter, should menace the coast between Venice and Rimini, and act according to circumstances. But the most remarkable part of the information brought by the Count de la Tour was this; that Austria was in correspondence with the *patriotti* of Italy; and she professed her readiness to afford them her aid not only in expelling the French, but in setting up a constitutional and independent kingdom!

The emperor at the same time could not help recommending, that one of his archdukes should be the constitutional and independent king. Whether such a correspondence was serious and in good faith on either part, and whether the scheme would have ripened if the Austrian arms had been successful, can never be known; but it is certain that there was at this time a fermenting spirit at work in all parts of Italy, and a very general desire to be rid of their French masters.

With regard to our own part in the play, it was obviously our best policy (and such was the earnest desire of Austria) that we should strike our blow as nearly as possible at the time when our Imperial ally should be making his main effort. (The *Memoir* presented by Count de la Tour on the part of the Austrian Government, ended with these words: "*Toute diversion est utile; le moment presse; et c'est le dernier.*") But it was less easy to decide as to place than as to time, hampered as we were by the necessity of keeping a sure hold of Sicily. The Austrians naturally desired that we should come as near to their army as possible, so that our movements might operate more immediately as a diversion in their favour: but Murat had still nearly 30,000 men in the kingdom of Naples (though not one half of them were French); and there was a weak division, under General Miollis in the Roman States.

On our side there was a lamentably large proportion of foreign soldiers, and as I have said before, a lamentable lack of general officers in whose abilities or experience any confidence could be placed. Sir J, Stuart could not have ventured to carry to the coast of Tuscany at this time more than seven or eight thousand men: while, if he began his work nearer home, he had the power of bringing to bear on King Joachim some 12,000 of our own, and 6,000 of the Neapolitan troops.

✶✶✶✶✶✶

To these, seven or eight thousand, perhaps, might have been added a couple of thousand Sardinians (good troops) from Cagliari; but still these would have been too few to raise and maintain a wide and lasting war, unless Leghorn could have been carried by a *coup de main*; and of this there seemed little probability. Still it is to be noted that Lord Collingwood was desirous we should go to the coast of Tuscany.

✶✶✶✶✶✶

It seemed therefore to be our best plan to strike quickly and sharply at the divisions which Murat still kept of necessity in the provinces distant from his capital; to reduce his strength, damage his reputation, and cripple his means as much as possible; and then to menace Naples itself; but, without lingering there, to pass rapidly on and strike a blow at Rome, or even farther to the north. We might feel at our ease about Sicily, when all the enemy's troops should have been rolled back upon Naples and Gaeta. However, the main point was promptitude in acting. Everything was ready on our part: the transports were ready for sea, guns and ammunition were on board, and our troops quartered close to the places where they were to embark. But our general could not make up his mind as to what he would attempt, or how, or where, or when he would try his fortune. The French held small garrisons in the castles of Reggio and Scilla, and a chain of posts up to Mileto and Monteleone, where they were believed to have three or four thousand men.

In Upper Calabria, the Principato and Basilicata they had five or six thousand more, widely scattered to keep down insurrections, but ready to march on the first intelligence of our being in motion. Their positions, however, were becoming uneasy; insurgents were shewing themselves and gathering strength in the Basilicata and Puglia; and others, quickened by the exploits of our seamen along the coast of the Adriatic, were up and daring in the march of Ancona, (Lord Collingwood to Admiral Sotheby, June 30, 1809), and across the Apennines even to Arezzo. Sir John Stuart appeared at times disposed to strike at least at the enemy in Calabria; but he could never make up his mind. He dawdled and fretted in his quarters; issued no orders, nor even looked at the troops. The spirit of discontent and even of contempt, to which I have before alluded, became every day more general and more mischievous in the army.

And thus passed away in worse than idleness the important month of April. Then we were roused from our sulky languor by repeated salvoes from the cannon of Scilla and Reggio; and by the French accounts of their victories at Eckmuhl and Ratisbon.

These events gave a new and a more dangerous turn to the spirit by which very many of our officers, including some of the highest rank were infected. They had persuaded themselves already that Sir John Stuart was incompetent for the command of an army on active service; and now they decided amongst themselves that it would be madness to go forth on an expedition, since our Allies had been defeated on the Danube.

But just before this period, Stuart had communicated to Lord Collingwood a small design which he had been nursing, of sailing to Ischia, taking possession of that island, and from thence threatening the city of Naples. The admiral answered frankly that he did not see that such an expedition could answer any useful purpose; but the general nevertheless did not relinquish his little project, in which he was encouraged by the Court of Palermo. The preparations for an expedition therefore went forward, and the cabal grew furious. The most unbecoming language was known to be current, and at length Sir J. Stuart, who had long avoided conversation with his adjutant-general, James Campbell, or myself, suddenly sent for me. I found him extremely agitated, and he poured forth his complaints apparently with full confidence.

He told me that a general officer had come to him, seemingly as the spokesman of several others, and had held to him a language of remonstrance and censure so strong and unbecoming, as to lead him to apprehend an open resistance to his authority, and a disobedience of his commands, if he should order the troops to embark! At Sir John's desire Campbell and I bestirred ourselves to ascertain the extent of the mischief: and we soon found out that though the spirit was bad, and the language in common use was indefensible, there was no danger of an open mutiny. Under the circumstances, however, the best thing to be done was to disperse the caballers, to get the troops on board their ships, and to sail away from Sicily.

The fleet which issued forth from the anchorage of Milazzo made a splendid show. It was a great armada. Innumerable vessels of all descriptions, convoyed by three ships of the line, and some frigates and brigs of war, covered the blue sea from the Lipari Islands to the coast of Calabria. Nearly 13,000 soldiers were embarked in the transports; and in outward seeming we might have vied with the proudest armaments which had carried the standards of England to fields of glory.

******

For a detail of our troops, see the Appendix. We carried 1,000 mounted dragoons, and above 400 artillerymen; 5,200 British infantry, 3,600 Germans and Swiss, 1,000 of our Corsicans and Calabrese, and General Nunziante's brigade of Neapolitan infantry, by no means bad soldiers, and led by a brave and earnest officer. We had good commanders of brigades; Oswald, Lumley, Airy, Honstedt, Hinuber.

******

But our general had done with fields of glory.

The movement of the fleet began on the 11th June, but the wind was light and unfavourable, and darkness fell before the whole of the vessels had cleared the bay. Early in the morning of the 12th the transports which had on board six companies of the 10th regiment and the *Chasseurs Britanniques*, parted company, and passed through the Faro of Messina, according to a plan which had been previously concerted for an attack on the Castle of Scilla.

******

The first purpose of this detachment was to afford greater security to Messina in case the French should make a dash at the town. Afterwards, it was to dismantle the enemy's batteries, and attack Scilla. So perfectly confident was Stuart of the success of this episode, that in making his report to the Secretary of State a fortnight afterwards, he says, "our appearance on the coast of Calabria had the effect of inducing the body of the enemy stationed in that province to abandon, for the purpose of immediate concentration, the greater part of their posts along the shore; when those upon the line opposite Messina were seized and disarmed by a corps under Lieut.-Colonel Smith, who had been detached." &c. (Sir John Stuart to Viscount Castlereagh, Ischia, July 5th, 1809.) Before Sir John wrote this official despatch. Smith had been obliged to fly to Messina.

✳✳✳✳✳✳

Large boats having heavy ordnance and engineer's stores on board were lying ready at Messina, and a part of the 21st regiment were prepared to join in this attempt, which was placed under the command of Colonel Haviland Smith. To what took place in this quarter I will return, after narrating the progress of the grand expedition. But it may be convenient to mention here what were the calculations of our commander with regard to the enemy's troops which remained in Calabria. It was known that General Partonneaux was still about Monteleone with four or five thousand men, and some civic guards. But Stuart expected too confidently that when his armament should be seen passing slowly along the coast of Calabria, the French would immediately draw to the northward from a fear of being cut off.

This, however, did not happen. Partonneaux held his ground, and we went on our way in ignorance; for though we held communication with the coast, the mass, who were again appearing in armed bands, always deceived us as to the numbers and stations of the enemy.

If it was Sir John Stuart's desire only to make a grand display, the weather certainly favoured him to the utmost. Day after day we floated on the still blue sea, with scarcely a breeze to help us on our way. Off Amantea our great fleet was joined by nearly a hundred more vessels, bringing Prince Leopold, and all the troops that could be sent forth from Palermo; the whole under the command of General Bourcard.

This officer immediately received Sir John Stuart's instructions to make a show of landing near Policastro, while the English expedition should proceed as directly as the calms and variable breezes would permit, to the Bay of Naples. But it was not till late on the thirteenth day that we came to anchor between Ischia and the mainland behind Baia. It was, indeed, high time; for our horses were beginning to suffer severely from the heat of the crowded vessels, and the lack of water, which was nearly exhausted. Without loss of time we reconnoitred the places of landing on Procida as well as Ischia; and we found the appearance of the batteries more formidable than we had expected. However, there was now no choice, and orders were issued for a debarkation at daybreak on the eastern side of Ischia.

After midnight the launches of our transports, having on board two battalions of light infantry, the 81st regiment, and the Corsican Rangers, assembled under the stern of H.M.S. *Spartiate*, 74 guns, the captain of which, Sir Francis Laforey, was appointed to lead and regulate the process of landing. The troops were under the command of Major-General MacFarlane and Brigadier Lumley. The *Warrior*, 74, the *Success* frigate, and a swarm of English and Sicilian gunboats were prepared to engage the enemy's batteries, and cover the approach of the troops; but the collecting and setting in order of the boats during the darkness, the heaviness of the launches, (see note following), and the want of power in the skiffs selected to tow them, occasioned so much delay that when the day broke on the 25th of June, the flotilla was still nearly a league from the shore.

★★★★★★

Although the British Army in the Mediterranean had been from the first destined to various services, all involving the chance of debarking in face of an enemy, no flat-bottomed, boats, or light craft fit for such services, had been provided by our successive governments. No expedition of troops by sea ought to be without such boats.

★★★★★★

However, the men-of-war and gunboats set to their work as soon as there was sufficient light to engage the batteries. The enemy made but a poor return, and his fire was shortly silenced. Our light infantry landed, and scrambling up the rocky banks they encountered as paltry a resistance as that which had been offered by the batteries. Though the enemy went off precipitately they left about one hundred and eighty prisoners in Lumley's hands, while on our part not a man was hurt. The landing of two brigades was effected without farther impediment; and a summons was sent in the evening to General Colonna, who held command in the Castle of Ischia. On his refusing to capitulate, we took measures immediately to bring some heavy guns on shore. But in the meantime, the moment our landing in Ischia was secured, a summons had been despatched to the Governor of Procida, requiring his surrender.

On the preceding evening King Joachim had come in person to the Punta di Miseno, and had made a strenuous effort to throw a reinforcement into Procida. About 130 men got across in the night, but nearly as many more were intercepted and captured on their way; and amongst these prisoners was included very fortunately the colonel whom Murat had sent to assume the command of the citadel.

This fort was so strong that it might have given us a good deal of trouble, if it had been defended with resolution; but the garrison was weak and ill composed; and the actual governor was a wretched old

Neapolitan, who knew nothing of war, and felt nothing of duty. Some shots from the *Cyane* and a few shells from the mortar-boats had already frightened him out of his wits, and he was ready to surrender the moment our summons was presented. Some of his officers however demurred; and while the hesitation lasted, the soldiers mutinied, broke open the stores, maddened themselves with brandy, and were on the point of committing every sort of atrocity, when General Oswald determined to arrest the mischief by landing his grenadiers without waiting for a capitulation.

******

The garrison consisted of about 500 men, partly invalids, but principally composed of the regiment of Isembourg, a corps formed out of foreign deserters and prisoners of war, Russians, Sclavonians, and what not.

******

He entered the fort, disarmed the mutineers, and saved the officers from having their throats cut. In the meantime, however, so alert had the people of Procida been, when the magazines were thrown open, that we found scarcely any provisions left, out of the stores for 1,500 men which Murat had deposited therein. Thus, in less than twenty-four hours were the British in possession of both the islands, excepting the old Castle of Ischia.

The night of the 25th of June, however, did not pass in quiet. Our shipping had been anchored between the islands and the main land, but nearer to the latter, from which they were distant less than a league. They stretched nearly two miles to the northward, and parallel to that part of the coast, which, skirted by swamps and thickets, is called the Fusaro. The passage between Baia and Procida was watched by the *Cyane* sloop of war, and several of our gunboats. The line-of-battle ships were lying under the high land of Ischia; and the vessels opposite to the Fusaro were almost entirely transports.

At three in the morning of the 26th, I was roused by a Neapolitan boatman, who told me that he had discerned nearly thirty of the enemy's gunboats stealing between our transports and the shore, and holding a course towards Cape Miseno. The intelligence was strange, but it was true. Murat had worked successfully to form a powerful flotilla. But when threatened by an invasion from Sicily, and uncertain as to the point where we might strike our blow, he sent one-half of his vessels to Gaeta to strengthen the means of that fortress, about which he seems to have felt much jealousy.

But when we pounced unexpectedly on Ischia and Procida, and our designs appeared to point at the capital itself, the warrior-king became anxious to recover the help of the stout gun-vessels of which he had unwarily deprived himself. The position of our great fleet seemed to cut them off from Naples; they could have no chance of making the passage in the day-time; and the nights were at their shortest. No attempt, however, was too hazardous for the spirit of Joachim Murat. He ordered his flotilla to start from Gaeta, where no English cruiser was then stationed, to creep close along the shore, and passing within the British shipping in perfect silence, to double, if possible, the Cape of Miseno, (the island and batteries of Procida were still in the enemy's hands when these orders were given); while the calm which always prevailed towards day-break, would prevent our ships of war from working. In the night the king came in person to the seacoast, with reinforcements for his batteries, and light artillery to work along the beach.

As soon as I had heard the fisherman's story, the alarm was raised. The *Volage* tried in vain to get under way: there was not a breath of air. Only six light gunboats, belonging to our flotilla, were at hand; but these commanded by Lieutenant Cameron, of the 21st Regiment, pushed for the shore. The first break of dawn shewed up thirty-four of the enemy's vessels, which had already passed the body of our fleets and were pulling vigorously for the Cape, Notwithstanding this disparity of force Cameron closed with them at once; and he fastened on them with so determined a valour and so much success, as to give time to Captain Read of the 27th to come up with the main body of our own, and the Sicilian gunboats; while a faint breeze rising, enabled the *Cyane*, of 24, and the *Espoir*, of 16 guns, to cross the enemy's van,

A battery near the Cape, which endeavoured to protect them, was silenced by the fire of the *Cyane*; and some of the rearmost of the enemy's vessels having run on shore under another battery, protected by a considerable number of French infantry, a very satisfactory interlude was played in the sight of our fleet, and probably within ken of Murat himself. One company of the King's German Legion, a party of marines, and 30 or 40 of the Calabrese free corps, pushed off to the shore; they charged and routed the enemy's infantry, killing a good many, and capturing an officer and thirty-six men; while our seamen destroyed the vessels.

The result of this morning's action was the capture of twenty-four of King Joachim's gunboats, and the destruction of five. Five others managed to scramble round the point, and they found shelter under the forts of Baia, though torn by the shot of the *Cyane* and *Espoir* On our side the loss of men was trifling; but we had to lament the death of Cameron, a young officer attached to my department, whose conspicuous gallantry in this day's service excited the admiration both of our navy and army.

There remained no other work for us on the island than the reduction of the Castle of Ischia. This picturesque old fortress is perched upon a rock washed by the sea on every side, save where a very narrow isthmus connects it with the mainland. General Colonna had a garrison of nearly 300 men, amongst whom were some well-trained gunners: they made good shots; and the first they fired, though plunging, sent one of our gunboats to the bottom. But the castle was commanded by the lower falls of the mountain opposite to it; and though our antagonist gave our people the trouble of cutting a road, and dragging some 24-pounders up the hill, he was obliged to surrender his fort on the 30th of June,

Thus, then at the end of six days there remained nothing farther to be done, as far as Ischia and Procida were concerned. Our feats had served to throw Naples into hot water, which had indeed been raised to boiling heat on the 27th, when an audacious attack was made by that gallant officer Thomas Staines, commanding the *Cyane* of 24 guns, assisted by the *Espoir* brig, on a large frigate, a *corvette*, and ten gunboats, which were endeavouring to escape from Baia to Naples. The enemy kept close along the shore, deriving support from the coast-batteries, and finally from the castles of the capital itself, till the action ended at the molehead of Naples.

In sight of the numbers who clustered on the sides of the hills and on the house-tops, in sight of Murat himself, who came raging into the batteries to excite the gunners, in despite of the thunder from the forts, Thomas Staines tore this 40-gun frigate so terribly, that in fear of being boarded, she at last cut the cable she had dropped, and staggered within the harbour. The fever which this action aroused in the city of Naples was such as to awaken in the mind of King Joachim the dread of a sudden insurrection; and he adopted immediately the severest measures to prevent or put down such an attempt. On our part we had to lament that our valiant countryman, who had given to the French and Neapolitans such a specimen of what English sailors are capable, that Staines should have been so severely wounded as to deprive our navy of his services for a long time.

Before I return to a consideration of what our army might have been expected to attempt after the reduction of the islands, it is necessary that I should give some account of what had been passing in Calabria, and almost within sight of Messina. It will be remembered that Colonel Smith had been detached first to cover our headquarters in Sicily against any possible insult on the part of the French, and secondly, after having waited a few days to afford time for General Partonneaux to march away from Lower Calabria (as it was presumed he would), to destroy the enemy's batteries along the straits, and finally to lay siege to Scilla.

Smith proceeded to act according to his instructions. The dismantling of the batteries on the beach was easy enough, for the French had left nothing there but a few old iron guns. The information respecting Partonneaux was false or vague as usual. It was believed that his division, or most of them, had marched towards Naples; and Smith invested the Castle of Scilla. He had six companies of the 10th, eight of the 21st regiment, and some of Watteville's; in all about 1,300 bayonets, exclusive of the artillery. Heavy guns had been held ready, and were promptly landed and dragged up the hill to batter the old fort.

But Colonel Smith did not feel himself quite at his ease with regard to the enemy, who was supposed to have left the province; and he therefore detached two companies of the 21st regiment under Captains Hunter and McKay to Palmi, about fifteen miles distant, with orders to keep a sharp lookout (with the help of the Calabrese) on the road towards Monteleone. Trusting to this watch upon the enemy, Smith applied himself to the siege of Scilla.

In the following night the picquet of the 21st in advance of Palmi was surprised, and Captain McKay badly wounded, and made prisoner with his men, by the advanced guard of Partonneaux's division, which broke without halting into the town, killed Captain Hunter and some of his people, and captured nearly the whole of the detachment. The French followed the chase, in the eager hope of catching Smith still before the walls of Scilla: but he luckily received news of the disaster just in time to throw all his men into boats, and to repass the straits, abandoning the guns and stores which had been brought over for the siege.

Haviland Smith was a good officer, and no blame was attached to him on account of this failure. He went to his work under the impression, conveyed by Sir John Stuart's orders, that the French troops would be drawn away from Lower Calabria by the operations of our army; nor was he responsible for the falsehood of the intelligence received afterwards at Messina, where Generals McKenzie and White were in command. But scarcely had Partonneaux driven the English from the Calabrian shore, when he received orders to abandon the province altogether, and to hasten with every man that could bear arms to the support of the war around the capital.

The Castle of Scilla, in which a fine train of heavy brass artillery had been collected for the invasion of Sicily, was blown up by the French; the guns were cast into the sea; the most valuable stores destroyed; and General Partonneaux set off upon his long march, carrying with him the late garrison of Scilla.

But we must now return to Ischia. There we were with 13,000 or 14,000 fighting men (including officers and followers) and some 1,500 horses and mules, upon a small island, extremely beautiful, but yielding none of those supplies which an army requires, excepting wine. Even of good water there was a scarcity. In a few days the inconvenience was increased by the arrival of Prince Leopold with his part of the expedition. They had threatened Policastro, and Agropoli, and finally Sorrento, and then they came to take up their quarters on the western side of Ischia, as we occupied the east and the north; and beds of lava have possession of the south.

As neighbours we were very disagreeable and troublesome to Murat. The swarming populace of Naples and its vicinity were in a ferment, and were kept down only by the severest vigilance and rigour. The principal places in the city were closed by barricades, and defended by strong posts of soldiery, and through the streets, patrols were pacing their rounds night and day. King Joachim called in his troops from every distant quarter, though flashes of insurrection were gleaming in several of his provinces. He summoned Partonneaux, as we have seen, from Scilla, and he recalled from Rome, by forced marches, some battalions which he had recently sent thither for purposes to which I must presently allude. Always in active exertion, encouraging his soldiery, daunting the disaffected by a display of his own intrepidity, and longing impatiently for the landing of the English Army, still Murat must have felt his position very embarrassing while the great war remained undecided in Austria.

Nor were his apprehensions of risings and conspiracies in his capital without a cause. Shortly after we had settled ourselves in Ischia, there came over two gentlemen who solicited an interview with our general, announcing themselves as accredited delegates from the "*Patriotti*" of Italy. Sir John Stuart would not even admit them to his presence. He turned them over to me that I might hear and dismiss them, and report the conversation to him. Nothing could appear more fair, straightforward, and explicit, than the language these two gentlemen held to me. It was to this purport:

> We are Neapolitans; and we come here more particularly on the part of the *Patriotti* of this kingdom, by whom we are authorised to treat: but we act in concert with similar associations which exist all over Italy. We are sent to ask what are the intentions of the British general in bringing his army to the Bay of Naples. If it be simply to drive the French out of the country, we will aid him to the utmost of our power; and our power is great. We wish to get rid of the French, and to make our country independent. But if you come with the view of replacing Ferdinand and his queen on the throne of Naples, we will to a man take arms with the French and fight against you. We will never trust King Ferdinand again, nor ever suffer Caroline to set her foot on these shores. To the hereditary prince we should not feel the same objections, provided he should come without his parents or their ministers, and would take his place as a limited sovereign in a freely constituted state.

But to this overture Sir John Stuart declined to make any reply whatever; and as the delegates saw that Prince Leopold was on the island, they could put no other construction on our general's silence and lack of courtesy than that his object was to replace King Ferdinand on his throne. Yet strangely enough, almost at the same time, Sir John Stuart, taking just umbrage at some acts of oppression and assumption of authority at Ischia on the part of Prince Leopold and his people, put a stop to them with a rough hand, and a very decisive tone. A change appeared to have come over the spirit of the Count of Maida, who had hitherto been a zealous defender and encomiast of the royal personages at Palermo. On the 3rd of July, there being many people at his dinner-table, he broke out into this tirade:

> As for the king, his cause is desperate; he has lost one kingdom, and he must lose the other. There is no alternative for England but to take Sicily for herself, or to abandon it altogether.

The guests were probably of the same opinion, but they could only wonder in respectful acquiescence. I wondered more than any of them, because I had been in the way of hearing Sir John's sentiments a long time, and in more privacy.

But I must return to our military position and its relationship to the general concerns of the war. Though we had merely set ourselves down in the islands of the Bay of Naples, yet even this late show of activity seems to have excited alarm in the French commanders in Italy. Napoleon had issued his decree, from Vienna, on the 17th of May, for the dethronement of the Pope, and the annexation of the Papal dominions to the French Empire. General Miollis had in consequence assumed the government in the name of his master; but Pius VII. had been allowed to remain unmolested in the Quirinal palace. The French forces in the Roman territory were few, and, as I have before stated, some battalions which had been despatched by Murat to their support, were recalled in haste on our appearing in the Bay of Naples.

On the 6th of July Miollis suddenly attacked the Quirinal, seized the person of the Pope, and hurried him off with the utmost rapidity to the Alps. The effect of this sacrilegious violence on the minds of the Italians was universal; and if, instead of eating grapes at Ischia, we had struck in at that moment on the coasts of Rome or Tuscany, the landing of a British Army might have been productive of a serious influence on the results of the general war. Napoleon had been defeated at Aspern on the 23rd of May; he won the hard fought Battle of Wagram on the 6th of July. But the Austrians were worsted only, not crushed; they did not yield to peace till October, and in August the war was raging in the Tyrol. If Italy had been roused by the landing of the British, Austria would have fought it out; though one must confess that she had little reason to rely on England when she looked at our tardy, ill-designed, and worse-conducted expedition to the Scheldt.

I pressed Sir John Stuart to attack either Civita Vecchia or Leghorn, or at least to try what might be the effect of a demonstration on the northern coast of Italy. But the general would not stir.

Now came from General Mc Kenzie the accounts of Smith's failure at Scilla, and of the panic which had in consequence seized on the people of Messina. Sir John Stuart immediately ordered Nunziante's brigade and a regiment of cavalry to return, and help to allay the alarm, though it was known that Partonneaux and his Frenchmen had quitted Lower Calabria. Two days afterwards he directed that Airey's brigade should likewise return to Messina; and though he countermanded this order the following morning, it became quite clear that our general was resolved to confine his campaign to the reduction of Ischia and Procida.

Therefore, as I had come on the expedition with a leave to return to England, on urgent family affairs, in my pocket, I now begged permission to avail myself of the commander-in-chief's leave. I went down in a boat to Messina in order to catch the packet; and two days after my arrival at my old quarters, I was surprised by the appearance of Sir John Stuart and his whole army; for he did not even leave a battalion to occupy the fort of Procida and so assist our navy in the blockade of Naples.

The immediate cause or apology for this sudden abandonment of places which our general had imagined to be objects worthy of the great armament he had put forth for their reduction, was the receipt of a letter from Lord Collingwood, containing the following paragraphs:

> Ever since the movement of the army from Sicily, there appears to have been a particular degree of activity at Toulon. They have a fleet of twelve sail of the line, seven frigates, and many smaller vessels, lying at the outer part of the harbour, where they never lay before, as if ready for a start.
>
> There is no destination so likely for them as to succour Murat, and counteract your measures. I do not think they would come out to fight the English squadron, which is ten sail of the line and a frigate; but they are strong enough not to require much caution to avoid it. In weather when I can keep close off the port, I do not think they will move; but ten days since we had a gale from the N.W. which drove the fleet almost half way to Minorca; and had they been ready then, they might have sailed, and probably have been near Naples before I could have known that they were out of port. This may happen again, and most likely will. It is a circumstance over which we can have no control; but it is for consideration whether the ships and transports are so secured at their anchorage at Ischia as not to be endangered by such a fleet, if enabled to make a sudden attack. But there are other objects for the enemy, not of less consideration. Why in such a case may they not go to Palermo? and if they did, what is there to resist them?"

This liability to the attack of a superior fleet on a small squadron, with a very large convoy, at anchor in an exposed roadstead, had existed from the moment when it became apparent to Murat that we held no designs of active hostility, but were merely making a parade of menacing his capital. There was a telegraphic communication between Naples and Toulon. If we had been sailing along the coast of Italy, the French fleet might have been at fault; but when our two hundred transports were fast at anchor, and our troops were cantoned in Ischia, the enemy could hardly miss his mark if he could make his escape from Lord Collingwood.

Thus, ended the expedition from Sicily in the year 1809. It cost England a very large sum of money, and no little reputation. Here also ends my personal acquaintance with military transactions in the Mediterranean. But the interest which I continued to feel in the affairs of that part of Europe, my constant correspondence with well-informed officers and others in Sicily, and the position which I came to hold as Under-Secretary of State for the War Department, hare enabled me to add an account, though more succinct, of what occurred there in 1810.

******

I finish with 1810, because at the close of that year Lord William Bentinck was sent to take the command of the army in Sicily; and from that time there began a totally different course of policy in that island. The protecting authority of England was vindicated; the intrigues of Queen Caroline were crushed with a strong hand; and by degrees the ancient constitution of Sicily was restored for a time, though it was again overthrown by the treachery of the perjured king, after the general peace.

******

Before Sir John Stuart led his army to the bay of Naples, Lord Collingwood, while throwing cold water on the general's project, had suggested the expediency of seizing on the Ionian Islands, which had fallen into the hands of the French in 1806. The reduction of these islands promised to give to England an influential command over the Adriatic on the one side, and the eastern sea on the other. After the return of our army to Sicily, the admiral renewed his proposal that a conjoint expedition should be directed to this quarter; and Stuart reluctantly acquiesced. (See Lord Collingwood's *Correspondence*, Oct. 30th, 1809.) Sixteen hundred of the troops were embarked under Brigadier Oswald; and Captain Spranger of the *Warrior*, 74, commanded the little squadron. They sailed from Messina on the 23rd September; and, after a slight resistance which cost a very few lives, the islands of Zante, Cefalonia, Ithaca, and Cerigo were surrendered to the British arms.

This part of the service was completed between the 2nd and the 11th of October. The enemy's works and garrison in Sta. Maura were found to be too strong for the small expedition which had been detached from Sicily; and the attack upon that island was postponed. As for the fortress of Corfu, well manned and amply provided, it was not to be meddled with till an army could be spared for its reduction, or till a close and constant blockade might work out this end by starving the garrison. One great good, however, was obtained by what had been already done, besides the advantage of ports and supplies for the English squadrons in those seas,—we had found warm friends in the islanders; a people hating the French, and earnestly desirous to assist us in driving them out.

The long armistice between France and Austria which had followed the Battles of Wagram and Znaim was at length terminated by the treaty of peace signed at Vienna on the 14th of October, the miserable issue of the British expedition to the Scheldt having probably extinguished the last hopes of the Imperial Cabinet.

******

It ought to be recorded, to the credit of the Duke of York's judgment, that he protested strongly against this expedition. It was Lord Castlereagh's own project; and the whole of the shame should be divided between him and Lord Chatham.

******

It was not till this treaty was concluded that the French legions broke up from the frontiers of Hungary and Bohemia; and while a great proportion set forward on their long march for Spain, many thousands took their route for Italy; but their van did not arrive at Naples before March 1810.

In the meantime, the Court of Palermo had engaged busily in intrigues, the object of which was to squeeze more money out of the impoverished people of Sicily. They were to be cajoled and deceived by the adoption of a measure which bore the outward semblance of liberality. The constitutional parliament of Sicily was summoned to assemble, as of yore, in its three estates of Barons, Ecclesiastics, and that which ought to have been the Commons of the realm, but was in effect quite another thing. This third chamber was composed of persons nominated by the corporations of certain large towns, and domains under the influence of the Crown. Amongst these men Medici, the minister of finance, had been busy beforehand, and with complete success.

It was not doubted that the patronage of government, and the influence of the archbishop would secure the Ecclesiastics; and thus, feeling confident of commanding majorities in two of the chambers, the Court did not fear the resistance which it expected to encounter from the barons, Still it was considered prudent to try whether the latter might not be softened by an affectation of deference and candour. Four of the principal *grandees*, Butèra, Cassaro, Trabbia, and Belmonte, were invited to meet the king's ministers before the assembling of the Parliament, and to form with them a committee which should investigate the state of the national finances, and make inquiry into their past administration. Prince Butèra, the first Baron of Sicily, was rough without being honest; and he returned this singular answer to the invitation:

> Neither I, nor my forefathers have ever known how to manage our own affairs as to money, and therefore I am not capable of serving His Majesty in this matter.

Cassaro and Trabbia declined to act; and Prince Belmonte alone offered to attend, but conditionally. He required, 1st, that sufficient time should be allowed for the investigation: 2ndly, that there should be good faith and sincerity in exhibiting the real deficit, and the extent of the claims: and, 3rdly, that all the departments of government should furnish whatever information might be required for the fulfilment of the duty. These conditions involved a scrutiny too rigid to suit the purposes of the queen and her ministers; and the scheme of a committee was laid aside.

The Parliament met. The third chamber at once voted taxes to the amount of 666,000 ounces, and presented their vote for the concurrence of the barons. Butèra, who had hitherto passed himself off as a patriot, supported the proposition; but only four of his order adhered to him. The mass of the barons rejected it; and they sent some of their number, with Prince Belmonte at their head, to explain their views to the Ecclesiastics. These reverend members of the church had been fully prepared by the influence of their archbishop to grant all that the government required; but the eloquence of Belmonte, and the proofs which he adduced of the state of the finances, produced a sudden conversion. The majority of the Ecclesiastics came over to the views entertained by the barons; and to the dismay of the archbishop and the discomfiture of the court, the Parliament granted but a slight addition to the taxes, modifying at the same time some of those which were already in existence.

******

These details were furnished to me by a Sicilian abbot of note and good abilities, with whom I long kept up a friendly correspondence. After this time, he obtained a place in the esteem and confidence of Lord William Bentinck.

★★★★★★

The disappointment and the rage of the queen were excessive. She had no money left to carry on her schemes in Calabria, or to complete the equipment of an expedition of 3,000 men which she had been preparing to send into that province under Moliterno. With Sir John Stuart she had been on very bad terms since the return of the British Army from Ischia: but when the Sicilian Parliament was about to meet, Her Majesty bethought herself that it might be of some advantage to her that the court should appear at least to be on a friendly footing with the English general, and she graciously and urgently invited him to Palermo. Sir John, however, would not go; and in his despatches to Lord Liverpool, written in February, (letters of the 6th, 8th, and 9th February, 1810), he expresses a marked distrust of the designs of the Court of Palermo, as well as his dissatisfaction at their conduct.

We find in them nearly the same sentiments, and the same grounds of complaint and suspicion, as in the letters written by General Fox in 1807; and with Stuart these opinions must have been the slow growth of experience, for all his predilections had been on the other side. To an urgent appeal for pecuniary assistance, on account of the extreme distress of the government, Sir John answers that he is not at liberty to divert the funds of the English Army to any other purpose. He states to Lord Amherst; (then Minister Plenipotentiary at Palermo) that his presence at the court could be of service only for military purposes; and as they allowed him no control or influence over their troops, his attendance under the actual circumstances would be useless. But to Lord Collingwood he adds this ground for his mistrust:

> The queen and the minister have recently held the language that Sicily would not be attacked; and if attacked our *naval* superiority was a sufficient defence.

In the month of March, a remarkable change suddenly appeared in the tone and in the spirits of Queen Caroline. Ever since the Peace of Vienna she had been depressed and seemingly desperate: now Napoleon's marriage with Maria Louisa being declared, and certain despatches having been received by the Court of Palermo from the ambassador Ruffo, the queen came forth as if inspired with new hopes, and intent upon new projects. She no longer confined herself to saying that naval protection was sufficient for the defence of Sicily; but she added that the British Army was useless and burthensome.

There arose the strongest suspicion that Her Majesty had opened, through the Austrians, a secret communication with Napoleon. Without any assignable object she began to fit out a number of transports as for an expedition; and she endeavoured to withdraw from the straits of Messina the gunboats, which were of great importance to the English for the defence of that narrow channel. A courier with, despatches for the queen passed from Calabria to Messina in the night, without its being made known to the British general.

The messenger, when detected, professed himself, to be an Austrian coming from Vienna: it turned out that he was a Neapolitan; and that he had been detained some weeks at Naples, probably to afford time for a communication between Murat and. Napoleon. (Sir J. Stuart to Lord Liverpool, May 23. Also, Colonel Coffin and the Abbate B. C. to Colonel Bunbury, April, 1810.) At all events, there was sufficient evidence that a correspondence with the Court of Palermo was carried on with the knowledge and connivance of the enemy.

※※※※※※

Colletta, in the seventh book of his *History of Naples*, alludes more than once to the secret correspondence which had, as it was believed, grown up between Napoleon and Queen Caroline, the grandmother of his young wife. It is pretty clear that Colletta gave credit to the report, and it must be borne in mind that he filled a high ministerial office under King Joachim; but he believed that even his royal master was kept in ignorance of the secret designs of the emperor, and the machinations of his new correspondent. It appears to have been the belief of the historian that Napoleon had gladly seized upon some overture made to him by Caroline on his marriage, and had encouraged her to engage in dark schemes for the destruction of the English, or for their expulsion from Sicily.

That this faithless and unscrupulous woman had promised to raise the islanders against their defenders when Murat should be ready for the invasion; a promise which she was, happily, unable to effect. But as, according to Colletta, Napoleon did not choose to trust Murat with the whole of his secret designs, the fiery warrior was made to play the part of an unconscious puppet in these transactions. With this view the emperor placed the main body of the French troops, which he had sent to aid his brother-in-law in the Sicilian expedition, under the special control of General Grenier. To this general the secret was confided; and to him was also given a discretionary authority (to be produced, if necessary) to grant or to withhold, according to circumstances, the co-operation of the French divisions.

Grenier was believed to have instructions to wait until the promised risings of the Sicilians might have embarrassed the British Army, and might render the invasion less hazardous. It is to these causes that Colletta attributes the failure of Murat to pass the straits with his army on the 18th of September, when a diversion had been made by 1,600 troops under General Cavaignac on the coast to the southward of Messina. Grenier, says the historian, refused to allow his French divisions to embark. If this be so, one cannot wonder that Murat should have posted off immediately to Naples, boiling with disgust and rage. It may not be immaterial to note, that a letter from Napoleon to Queen Caroline had been intercepted in Spain, and was published at Cadiz in June. Though this letter contained nothing material, it proved the fact of there being a correspondence, and this correspondence not carried on by a direct course, but through some secret channels in Spain.

******

And this was at the very moment when 6,000 French troops having arrived at Naples, and many more being on their march from the north of Italy, Murat was despatching division after division into Calabria, and was making the greatest exertions to collect vessels for the invasion of Sicily. The belief amongst the English and the best-informed Sicilians was general, that the queen was collecting transports and gunboats expressly for the service of our enemy. At Palermo, and in the great towns, disaffection was rapidly gathering head: and sullen murmurs against the English, stigmatising them as men who were asleep, and who took no heed to the condition of the country, gave evidence that the Sicilians were losing their last hopes.

Before the French Army in Calabria had been greatly reinforced, Sir John Stuart had detached a few of his troops, with an ample proportion of artillery and engineer's stores to Zante; and Brigadier Oswald, with a small squadron commanded by Captain Eyre, proceeded immediately to attack the fortress of Santa Maura. The troops employed on this service were the 35th Regiment, De Roll's, and the Corsican Rangers, with detachments of the Royal Marines, and of the Calabrese and Greek sharpshooters. Captain Thackeray was the chief engineer, and Captain Williamson commanded the artillery.

The position of this fortress, on a long narrow isthmus of sand, renders it difficult of approach. The castle was well supplied: it contained casemates amply sufficient for the garrison; and it was defended by General Camus with about 800 men. The strength of the place and the difficulties of the undertaking were found to be greater than had been anticipated; but the operations of the assailants were conducted with skill and vigour; the outworks were carried in succession, and with the greatest gallantry, by assault; and heavy batteries having been brought to bear upon the fortress during nine days, the French General surrendered on the 16th of April. This service cost the British about 160 men, including a remarkably large proportion of officers. (The conquest of Santa Maura brought the English into a close communication with that celebrated savage, Ali Pacha of Jannina.)

The despatches from Sir John Stuart during the months of March and April, 1810, (to the Earl of Liverpool, March 24th, and April 18th), dwell strongly on the grounds he finds for distrusting the intentions of the Court of Palermo, and even those of the Sicilian troops; though he feels that if the latter were placed under his command, and were paid and fed by him, they might be turned to account in defending the island. In the meantime, says the general, columns of French troops are arriving at Naples; large bodies are moving down to Calabria; and a law of conscription has been issued by Murat, and is already coming into effect.

A few days afterwards Sir John transmits intelligence received by him from the coasts of the Adriatic and from Calabria, serving to shew the great scale on which preparations were being made for the invasion of Sicily, and the active energy with which they were pushed forward. (The same to the same, April 27th, and May 1st.) He repeats and dwells upon his suspicion of the persona who possess full influence at the Court of Palermo, and he represents the utter inefficiency of their marine, of their army of 7,000 starving and discontented men, and their imaginary militia, to render any help to the British in the event of an attack from the enemy, even if the government were sincerely desirous to afford it.

Under these trying circumstances. Sir John Stuart had received orders from Lord Liverpool to send four battalions to Gibraltar, upon their being relieved by a smaller number of sickly soldiers from England. Deeply impressed with a sense of the present dangers, and the responsibility of his position, the general had resolved to detain, for the present, not only the troops which he was required to detach, but those likewise which were announced as being on their way to relieve them.

The British Government had by this time engaged themselves deeply in the war of the Spanish peninsula. Though there were doubts and misgivings amongst them as to the soundness of Lord Wellington's undertaking to defend Portugal against the power of France, yet he was just entering on the immortal campaign of 1810, and our ministers were anxious to strengthen his army by all the troops they could collect from every quarter. It was for this purpose that they called for four battalions from Sicily and Malta, forgetting, in their anxiety for Portugal, the interests of England in the former country, and even the dangerous circumstances in which Stuart's army was actually placed.

With less than 14,000 men, (about 2,000 being now detached to the Ionian Islands), nearly one half of whom were foreigners, he had to garrison four fortified places, and to make head with the remainder against Murat, who was about to assemble 20,000 or 30,000 French on the Straits of Messina. Whether it was wise in the British Government, now that Austria was crushed, and Russia still in alliance with Napoleon, to attempt the defence of both Sicily and Portugal, may perhaps be doubted, though the issue has appeared to justify the resolution. The military means of England had been crippled by the consequences of the expedition to the Scheldt. Of that noble army which was sent to sicken in the marshes of Walcheren, few were the battalions which recovered from the fever sufficiently to be fit for service in the following year; and when Wellington was urging upon the attention of ministers the vast importance of collecting as large a force as possible at Lisbon, there were but few regular regiments in England capable of taking the field.

Lord Liverpool therefore reiterated his order to Stuart to detach the four battalions; and great was the anger of our Cabinet when the general again declined to yield obedience. Yet, considering the circumstances in which his army was placed, (Sir John Stuart to the Earl of Liverpool, June 9th, 1810), it would be unjust to censure him, or to cavil at his declaring that if the numbers of the British were to be farther reduced, and the means of calling forth and directing the resources of Sicily were still withheld, the confidence of the people in the British would be chilled, and he could not consent to hold himself responsible for the result. In fact, the preparations of Murat appeared in the month of June to be nearly ripe for his attack upon Sicily; and very formidable these preparations were.

From 20,000 to 25,000 French were massed at the extremity of Lower Calabria, and many more were behind them. Large boats, many of them carrying guns, were being gathered in great numbers, and making their way from post to post till they reached their rendezvous, under cover of the numerous batteries which now lined the shore from Palmi to Reggio. But the enemy was not always allowed to carry forward these preparations with impunity: the gallantry and success by which one action in particular was attended, make it deserving of record. A part of our army-flotilla, commanded by Captain Read of the 27th Regiment, (the late Sir Thomas Read, and Consul at Tunis), attacked a large convoy coming from Naples, which was resting under the shelter of batteries between Bagnara and Palmi. Eight of the enemy's gunboats were sunk, and three others, together with eleven vessels laden with field-artillery, ammunition and stores, were captured and carried into Messina.

******

Another of the enemy's convoys was intercepted by Captain Waldegrave of H. M. frigate, *Thames*, with two brigs of war in company, on the 25th of July; when twelve gunboats, and thirty-one transport vessels, were taken or destroyed after an action gallantly fought by the British marines and the crews of the boats led on by Captain Prescott.

******

However, it was calculated that by the beginning of July nearly 500 of these large boats were assembled on the shores of Lower Calabria, and they were held in constant readiness to cross the straits. Murat had arrived in person, and with that love of pompous display which belonged to his character, he pitched a magnificent pavilion, and a gigantic standard on the brow of the point of Pezzo, overlooking the whole of the channel, and full in the view of every British post from Messina to the Faro. Close behind this gaudy abode of the warrior-king were grouped the huts of the thousands which formed the flower of his army. There could be no doubt that the fixed determination of that valiant chieftain was, to quit his position only when he should step on board his barge, and lead his forces to the hostile shore.

By this time, however, the aspect of that shore was greatly changed. The engineers and staff officers of the British Army had not been idle, however careless and indifferent their general might appear. A chain of heavy batteries connected the Faro point with the fortress of Messina, and these were supported by fortified posts and barracks. A squadron of four sail of the line, and three brigs of war were anchored along the coast, and covered those parts of the beach which were most exposed to attack, while our flotilla, now mustering nearly one hundred boats, since the Neapolitans had been taken into British pay, lay clustered round the Faro, ready to be let slip upon the flank and rear of the enemy's armada. The peasantry of the Val Demone displayed a hearty good will towards the English, and an anxious desire to render all the assistance in their power. They came down by hundreds, with their long spades (*zappe*) to the shore, shouting, "*Viva 'l Rè Giorgio!*" and proffering their voluntary labour in throwing up works of defence.

Two strong regiments, the 31st and 39th, were brought from Malta to increase the strength of the British line; and not a day passed without a skirmish more or less brisk between the opposing flotillas. And thus stood the English and French in battle array, army against army, on either side of a strait so narrow that every movement of the smallest body of troops could be observed by their opponents; individuals could be recognised by means of spying glasses; and the heavy guns from Murat's batteries sent plunging shot over the British works. But while the opposing hosts lay in this close proximity, and the enemy's attempt to pass was expected every night, the Court of Palermo gave no sign of care or alarm. (The adjutant-general to Colonel Bunbury, 12th July.)

> The court makes no effort, sends no succour, takes no notice, and laughs at Lord Amherst. Ferdinand 4th goes a tunny-fishing, and his wife continues her usual pranks; pronounced by her own subjects, and convicted in my mind, of acting in concert with Murat for our expulsion.

Every mark of attachment to the English became distasteful to the court; the zeal shewn by the peasantry drew forth expressions of reprobation; and when the wealthier classes in Messina tendered the use of their horses to drag the British guns, the governor was instructed to interfere, and if possible prevent the accomplishment of this service. (L'Abbate B.C. to Colonel Bunbury, August, 1810.)

This state of things continued with little variation through nearly three months. Even the fearless Murat hesitated to lead his five hundred boats and 20,000 men across the narrow channel, when every day shewed him the formidable and still improving means of resistance which he must overcome or perish. Nor, whatever might have been the treacherous designs of the Sicilian Government, did there appear in the Sicilian people the slightest falling off in their attachment to the English.

During this time Lord Amherst, in obedience to his orders from home, pressed the Court of Palermo strongly to place their troops under the command of the British general, who would in that case have taken care that they should be regularly paid, and sufficiently fed. As our minister became more than usually urgent in the matter, the queen and Circello, puzzled to evade the demand of the English Cabinet, hit upon the notable expedient of making King Ferdinand declare himself *generalissimo* of all his forces by sea and land. The excessive absurdity of this manoeuvre did not excite ridicule alone; it aroused a very angry spirit in the Palermitans, and even in so calm a man as Lord Amherst. (The adjutant-general, and the Abbate B.C. to Colonel Bunbury, August, 1810.)

In warm terms our ambassador expressed his indignation at this unworthy subterfuge, and announced officially his intention of representing the measure in this light to the British Government. It was believed that the court adopted this poor expedient merely from the fear of offending the Emperor Napoleon; and to the same motive had been attributed a prior evasion, contemptible in itself, but adding strength to the general impression which was entertained as to the perfidy of the court. Lord Amherst's remonstrances had wrung from Ferdinand the promise of a Proclamation, calling on the people of Sicily to aid the English in repelling the expected invasion.

A short address to this effect was at length drawn up, and a copy was placed in the hands of our ambassador; but it was not placarded or circulated through the island as a royal proclamation; nor did the paper exhibit to the public the signature either of the king or any of his ministers. And at the very time when the court entered on this course of perfidy, and of underhand hostility to the English, the Cabinet of St. James's had granted to Ferdinand an additional subsidy of £100,000 a year.

But to return to the theatre where some 14,000 of our troops lay watching and wishing for the attack with which they had been so long threatened. The autumn was come, and the season was not distant when our ships of war would no longer be able to hold their anchorage along the shore without great risk. More than one experiment had satisfied our naval officers that the enemy's boats, even where they lay clustered in great masses on the beach, could not be destroyed, covered as they were by numerous batteries and guns of the heaviest calibre. Our army was beginning to look forward with some uneasiness to the chances which the dark nights of winter might afford to the superior numbers of the enemy, led by such generals as Murat, Grenier, Lamarque, Partonneaux, Cavaignac, &c.

But the foe was become still, more impatient of the long delay. In the night of the 17th, of September, two battalions of Corsicans and; four of Neapolitans (reckoned at 3,500 men), commanded by General Cavaignac, crossed the wider part of the straits, and reached the Sicilian shore about seven miles to, the southward of Messina. This movement seems to, have been intended as a diversion; for when the day broke the enemy's troops were seen to be embarking, in their boats at Scilla and round the Punta del Pezzo; and Cavaignac's object, though very early and) rudely interrupted, appeared clearly to have been the gaining of the mountain ridge, from whence he might, have come down on the rear of our army while it, should be engaged in front by the main, body of the French.

But the diversion failed. General Campbell, the adjutant-general, had galloped to the south on the; first rumour of the approach of boats, and assumed the command of the British troops in that quarter. He found the enemy landing from their vessels: the two battalions of Corsicans, indeed, were: already onshore; and one of these had pushed forward immediately up the ridge in their front, which rises to the; mountain chain of Dinnamare, The beach where the, disembarkation was taking place lay between Mili and San Placido, two posts occupied by our troops. Between the invaders and Messina stood the 21st; regiment, commanded by Colonel Frederick Adam, with two six-pounders; and a part of the 3rd battalion of the German Legion, with two companies of riflemen, were coming fast to his support.

On the other side of the enemy, hastening from San Placido, were the light companies of our foreign regiments, about 400 men, commanded by Colonel Fischer, who had already opened his fire on the boats, while he detached a part of his little corps to flank and harass the enemy's battalion on the hill. The day was breaking, and it displayed to Campbell's view the whole state of the affair. He immediately sent parties to secure the rugged paths through the mountains; keeping the 21st and a part of the Germans in hand for a decisive stroke. The bells clanged forth from every little village; and the peasants grasping whatever weapons they could find, were clustering on every height, shouting, "*Viva 'l Ré Giorgio!*" and exhibiting by their gestures the fiercest hostility to the invaders.

The Corsicans upon the hill halted as if waiting for support; while upon the beach Cavaignac's main body, galled by the sharp fire of Fischer's light infantry upon their left, and threatened by Adam's position on their right, began to fall into some confusion. Their rearmost battalion seemed to be unwilling to quit their boats; and Campbell, observing their hesitation, ordered Adam to push forward with his guns and his column of eight or nine hundred men. Weak was the resistance offered to this attack. Crowds of the enemy's soldiers scrambled back to their boats, and the boats put off from the shore in hurried confusion, leaving a mob of more than 200 men to throw down their arms and cry for quarter.

There remained the battalion of Corsicans on the heights, their retreat to the sea cut off by the position which Colonel Adam had now taken. They were summoned to surrender, and for a moment they demurred; but the 21st drew near prepared to charge with the bayonet, while Fischer's light infantry approached on the other side. There remained little time for hesitation, and the Corsicans laid down their arms and their colours. A French colonel, a *chef de l'état-major*, one of General Cavaignac's *aides-de-camp*, forty other officers, and above eight hundred men, were made prisoners on the shore: a good many more were captured in four of the enemy's small vessels which were intercepted in their retreat by Captain Robinson of the Royal Marines, who pushed out from Messina with some of the fast rowboats belonging to the army flotilla. But it happened, unfortunately, that all our ships of war and all our large gunboats were at anchor at their stations near the Faro. (See General Campbell's letter to Colonel Bunbury, in the Appendix.) The loss of the enemy in killed, wounded, or drowned was considerable; while, on the part of the British, only three men were hurt!

While this affair was going on to the southward of Messina, the main army of King Joachim was embarking leisurely under the eyes of our forces, in their vast flotilla which stretched from the Punta del Pezzo to Scilla; and on our side every battalion was at its post, and every artilleryman at his gun. Some hours wore away: the enemy discovered no sign of Cavaignac's having gained the mountains in the rear of the British line, and, according to the authority of Colletta, General Grenier refused to allow the French divisions which were subject to his particular control to risk the attack. Before the evening closed the whole of the enemy's troops had returned to their huts.

Such was the poor conclusion of Murat's boastings and of the great preparations he had made for the conquest of Sicily. A very few days afterwards he set off for Naples, leaving orders for the gradual withdrawal of his army, and the return of his flotilla by divisions, seizing from time to time the best opportunities which might present themselves of eluding the British cruisers. By the middle of October there remained not more than 8,000 of the enemy's troops under General Lamarque, who were busily employed in erecting barracks, and fortifying a position on the heights behind Scilla; but as their train of siege-artillery was left in this fortress, and as many troops remained in the two Calabrias, Sir John Stuart continued to hold the belief that it was Murat's intention to return and to renew his attempt.

The flotillas of the enemy were more fortunate on their retreat than could have been expected: only one of their divisions met with a serious disaster, when a squadron of British frigates and brigs of war, under Captain Ayscough, destroyed between fifty and sixty of the transport vessels, and two large gunboats. All the rest of Joachim's great armada reached Salerno or Naples in safety.

The prospect of an immediate invasion was at an end: and now the Court of Palermo despatched General Fardella, the chief of their staff, to propose to Sir John Stuart measures of co-operation, and plans of future defence. (Sir J. Stuart to the Earl of Liverpool, 25th October; and the Abbate B.C. to Colonel Bunbury, 26th October, 1810.) But even now, the principal suggestion was fraught with the most insidious designs. The court proposed that twelve battalions, picked out of what were called the "Volunteers" of the kingdom, should be embodied, drawn away from their respective homes, and placed under Stuart's command.

This would have excited a ferment of dissatisfaction throughout the island; and the belief that it was done in compliance with the wishes of the British general, would have drawn upon him a large share of the obloquy. Sir John had the good sense to withhold his assent; and in writing to Lord Liverpool the general recapitulated his views of the danger which was still to be apprehended from a French invasion, and of the suspicious conduct of the Court of Palermo. (Sir J. Stuart to the Earl of Liverpool, Oct. 23rd, 1810.) He represents, that when he was appointed to the command of the army in Sicily, he had been led to expect he should have a control over the military resources of the country, and over the application of the British subsidy. He is still of opinion, that if he were invested with such a controlling authority, and were strengthened by a small addition of British troops, the defence of Sicily might be made good; but under the actual circumstances of his position, he must fed it his duty to resign the command of the army.

This intimation was perfectly acceptable to the Cabinet of St. James's. They had been for some time past desirous to confide the British force in Sicily to other hands, and to unite the military with the diplomatic authority; so as to insure a sufficient control over the mistrusted Court of Palermo, and to attach the people of the island more effectually to the common cause. After the comparative fitness of several general officers had been considered, our government decided on appointing Lord William Bentinck to this high and arduous post. Nor could they have pitched upon a man of greater zeal, of purer motives, or of more untiring energy. But it is not the purpose of my present narrative to treat of the measures pursued by that thoroughly honest and inflexible public officer, during the three years in which he exercised and rendered effectual the British influence in Sicily.

Before I close my account of transactions in the Mediterranean, it may not be thought irrelevant to make some mention of the detestable cruelties which were exercised in the two provinces of Calabria, after Murat had broken up his army of invasion. He probably had returned to Naples in a very bad humour; and, on the other hand, the exactions of his troops had reduced the people of those provinces to severe distress. The consequence, usual with the Calabrese, was that many of the starving villagers betook themselves to the mountains, and resumed those practices of robbery and violence which had been suppressed during the preceding year.

Small parties of these brigands were already infesting the highways, and skulking in the ravines and thickets, while the French Army were still lowering over the straits of Messina, and Colletta gives us one anecdote which regarded Murat personally, and afforded him an opportunity of displaying his magnanimity as an individual, though it might have been the offspring of a gratified vanity. One day while the king was riding near Palmi, he met some of his *gendarmes* bringing a prisoner in their custody. "Who is this?" asked the monarch.

The captive answered for himself: "I am a brigand, but I deserve pardon from you. Yesterday, as your majesty was climbing the mountain behind Scilla, I was lying hid behind an old building, and I could have shot you. I had a mind to do so, and I levelled my gun; but your bearing was so grand and royal, that it made me desist. Oh, if I had killed the king yesterday, I should not have been a prisoner and on my way to death this morning." (Colletta, *Storia di Napoli, lib. vii 27.*)

Murat directed that the fellow should be released immediately. It would have been better for his fame and for his conscience if he had allowed his clemency to take a wider range, and had restricted the powers and modified the conduct of the French general whom he selected, on his return to Naples, for the express purpose of extirpating the brigands.

It is with disgust that I enter on a recital of the atrocities which ensued; but while great and generous actions ought to be kept in remembrance as examples and stimulants to future generations, so on the other hand it is the duty of every writer, however humble, to record those crimes of public men which brand their characters with shame, and merit the abhorrence of mankind. Perchance some future historian may turn to this little narrative for particular facts; and the course adopted and pursued by the French in the two Calabrias during the winter of 1810, and the spring of 1811, is too closely connected with the subject on which I have been writing to be passed by without notice.

I have already said that Murat returned from his abortive attempt on Sicily in a very bad humour. He turned his vindictive spirit on the brigands and starving insurgents of the two Calabrias. The man upon whom he pitched as the fittest instrument of his severity was General Manhès, a name which will be long remembered in those countries with horror and detestation. During several months the letters which I received from my correspondents in Sicily alluded more or less to the unexampled cruelty with which this Manhès was persecuting the wretched Calabrese. But we have more direct and unexceptionable evidence. Pietro Colletta, a man of high character and talents; himself a Neapolitan, and Minister of War under Murat, gives us the following account of the course pursued under the authority, though possibly without the knowledge, as to particulars, of his royal master.

> Joachim, since he saw that the brigands were capable of committing all sorts of crimes, gave orders that a general should be invested with supreme power over all matters, whether military or civil, for the destruction of brigandage in the Calabrias. General Manhès, who was selected for this service, passed the month of October in making his preparations; waiting till the fruits and even the leaves should have withered, as the one yielded to the brigands the means of subsistence, and the other afforded hiding-places. Then he opened his plan. In every district the names of the persons considered to be '*banditti*' were

published, and the citizens were called upon to slay them or make them prisoners.

All men capable of bearing arms were summoned to take their weapons and go forth upon this service. Death was proclaimed as the punishment of any sort of correspondence with the brigands, without pardon, even between a wife and her husband, or a mother and her son. The unoffending father was to take arms against his outlawed sons, and brothers against brothers. The sheep and goats were to be brought in from the country and kept in certain places under watch. The cultivation of the fields was suspended; or where exceptions were allowed, the carrying out of any sort of food was forbidden. Soldiers and *gendarmes* were stationed in every town and village, not so much for the purpose of following up the brigands, as for that of keeping a severe and vigilant watch over the inhabitants.

Throughout the vast extent of the Calabrias there began at the same moment one universal hunt after the outlaws. So fearfully severe did those ordinances appear, that men imagined at first, they were issued only for the purpose of striking terror: but incredulity very quickly vanished before the facts which were spread by report or published by the general himself. Eleven persons of the town of Stilo, women and children (for the men were out in search of brigands) going forth to gather the olives at a farm at some distance, carried in their pockets a little bread, that they might refresh their strength at mid-day after the labour of the morning. Encountered by the *gendarmes* who were on the watch under the orders of Lieutenant Gambacorta, these poor wretches were stopped, searched, and being found to have these scraps of food on their persons, they were all put to death upon the spot.

I will not relate the miserable tale which was told of what one of these women said and did in the vain hope of saving, not herself, but her boy of twelve years old. In a wood near Cosenza, a peasant hoary with age was seen giving some food to a young man lean with hunger, but armed. This was a fugitive brigand; the other was his father. Both were seized, condemned and executed in the public square of Cosenza; and in order to render the punishment of the old man the more painful, he was made to be present at the execution of his son, before he was allowed to die himself. In the woods of San Biaggio, a woman who was flying with her outlawed husband gave birth to an infant. The little creature was a clog upon their flight, and its cries might betray their hiding places. The mother, therefore, carried it in the night time to a house in the town of Nicastro; awakened a friend, confided the child to her care, and hurried back to the woods.

This occurrence came to be known the next day; and General Manhès, though he spared the infant, ordered that the nurse who had shewed this compassion to her friend should be put to death. And here I pause, for my mind cannot bear to continue the narration of other deeds, which proved that the dreadful threats of Manhès were followed up by a fulfilment, certain, inflexible, and even exceeding the menaces themselves. Great was the horror which spread through all classes of the people; such indeed, that the dearest ties of nature and of society seemed to be cast loose. Relations and friends denounced by their friends and kindred, persecuted, slain; men, as in earthquakes, shipwreck, or pestilence, oaring for themselves alone, and regardless of the rest of human kind. The morals of the people sank lower and lower amidst such deeds and such examples; and the subsequent rebellions, the public miseries, and the exercise of tyranny, sprang from this source.

The brigandage increased, but it was extinguished. This excess of violence was of short duration: all the Calabrese, whether the persecuted or the persecuting, acted as desperate men; and as the outlaws were by far the inferior in numbers, engaged in a bad cause, scattered, betrayed, they were crushed. So that out of three thousand, whose names appeared on the list of proscription in the beginning of November, not even one remained at the close of the year. Many were killed in fight, many were executed, many perished by hunger, some escaped into Sicily, and a few remained after these trials of fortune alive, but immured in dungeons.

Such deeds could not be done, such cruelties could not be practised even under the mask of justice, without producing a revulsion in the minds of men. No necessity of circumstances could be adduced at this time as a plea for the extermination of thousands of men, women, and children. The Neapolitans, who had been accustomed to view the savage mountaineers of Calabria with aversion, came now to regard them with pity. Murat, who had been looked up to with hope, and even with some affection by the middle classes of his kingdom, became now an object of dread; and he, and the French in general, shared in the abhorrence which Manhès and other individuals had inspired.

The French had driven from Naples a set of corrupt and contemned tyrants; they had introduced a better system and administration of law; in several respects they had bettered the condition of the people; and they were for a time welcome in the land. But their insulting airs as conquerors, their arbitrary exercise of power, and above all the introduction of a military conscription, had already tended to alienate the minds of the Neapolitans from French dominion. The atrocities committed by Manhès, under the authority of King Joachim, filled the measure of discontent; but impatient as they had become of the yoke, they were unable to shake it off. Military strength and suspicious vigilance kept them down.

But from this time the provinces, and even the great towns of Naples, became at heart thoroughly hostile to the domination of France. A similar aversion, though not quickened by similar cruelties, had already spread through the people of Rome and Tuscany; and the Italians yet live who have from that time taught their children to dread and deprecate the interference of the French in the interests of Italy.

Appendix: Papers Referred to in Military Transactions in the Mediterranean

A. Lord Castlereagh's letter, "most secret," regarding Gibraltar, ... 19th July, 1805.
B. Sir James Craig to Lord Castlereagh, 9th Dec., 1805.
C. The same to the same, . . . 11th Feb., 1806.
D. The same to the same, . . . 11th Feb., 1806.
E. General Orders, ... 6th July, 1806.
F. Sir John Moore to General Fox, . 24th Aug., 1806.
G. Sir J. Stuart to General Fox, . . 26th Aug., 1806.
H. Extracts from the Letters of Paul Louis Courier, Aug. and Sept., 1806.
K. Mr. Drummond to General Fox, . 27th Jan., 1807.
L. Intercepted Letters from King Joseph to Napoleon, and to his wife, then Queen of Naples, . April, 1807.
M. Lord Castlereagh to General Fox (secret), 21st May, 1807.
N. Sir John Moore to General Fox, . 25th July, 1807.
O. The same to the same, . . . 28th July, 1807.
P. The same to the same, . . . 19th Sept., 1807.
Q. Instructions for General Officers . 21st Sept., 1807.
R. Returns of the British Forces in Sicily at different periods, 1805 to 1809.
S. Extracts from private letters to Colonel Bunbury, March to October, 1810.

Appendix A.

Most Secret.   Downing Street, 19th July, 1805.

Sir,

I think it right to apprise you that secret information has been received that every effort will be made by the Prince of Peace for the recovery of Gibraltar to Spain by force, by surprise, or by treachery.

An agent, whom he meant to employ, has recently had several interviews with him at Aranjuez. The prince gave him a paper, signed by himself, promising half the property of the fortress to such of the garrison as would join in betraying the place, and a gratuity of £100,000 to those who should effect its surrender. An agent was to go to Gibraltar with this proposal, who was to correspond with the general commanding at Cadiz.

A scheme of taking off the garrison of Gibraltar and the chief officers by poison was mentioned; another was to take advantage of a great festival to get the garrison as much intoxicated as possible, when a party was to spike the guns of the chief batteries, and an attempt to be made for surprising the town. The Prince of Peace said that he had a person in his pay whilst General Sir T. Trigge was in the garrison; and he mentioned that the attempt of which you gave an account in January last was true.

The information adds that a very large force was prepared against Gibraltar, and that General Moreau was employed by the Spaniards.

You will preserve entire secrecy as to the channel through which this information comes, and as to the point of an agent having been appointed to carry offers to Gibraltar, lest such particulars being public might affect the channel of intelligence; but you will make use of this notice for the purpose of increasing vigilance, watching the disposition of the garrison, and the appearance of suspicious strangers, or the conduct of suspected residents.

I am. Sir,
Your most obedient and humble servant,
(Signed) Castlereagh.

The Right Honourable and Honourable
General Fox, &c. &c. &c.

APPENDIX B.

From General Sir James Craig to Viscount Castlereagh.

Naples, 9th December, 1805.

My Lord,

I have thought it more proper to reserve for a separate communication the observations that I might have to offer to Your Lordship on the subject of our situation here; as arising, in the first instance, from the step which His Sicilian Majesty has thought it expedient to adopt, in signing a treaty of neutrality with France, under a declaration delivered at the same moment to the Russian minister, that he considered it extorted by force, and consequently no ways obligatory on him, but, on the contrary, that it was his intention to adhere to his prior treaty with Russia; and in the next, from the unforeseen, and, as they appear to me, equally unaccountable events that have taken place in Germany, and the consequent evacuation of the North of Italy, by the army of the Archduke Charles.

Of the first of these events I had no notice till after I had received General Lacy's requisition to repair to this place; and, until the period when the arrival of the Russian fleet at Syracuse, for the purpose of forming a junction with us, was in hourly expectation. I beg to be perfectly understood as not meaning to convey the slightest complaint or reflection on Mr. Elliot, when I add that the notice he sent me of this event was unaccompanied with any detail or comment of any sort that might have assisted me in forming a judgment as to the nature of the transaction; for the fact was, he was not officially informed on the subject, and was totally unconcerned in the business; and in order to set this part of the subject in as clear a light as possible to Your Lordship, I beg to enclose an extract of the letter from that gentleman to which I allude. His sentiments on this subject perfectly concur with mine.

Thus circumstanced, it was still a matter of serious reflection to me. It was impossible that any instructions that His Majesty had thought proper to give me for the guidance of my conduct, could advert to a circumstance that could not be foreseen, and I certainly felt myself left in a great measure to the exercise of that discretion on which, on other points, His Majesty had thought proper to place reliance. I felt a very great repugnance to stand forth either as directing the public operations of my country on this occasion, or even in my individual capacity, as the supporter of what in its outline, and under the circumstances of a total ignorance of its detail, could not but appear an act of perfidy; and had the transaction stood simply on its own bottom, unaccompanied with any other consideration than the consequences which might arise from it to the government with whom it originated, I should not have hesitated to have declined giving my support or protection to it.

Under the present situation, however, I was not to stop at that consideration only; His Majesty had thought proper to enter into an alliance with Russia, and I was enjoined to co-operate with the army of His Imperial Majesty; it was by the general of that army that I was called on to proceed here, I had all along during my communication with that general, for the space of three months, given him to understand that I should acquiesce in his requisition to join him; and I of course must be aware that in any arrangement he had made for his future operations, he must have relied on that junction: that junction must even be of the more importance to him now that a considerable part of the reinforcements which he had expected from the Black Sea had not arrived, and a failure in it might go to the length of the ruin of his army.

A strict adherence to my engagement with the Russian general appeared, therefore, to me my first and greatest duty. I viewed it as a call on national honour, of more weight than the abstaining from abetting an act that I could not approve, but which, in the loose morality of the present times, might, perhaps, find many defenders. Upon a more serious reflection, it appeared to me, even that without subjecting myself to the imputation of an unworthy equivocation, I might consider myself as acting totally independent of the objectionable transaction on the part of the Court of Naples.

I appeared, and in fact came here, as the ally of Russia; and if the operations of that ally, to whose assistance I came, carried him into a country which, from a previous transaction of its government, had placed itself in a particular situation with respect to the enemy, I do not feel that it became any consideration of mine, or that I was at liberty, from that circumstance, to refuse performing my engagements to His Majesty's ally.

Since my arrival here no circumstance whatever has occurred to call for any official declaration of my sentiments on this business; and it has not appeared to me necessary that I should voluntarily enter into any unavailing discussion now, in which it would be scarcely practicable to avoid offending the Court of Naples: in my general conversation, however, I have never hesitated to express my opinion. I have always considered the Treaty as unnecessary; but being made, it ought not to have been broken.

My sentiments are, I believe, perfectly understood; and I know that General Lacy individually concurs in them, though he submits to the act of the Minister of his Court. I leave Your Lordship to judge of the astonishment with which I heard the very confused accounts that were given me on my landing of the fate of the Austrian Army in Germany.

Its immediate consequence in the retreat of the Archduke Charles was of course the circumstance that, as affecting us the most, became the object of our principal attention. The French, who had marched out of this kingdom, and who seemed to have no other view but that of joining Massena as rapidly as possible, were immediately stopped, (though part of it has since proceeded), and about 4,000 men remain in Ancona.

I do not know that there is at this moment anything else between us and the Po—at least anything of any consequence. Massena and the gross of the French Army appear at present to be employed in following the archduke, and our latest accounts from Upper Italy are, that the viceroy, Eugene Beauharnois, is collecting a corps of 30,000 men at Bologna, for the avowed purpose of coming this way.

There is no disadvantage under which we labour that affects us so materially, as that of the want of communication. The consequence necessarily being that we get no intelligence or account of either the progress of the war or the negotiations that may be going on, but those that the French choose to circulate; and on these I am not inclined to place the reliance that a great many people do. However, that may be, until we receive further instructions arising out of the new system that must probably be adopted on account of the change of situation from the destruction of the Austrian Army, it must be on the intelligence that we do get, such as it is, that we can alone take our resolutions.

It is obvious that Massena can have no difficulty in detaching what may be necessary to render the viceroy's army formidable as to numbers. The frontiers of this kingdom are indeed represented as strong; and Your Lordship is in possession of the strength of the army we shall have to defend them.

This is certainly inadequate, and the Neapolitan part of it is still to be raised; and when raised can for the campaign be considered in no other light than recruits, on whom certainly very little reliance is to be placed.

In short, my Lord, I have little hesitation in giving my opinion that if France chooses to take the present opportunity of becoming masters of the kingdom of Naples, it will not be in our power to prevent it; nor could we expect to protract our resistance so long as to enable us to receive the reinforcements that would be necessary to secure it from them.

My present advice to General Lacy has therefore been to take up the cantonments we propose to occupy, and there wait for either instructions from our respective governments, or at least a more perfect knowledge of what is going on in other parts of the world with which our own fate is intimately connected. In the meantime, to be prepared for every possible event, we keep our transports here,

I do not enter more at large on this part of my subject, because at present we really are too little acquainted with it to be able to reason soundly on it. We do not precisely know where Massena is. The *Lively* frigate, however, is to sail in a few days, which will furnish me with another opportunity of addressing Your Lordship, when I hope to do it more fully.

  I have the honour to be, my Lord,
    Your Lordship's most obedient humble servant,
      (Signed)   J. H. Craig,
Right Honourable Lord Viscount
Castlereagh, &c, &c.

Appendix C.

From General Sir James Craig to Viscount Castlereagh.

           Messina Harbour, 11th Feb., 1806.

My Lord,

  My despatch, No. 22, by the *Jalouse*, was a very short one, and was not written under circumstances that would admit of my entering into any of those details with respect to our evacuating the kingdom of Naples, which I am aware are requisite for His Majesty's information on a subject which is likely to be attended with important consequences. I was under the necessity of deferring these for a future opportunity.

  So early as by the first despatch which I had the honour of addressing Your Lordship after our landing in Naples, Your Lordship will have perceived that under the then existing circumstances of the first defeats of the Austrian armies and the consequent movements of the Archduke Charles, I began to entertain great doubts of the possibility of our defending the kingdom of Naples; and nothing had certainly occurred that could tend in any degree to weaken this opinion, when I found myself called upon to apply it under a more detailed consideration of the circumstances of our situation, as they arose from the intelligence we had received that the French Army appointed to act against us was actually on its march.

  I have already in my despatch of the 2nd of January, informed Your Lordship of the meeting that took place at General Lacy's Headquarters the preceding day, and though I have mentioned the result of the meeting, as well as that which I foresaw likely to take place in consequence, I had not, however, the time that would have been necessary for me to enter into the motives and reasonings which guided our opinions, particularly those on which my own were founded, and for which I am the more immediately accountable to His Majesty.

  It was very clear that Massena, left at full liberty, had it in his power now to detach against us any force that he might deem adequate to the object he had in view; and if that which originally destined for the purpose was found unequal to it, no reason could be found to exist why he should not either from his own army or from any of the other resources which France so eminently possesses, increase it to any further magnitude that might be necessary to insure his success. We, on the other hand, with numbers that were ill calculated for the defence of so extensive a frontier, found ourselves besides, from accidental causes, so hampered and embarrassed with difficulties with respect to movement, as greatly to detract from the real efficiency of that force, such as it was.

We were still short by 600 horses of the number that had been promised us by the Court of Naples, so that after leaving a considerable portion of our artillery behind us at Castel-à-Mare, that which accompanied the line to our cantonments was still but ill-supplied and little capable of movement, and as to camp equipage, or officers' baggage, we had no means of transporting either. The Russians were pretty much in the same situation, excepting that their deficiency of horses did not exceed 300; and as to the Neapolitans they had literally nothing; but in their march to their position had relied entirely on the resources of the country, pressing mules and asses for their service the whole way, and leaving the roads covered with the carcases of those that perished under the severity of ill-usage.

But even these wants and difficulties, great as they were, were still of inferior consideration to those which arose from our deficiency in cavalry. Nothing could prevent the enemy from bringing what number he thought proper, and this, in a country great part of which is extremely well adapted to that arm, would have given a decisive turn against us; defeat would have been certain ruin to us, while success would have been nugatory from our inability of pursuing it.

Obliged to abandon the frontier which General Lacy supported by the opinion of General Oppermann, his quartermaster general, declared to be indefensible, no other position which was within our means of attaining presented itself, but one which, though not a position of strength to compensate for deficiency in numbers, covers in some degree the entry into the plain on which Naples is situated. This, all things considered, seemed the most advantageous spot on which we could have made a stand; and however superior in numbers he may be, there were still no grounds for despairing of our repulsing the enemy's attack in it; but it did not appear that we should gain much by doing so: covered by his numerous cavalry, he would have retired without our daring to pursue him, and renewing his attacks day after day, it was more than probable that he would have found one fortunate in the end; or, if not, he might have awaited quietly till he brought down further reinforcements, of whose march we might have remained ignorant, till we saw them in their line.

While we on our parts had no succour to look for, and what was of more consequence, had no point on which we could retire; retreat was to us impossible, for though the transports were at hand to receive us, yet an embarkation in the face of an enemy is a bad resource. Our transports too were particularly unfavourably situated for hasty embarkation, which was scarcely practicable, and under certain winds, which are precisely those that most prevail at this season of the year, we might have remained eight or ten days under the enemy's fire, without a possibility of getting away from it.

With respect to the Neapolitan Army, or the internal resources to be drawn from the armed population of the country, General Lacy laid but little stress on either. The former consisted of about 7,000 men; I rather think that after the arrival of two regiments that were drawn from Sicily it might somewhat exceed that number. For Your Lordship will observe that its real strength was never ascertained; nothing being less to be relied on than a Neapolitan return, and no possibility of personal inspection having ever existed. But when we deduct from this number what must necessarily have been left for the guard of the royal family, and for the security of the forts of Naples, with the garrison of Gaeta, I do not imagine they could have brought above 4,000 into the field.

This army it is to be observed had been ordered to be increased by an addition of 30,000 men; and of these it was said that about half were actually assembled. But only a small portion of that half had even joined the regiments to which they were appointed, so that the whole were in fact recruits of the rawest and most untrained description.

Upon the levy *en masse* both General Lacy and General Oppermann seemed to place no sort of reliance. They had very lately visited a considerable tract of country, and their report as to the state and disposition of the people was most unfavourable. I had no opportunity of forming a judgment on my own inspection, but the accounts I had received from the inquiries I had made, did not lead me to expect that they would turn out with the alacrity which the Court seemed to expect they would shew. Indeed, they had already manifested a considerable degree of backwardness in the only part in which they had been called upon to embody themselves.

All these considerations which I have presented to Your Lordship's view were general, and I believe operated upon the minds of all; but with respect to myself, I felt the force of others which concerned the interests of Great Britain only. I considered the defence of Sicily as an object of considerable more importance than that of Naples could be; and I was loth to hazard the means of securing the former in what we seemed all to be convinced must be an unavailing attempt to insure the latter.

If we failed in Naples nothing could save Sicily. Whereas, by giving up the former, and transporting the army to that island, we at least secured that which appeared to me by far the most important object of the two. I could not, therefore, but be exceedingly desirous not to hazard the corps I commanded, where I considered its destruction as so probable, and for an inferior stake to that which might soon be at issue with so much better founded hopes of success.

These were the considerations, my Lord, which guided the opinion which I gave from the first of its becoming a subject of discussion. I always, however, took care to mark as strongly as language could do so, that it was only an opinion, which, feeling as I did, I thought myself bound to give frankly and without disguise; at the same time, I desired it to be perfectly understood, that if General Lacy thought otherwise, and chose to undertake the defence of the kingdom of Naples, the troops under my command were at his orders, and perfectly ready to take their share of the task on whatever point he might direct.

To this opinion I have always added another, which was, that if a re-embarkation of the combined armies was once resolved on, no time should be lost in carrying it into effect. This I insisted on the more because I saw that the subject was little understood, and the dangers of an embarkation in the face of an enemy not so apparent as could have been wished, at the same time that the local disadvantages of the situation in which our part of the transports lay, increased to us in a tenfold degree the danger that might have arisen from delay.

Under these circumstances I thought myself warranted in stating to Your Lordship, as I did in my despatch, No. 21, the great probability that I foresaw of our ultimately coming to the resolution of evacuating the kingdom. A subsequent meeting, however, having taken place two days after at Naples, by General Lacy's desire, at which, in addition to Sir John Stuart, General Campbell and Colonel Bunbury attended, another proposal was there made and acceded to.

It was here proposed that we should retire into Calabria, and taking advantage of the natural strength of the country, defend ourselves there, for the chance of a more favourable turn of affairs; or, what I confess appeared to be still more to me the object, till the arrival of orders or instructions from the Emperor of Russia, without which it seemed now to be doubtful with the officers of that army whether it would be justifiable to take any decisive step. At this meeting it was my misfortune to differ entirely from the whole of the officers assembled, except Brigadier-General Campbell; for as by this measure we left the capital and all the richer provinces of the kingdom entirely uncovered and at the mercy of the enemy, I could not, I confess, see any possible motives that could induce us to run the still greater hazard of it, than those which would have attended our meeting the enemy on the frontier.

As it was impossible to form any magazine or depot, we should have starved in a week's time. I found, indeed, that a reliance was placed on a constant supply by sea of flour or bread from our transports, by means of a small port in the Gulf of Policastro, which is the only one that exists in the whole tract between Reggio and Salerno, at the entrance of the Gulf of Naples; while Messina was the nearest port in which our transports could have remained. There was confessedly no road to this harbour, the communication with which for the last five miles was only by a track up a strong steep mountain practicable only for mules.

I could not but give my opinion upon the danger at any rate of relying upon such a communication for the supply of an army; but besides this, having accidentally had occasion to make enquiry as to what harbours there might be on the coast of Calabria, though without any view to the present question, I thought I recollected this one having been mentioned to me as fit only for the very small craft of the country.

However, I was not sufficiently certain to feel myself competent to combat the assurances that every enquiry had been made from able pilots, and that though small it was sufficient in other respects for the proposed purpose. At my desire, therefore, Captain D'Urban was despatched the next morning in the ambuscade, to examine into this point, which would have been of no small importance to us; and on his return he reported the harbour to be totally unfit for the purpose for which it was proposed to employ it; unsafe, and capable at most of receiving two transports, which must lie at the point liable to go ashore every moment that the wind was a little stronger than usual.

With regard to the Calabrians, their attachment or willingness to give any effectual assistance was, I knew, extremely doubtful; but I felt also, although I did not well know how to bring it forward in argument, that there existed a circumstance which would probably very materially affect our situation with regard to them, whatever might be their original disposition.

Although we had found a communication with our ships, the fact was, the Russians had no provisions in their ships, neither had they any money nor credit by which they could have procured it. The consequence would have been that they would have supplied themselves; in three days' time not a Calabrian would have come near us, and in six, I should have expected to have found them in arms, cutting off all our small parties without distinction to whom they belonged, and instead of giving us help acting against us.

The country into which it was proposed we should retire is very strong; and as to the mere circumstances of our being able to defend ourselves there, it offered such facilities that I imagine there could not have been much difficulty in it; although of all the nations of Europe the Russians are the least adapted to war in a mountainous country. Retreat, however, should such become necessary, was scarcely practicable; for about 90 miles there is a very good road, but beyond that there is no communication but by a track passable only by mules, over mountains and across watercourses and valleys, in such manner that at the first step we must have abandoned artillery, stores, sick, in short, everything that could not be carried on the backs of the animals for 200 miles more.

However, the other officers present, seeing these circumstances in another point of view, or not giving to them the same weight that I did, General Lacy declared his determination to embrace the proposal, and to march immediately into Calabria. I again took the opportunity to assure him that whatever might be my opinion as to the expediency of the measure, he would hear no more of it from me, but that my sole object would now be to use my best endeavours to carry it into effect according to the directions I might receive from him: and I the very next morning began the previous arrangements for that purpose. These were, however, soon rendered unnecessary, by the court having given their decided negative to the measure, which could be of no possible use to them.

The paper in which their opposition to this proposal was announced, was never communicated to me. General Lacy only told me that it was conceived in such terms of indiscreet invective, that he had returned it, and had not kept any copy.

General Lacy then determined to concentrate his cantonments behind the Volturno, preparatory to our embarking, as the country beyond that river is a plain most favourable to cavalry, in which we were so weak. Some variation in our intelligence relative to the numbers and movements of the French, and a desire, as far as was found possible, to accord to the wishes of the court, induced him, however, afterwards to come to the resolution of suspending the (?), and of waiting in the position I have formerly mentioned, till these were more precisely ascertained. Precisely at this moment, *viz.* the 7th January, and while General Oppermann was with me at my headquarters, conversing on the subject. General Lacy received a despatch from the Emperor of Russia, dated the 7th of December, detailing the unfortunate Battle of Austerlitz, and directing him to provide for the security of the corps under his command by immediately retiring to Corfu.

As this order was precise, and left nothing to his discretion, the general did not consider himself any longer at liberty to delay embarking beyond the time that would be indispensably requisite to do so; and having, therefore, sent for me, to communicate this order to me, the necessary arrangements were made; and, as we had by far the longest march, it was agreed that we should commence the movement on the 10th. The head of our column arrived at Castel-à-Mare on the 13th, and having embarked everything, we were able to put to sea on the 19th.

While the embarkation was going on, Mr. Elliot and Captain Sotheron, having come over to Castel-à-Mare (previous to which I wrote the letter to Mr. Elliot, a copy of which Your Lordship will find enclosed, as also a letter from that gentleman to me, and of my answer, as they passed during the march), among other conversation, assured me that they had good grounds for saying that the Russians could not possibly embark under ten or twelve days, as it would require at least that time to get their vessels ready, and supplied with provisions. It may be necessary to observe to Your Lordship, that during our march General Lacy had written to me, to propose to me to halt for a few days: a copy of this letter I do myself the honour to enclose.

It so happened that it was not delivered to me till the following day; when, being sent to me, it was put into my hands in the general's presence. I made no hesitation in concurring with his desire, but I submitted to his consideration the very great inconvenience to which it would subject me. The general immediately acquiesced in the force of my representation, and seeming to me to lay as little stress on any success to be expected from negotiation as I confess I did myself, be desired me to continue my march. The next day I thought it right to answer his letter, a copy of which I also enclose.

I certainly at the time considered this as of very little importance, and as an occurrence only between General Lacy and me; nor should I probably have mentioned it to Your Lordship, had it not been, to my great surprise, that I have since found that it has been represented as a refusal on my part to support the Russians. I did not, indeed, know that this malignant turn had been given to it, till after the following circumstance had taken place, completely to refute the imputation.

This halt that had been proposed went, as Your Lordship will observe, no further than for three or four days, as, by the postscript in the general's letter, which was written in his own hand, he says he shall be ready to embark on the 16th; but the accounts given by Mr. Elliot and Captain Sotheron, extending the period of their detention on shore to ten or twelve days, which might even be prolonged, from the same impediment of bad weather, the situation of the Russians appeared to me to be more serious, and very far from being free from danger. I therefore immediately suspended our embarkation, which was then begun; and proceeded myself to headquarters, where, acquainting the general with what I had heard, I added that I came again to put myself under his orders (for he had given up the chief command of both us and the Neapolitans immediately on our beginning our march), and that if he thought it necessary, I would immediately disembark what was on board, and either march towards him to support him, or remain in constant readiness to do so whenever he thought proper to call for us, as he might think best.

The general expressed himself in warm terms of acknowledgment, but assured me that he did not see the slightest necessity for my delaying our embarkation a moment, the possible consequence of which he was well aware of;—that no consideration should make him defer his, and that he proposed beginning the day after the following. His embarkation actually commenced on the 17th.

I have now, my Lord, given Your Lordship every circumstance of detail relative to this event, which I am aware of, as being necessary to convey to His Majesty every possible degree of information, in its military point of view, that I think His Majesty would wish to be in possession of. The clamour of the Court of Naples has been great, and in the style of invective which has been assumed, I shall not be surprised if much misrepresentation has taken place. On the other hand, though I owe every acknowledgment to General Lacy, whose candour, frankness, and honour, have been shown on every occasion, yet I cannot extend the same to the Minister of the Russian Court.

From him I am sure no steps will be omitted that may be wanting to represent circumstances as he may think necessary to his own views; unfortunately, too, from the situation in which General Lacy was placed, all our military communications with the court were made through him; so that I ascribe not a little of the violence of the latter to the light in which he has placed circumstances to them. His Majesty will, I am sure, do us the justice to believe that it was not without sentiments of extreme regret, and under every feeling becoming soldiers, that we found ourselves thus compelled to abandon the field to the enemy, although from causes with which we had no concern. The responsibility of it however I take entirely on myself, and therefore have been anxious to detail the grounds on which I have proceeded.

Until the arrival of the orders for the Russians retiring, I held myself bound, by every sentiment of duty and of honour, to co-operate with them; and nothing should have been wanting on my part to do so.

After that period, and from the moment that General Lacy had given up the chief command, the line of conduct to be pursued regarded ourselves only; and I could have under consideration no other motives but those of protection to His Neapolitan Majesty's dominions, and the safety of my own army.

Could I have seen the slightest grounds for any hopes of success in the former,—had there appeared in the court any of that energy that was necessary to meet the peril of the moment, or in the people of that public spirit and attachment to the government, that could lead to an expectation of exertion on their part—had there been the smallest trace of a spirited nobility, generously devoting themselves to the safety of their prince and country,—however unavailing I might have considered all these as likely to be in the end, against a force that would be increased so infinitely beyond what they could have resisted, I should, nevertheless, have trusted to the indulgence of His Majesty and of my country if I had so imminently hazarded the troops under my command, by sharing all the dangers of the attempt with them. Of their cheerful concurrence I have not the smallest doubt.

But, my Lord, the prospect that presented itself to our view was widely different from this picture; different in every respect; nor would it, under these circumstances, have been an object of other than serious consideration to me that their army is commanded by an emigrant French officer.

I have no reason to doubt the individual honour or fidelity of that officer; but there are few or none of these gentlemen who do not pant after an opportunity to return to their country, and more particularly just now when they seem anxious to partake of the sort of splendour that it enjoys from the late successes that have attended its armies. The permission to do so must be purchased by some great service; and I confess I could not feel very secure while depending so much on a temptation so strong.

I have the honour to be, my Lord,
Your Lordship's most obedient humble servant,
J. H. Craig, General.
The Right Hon. Viscount Castlereagh, &c. &c. &c.

P.S.—I have written this long letter, my Lord, under such circumstances of ill health as will I am sure plead my excuse for any inaccuracies that may have occurred in it. Nothing indeed but my anxiety that His Majesty should receive every information on the subject could have enabled me to support the exertion. On reperusing it I find I have nowhere adverted to the numbers of the enemy.

Our original intelligence made them from 32,000 to 35,000 men; the latest accounts, however, and those on which I most depend, made those who were actually arrived in cantonments in the vicinity of Rome 22,000; and the division at Ancona not being in those cantonments, as it was probably meant to advance along the Adriatic to keep the Neapolitans in check, is not included; it amounted to near 4,000 men.

To these is to be added a second line which was always alluded to in all our accounts as being on its march, and which Mr. Jackson expressly mentions to be composed of three divisions of Massena's army. These were greatly impeded in their progress by bad weather and the difficulties of the roads; and the troops about Rome halted a considerable time for them. They are stated by several concurring accounts at 16,000 men, and it is scarcely possible to suppose them less. The total of these something exceeds 40,000 men.

J. H. C.

APPENDIX D.

From General Sir James Craig to Viscount Castlereagh.

Messina Harbour, 11th Feb., 1806.

My Lord,

Upon our leaving Naples, the measures to be pursued for securing the Island of Sicily from falling into the hands of the enemy became of course the object of my most serious consideration; and I was the more anxious on the subject because it was obvious that the French having turned their views to the possession of His Sicilian Majesty's dominions would not omit any effort for obtaining possession of that part of them which are not only so valuable in themselves, but in which they know we are so much interested. I therefore could not but consider the danger as imminent, and the expediency of guarding against it as great.

These will certainly increase in proportion as the enemy succeed in establishing themselves in the kingdom of Naples, and particularly in Calabria; but as they must be well aware that we should not be wanting in our exertions for the security of that point to which these more immediately lead—I mean the citadel of Messina—the anticipating us in the possession of that fortress must be an advantage not likely to escape them.

Four or five thousand men slipped down the coast in the small vessels of the country were quite sufficient for the purpose, and the little preparation necessary for such an undertaking, at a time when all Italy was full of troops in movement, might have been made at Genoa, Leghorn, or Civita Vecchia, unknown to us at Naples. Unfortunately too, just at that period we received accounts of Lord Collingwood having again quitted the Mediterranean, and being cruising off Cadiz; so that these seas were left entirely open to the enemy, and there seemed nothing to prevent his coming in greater strength from Toulon or Genoa.

Under these circumstances a direct movement to Messina was the most obvious measure of security that could offer itself, and, in fact, the only certain one that could be pursued. I, however, knew too well the jealousy of the Court of Naples on this head to propose it at once; but I wrote to Mr. Elliot a letter to be laid before His Sicilian Majesty, offering in general terms my assistance for the protection of the Island of Sicily.

As a difference of opinion had existed between Mr. Elliot and me on the subject of my coming to Sicily, I have thought it best for

Your Lordship's information, as well as in justice to that gentleman, to enclose to Your Lordship copies of all the letters that have passed between us upon it.

I trust that those letters written upon the spur of the occasion will convey to Your Lordship every information that may enable Your Lordship to form a proper judgment of what has passed.

When I left Naples my intention was to have gone to Agosta, there to wait till a more determined state of affairs might point out a decisive line of conduct for me; but upon a more serious reflection of the extreme importance of this point, and in the unwillingness to run any possible hazard as to its safety, I afterwards determined to come to an anchor here, though not to land, and we have now been here since the 22nd *ult*. I have not permitted any soldier to go on shore, and but a very few of the principal officers. I have not landed myself.

I lament that there should have existed any difference of opinion between Mr. Elliot and me. His advice has always been of great weight with me; but upon the present occasion we have unfortunately seen the subject under points of view so widely different from each other, that it was impossible for me to act upon his while I remained unconvinced of the falsity of my own.

It has appeared to me that Mr. Elliot is too much inclined to place a confidence in the sincerity of the court, that I have found myself obliged to deny to it.

I am free to confess to Your Lordship that I place no reliance on it; constituted as it is, it is impossible that I should do so; and I will acknowledge that under the conviction of the extreme importance to the interests of Great Britain that Sicily should be in any other hands than those of France, I have been not a little actuated in my present conduct by a belief that it is as well to guard against the want of good faith in our friends as against the open projects of our enemies.

If the importance which I attach to the possession of Sicily was felt by His Majesty's Government when my instructions were framed, how much more must it appear in that light now, and how much more will it justify strong measures under the present circumstances, when the cession of Venice, and all its ancient possessions, by Austria, has given to France such an immediate and ready access to the Levant. The addition of Sicily would completely shut us out from that part of the world; but neither will the limits of a despatch admit, nor, writing to Your Lordship, is it at all necessary, that I should enter into the incalculable evils of such an event.

Mr. Elliot very early embraced the idea of negotiating with the French, which he wished the court to permit him to undertake, and towards which I believe he did take some steps, though without committing himself to any precise proposal. I confess I saw no great prospect of any success in his endeavours; but in a negotiation conducted by him there could be no danger, and therefore I only waited with anxiety for the results; but when the court itself began a negotiation, at a moment when, without the means of defence, an irritated (and I am sorry to add in this instance not unjustly irritated) and vindictive enemy was within three marches of its frontier, and when it had nothing of its own to offer, the case was widely altered; it carried suspicion in every line of its progress.

At whose expense but at ours could it expect to purchase the advantages it sought by a treaty. The object was to save Naples, if not to the present possessor of the throne, at least to the hereditary prince; and to accomplish this I have no doubt that both that kingdom and this island would have been placed under French influence; their ports immediately shut against us; Malta in a manner blockaded; and indeed their government in hostility to us.

But the truth is, my Lord, I never could form an idea of the possibility of any treaty taking place under the present circumstances. Bonaparte evidently seizes the opportunity of manifesting by a public display of his greatness, that justice of which he at this moment so loudly and insolently boasts; and while he on the one hand affects to reward those who have adhered to him, he on the other greedily lays hold of the occasion of punishing what he holds up as an act of perfidy in a faithless government. This is a gratification to his arrogance and vanity that I am persuaded no consideration would induce him to forego, even if it were not attended with the advantage of another kingdom in his family.

I should apologise to Your Lordship for detaining you with all this speculative reasoning, but I am in hopes Your Lordship will excuse it, as it is on it in a great measure that I ground the opposition that I have hitherto made to the king's wishes of retiring to Malta; for however convinced I may be of the great consequence to us of the security of this place, yet if I could see any real probability of a treaty taking place by which their dominions might be preserved to the present Royal Family, and if I had assurances from Mr. Elliot that he was satisfied that such a treaty would not be productive of all the consequences I have alluded to, I believe I should be answering His Majesty's intentions, if

I did not interpose any impediment by any further opposition to what is considered as so essential to its completion.

The last accounts I have from Naples are by Mr. Elliot's letter of the 3rd, by which Your Lordship will perceive that I am given to hope that the citadel at this place will be put into my hands in the course of a few days. General Campbell writes me at the same time:

> In the meantime I am authorised to say that all parties here are now well satisfied you are at Messina; and, though not authorised to say it, I have little reason to doubt they would be equally well satisfied you should be in possession of the citadel.

This letter from him was of the 1st instant. The king being landed at Palermo, I have sent Sir John Stuart there to pay my compliments to His Majesty on his safe arrival, and accompanying my letter to Sir John Acton with a copy of Mr. Elliot's of the 3rd, which must probably be of a later date by two or three days than anything they could have received from Naples. I have proposed to His Majesty to permit us to land and take possession of those points that are necessary for the defence of these parts of his dominions. There has not yet been sufficient time for me to hear of Sir John's arrival at Palermo.

Your Lordship will observe by the enclosed series of letters that the Court of Naples is impressed with the idea of its being my intention to land here without their concurrence, or rather in direct opposition to it; and Mr. Elliot seems to have adopted the same notion. It is certain that in conversation with Mr. Elliot I did once mention that, as a measure to which it was not impossible I might feel myself obliged to have recourse; but nothing further to my recollection ever passed, and I am positive no communication with the court of any sort from me was ever calculated in any shape to countenance the idea of such being my intention.

However, as I have perceived that its existence among them has rather a tendency to forward my views than otherwise, I have never noticed it, as I should in that case be obliged to deny it.

The truth is that under the present circumstances I never had such an intention, our being in the harbour as we are answers every purpose of security to it; and it has been solely my intention to remain here till their situation was finally decided on, by which to guide my future conduct.

I am happy to add that, from every information I am able to procure, the attachment of the inhabitants of this island towards us remains unshaken.

I am assured that there are none but a part of the nobility and a few principal merchants who are supposed to be in any ways inimical to us. The clergy are very generally in our favour, and as to the inhabitants of this place they are clamorous for our landing.

I have the honour to be, my Lord,
Your Lordship's most obedient humble Servant,
J. H. Craig, General

The Right Hon. Lord Viscount Castlereagh,
&c. &c. &c.

Appendix E.

Plains of Maida, 6th July, 1806.

Parole Messina,

Major-General Stuart finds himself incapable of expressing to the troops the sentiments excited in him by their brave and intrepid conduct in the late action of the 4th, in which they gained so signal a triumph over a boasting and insolent enemy. Their distinguished behaviour on this memorable day will endear them in the breasts of their grateful countrymen—it will ensure to them the applause of their approving sovereign, and will add another immortal wreath to the laurels of the British Army.

The light brigade under Lieut.-Col. Kempt, who led the attack, and who charged and broke the enemy's favourite 1st light corps, displayed a combined instance of gallantry and discipline, of which military records have furnished but few examples.

The 78th and 81st Regiments, which formed the brigade of Brigadier-General Acland, shared the first and severest part of the action, with the light infantry, whom they were ordered to support. The gallantry and good conduct of the brigadier-general in fulfilling this duty, were most nobly seconded by the brave regiments under his orders.

The battalion of grenadiers, and the 27th Regiment, under the orders of Brigadier-General Cole, made a firm and intrepid resistance against a superior force; and a manoeuvre of the 27th Regiment, in throwing back a wing to receive the enemy's cavalry, was the strongest token of the excellent discipline of that corps.

The 58th and Watteville's regiment, which formed the brigade under the orders of Colonel Oswald, and which were brought up as a second line, sustained the advanced columns with the greatest spirit and intrepidity.

The conduct of Lieut.-Col. Ross in throwing the 20th Regiment into the wood on the enemy's flank, while the latter were attempting to turn our left, was a prompt display of gallantry and judgment to which the army was most critically indebted.

The artillery was well provided and most effectually served, under the direction of Major Lemoine, commander of that corps.

From the various public departments of the army, and especially so from Lieut.-Colonel Bunbury, Deputy Quartermaster-General, Sir J. Stuart has to acknowledge the most marked and able assistance, not only during the continuance of the action itself, but in all the arrangements preparatory to its commencement.

No language that the major-general could adopt would bear any proportion to the feelings with which he recurs to all the circumstances of this great, this signal day, to offer the expression of his own humble thanks on so memorable an occasion, would be presumptuous.

The army will receive the only acknowledgments that are adequate to their deeds, in the approbation of their sovereign, and their country; and every soldier whom the general has now the honour of addressing, will have an equal right with himself to make the boast hereafter, that he bore a part in the glorious Battle of Maida.

APPENDIX F.

From Lieut.-General Sir John Moore, addressed to General Fox.

24th of August, 1806.

Memorandum.

The annexed is a copy of the letter I left with Sir Sidney after the conversation I had with him; but it will be necessary for you to express your sentiments much more decidedly if you wish him to discontinue his interference in Calabria, where in his imagination he is directing the operation of armies, but where in reality he is only encouraging murder and rapine, and keeping up amongst that unhappy people, whom we have no intention to support, a spirit of revolt which will bring upon them the more severe vengeance of the French Government.

As long as Sir Sidney had money, he distributed it profusely; and now, with as little judgment, he is distributing arms, ammunition, and provisions. Transports are employed all along the coast with orders to receive and victual all the men, women, and children who apply to them; to reland them in Calabria, or carry them to whatever part of Sicily they direct. You will judge, in some degree, by Sir Sidney's orders to Captain Fellowes, of the style he has adopted. It will be necessary for you to send him a list of the transports, stating names and number, which you wish to be left at Messina subject to your call.

Appendix G.

Palmi, 26th of August, 1806.

My dear Sir,

I transmit for your perusal the enclosed letters from Colonel Philippis, *Presidé* of the province of Lower Calabria, by which you will find into what a scene of anarchy and confusion the whole population has been thrown by the conduct of the chiefs of the *Masse*, by whose dastardly flight from before the enemy the perpetrators of rapine have been brought into the interior, and every appearance of government dissolved. It is the attack of the poor, the worthless, the needy, against the better class of society.

Wherever the smallest party of our troops appear, tranquillity is restored. I reached this place last night with a subaltern's party and twenty men, at a moment that a numerous horde of brigands consisting of near 800 men were entering the town, with a demand of rations, &c.; and an universal pillage was expected by the terrified inhabitants. I sent to direct the chief of these brigands to retire with his people, and to call upon me *alone* this morning; to which he was perfectly obedient. I have desired him to abstain from entering the towns, and immediately to repair to and put himself under the orders of Colonel Cancellieri, who has been appointed by the king to the chief command of all these disorderly ruffians.

It is unfortunate that the people have no confidence in their own national troops, otherwise a disposition of men might be made for all the purposes of police: a few detachments at principal places by means of patrols would easily control the whole country.

I have exhorted the better class of people to establish themselves in civic guards; and to an institution of this nature, which I made at this place the last time I passed, has its peace been hitherto owing, amidst the general confusion around it. But last night its position was certainly critical. I remain, with great regard and respect,

My dear Sir,
Your faithful and obliged servant,
(Signed) J. Stuart.

To General the Rt. Hon. H. E. Fox,
&c. &c.

Appendix H.

Extract from the Letters of Paul Louis Courier

Cassano, le 12 Août, 1806.

Chacun après le dé vous montre comment il fallait jouer. S'il n'eût pas attaqué il n'y aurait qu'un cri—'Quoi, voir les Anglais, et ne pas tomber sur eux!'—L'aventure (the assumed name of one of the chiefs of the Masse), est facheuse pour le pauvre Reynier. Nulle part on se bat; les regards sont sur nous. Avec nos bonnes troupes, et à forces égales, être défaits en si peu de minutes! Cela ne s'est point vû depuis la révolution!

Scigliano, le 21 Août, 1806.

Or écoutez, vous qui dites que nous ne faisons rien. Nous pendîmes un Capucin à San Griovanni in Fiore, et une vingtaine de pauvres diables qui avaient plus la mine de Charbonniers que d'autre chose. Le Capucin, homme d'esprit, parla fort bien à Reynier. Reynier lui disait, 'Vous avez prêché centre nous.' Il s'en défendit; ses raisons me paraissaient assez bonnes. Nous voyant partis en gens qui ne devaient pas revenir, il avait prêché pour ceux à qui nous cédions la place. Pouvait il faire autrement? Mais si on les écoutait on ne pendrait personne. Ici nous n'avons pû pendre qu'un père et son fils, que l'on prit endormis dans un fossé. Monseigneur excusera: il ne s'est trouvé que cela. Pas une âme dans la ville; tout se sauve, et dans les maisons il n'est resté que des chats.

Nous rencontrons, par-ci par-là, des bandes qui n'osent pas même tenir le sommet dés montagnes. Leur plus grand audace fut à Cosenza, où l'Anglais (Battle of Maida) les amena. Il les fit venir jusqu'à la porte du côté de Scigliano, et ils y restèrent toute une nuit sans que personne dedans s'en doutât. S'ils fussent entrés tout bonnement (car de gardes aux portes, ah! oui, c'est bien nous qui pensons à cela!) ils prenaient au lit Moaseigneur le Maréchal avec la femme du Major. L'Anglais fut tué là. Le matin nous autres desconfits, qui venions de Cassano, traversant Cosenza nous sortîmes par cette porte à la pointe du jour, et les trouvâmes là dans les vignes. Il s'était avancé lui; mais sa canaille l'abandonna. Je le vis environné. Il jeta son épée en criant "Prisonnier." Mais on le tua. J'en fus fâché; j'aurais voulu lui rendre un peu les bons traitemens que j'ai reçus de ses compatriotes. C'était un bel homme, équipé magnifiquement. On le dépouilla dans un clin d'oeil; il avait de l'or beaucoup. Nous allons a la Mantea—&c.

★★★★★★

Amantea was a rugged little place upon the coast, and in communication with Sir S. Smith. The French were beaten off with loss in this attempt; but they took Amantea in the following January,

★★★★★★

Mileto, le 10 Sept., 1806.
À M. Le Général Mossel,
J'ai reçu, mon Général, la chemise dont vous me faîtes présent. Dieu vous la rende, mon Général, en ce monde-ci, ou dans l'autre. Jamais charité ne fut mieux placée que celle-là. Je ne suis pas pourtant tout nu; j'ai même une chemise sur moi, à laquelle il manque, à vrai dire, le devant et le derrière, et voici comment. On me la fit d'une toile à sac, que j'eue au pillage d'un village; et c'est là encore une chose à vous expliquer. Je vis un soldat qui emportait une pièce de toile. Sans m'informer s'il l'avait eu par héritage ou autrement, je lui donnai l'écu, et je devins propriétaire de la toile, autant qu'on pent l'être d'un effet volé. On en glosa: mais le pis fut que ma chemise faite et mise sur mon maigre corps par une lingère suivant l'armée, il fut question de la faire entrer dans ma culotte, la chemise s'entend, et ce fut là que nous échouâmes moi et ma lingère. La pauvre fille s'y empioya, et je la secondai de mon mieux; mais rien n'y fit: il n'y eut force ni adresse qui put reduire cette étoffe à occuper autour de moi un espace raisonnable.

Je ne vous dis pas, mon Général, tout ce que j'eus à souffrir de ces tentatives, maigre l'attention et les soins de ma femme de chambre, on ne put pas plus experte à pareil service. Enfin nécessité, mère de l'industrie, nous suggéra l'idée de retrancher de la chemise tout ce qui réfusait de loger dans mon pantalon, c'est-à-dire le devant etle derrière, et de coudre la ceinture au corps même de la chemise, opération qu'exécuta ma bonne couturière avec une adresse merveilleuse. Il n'est sorte de calembourgs et de mauvaises plaisanteries qu'on n'ait fait là-dessus; et c'était un sujet à ne jamais s'épuiser, si votre générosité ne m'eût mis en état de faire désormais plus d'envieque de pitié.

Je me moque à mon tour des railleurs, dont aucun ne possède rien de comparable au don que je reçois de vous. Il n'y avait que vous, mon Général, capable de cette bonne oeuvre dans toute l'armée; car outre que mes camarades sont pour la plupart aussi mal équipés que moi, il passe aujourd'hui pour constant que je ne puis rien garder; l'experience ayant confirmé que tout ce que l'on me donne va aux brigands en droiture. Quand j'échappai nu de Coregliano St. Vincent me vêtit, et m'emplit une valise de beaux et bons effets, qui me furent pris huit jours après sur les hauteurs de Nicastro. Le Général Verdier et son état major me firent une autre pacotille, que je ne portai pas plus loin qui Ajello, où je fus dépouille pour la quatrième fois. On s'est donc lassé de m'habiller et de me faire l'aumône: et on croit généralement que mon destin est de mourir nû, comme je suis né. Avec toute celà on me traite si bien, le Général Reynier a pour moi tant de bonté, que je ne me répens point encore d'avoir demandé à faire cette campagne, où je n'ai perdu après tout que mes chevaux, mon argent, mon domestique, mes nippes, et celles de mes amis.

Appendix K.

(*Private and Secret.*)

Palermo, Jan, 23rd, 1807.

My dear Sir,

The *Ajax* is just arrived here, and has brought despatches of the greatest importance. Sir John Duckworth will follow immediately. I tremble for his seeing ———— before I have time to speak to him, as otherwise your most secret orders will be no longer so. Things go on here as ill as possible, but if I had one person out of the way I could soon bring about an alteration. In the meantime, as we are going upon new enterprises it becomes absolutely necessary to secure ourselves in Sicily. For this reason, I am very desirous of going to Messina with Sir John Duckworth to combine with you and him the plans that it may be necessary to adopt. I enclose Sir John's letter to me.

I have the honour to be, my dear Sir,
Your most faithful humble Servant,
(Signed) W. Drummond.

His Excellency the Rt. Hon. General Fox.

(*Private.*)

Palermo, Jan. 27th, 1807.

My dear Sir,

I have delayed writing to you for these two days in hopes of having some communication with Sir John Duckworth, who arrived off Palermo the day before yesterday with the *Repulse* and *Windsor Castle* in company. His anxiety to proceed on his voyage induced him not to land, and I have been obliged to correspond with him the best way I could. Yesterday I sent Lord Burghersh (being confined myself with a cold) on board the *Royal George*, and desired him to detail my feelings and views to the admiral, whom I wish much you should see, as he passes by Messina. He seems not inclined to give entire credit to the report of the war having broken out between Russia and Turkey. In this he may be right, for we have nothing official on the subject.

Still, however, I am of opinion he would do well to take troops with him, or at least to have them follow him, when he goes up to the Dardanelles. If this should be your opinion likewise, which is of much more consequence than mine, it would be highly important to communicate with the admiral before he arrives at Malta. In all events I trust you will have time to write to him before he quits that island. Now as to the number of troops to be sent from Sicily, I think we ought to be extremely cautious. The court here will certainly be too happy to take any advantage of our weakness. I have no doubt in my own mind, though I cannot prove it, that the queen and her minions had applied to the Court of Petersburgh for a very large force to be sent to Sicily; and that since the diversion occasioned by the Turkish war will occupy the Russians, they have made propositions to Bonaparte.

That they have been negotiating with him for some time is a thing of which I am quite persuaded. I now have reason to believe that they are corresponding with the French government through Spain. Of this I have been informed by a respectable person here, who has generally pretty accurate intelligence. The reason of this detestable treachery arises partly from the abhorrence of the queen and her minions to everything English; and partly from the belief that France is stronger than England, and that sooner or later France will become masters of Sicily. They openly say, indeed, that we have not a sufficient force to protect the island. Under these circumstances you will judge whether it may be prudent to detach a large force at present. I rejoice to hear that reinforcements are coming out. Still, however, we must remember the enemies with whom we have to contend both without and within the island of Sicily.

It gives me great pleasure to announce to you the departure, and I hope for ever, of a person (Sir Sidney Smith), who has been acting a most extraordinary part here. I have frankly spoken my opinion to Sir John Duckworth about him. He continued his miserable intrigues to the very last, and was closeted with St. Clair for many hours the day previous to his departure. For all this he is rewarded with the Order of Ferdinand. By accident or design a letter was left on my table from the queen containing the following words:—

> *Je reçois la desagréable nouvelle que l'infernale intrigue et cabale a provoqué, quelquonque en sera le résultat, de loin ou de près, je serai toujours voire éternellement attachée et reconnoissante amie* (Signed) Charlotte. (With an ingenious device by way of flourish, where a heart is represented in the midst of flames), *ce 23 Janvier*, 1837.

It is easy to guess, though the cover and the direction are wanting, to whom this tender and delicate epistle was addressed. You, Sir John, Moore, and myself, are evidently understood to be the authors and abettors of the infernal intrigue and cabal against this naval Celadon.

There is another curious circumstance. The letters for you were sent to me by Sir Sidney Smith. I wrote a short letter to you, not to detain the messenger. Sir Sidney informed me he had despatches of consequence, and kept my messenger back for three hours. He then came himself, and sat down at the table where all my papers were. He pulled a packet from his pocket, and did me the favour to read one or two letters. Impatient to send off my messenger I got up, and he followed me out of the room. The next day I found the letter addressed to Captain Cochet on my table. I cannot swear that it was not among those sent to me, but I certainly read over all the directions, and do not remember to have seen this. The circumstance appears the more extraordinary, that Sir Sidney wrote instructions to Captain Cochet himself.

His conduct about Raphael Silvestri is of a piece with all the rest. He assured me he had never acted as Commander-in-Chief of the forces of the King of Naples since he got a well merited rebuke from the Admiralty; and yet here is his passport with his almost royal titles, dated the 6th of November, 1806.

I think it so important that you should have this intelligence that I shall close this letter without adverting to some other things that might be otherwise interesting for you to learn.

  I have the honour to remain, my dear Sir,
    Most faithfully yours,
      (Signed)   W. Drummond.
To the Hon. and Rt. Hon. General Fox,
&c. &c. &c.

Appendix L.

The two following letters (intercepted) from King Joseph afford evidence of the weakness of the French Army in the south of Italy, at the very time when our forces in Sicily were reduced by the detaching of 5,000 men to Alexandria, and were thus rendered unable to take advantage of the opportunity which presented itself. The first of these letters, addressed to the emperor, evinces the trembling submission with which Napoleon's brother was content to act as a nominal King of Naples.

Venosa, le 9 Avril, 1807.

Sire,

Je reçois les lettres de V. M. du 20. Je suis affligé de penser qu'Elle aura cru jusqu'au raoment qu'Elle recevra cette lettre, que je me suis permis d'ôter des régimens Français, pour faire entrer dans ma garde, des cavaliers d'élite ou des grenadiers. Je donne ina parole à V. M. que depuis la formation de ma garde, il y a aujourd'hui un an, temps où j'ai connû sa volonté, je ne me suis par permis de prendre un seul tambour Français; et je m'en garderai bien, et par le respect que je dois à ses ordres, et parceque je sens moi-même la nécessité et la justesse des dispositions qu'Elle me present.

Je vais faire partir pour l'Italie un régiment de cavalerie Française, et un régiment de cavalerie Napolitaine. Il ne me restera alors qu'un régiment de cavalerie, et un d'infanterie. Je n'ai pas d'autres troupes. Ainsi V. M. voit qu'Elle s'est trompée par les gens qui lui écrivent que le Général Dumas me fait faire beaucoup de levées de régimens. Je remercie V. M. de vouloir bien me donner tous les ans cent conscripts.

Voici le rapport que je reçois de la Sicile. M. Anthoine, que V. M. a toujours distingué m'écrit la lettre ci-jointe.

Je suis avec respect, Sire,

De V. M. le très-raffecti^e frère,

Joseph.

A Sa Majesté L'Empereur et Roi
à son Quartier Général.

Venosa, le 9 Avril, 1807.

Je reçois votre lettre du 31. Laborde sera le bienvenu: je ferai ce qu'il désire. Le Gén. Macdonald ne doit pas s'attendre à commander beaucoup de troupes. Je ne vois pas que je puisse lui donner plus de 2 à 3 mille hommes. Ce n'était pas non plus pour cela que je l'avais demandé. Le Maréchal Jourdan commande 5000 à Naples. Reynier (Illegible) Tout est en garnison. C'est pour cela que taut de Généraux ont dû partir. Je désire que vous ne cachiez rien de cela au Général Macdonald, pour qu'il ne se trouve pas abusé en arrivant. Je me porte très-bien.

Adieu, ma chère. Il faut que——se decide en homme, oui, ou non.

Joseph.

A sa Majesté La Reine de Naples
& de Sicile à Paris.

APPENDIX M.

Downing Street, 21st May, 1807.

(Secret.)

Sir,

Your letter of the 5th *ult.* has been received and laid before the king.

Considering the little probability there now exists of any further military operations being undertaken against the Turkish Empire, and hoping that no occasion will arise for sending more of our disposable force to Egypt, I am to convey to you instructions with respect to the troops at present stationed in Sicily, and the more immediate objects to which they may be considered applicable.

The strength and efficiency of the corps lately assembled under your orders having been considerably reduced by the detachment of the troops under the command of Major-General Fraser, to Egypt, it is impossible not to feel how much the power of what remains in Sicily to undertake offensive operations has been impaired.

As, however, an active exertion on the continent of Italy, either directed against Naples or some other point of that coast, may in the course of the ensuing campaign be of the utmost importance to the cause of His Majesty's allies, and as it is conceived that, consistently with a due attention to the precautions hereafter to be stated, a force of about 20,000 men, British and Neapolitans, may be made applicable to such a purpose, it is the king's pleasure that you do use every possible exertion, not only to prepare the British, but the Neapolitan troops, for such an enterprise. And although the quality of the latter is in all respects inferior to what could be wished, yet as numbers are in themselves of great importance, they must be encouraged, improved, and made the most of, with a view to this important object.

The strong desire that has always been evinced by the Court of Palermo that an effort should be made for the recovery of Naples, will enable you, so far as their army can be rendered effective, to prevail on them to take their full share in such an operation; and it certainly is desirable, for several reasons, that the Neapolitan troops should be brought as much forward, and employed as numerously as possible in any attempt of this nature, and that the British troops should be understood as co-operating rather than as prepared to take such an enterprise chiefly on themselves.

From the jealousy which has appeared on more than one occasion, with respect to our position in Sicily, it certainly would be imprudent to carry the whole of the British Army to the continent of Italy, leaving the Neapolitan troops in force in Sicily. In the event of such an expedition, it will therefore be expedient to leave a proportion of the king's forces to occupy one or two of the principal fortresses, so as secure the re-entry of our troops into that island; whilst it is desirable that the Neapolitan troops should be employed as largely as possible, not only as a pledge of the interest taken by the Neapolitan Government in the success of the operations, but also with a view to reserve the military power of the island more completely in our hands.

The last despatches from Mr. Drummond gave us reason to hope that an improved disposition has taken place in the Government of

Palermo. I trust that you will encourage and profit by it as much as possible; and as a means of doing so, that you will intimate to that court that you are instructed to invite them to co-operate with you in making the most active exertions with a view to offensive operations. You may acquaint them that measures have been taken for immediately replacing to the extent of 10,000 stand of arms the loss they have lately sustained; and that the king looks to His Sicilian Majesty's troops for bearing a distinguished share in any active operations which may be undertaken.

Under the uncertainty which prevailed with respect to the turn affairs might take to the eastward, when Mr. Drummond's proposition of sending a force against Naples was communicated to you, and considering the doubts you felt as to the course of measures which the government at home might, as things then stood, wish to pursue, His Majesty entirely approves of your having declined at that moment taking any steps for carrying such a plan into execution. As there is now, however, every reason to presume that the war with Turkey is reduced, on our part, to one of mere blockade; and as we may indulge the hope that Egypt will not be suffered to operate as any further drain upon our army, I am to impress upon your mind the importance of every exertion in your power being used to create the means of striking, under favourable circumstances, a blow against the enemy's power in Italy.

Much of the prudence of such an attempt must depend upon the information you may receive at the moment, of the precise state of the enemy's strength within the kingdom of Naples, as well as the means he possesses of speedily receiving reinforcements from the French forces which may be assembled in the North of Italy, whether with a view to enter Turkey, to watch Austria, or eventually to strengthen their army in the north of Europe.

Should the campaign open advantageously in Poland on the part of the Allies, and the French be weak in the north of Italy, the recovery of Naples might be undertaken with some hopes, if successful, of a permanent occupation being therein maintained; if, on the contrary, the French should be successful in Poland, and the troops in the north of Italy and Dalmatia be at liberty to turn themselves against the English and Neapolitan troops, no reasonable hope could in that case be entertained of holding Naples; and the operation must then be looked at, not as likely to lead to the re-establishment of the Neapolitan Government, but as a diversion calculated to draw off the enemy's forces and attention to a distant point.

In this case the advantage to be gained is certainly less considerable, but by no means to be disregarded, if it can be combined with a reasonable hope of destroying the French corps stationed in the kingdom of Naples before it can be supported; and also provided the attempt can be made without incurring too much military risk.

Upon the whole, it is His Majesty's wish that you should put yourself in a situation to move with the utmost conjoint force that can be assembled of the troops of the two powers, consistent with the principles above stated; so as to profit by any opening which may present itself, either to make a useful diversion in favour of our allies, or to re-establish His Sicilian Majesty's power in the kingdom of Naples.

To your zeal and discretion His Majesty is graciously pleased to confide the prosecution of these measures; and you may rely on receiving from me, not only every information which I may conceive can be of use to guide your judgment, but such explicit instructions, from time to time, as circumstances may point out, and as it may be possible to furnish from home, with respect to measures necessarily requiring a latitude being given to those intrusted with their execution.

   (Signed)   Castlereagh.

P.S.—Since the above despatch was written, intelligence has been received that the greater proportion of French troops assembled in the Venetian territories and in Dalmatia have been moved into Germany. As this distribution of their force must render them less strong with a view to the defence of Naples, I think it right to call your attention to it, in order that it may have such influence on your determination as the facts may appear to justify; of which it is reasonable to presume that you will be more accurately informed.   C.

To General
The Rt. Hon. Henry Edward Fox,
&c. &c. &c.

Appendix N.

Sir John Moore to General Fox.

             Palermo, 25th of July, 1807.

My dear General,

Yesterday I had my audience with the queen. As I wished to see her by myself, and to avoid all discussion with Drummond on the subject of it, until it was over, I applied to Sir John Acton to know what steps to take in order to see Her Majesty. He offered to write to her, which I accepted; and she fixed yesterday at three o' clock. In the meantime, as this is not the country of secrecy, Drummond got hold of it. He wrote to me, complaining that I had asked a secret audience without the knowledge of him or Circello. I answered, that I was sorry he had heard it from anybody but myself, as it was my intention, the moment it was over, to have told him what had passed, and my reason for applying for it through another channel than him; but, as it was, I must submit for a few hours to be thought what I was not—a bit of an intrigant; that I had no doubt of clearing myself to his satisfaction when I was at liberty to explain the truth. I went to the conference.

She received me as usual, most graciously, and allowed me full time to make my speech, which I need not repeat. She expressed herself satisfied, and she appeared to be so; and after more than half-an-hour's conversation, I retired. What effect this will have I know not, but I feel easier after it, as I feel I have fully acquitted myself of my part. Before I left her, she shewed me a letter from Drummond, complaining of having granted me an audience without his knowledge. I told her that the explanation I had had was of a personal nature, with which Mr. Drummond had no concern; but, at any rate, in the station I held, I could not consider myself in the light of an ordinary English subject here, but had a right to ask an audience of Her Majesty when I thought proper, quite independent of Mr. Drummond.

From the queen I drove to Drummond's. Our conversation very soon grew warm; for he began by laying down the law about himself as minister, which I did not like. I, in the first place, explained to him quietly enough my reasons for having acted on this occasion without his knowledge; that I probably should never do so again, for I had no wish to disoblige him, and should probably never have a motive for seeing any of the Court or Cabinet on business with which he was not previously acquainted: but I begged not to be considered as admitting his law; for should I command the forces, though probably I might never exert it, I should consider myself at liberty to communicate with Their Majesties when and how I thought proper.

One thing led to another: at length he complained of the manner I had spoken of him. He said there was nothing too contemptuous I had not expressed. I told him I had always thought his conduct weak and pusillanimous, and had always said so. He harped on this so long, that I at last told him that we had not heard of his speaking very respectfully of the generals.

I then told him of his conduct before company, on receiving a letter from you, declining the expedition to Naples, as well as the general tone of conversation at his house, which we had from Lord Burghersh and others, as well as his having revealed a conversation which passed between himself, you, and me; and his having represented, as a proposal on our part, that which was only mentioned in a passing manner (I mean what I said—that the best thing which could be done, was to send the queen to Trieste).

This was never proposed to be adopted, either by you or me, but only mentioned; that if possible, to be done, it would be the surest way to quiet Sicily. He denied the exclamation on the receipt of your letter, and also the having revealed the conversation to Lord Burghersh; this last he was, however, at last obliged) to allow. After much heat, we parted quietly. He has written a letter to you: when you compare it with what you know of the contents of his letters to Leckie, you will know the credit to be given to the assurances he now gives you.

I am sorry, however, that I was led into this scene: it was my wish to have avoided all allusion to the past; and as I wish, however much I despise him, to continue upon good terms with him, I expressed myself obliged towards him, and said I was sorry he was hurt at my having seen the queen without applying to him, but that I meant him no sort of slight. He is furious against Burghersh; and I must beg of you to explain to His Lordship that his name was drawn from me in the heat of argument, but that of course I said nothing but what he had said to you and to me. All this is very tiresome.

I have seen this morning the state of the troops for the field, which amount, of all arms, to 4,400 non-commissioned and privates only. On this subject I shall write to you more fully in a day or two.

In the meantime, believe me.

My dear General, very faithfully,
(Signed) John Moore.

Appendix O.

Sir John Moore to General Fox.

Palermo, 28th of July, 1807.

My dear General,

I had the pleasure of your letters of the 24th and 25th, with the enclosures. Mr. Drummond sent of the messenger with the letters for Girgenti yesterday afternoon, so I had but little time to write. I wrote a private letter to Lord Castlereagh, that he might be a little in the current of affairs here; but I had not time, nor are things here sufficiently decided yet to write fully.

I saw, yesterday, the greater part of the infantry; but the Prince Royal, as Inspector-general, would be present, which did not make me see the better. The men are good, but, upon the whole, they resembled the London Volunteers, with rather less discipline, and without their zeal and personal bravery.

This day I see the reserve, which St. Clair commands, and which is composed of the grenadiers and foreign regiment; tomorrow I see the cavalry; and in the meantime, I am getting returns of their whole military establishment. When this is done, I will bring them to a decision with respect to the command; and shall also settle with respect to the citadels of Syracuse and Messina, &c.; and I should hope to leave this the end of the week, and still to see you before you embark.

I had the curiosity to ask Captain Rowley whether the scene reported by Burghersh, which passed before Tatischeff, on the receipt of a despatch from you, was correct. He told me it was, and that at all times his language was disrespectful. This I tell you merely for your satisfaction and mine, but I wish to quote no more; therefore, unless you think it necessary for Lord Burghersh's peace of mind, do not name Rowley, who was averse to speak. I was anxious to make him; for, though I was convinced that Drummond lied, I was curious to ascertain it. You have not an idea of the solemn manner in which he denied the scene before Tatischeff, or of having ever spoken disrespectfully.

I have seldom met, in the character of a gentleman, with a more mean or unprincipled fellow. Drummond has told me that since he was at Messina, until the receipt of your letter respecting the command, he had never seen the queen, nor communicated with her; that he and Circello worked alone with the king, and nothing was ever communicated to the queen. I have been told, from authority I think undoubted, that seldom a day has passed without Drummond seeing or receiving notes from her; that Circello, nor no minister, ever dare present a paper, or make a proposal to the king, without previously showing it to the queen, and receiving her approbation; that Serrati alone did so, and she has made Drummond an instrument to get him turned out, and now laughs at him.

In short, it is impossible to believe a word he says. I shall write again in a day or two. Whatever you wish me to do when you are gone, either for individuals or otherwise, leave a memorandum, and it shall be done, as far as depends on me. Wherever you wish the 10th to be, either here or at Malta, order them accordingly, and tell Oakes

that he may arrange.
> Believe me always faithfully,
> (Signed)   John Moore.

Admiral Thornborough gave me the letter which accompanies this. He sailed on a cruise off Toulon the night before last.

Appendix P.

Extract of a letter from Lieut.-General Sir John Moore to General Fox.

Messina, 19th Sept., 1807.

My mission to Palermo ended much as you expected; they did not give me, nor ever intended to give me, any command over their troops; and it is as well they did not, for I could have done no earthly good, and might have got myself into a scrape, unless I had got at the same time the command of the government. My journey was, however, so far of use that I satisfied the king and queen that you and I were not Jacobins, of which we had been both accused; and I believe it did not pass unobserved that Drummond did not open his mouth all the time I stayed.

I send you enclosed copies of a correspondence I had with Circello whilst at Palermo, because it is the only occurrence, since you left this, in which your name, or the circumstances of your command, have been brought forward. I know not why Circello chose to write at all, unless it was to bring out his impertinence, for everything else had been settled at the conference, and did not require his confirmation. Since my return from Palermo the Peace of Tilsit has been promulgated, and I have been much occupied in measures for defence. I did not expect to be interrupted by a proposal at such a time to invade Italy; but so, it is!

You were never more pressed than I was on this occasion. They wanted the admiral to convoy even the Sicilian troops; for they were told and believed the French had sent all their soldiers to take possession of the Seven Islands, or to Upper Italy. Drummond played, as usual, a double and a dirty game; luckily Thornborough is an excellent man; he has had an opportunity of seeing Drummond's falseness, and has given him up.

He and I go on by ourselves, without troubling ourselves with Drummond. We see plainly in case of attack we have our own forces alone to depend on. We have not had a line from either Lord Collingwood or Sir A. Paget since they passed this, and the troops from Egypt are not arrived.

I am anxious for their arrival, for I believe nothing but the sickly season prevents the French entering the Calabrias. Massena, it is said, is upon his march with a large force; and when threatened from Tarentum, Corfu, Calabria, Naples, Toulon, &c., our situation, with a foolish government and a disaffected people, will not be a quiet one.

Appendix Q.

Instructions for General Officers commanding Brigades.

Headquarters, Messina, Sep. 21st, 1807.

The General Orders of the 14th instant detail many particulars respecting regimental preparations for service, to which a rigid adherence is expected. But there are other subjects of previous consideration and arrangement, upon which it is necessary that general officers should bestow their immediate attention, to enable them to bring the corps under their command to the point of assembly for the army, furnished with all that is *necessary*, yet encumbered with no superfluity.

A general officer, leading his brigade to the common rendezvous, or to such point as his instructions may direct, is to consider it as if it were a complete and independent body, for all the wants of which he himself must provide; and he is expected to bring it up well supplied and well-organised in all its branches. He is not to rely upon the assistance he may meet with when he joins other corps, but is to consider the possibility of his being isolated. A perfect whole can only be formed by a union of perfect parts.

To insure the requisite degree of preparation for the most sudden calls of service, the minds of general officers must be turned to every particular which such service may involve; and it is only by clear and early arrangement, and by explanation to the corps under their command, that they can expect to produce their brigades in that state from which alone we can hope a fortunate result in the impending conflict. Without entering into the multiplicity of considerations which will of course present themselves to every general officer, the Commander of the Forces deems it necessary to explain his wishes on a few general subjects.

Baggage.

It is expected that every regiment should be ready to march at the shortest notice; and as the men must not on any account be fatigued at such a moment with carrying burthens, it is necessary that as much of the heavy baggage as possible should be constantly kept in the stores; and that officers, when ordered to march, should employ Sicilians or other private means in removing their own superfluities to the magazine. The light baggage at out-quarters must not be suffered to accumulate; when the detached corps take the field, its surplus may either be collected as pointed out in General Orders, or if boats are at hand and such a measure appears preferable, the magistrates may have been previously instructed to send it by water to the nearest of our fortresses.

Sick.

A previous and clear arrangement must be made for the well-being of the sick (which the corps may leave behind), and instructions prepared for their guidance until they can be transported to a place of security. The attendants left should be as few as possible, and chosen from among those men least equal to fatigue.

Provisions.

Each general officer will make arrangements that the troops when called upon to move may start with provisions for three days and wine for one upon their persons. Beside this it is desirable that a good stock in reserve should always accompany the brigade. Oxen may at all times be driven with the troops without delay or difficulty; and whatever numbers the contractor may have in possession, or can readily procure, should be made to move with the column.

As to other supplies which must be carried upon mules, the general officer should regulate the quantity he takes with him according to the description of provisions and their plenty or scarcity in the country through which he is about to move. Biscuit is always a desirable article; salt pork, when meat is likely to prove scarce; and even wine if it cannot be found upon the road. The commissary must be prepared to answer these calls, and mules will be required in proportion to the quantity to be carried. Economy should be observed in the use of this reserve stock, which is never to be broken in upon when provisions can be obtained in the country.

The comfort of a soldier on his march, and consequently his ability to sustain it, depends in a great measure upon good management with regard to his food. The assistant commissaries should (if possible) be in advance, that the troops may find their fuel, as well as their provisions, ready and upon the spot when they halt; and no opportunity of procuring oxen should be lost, as though one brigade may be overstocked it may find another corps in want.

Mules.

Every general officer must accurately ascertain the number of mules in his neighbourhood upon which he can lay his hands at the shortest notice for all the wants of his brigade. The quartermaster-general will transmit the details of the number of mules requisite for each corps, what conductors, &c. &c., as well as the rations and pay that will be allowed them. It is advisable that, by arrangement with the magistrate, each mule may start with two days' barley. In this as well as in every other transaction with the Sicilian people, pains must be taken to conciliate them to the utmost. Gentleness and civility must be blended with the necessary firmness.

Officers' Horses.

As it is probable that many regimental officers are possessed of horses which, according to the General Order of the 14th, they cannot be permitted to use, and of which they would not be able to dispose at the moment, the Commander of the Forces recommends that as far as these go they should be applied as bat-horses for the light baggage of officers.

Ammunition Boxes,

A proportion of boxes of musket ammunition will be distributed to brigades as soon as possible, as a stock in reserve. These are to be carried on mules; and another mule is to be laden with the pioneers' and entrenching tools of the brigade.

When a detachment of artillery is attached to the corps the charge of these ammunition boxes and their mules should be given to the officer commanding it; but if there is none, the major of brigade (or other officer selected for that purpose) must have the care of these, as well as of the mule carrying tools.

The annexed papers will serve to shew the place of the mules when the brigade is in column of march (under common circumstances), and also when it has taken up its ground for the night, as well as the general arrangement of the whole corps; but there are of course many cases where it becomes expedient to deviate from these orders of march and encampment, and when the general officer must exercise his own discretion.

Marches.

The Commander of the Forces expects that a march shall always be conducted in the most soldier-like manner, even though the enemy may be distant. Whenever the country allows it, the corps are to march *by divisions, never by files of any sort, except when it is absolutely impracticable to move upon a larger front.*

✶✶✶✶✶✶

I drew up these instructions after having received the verbal orders of Sir J. Moore. When I carried the draft to him for approval, he smiled when he came to the words, "march by divisions." "What do you mean by divisions?" said the general. "Any complete part into which a brigade, battalion or company may be told off," answered I. "Just so," replied Sir John, "that's it; you are right; but half of the blockheads will not understand what is meant by '*divisions*.'"

******

The column is to have its advanced and rear guards; and where the description of the country makes it necessary flankers should be thrown out. When the brigade halts for the night, it must take up its position regularly, place its piquets, &c. &c. This is evidently *necessary* when the enemy is within the possible reach of a forced march; but it is at all times useful, as serving to instruct the men and officers, and tending to prevent marauding and disorders of all kinds. The established regulations of the army contain such excellent instructions on the subject that the Commander of the Forces deems it unnecessary to say more. General officers should previously accustom their brigades to *marches of all kinds* that the readiest and least fatiguing modes may be ascertained, and that both the soldier and the officer may be familiar with all the preparatory arrangements.

Major of Brigade.

It is the brigade major's duty to see that the corps moves off its ground with its baggage and every appendage in strict conformity to the orders laid down. While the general officer heads the column (marching at a very slow pace), the major of brigade should remain halted, to see the rear fairly and properly in motion. It is then his business to proceed leisurely to the front, attentively remarking and correcting errors as he goes; and at his arrival at the head of the brigade he will make his report to the general officer.

The fatigue of the soldier may be greatly diminished by judicious arrangement beforehand, and by his being prepared for all the occurrences of sudden and rapid movement. It is therefore highly incumbent on general officers to give their earliest attention to these subjects, and to impress these principles through every branch of the corps under their command.

In short, the Commander of the Forces desires that the minds of the general officers should be attentively turned to put everything into such a state of preparation, that the brigades may move from their cantonments at the shortest possible notice, yet without hurry or confusion; and the whole arranged in so soldier-like a manner, and so judiciously supplied with what is necessary, *and only this*, that they may continue their movements and maintain the field without distress as long as the most arduous service may demand.

Headquarters, Messina, Sept. 21st, 1807.

Appendix R.

RETURNS OF THE BRITISH ARMY IN THE MEDITERRANEAN (EXCLUSIVE OF THE GARRISON OF MALTA) AT DIFFERENT PERIODS.

1st.—Troops embarked for Naples, Nov. 1st., 1805.

	Rank and File.
20th Light Dragoons	307
R. Artillery	469
R. Engineers	14
20th Regiment	714
27th	939
35th	982
58th	848
61st	753
Flank Companies of 39th, 44th, and 81st	480
Watteville's	641
Corsican Rangers	709
Chasseurs Britanniques	562
Total	7368

There was little alteration in the numbers till April, 1806, when the 81st Regiment and the 2nd Battalion of the 78th (Highland) Regiment joined the army at Messina; the two mustered about 1870.

2nd.—Army on the Straits of Messina, Aug. 1st., 1806.

	Rank and File.
20th Light Dragoons	311
R. Artillery and Engineers	436
Grenadier Battalion	757
Light Infantry do	764
20th Regiment	616
21st „	609
27th {1st Battalion	797
{2nd do	615
31st „	776
35th {1st Battalion	780
{2nd do	419
61st „	609
Watteville's	629
Sicilian Volunteers	400
	8518

Detached.

58th Regiment	706
78th „ (2nd Battalion)	757
81st „	612
Corsican Rangers	656
Total	11,249

In the course of August De Roll's regiment joined the army, and the Chasseurs Britanniques rejoined,—thus adding 1516 Rank and File to the above. Memorandum.—A great proportion of sick in the army at this time.

4th.—Army in Sicily, December, 1st., 1806.

20th Light Dragoons	287
R. Artillery, Engineers, &c.	736
1st Guards ⎰ Flank Battalion	725
1st do.	919
3rd do.	915
Grenadier Battalion	763
Light Infantry do.	756
20th Regiment	767
21st Regiment	608
27th ⎰ 1st Battalion	721
2nd do.	604
31st „	773
35th ⎰ 1st Battalion	708
2nd „	458
52nd Regiment	961
58th „	698
61st „	657
62nd „	498
78th „	965
81st „	635
R. Staff Corps	44
De Roll's Regiment	658
Watteville's „	891
Chasseurs Britanniques	867
Sicilian Volunteers	487
	16,831

Detached.

Corsican Rangers (at Capri)	728
Total	17,559

Army in Sicily, 1st July, 1807.

20th Light Dragoons	209
Artillerymen and Drivers	594
Engineers and Staff Corps	54
1st Regiment of Guards (3 Batt$^{ns.}$)	2528

20th Regiment	.. ..	710
27th „	.. (1st Batt.) ..	1040
52nd „	.. ..	957
58th „	.. ..	896
61st „	.. ..	875
81st „	.. ..	908
Watteville's do.	.. ..	861
Army in Sicily	..	9632

		Rank and File.
Corsican Rangers (at Capri)	.. ..	700
Convalescents of absent Regiments	..	334
Total	..	10,666

Gross numbers of Rank and File in Egypt 6,048

Expedition to the Bay of Naples, June, 1809.
Troops Embarked.

Cavalry { 20th Light Dragoons	.. ..	300
Neapolitan do.	.. .. ..	700
Do. Horse Artillery	..	120
Artillerymen, &c. (British)	.. ..	400
Grenadiers (do)	.. ..	900
Light Infantry (do)	.. ..	900
Foreign do. (including 340 Calabrese)	..	700
27th Regiment, 1st Battalion	.. ..	720
44th „	.. ..	600
58th „	.. ..	700
62nd „	.. ..	650
81st „	.. ..	700
German Legion (3rd, 4th, and 6th Batt.)		2070
Watteville's Regiment	.. .. ..	720
Chasseurs Britanniques	.. .. ..	550
Corsican Rangers, including Calabrese attached	.. ..	730
Nunziante's Brigade of Neapolitan Infantry	.. ..	1600
		13,060

Colonel Smith's Brigade, which returned to the Straits of Messina.

10th Regiment (part)	.. .. ..	570
27th do. (2nd Battalion)	.. .. ..	620
Total embarked	..	14,250

Left in the Garrisons of Sicily.

	Rank and File
Artillery, &c.	300
Cavalry (Neapolitan)	300
10th Regiment (part)	230
21st Regiment	630
35th (1st Battalion)	670
De Roll's Regiment	900
Dillon's Regiment	500
Calabrese Free Corps	400
	3,930

Besides the convalescent and sick of the absent corps.

APPENDIX S.

Extract from Private Letters written by the Deputy Quartermaster-General of the British Army in Sicily to Colonel Bunbury, Under Secretary of State for the War Department,—March, et seq., 1810.

That negotiations of a conciliatory description are on foot between the two Imperial Courts and Ferdinand of Sicily, the most sceptical no longer hesitate to admit. How then are we situated here to meet such a combination at the present juncture? Lord Collingwood gone! our army in the hands where you left them—the laughing-stock of the community, the sneer of the lowest ensign in its ranks. Confidence and respect quite gone away; and nothing remaining but the good conduct, submission, and discipline which was impressed upon us by abler men."

Public business of every kind lies over, and is neglected. His troops he never saw, or knew much of; and now he knows no more of them than the forces of the Chinese Empire, &c., &c.!" ..."The national name and character suffers much by this parade of folly; and, humble as I am, I feel ashamed of pulling an oar in the same boat with so silly and trifling a steersman. I am positive I utter the sentiments of every reflecting man in the army."

With such leaders and such employments are we occupied, while treachery and designs inimical to the best interests of the British Empire are openly entered into! One way or another, however, it must soon terminate; and that crisis so long expected is now, and decidedly, most rapidly approaching." "Queen Caroline has *beau jeu* amidst such a tissue of folly and incapacity: she knows it, she says it, and she profits by it. I almost fear any orders from home will come too late to save this island:—we shall have a scramble for it, however, to shew at least what we could have done had we been better handled."

Measures of vigour you will not expect from *us*—we seem aware of our danger, but choose to blink at it, shutting our eyes like children in the dark, lest we should see Raw-head and Bloody-bones! The farce of Moliterno's *expedition* is still allowed to go on; their gunboats, &c., are all to be collected at Palermo; their troops will probably be embarked and landed near Naples: their place on board the transports will be filled with French troops; and then, as well as all the shipping at Naples, will return to take possession of the capital: while, with a superiority of force in the island, we shall be unable to move against them, and be shut up in our garrisons. We shall then have 'treachery' loudly vociferated by our ambassador, our admiral, and our general: while, in fact, the queen's betraying us has only been a consequence of our betraying ourselves, who would act with her as if she were all loyalty and honour, instead of all villainy and deceit.

Extracts of Private Letters from the Adjutant-General of the Army in Sicily to Colonel Bunbury,

Messina, 12th July, 1810.

You will already have heard of us through the foreign journals and other channels; and *as how* we are standing in battle array; army against army like the Israelites and Philistines in the Book of Samuel. Murat's large pavilion tent is pitched, his tricolour flag flying, and his eagles posted at the ridge above the Punta di Pezzo. Campo in his rear; a large encampment surrounds him, and the plains of Melia are white with tents; and the shore from Scilla to Pezzo and round that point is studded with gunboats and boats of debarkment. I send you a rough sketch done by A'Court. You know both sides of these narrows so well that it is needless for me to expatiate. I send you also a detail of our force, and how posted upon the front menaced by the enemy, from Faro to Messina.

Our sandbag batteries have sprung up like mushrooms, and present a very formidable aspect, with the intermediate positions taken up by the ships of war; and round the point to Rasocolmo are Canopus and Cumberland, with a portion of the flotilla, to secure any diversion to that flank while we may be engaged to the front. Melazzo is left with one battalion. Everything else you will perceive has moved in this direction; and as every day adds to our means of resistance, we can only imagine Murat postpones his attack in the expectation of a conjunct operation on the part of the Toulon fleet, who may escape the vigilance of Sir Charles Cotton, and push out with troops of debarkment, and throw themselves ashore on some of the various defenceless points of the island.

If so, our situation will be very critical. During all this time the Court of Palermo makes no effort, sends no succour, takes no notice, laughs at Lord ———. Ferdinand IV. goes a tunny-fishing; and his wife continues her usual pranks, and is pronounced by her own subjects, and convicted in my mind, of acting in concert with Murat for our expulsion. I believe the latter (indeed our information states it) placed much reliance upon the popular commotion and ferment his formidable display of force would occasion; but the peasantry of the country have shewn the most favourable disposition towards us, and come in hundreds, as many as we want, with their *zappas* to the construction of our works and batteries, vociferating "*Viva Ré Giorgio,*"—and getting well paid for their labour. Roads of communication are made from Curcuracci heights to the telegraph hill above the Faro, and also along the shore from the Grotto to St. Agatha (avoiding the heavy sand), and all matters made and making ready for a vigorous defence.

Thus situated, I presume if we succeed in *fending off* the foe, that government will at length be induced to come to some definitive resolution as to this island. To remain as we have been for the last four years is discreditable to our name and character; and in the next place *impossible* for any length of time longer. Our army is too respectable to be sacrificed, though infinitely too few and inadequate to the defence of the island, which we ought at once to abandon, if you do not mean to sustain it and ameliorate its government. In short, you must do so, or give up the matter at once. I need not dwell upon this subject with you, my good friend, you know it, and all the arguments that can be made use of full well already.

Meanwhile, if the matter was not so serious, here is fund for amusement in abundance; nor can I help being so for the soul of me at the scenes I daily witness. We have so many and renowned commanders and there is so much good sense, good system, and regularity amongst us, as would, under any other circumstances, prove most diverting!

Our army is well, hearty, and full of spirits. Under arms two hours before daylight, and remain so till we see our way well across the channel. I am out every night down towards Faro, as is everybody else; and wo sleep and refresh early in the evening; early in the morning, or at some interval of leisure through the day. The flotilla (I may say your flotilla) has proved of essential use, and is much increased. We have also taken all the Sicilian gunboats into our pay, as they were starving, that is to say their crews—and Captain Sturt, of the *Termagant* sloop of war, is nominated commodore, and appointed to direct its operations and services.

I have just come from the flotilla office on the Marino, where they have an excellent telescope, with which I have been staring at Murat in front of his tent, surrounded by his suite, with a spy-glass and a map or chart in his hand, looking and gesticulating towards the Faro. A report is prevalent of 8,000 more troops, under Caesar Berthier, having reached Monteleone.

Messina, Aug. 19th, 1810

Strange to say, we still remain just as when I wrote to you on the 27th of July.—Murat and ourselves staring at each other across the straits. He no way diminished in force, barring deaths and desertions; and we in no degree relaxed in our vigilance or preparations to give him such a reception as he has never yet met with in all his various and successful military course. I believe he is well aware of it, and does not know well what to do with us; whether to put his established fame to the issue of an attack, or to commit his kingly reputation, as he certainly will do, if he retires and declines the contest.

He acted like a blockhead too in coming down and making such a grand *splash* and display, without knowing his ground better; in which he was, I have no doubt, encouraged and misled by the female fury at Palermo, who, judging of our abilities from our leaders, gave him to understand we should make a Cintra Convention with him on his mere appearance; and that the population would revolt at our backs, and quicken our evacuation.

In this, however, she has been woefully deceived. Circumstances, and our quiet unshaken countenance towards the enemy, have raised our name and character in the estimation of the Sicilians. Instead of tumultuously assembling against *us*, I am fully persuaded, and so are you also, I know, that nought but our presence prevents them from driving forth Caroline, as a demon of discord and tyranny, to live by the alms of such of her relations as might afford her an asylum.

And here's your friend Johnny, who because he has once mounted to Curcuracci heights, ridden some half dozen times to the Faro and Ganzirri, driven Madame —— every other day down to the Grotto in his *tim whiskey*, and signed the money warrants for extra expenses— why Johnny thinks all that's been done is his doing, and looks around him with a degree of complacency and content which is really amusing, when to my certain knowledge he is ignorant of the names of the corps, their stations in the line, or their numbers for battle, between this and Paro; or the nature, number, or calibre of the cannon on any one battery from Cape Pelorus to Scaletta.

We have some part of every day occupied in a fight or cannonade, which has at length become so familiar that the porters on the Marino do not turn their eyes aside to witness it. The shore from Scilla to Reggio, more particularly about Punta di Pezzo, is garnished with batteries, and the 36-pound shot from each side reach at the narrows, and are thrown across daily. One of these same missile weapons kicked up the dust round me and my horse about a week ago, as I was looking about me near our mortar battery at Ganzirri about gun-firing in the morning. They fire at everything that goes through; but as yet our men-of-war and transports have persevered to run the risk and without loss. We have had three or four soldiers killed, and as many wounded by the plunging shot; but they are fired at such elevations as to render their effect very uncertain; ours has been principally directed at their gunboats, and boats of transport, as they lie along-shore; and our shells have appalled in no small degree the Neapolitan mariners.

You will learn by this mail that Her fiend-like Majesty of this isle, after having shifted, contrived, and evaded as long as she could, has at length resorted to the bare-faced subterfuge of creating her weak helpmate the *generalissimo* of his own forces, seconded by his two august sons, and aided by Bourcard! The measure, as you may imagine, is laughed at and reprobated, and has at length unsealed the drowsy ideas of the *bon homme* Lord —— whom they neither respect nor attend to, such has been the insipid timidity of his conduct. Such a fellow as our old Commander, John Coape Sherbrooke, K.B., is the only character to guide and govern so corrupt and treacherous an ally, as we (not we but Murat) have in Caroline.

You remember a fellow named *Casetti*, whom you and I hunted out here at one time, and who was going back and forward between Ponza, Naples, Capri, and Palermo. This same vagabond is the grand channel of intercourse with the enemy. He is a captain of horse and captain of marines now-a-days, and *aide-de-camp* to that worthy character, Moliterno. As a mariner he has a small armed *xebecque*, with which he goes back and forward between Palermo and Naples with as much composure as if all Europe was in *the status quo ante bellum*; what still is more extraordinary our great authorities know this, and no notice is taken! The State of Denmark has many rotten symptoms about it, and we want a complete weeding.

!   14th of September, 1819.

After 52 days of a passage from Falmouth to Sicily, came at length the long-expected packet which we had looked forward to for conveying hither certain and interesting intelligence of the views and intentions of the British Cabinet respecting this miserable isle. This bark, with two defective rudders and no competent commander—this same packet reached us yesterday; and by her I have your note of the 20th of July. She brings to the British resident Minister at the Court of Palermo not one public letter or document of any kind; and to the military chief she has brought one despatch from Downing Street.

No material alteration has taken place since I wrote you last, on or about the 23rd of August; the opposing hosts are just as we then were; and we are beginning to be very tired of the incessant watchfulness, which, as the season draws to a close, has become more laborious, and, during the dreary, long, dark nights of winter must still be more so. We wish, therefore, very sincerely, that the matter was settled some way or another. Both armies have had their share of the malady peculiar to the season; but Murat, by many degrees, more severely a sufferer than we are.

The flotillas have daily skirmishes, and a few days past, we had an attack somewhat upon a greater scale; when the *Warrior* and *Victorious* went over, in consequence of the enemy having made an assembly of gunboats, and other craft, under the protection of batteries in front of Contessa, at Pentimele. You will better recollect it as the country-house and long vineyard-wall, near to which poor Handfield lost his brig and his life in February, 1808. But what is the use of all this, if government means to do no more, or no less, in regard to Sicily.

In time we must be worn down by watching if you leave us to our fate, while our enemy recruits his army and repairs his losses daily; and it has been found here, as it was in regard to Bonaparte's flotilla at Boulogne, that the united efforts of the British Navy cannot counteract the assembling of boats, and the placing them under the protection of heavy batteries, beyond the reach of being destroyed by any fire our gunboats or men-of-war can bring upon them.

They make holes in the boats and they knock about the batteries; but these are repaired and in activity very soon again. Landing to burn the boats by main force must be done, after beating Murat in the field;

for wheresoever he sees our maritime attack about to be directed, he forthwith marches a considerable division of his troops and artillery, who lie, perdue, in the vineyards and garden-walls adjacent, ready to assail any debarkation that we may have in agitation; and we have not people enough to run the risk of loss or of repulse, by venturing on such attacks.

Any reverse might have the most serious consequence in the minds and upon the conduct of the frivolous and fickle people among whom we are situated, tampered with, as we know them to be, by the artful insinuations of French emissaries, and farther discouraged in their natural goodwill towards us by the open and undisguised treachery of the Court of Palermo; who, by every means short of proclamation, are known to favour and to promote the views of the enemy.

Our disposition of troops remains as when I last wrote you, and we have covered, and are proceeding to cover our corps nearly upon the ground whereon they were encamped. As the season closes, I grow uneasy about our left flank between Gisso and the Faro, Cape Rasocolmo, Arena Bianca, Aqua di Ladrone, and all that long extent of practicable beach from Melazzo to Cape Pelorus, where at present we have nothing beyond a mere lookout; nor have we aught to spare to it from our immediate front of defence; and as the nights wax longer and darker, such fellows as Grenier, La Marque, or Partonneaux may be disposed to make a conjunctive effort in that direction, embarking either at Bagnara or the Bay of Gioia, while Murat threatened or assailed in front.

19th of September.

I could not possibly foresee when I wrote you the few preceding lines of the 17th, that I should have to state to you my having had a dust with our old acquaintance Cavaignac. That I may not be repeatedly the hero of my own tale, I enclose you the report upon it which I made to headquarters immediately after it occurred. It was my good fortune to have early notice, which brought me betimes to the ground, and I was also so lucky as to have settled the whole affair before the troop Doreè and all the *generales* and their attendants sallied forth from the city, together with Dalrymple, Benedetto, La Rocca, and a long train of *etceteras*, not forgetting old Danero in his carriage, with his *couteau de chasse* ready drawn for action.

You would have been amused to have seen A' Court, De Freuller, and myself, with half-a-dozen men of Fischer's Light Corps, bringing the Corsican battalion down from the hills to the beach, about 600 devilish able fellows, fully armed and accoutred. They pretended to make a waver about surrendering without terms; but a glance at the bayonets of Adam and his fusiliers on one side, and some companies of Fischer's edging down and nearing them on another, soon settled the matter; for they would have been in upon them *with the steel* in ten minutes longer; so you see, Sir, I am the little warrior of the day.

A' Court is a treasure; active, intelligent, self-possessed, and forward. In short, I had proper stuff both behind me and before me; and if I had fortunately moved forward a little sooner, I think I should have nabbed the *general de division* himself. It was unfortunate, too, that every man-of-war and cruiser we had was in Messina harbour. It is to be regretted also that, of our huge flotilla, not a single sail was out (our naval friends have assumed its entire direction). The weather was fine—a light working breeze—and not a boat of them ought to have reached Calabria.

As it was, some of our light *scampavias*, under Robinson of the marines, pushed out and intercepted four. I could learn nothing certain about the motive or plan for this debarkment from the prisoners; they conceived it must have been combined with an intended attack at the Faro, or thereabouts; but no such thing appeared to be in Murat's contemplation, otherwise than by shewing some of his corps embarking aboard their boats, and disembarking again—a ceremonial of daily occurrence. These people that came to the south had their camp-kettles with them, and certainly had in view to stay and kill their own mutton, had they been permitted. Notwithstanding they do everything but spit in his face, the Capo means to lay the colours of the Corsican battalion at the feet of His Sicilian Majesty. I think honest George full as good a man, and much better entitled to this trophy, and could not refrain from telling him so.

If you could do me the favour to get me out of the scrape altogether, before all matters go to the devil here, I should not be sorry; for, *all men and things considered*, our situation is critical and perilous; and infinitely too much, almost all, is left to the chapter of accidents; no system, no management, no provision or preconcerted measures for very probable occurrences.

Messina, 20th October, 1810.

You will have learnt, long ere this reaches you, of our comparative state of tranquillity since the commencement of the present month, our enemy having employed the last ten days of September in breaking up his camp and establishments opposite, and partially withdrawing his army. But where that army is gone, and how disposed of, except it be those in our immediate front, we remain in ignorance; and equally so (you will wonder, no doubt) are we whether his gunboats and armed craft have gone beyond Pizzo or Tropea.

We know there are about 8,000 French, under Lamarque, extending from Monteleone to Reggio—Lamarque's own quarters at St. Giovanni, over against us; and that artillery of siege and battery, with stores of every description for their use, spare carriages, and "all appurtenances and means to boot," are laid up in the Castle of Scylla and the cathedral church close to it. The foe is entrenching the position of Piale, above Giovanni, where Murat displayed his pavilion and tricolour for four months. He is likewise throwing up several works of defence for the roads which lead up from the beach opposite Faro to Melia; and upon Melia are two large, respectable, strong redoubts, with barracks inside, not yet finished, but I can see them at work with my glass, fraising, stockading, and all the rest of it. Upon the whole, you may take my word, we shall have them back again in no distant period.

The Battle of Maida
By Charles Oman

The Battle of Maida is essentially of tactical and not of strategical importance. It was the forerunner of all the great battles of the Peninsular War so far as tactics go; it only differed from them in results because the British Army was commanded by Sir John Stuart and not Sir Arthur Wellesley. The troops and the tactics were the same if the generalship was different. The first clash of Kempt's British light brigade and Compère's heavy battalion columns of which I have to tell in this screed, gives the key to the whole tactical superiority of the British infantry which lay at the base of Wellington's victorious schemes during the years 1808-15.

The battle passed without much notice at the time, because the Neapolitan campaign of 1806, forms a piece of by-play between the campaign of Austerlitz and the campaign of Jena; which few British and hardly a single continental commentator have cared to investigate. Its strategical and political results were nil; its moral results passed unperceived at the time, save among the handful of British officers of ready intelligence who laid to heart what they had seen and stored up its teaching for future use.

It is unfortunate that we have few independent narratives of the Battle of Maida either from the English or the French side. There are Peninsular fights of which the tale can be reconstructed from the evidence of a full score of eyewitnesses on the one side or the other, especially during the later years of the war. But at Maida the numbers engaged were small, only 5,200 on the side of the British and 6,400 on that of their adversaries. The latter were not so proud of the result that they should be eager to commit their experiences to paper. The former were so few that it is not surprising that few narratives survive Bunbury's is the only one which runs to great length, though de Watteville's notes (sent me by his grandson, to my infinite gratitude), an invaluable letter from Colborne (later Lord Seaton), then a lieutenant in the 20th, and the interesting screed of Colonel Stewart in the regimental history of the 78th, with the diary of Charles Boothby of the Engineers, have helped me much. Reynier's dispatch has never been published; it is of great length, and along with the complete set of "morning states", and the headquarters correspondence of the army of Naples, all in the French archives, has enabled me to give the fight from the point of view of the vanquished side pretty fully.

Especially I find that I can account for the exact numbers present under Reynier, a thing that was never certainly known before. Of maps there is only one available-the very pretty and rather too detailed one which I used as the base of that of The Battle of Maida. It is contemporary, and therefore invaluable.

Over the political preliminaries of the Calabrian campaign of 1806 I pass as lightly as possible. The imbecile king and the reckless, immoral Queen of Naples had resolved (too late to give help, but not too late to ruin themselves) to engage in the great coalition of Austria, Russia, and England against Napoleon, whose landmarks are Ulm, Trafalgar, and Austerlitz. The Queen of Naples summoned English and Russian auxiliaries to her kingdom, and defied the emperor just four days before the disaster of Ulm.

This small and miscellaneous army, hastily gathered, had not yet crossed the Neapolitan frontier when the news of Austerlitz came to hand. Almost with it came the tidings that Napoleon had decreed that the Bourbons of Naples should cease to reign, and, freed from the Austrian war, was about to launch a great army under Masséna into southern Italy. The Russians went home; the 7,000 British troops, who had been landed at Naples, were ordered by their government to retire to Sicily, which was defensible because it was sea-girt and protected by our naval power.

Thither, too, the king and queen ultimately retired, but they left their army behind, to be smashed up by the oncoming French. The main body was utterly defeated and dispersed at the Battle of Campo Tenese in March 1806. Only 2,000 men out of 20,000 escaped to Sicily. The sole place in the kingdom that held out—the sea-girt fortress of Gaeta, far north of Naples—was maintained by the one capable general whom Queen Caroline owned, the hard-drinking hard-fighting Prince of Hesse—Philipsthal. He held out against Masséna and the French main army from March to July, contrary to the expectation of both allies and enemies, for no one had believed that Neapolitan soldiers could fight, even behind stone walls. Meanwhile Napoleon appointed his brother Joseph King of the Two Sicilies, and bade him complete the conquest of the kingdom given him.

The French Army, marching far and wide to receive the easily won submission of the Neapolitan towns, gradually got divided into three sections, connected with each other only by insignificant posts of communication. Masséna with 15,000 men was busy in the siege of Gaeta; near him were 3,000 more men, garrisoning Naples for the new king. But St-Cyr with 1,2000 men was far off, busy in occupying Apulia and the Capitanata, while the third force of 10,000 men under Reynier and Verdier, who had won the Battle of Campo Tenese and overrun all the peninsula of Calabria as far as Messina, was still more distant from the capital and the commander-in-chief.

The Neapolitan *bourgeoisie* of the county towns had accepted the nomination of King Joseph and the annexation of the kingdom with apathy. Not so the peasants of the Apennines, and especially the Calabrese, who regarded the French as atheists and aliens, and remembered the final triumph of the Bourbons and their first restoration to their kingdom in 1799. Fifty thousand soldiers might overrun the whole kingdom of Naples and occupy its chief towns, but they could not occupy every village or guard every defile. Hence, when the first panic that followed Masséna's invasion was over, insurgent bands began to show themselves in the hills, and the Army of Occupation found plenty of work in hunting them, and failed to extirpate them.

The Bourbon Government, in its refuge at Palermo, and the English general, who now commanded 11,000 men in Sicily, found the temptation to *try* a sudden blow at the scattered French columns too great to be resisted. They undervalued the number of the enemy, whom they estimated at 30,000 instead of their real 50,000, and also believed them to be far more scattered than was really the case. The belief that Reynier had only 5,000 in Calabria, and these scattered over the whole province, was the false conception that lay at the base of Sir John Stuart's expedition, which sailed from Messina on June 30, 1806, with no greater ambition than that of beating up the enemy and aiding the insurgents to drive him out of Calabria. No greater scheme was at the bottom of the design, and (it may be added) neither the Sicilian Government, nor the brisk, fussy general in command, nor Sidney Smith, the active volatile admiral who was to aid him, was capable of framing a more ambitious plan. In short, it was to be one of the pin-pricks which (down to the outbreak of the Peninsular War) were all that we ever tried against Napoleon's vast Continental power.

The expeditionary force was wholly destitute of cavalry—sixteen orderly dragoons, told off to the brigadiers, constituted its whole mounted force. There were ten mountain guns packed on mules, and one field battery of six guns (four six-pounders and two howitzers) with about 150 artillery men. The infantry consisted of six infantry battalions (20th, 1/27th, 1/58th, 2/78th, 1/81st, and de Watteville's Swiss corps). But from the flank companies of these, (only the 2/78th had been allowed to keep its flank companies, and so took the field complete), aided by the flank companies of two other regiments in Sicily, which did not sail (the 1/35th and 1/61st), there had been formed a light battalion and a grenadier battalion of seven and six companies respectively. This left the main units shorn of their picked men and short of two companies each; their numbers were very low, therefore—the 58th had only 550 rank and file left, the 1/81st, 570, Watteville's only 520, when sick and detached were deducted—and the sick in a Sicilian summer were always very numerous in the British regiments.

It resulted that the battalions sailed with an average of not over 600 men in the ranks of each, save that the light battalion had been abnormally increased by adding to its seven companies 250 picked sharpshooters from the Corsican Rangers and the Royal Sicilian Volunteers, besides nearly 150 men from the battalion companies of the 35th regiment, called "flankers". For, by an evil device invented by Sir James Craig and discontinued next year by Sir John Moore, the regiments of the Mediterranean garrison, after having been skimmed already to make these light and grenadier battalions, were depleted again by some twenty of the best shots being chosen from each of the eight battalion companies to act as skirmishers, alias flankers. When the "flankers", as in this case, were deducted from a regiment as well as its grenadier and light companies, the remainder was left weak in numbers as well as in efficient men. It thus resulted that the light battalion (or the light brigade, as some called it) of Colonel Kempt was raised to very nearly 1,000 rank and file-of whom 320 were not British, *viz.* 70 men of de Watteville's battalion and 250 Corsicans and Sicilians.

The total rank and file of the expeditionary force, including the artillery, was 4,960 men; if we add the officer's, whom Stuart omits in his return, after the tiresome custom then prevalent, which gave only rank and file, the force must have been about 5,200 strong of all ranks. (See table in Appendix of the regimental strengths). This exactly tallies with the report of Colonel Bunbury, the most accurate statistician among those who sailed from Messina on June 29, 1806. That same officer adds:

> The 1/27th was the only battalion of old soldiers; the flank companies of the 20th, 35th, and 61st were also hard biting fellows of old standing; but the 1/58th, 2/78th, and 1/81st were young regiments.

Of de Watteville's regiment it must be said that Louis de Watteville, its war-tried colonel, and most of the officers were Swiss patriots, who had quitted their native land after its wanton conquest by the French in 1798, and that the core of the rank and file were old Swiss soldiers of a similar sort, but the corps had only been kept up to strength by enlisting prisoners and deserters, some Swiss, but many Germans and others of doubtful zeal. The Corsican Rangers in a similar way were full of French deserters, and some doubt was felt as to their loyalty. But the Corsicans did fairly well in the end. Some of my readers may remember that Sir Hudson Lowe was long the colonel of this regiment, and that some wits or wiseacres accounted for his being made Napoleon's jailer in 1815, by observing that "he was accustomed to deal with refractory Corsicans and so chosen for this job".

The force was organised into four brigades, each of the absurdly small strength of two weak battalions, with an advanced guard composed of Kempt's light infantry. Of the rest, Acland's brigade consisted of the 2/78th and 1/81st, Cole's of the 1/27th and the grenadier battalion, Oswald's of the 58th, de Watteville's, and the 20th, which was expected to come up late, as it had been told to threaten a landing near Scilla, at the toe of the Calabrian promontory, in order to distract Reynier's attention. As a matter of fact, it landed three days later than the rest of the army, on July 4th, the very day of the battle, yet arrived in time to take a distinguished part in the engagement. The expedition was convoyed by Sir Sidney Smith, who had with him one line-of-battleship, the *Pompée*, and the *Apollo* frigate, with two smaller vessels of war. There was no French naval force in the neighbourhood which could threaten any harm.

The expeditionary force landed, quite unopposed, on a shingly beach, a mile below the high-lying village which gives its name to the Gulf of Santa Eufemia, on the dawn of July 1st. Calabrese peasants rowed out to the ships to warn Stuart that there were a few French troops in the neighbourhood, but no force that he need fear. The place of honour in the disembarkation should have fallen to the light battalion, but a large transport which carried Kempt and the British portion of that corps had not arrived at the rendezvous, so General Oswald started the landing with the 250 Corsican Rangers and seven companies from the 78th, 58th, and 81st. Oswald spread out his men, and advanced cautiously towards Santa Eufemia, through a scrubby wooded rising ground. When he had nearly reached it a brisk fire broke out in his front, and the Corsican Rangers were driven in by a rush of some three hundred of the enemy. This force consisted of three companies of Poles, who had just come up from Monteleone, and did their best to disconcert the landing party by a sudden attack. But, as Bunbury remarks, "they showed want of judgement in risking a contest in the wood; their true opportunity of doing us mischief was while our boats were struggling through the surf". They were driven back by the supports after a brief scuffle, in which they lost two officers and fifty men prisoners. It may seem incredible, but is stated, alike in the official report and in Bunbury's narrative and Boothby's diary, that Oswald's force lost only one sergeant wounded.

The victorious advanced guard then passed on, and took possession of Santa Eufemia, while the disembarkation was continuing. It was completed during the day, every man, gun, and artillery mule being ashore by the evening of July 1st. That evening the advanced guard took possession of the little town of Nicastro, five miles inland, which is the chief place of the district. The Calabrese showed great pleasure at the arrival of the expedition, and in the course of the next two days some 200 armed men joined the British; they are described by Bunbury as "ruffians of the lowest type". The better class of inhabitants, though perfectly friendly, had not yet made up their minds to risk themselves, by taking up the cause of an ally whose force was small, and might (as they guessed) take to the sea again the moment that Reynier came up in full strength.

It is clear from the general strategic position of affairs that Stuart ought to have marched at once, to catch the enemy while he was still supposed to be in a state of complete dispersion. Every day that he remained stationary gave Reynier more opportunity to concentrate. Nevertheless, he lingered three days on the shore; the explanation given is that a heavy surf had sprung up on the night of July 1st, and that it was hard to get ashore the reserve ammunition, stores, and baggage-animals. Meanwhile Stuart employed his time in throwing up an entrenchment on the beach. A ruined tower called the Bastione de Malta was taken as the centre of the work, and it was surrounded with a ditch and a semicircle of sandbags touching the shore at both ends.

Reynier meanwhile showed a very different sort of energy. His army was much less scattered than the British had supposed. At the moment that the expedition sailed he had seven of his ten battalions in the very toe of the Calabrian peninsula—two of the 1st Léger at Reggio, two of the 42nd Ligne at Pontemolle near Reggio, two of the 23rd Léger at Scilla, one of the 1st Swiss at Palmi, only eight miles north of Scilla. All his artillery were with him. To keep up his line of communications with the north and Naples he had only left his three Polish battalions and part of his cavalry, dotted at intervals along the road to Cassano. One battalion of the Poles was at Tropea, on the high road, thirty miles north of Palmi; another at Monteleone, ten miles farther up the road than Tropea, on the headland looking out into the Tyrrhenian Sea. It was three companies from this unit which had attacked Stuart's vanguard on the morning of the disembarkation— Monteleone is only about fifteen miles from Maida beach.

Lastly, the 3rd battalion was far to the north, at Cosenza with General Verdier. It had three companies detached at Cotrone (Croton), where the division had its central hospital. Of the 9th Chasseurs, one squadron was at Catanzaro on the east coast of Calabria, the other two were near the main body of the division at a place called Maddalone, which I cannot find on the map, but which must be somewhere in the Reggio direction. Thus, when the British landed at Maida there lay north of them only one Polish battalion at Cosenza and Cotrone, and one *Chasseur* squadron at Catanzaro. Instead of cutting into the middle of Reynier's army Stuart had 8,000 of its 9,000 men south of him and only 1,000 north. It may be remarked, by the way, that Reynier in his dispatch says that he had but 7,000 men at the moment, of whom there were 1,000 out of reach at Cotrone and Cosenza.

But his own morning state gives him the lie, as it shows 9,166 officers and men present on July 1st, three days before the battle. The news that a British fleet of transports had sailed north from Messina on the morning of June 30th started him off at once for the direction which the enemy had taken. He would not be cut off from Verdier, but would draw near his base and fight the British at once, unless they were in overwhelming force. "Five thousand men", as he pleasantly remarked, "were enough to thrust 6,000 or 7,000 English into the water."

So, he threw 632 men from the 1st and 42nd into Reggio, and 281 of the 23rd into the Castle of Scilla, with a small contingent of artillery, and marched with 4,122 men remaining of these regiments, and his horse battery and two squadrons of cavalry, along the coast road to Maida. At Palmi he picked up the Swiss battalion 630 strong; at Tropea the 1st Polish battalion; at Monteleone the second——the one whose detachment had skirmished with Oswald on the 3rd—which gave him 1,600 men more. The *Chasseur* squadron from Catanzaro also rode across the peninsula and joined him, so that he had now his whole army assembled, save the one Polish battalion in the north and the garrisons that he had chosen to leave at Scilla and Reggio; 7,000 of his total of 9,000 men were mobilised.

He depleted himself, however, of a few additional men by leaving them at Tropea and Monteleone, as posts of connection, to keep him in communication with his southern garrisons—half a battalion of Poles and half a squadron of *Chasseurs*, 470 bayonets and 100 sabres. This reduced his fighting force to 6,440 men, though he underrated their numbers in his report, calling them a little over 5,000 in one place, 5,150 in another, and finally 5,360 in a third passage of his long report. There is no doubt, however, that 6,440 is the right number. The troops at Tropea and Monteleone he obviously thought would be useful for keeping down local Calabrese insurrection while he went, as he frankly confessed, with complete confidence to drive the English into the sea.

The field force, then, consisted of six French battalions or 4,122 men—the battalions averaging nearly 700 men, one Swiss battalion of 630 men and two weak Polish battalions with 937 men, each of these last having left a company or so at Tropea or Monteleone. The cavalry was about 328 sabres, the artillery consisted of one horse battery with sixty-two men. There were 311 men of the sappers and artillery train. (See table at end for the exact calculation. Where was the divisional field battery? Reynier denies its presence at the battle, yet it had been with him at Reggio, and had left behind only ten men at Scilla). The total made 6,440 of all arms and ranks, and the two infantry brigades were commanded by Compère, who had the 1st Léger and 42nd, and Digonet who led the 23rd Léger, the Swiss, and the Poles. The cavalry were under Peyri.

Reynier's march from Reggio to Maida had been very swift. The distance is about eighty miles, and he had covered it in three days, a fine achievement over bad Calabrian roads in scorching weather. In the corresponding three days Stuart had done no more than get his men ashore and seize Nicastro, which was only five miles from his landing-place. On the evening of July 3rd, the two armies discovered each other; Stuart reconnoitring in person across the shore plain, with a company of grenadiers, perceived the French Army just taking up its position on the heights below the village of San Pietro de Maida; Reynier ranging about with forty *chasseurs à cheval* saw the large British encampment on the shore; Bunbury says that the generals nearly met, having passed through the same thicket on the plain of Santa Eufemia within ten minutes of each other.

Next morning both sides, being equally confident, prepared to advance. Reynier thought he was strong enough to drive Stuart into the sea. Stuart had been told that Reynier had little over 3,000 men, and had not yet been joined by his outlying troops. If the one had not advanced the other would have done so; but Stuart started first, at daybreak, leaving four companies of de Watteville's regiment and three of his six field pieces to guard his camp on the shore, at the Bastione de Malta. Deducting this small force of 300 men, and the 20th regiment, which (except its grenadier and light companies) had not yet arrived, the British force consisted of pretty nearly 4,400 men, officers included. Stuart marched them in two columns along the shingly beach which separated his landing-place from the French camp below Maida. Kempt's light brigade led the inland column, with Cole's behind him; Acland led the inshore column, with Oswald following; the three field guns were with this column; each brigade had two mule guns with it. As long as they were on the actual beach line Sidney Smith followed with the *Apollo* frigate and two other vessels, to cover the flank of the marching columns with his fire, in case the French should come down and fight close to the water, intending to drive the British force actually into the sea.

Stuart's purpose, as stated in his dispatch, was to attack the French camp on the heights of Maida, unless he was himself assailed meanwhile on the march. Reynier's position, he observes, was good, the front being protected by the shallow stream of the Lamato (everywhere fordable but still an impediment), while its flanks, especially that on the French right, were covered by thick underwood, impervious to formed troops. The left flank seemed the weaker point, and it was this that Stuart intended to attack, forcing the enemy, unless he should decide to fight in the plain, to form front to flank, in order to receive the British attack. The march of nine miles along the beach was very fatiguing, the column being compelled to shuffle along ankle-deep in shingle. The grenadier battalion, who had garrisoned Nicastro and had marched back five miles to join the main force, was especially jaded.

It was a hot morning, so hot that there was a certain amount of mirage on the plain, and nothing could be made out clearly. The only touch with the enemy was produced by the fact that parties of French horse were continually seen riding parallel to the flank of Kempt's (the left) column. On reaching the mouth of the little river Lamato, Stuart had to change his direction and wheel inland, in order to approach (and outflank) the French position. This movement took him out of the protection of the guns of Sidney Smith's vessels, which could no longer help him when he turned inshore.

The brigades now advanced in echelon, Kempt leading, then Acland, the late head of the inshore column, then Cole. Oswald, who was to form the reserve, with his weak force of eight companies of the 58th and four of de Watteville's regiment, only 850 men, was placed behind the interval between Cole and Acland. He had (as already mentioned) the three field guns with him. The march of two miles from the beach towards the French camp was far more fatiguing than the first seven miles, for the Lamato spreads out into marshes at its estuary, there was no road, save a track followed by Kempt, and many of the battalions were ankle-deep in black slime.

At this moment—it was now a quarter to nine—the whole face of affairs was changed by Reynier's army suddenly leaving its position and descending into the plain with remarkable celerity and admirable order. The French general, confident in his strength and exactly acquainted with the position of the British by means of his cavalry vedettes, had been intending to attack all along, but he had deliberately waited till Stuart should have advanced far enough from the sea to put him beyond the protection of the guns of the British squadron. He then descended upon his adversary, intending, as he says in his dispatch:

> To make a vigorous charge, which should smash up a section of the enemy's force, so that the remainder would not be able to re-embark, and would have to surrender, especially the part which had been turning our left.

Sending out his 300 cavalry and his horse artillery guns to cover his movement, Reynier came rushing down from his camp in three columns. The southern one was to give the main blow; it consisted of the two best French regiments, four battalions of the 1st Léger and the 42nd Line, veteran troops with an old record of victory from Bonaparte's first Italian campaigns. They counted in all 2,880 men. The second column, intended to form a support for the first, or to continue its line northwards so as to form a centre for the army, was composed of the three foreign battalions, two of Poles, one of Swiss; it was much smaller than the first, counting only a little over 1,500 bayonets under General Peyri. The third column, which was led by Digonet, had a much fuller curve to make, in order to get into line; it was composed of the 1,250 bayonets of the two battalions of the 23rd Léger, and had the cavalry and guns attached to it—for Reynier's right was his weak point, being out in the open plain, and not covered (as was his left flank) by the wood lying below the French camp.

The three columns coming down the hill at the same moment, but having very different distances to cover in order to get into line, it soon resulted that the French Army, like the British, fell into an echelon of brigades, with the left advanced, Compère leading, Peyri some way to his right flank and rear, and Digonet, again, some way to Peyri's right flank and rear, except that his cavalry and guns, which were already down in the low country, were far ahead of the whole of the rest of the army. These 300 sabres found themselves opposite Cole, on the left of the British line; they endeavoured to stop his progress by ostentatious preparations to charge, and brought up four horse guns to play upon him. Cole replied by changing from column into line, and bringing up the three British field guns of the reserve, which engaged in a harmless but noisy duel with the French battery. The result was that Cole's brigade got a little delayed, and that the echelon which it formed became separated by a considerable gap from Acland, the brigade next on its right.

Since Stuart was advancing with three brigades in echelon from the right, and Reynier with three brigades in echelon from the left, it was clear that Kempt and Compère would meet long before Acland faced Peyri, and that Acland and Peyri would be at close grips long before Cole came near Digonet's two infantry battalions. Oswald was still far to the rear of Cole and Acland, as was indeed intended. This fact settled the general shape and course of the battle, which was fought in three separate sections, starting from the east and ending in the west.

Kempt, on seeing Compère's brigade descending from the hills, formed his seven British companies in line, and threw out his 250 Corsican and Sicilian sharpshooters on his right, to cover his flank and explore the scrubby thickets beyond the Lamato, which lay below the deserted French camp. The light battalion, according to the rules of regimental seniority, which were strictly observed, had the company of the 20th on the right, next it the two companies (flankers, etc.) of the 35th, next de Watteville's company in the centre, and finally the

61st, 58th, and 27th, the last on the extreme left.

Kempt had done well to cover his right with the Corsicans, for just as these had crossed the almost dry bed of the Lamato, and advanced among the bushes, they were charged by two companies of *tirailleurs*, whom Compère had placed under cover to protect his left flank. The Corsicans, receiving a sudden volley, broke and fell back into the open ground in disorder, followed by the French. But Kempt detached his two right companies, the light company of the 20th, and the "flankers" of the 35th, who crossed the Lamato, rallied the Corsicans, drove back the *tirailleurs* into the wood, and left the foreign light companies to "contain" them, while they themselves returned at the double to take their place on the right of the light battalion. They had hardly re-formed when the crash came. The 1st Léger in two battalion columns was now coming down upon the right and centre of Kempt's line. Deducting the skirmishers on the eastern flank of each force, who were now bickering in the woods, the two French battalions had 1,600 men in line, the seven British companies only 700, so that the numerical advantage in favour of Compère was overwhelming.

Neither side had any skirmishers out in their front, all having gone off to the flank. The ground was level and sandy, bounded by the shallow Lamato on its western side. The two forces were quite isolated for the moment, though if Kempt looked to his left rear he could see Acland coming up with two battalions in line a quarter of a mile behind him, while if Compère looked to his right rear he could see the 42nd Ligne, also two battalions, coming on in column at a similar distance. The French 42nd, it may be remarked, had 1,046 men, Acland's 78th and 81st a decidedly superior force, the Highland regiment with about 700, the 81st with about 600 men in line. But Peyri with 1,500 Swiss and Poles was not very far in the rear of the 42nd. The rest of the troops on either side were almost hidden from the earlier combatants by the dust and the shimmering mirage which lay over the plain on a hot day.

The whole fate of the battle turned on the first clash of arms between Kempt and the 1st Léger. It was the fairest fight between column and line that had been seen since the Napoleonic wars began—on the one side two heavy columns of 800 men each, drawn up in column of companies, i.e. with a front of some sixty men each, and a depth of fourteen (each battalion having seven companies present). The front of each was not more than sixty yards. Kempt, on the other hand, had his battalion in line, two men deep only, so that, even deducting officers, sergeants, etc., he had a front of 350 yards, only 120 yards of which had Frenchmen directly in front of it. The two battalions of the 1st Léger being a little way apart, the 1st battalion faced the 35th flankers, the 2nd the light companies of the 81st and de Watteville. Be it noted that every man in the British line was a picked marksman (all being light company men), and that every one of them could use his musket against either the front or the flank of one of the two French columns. Of the 1st Léger, on the other hand, only 240 were in first or second line and therefore able to fire.

But of course, Compère, who was riding between his battalions with his Staff, had no notion whatever of winning by fire; he was, in his own estimation, about to break through the British line by sheer impact, as he had broken through Austrians many a time in the old wars of Lombardy. His columns came down, a formidable sight from their depth and their rapid pace, looking like rolling boulders which must inevitably crash through the thin red wall in front of t hem. For Compère had put on full speed, knowing that the shorter time he was within musketry range the less would be his losses. The trumpets were all blaring and the men shouting, "*Vive l'Empereur! À la baïonnette*". (Boothby). Kempt, on the other hand, halted as the enemy drew near: "Steady light infantry. Wait for the word. Let them come close." And then, when the columns were within half musket shot only: "Now fire!"

What followed was a puzzle to Compère and Reynier, a surprise even to the British themselves. The French received three volleys, at 150 yards, 80 yards, and 20 yards. The first laid low almost the whole first line, but the mass still came on. The second tore well into the heart of the disordered crowd, whose impetus was still carrying it forward. The third turned the whole to flight. Reynier, who was watching from the rear, writes in his dispatch:

> The English remained with ported arms till the 1st Léger came within half musket shot; they then opened a tremendous fire, which did not at first stop the charge, but when the columns were only fifteen paces from the hostile line and could have broken it by one more thrust, the soldiers of the 1st turned their backs and ran to the rear all together.

He thought that he had been beaten because his men had flinched at the last moment.

So, did Compère, who actually rode into the British line, with one bullet in his shoulder and another in his left arm, "and was captured, menacing with the action of his other arm, and cursing and swearing with the most voluble bitterness". (Boothby. In Colonel de Watteville's notes it is mentioned that he was shot by a man of the light company of the Swiss regiment, who had taken deliberate aim at him).

Reynier ought to have known better what to expect; he had seen the battles in front of Alexandria, but evidently had not learnt the lesson which they might have taught him; there, indeed, line and column had not been pitted against each other with the beautiful simplicity that was witnessed at Maida. What is odd is that even Maida did not teach him the truth. Three years later he tried the same old tactics at Bussaco, with equally disastrous results, so that Bonaparte exclaimed: "Ney and Masséna had never seen the English before; but that Reynier, whom they have already thrashed twice, should have attacked in this way is simply astounding." (See Foy's autobiography). Even after his Calabrian experiences he remained with the comforting belief that a courageous column could smash any line, and that if the experiment did not come off it was the fault of faint hearts in the rank and file.

Of the purely physical aspect of the attack of column on line I have already spoken. Eight hundred men in line cover more than twice the front of 1,600 in column, and can put in 700 shots per volley against 240, and that at a target which even with Brown Bess it was hard to miss at 100 yards. But the physical aspect of the affair is only one side of it. There remains the moral. What did the men in the column feel while attacking the line? That is harder to find, for not one Frenchman in a hundred thousand wrote down his mental experiences of the trial. One did, however, and though he wrote, not of what he saw at Maida (where he did not serve), but of memories of Castalla and of other fields in Spain, the moral is so much the same that I may be permitted to quote Marshal Bugeaud:

> Why did we engage in so many general actions during the seven years that I was in the Peninsula and never get the better of the English save in an insignificant number? The reason was plain enough. We attacked them, without bearing in mind that tactics which answered well enough against the Spaniards and others, failed with an English force in front. The usual matter-of-fact cannonade would commence the operation. then hurriedly, without reconnoitring the ground, we marched against the enemy, 'taking the bull by the horns'; as men say.
>
> As soon as we got about 1,000 metres from the English line, the

men would begin to get restless and excited. They exchanged ideas with each other, the march began to get somewhat precipitate. Meanwhile the English, silent and impassive, with ported arms loomed like a long red wall—an imposing attitude which impressed novices a good deal. Soon the distance diminishes; cries of *'Vive l'Empereur!' 'En Avant', 'À la baïonnette'* broke from the mass. Some men hoisted their shakos on the top of their muskets. The march turned into a run. The ranks began to get mixed up. The men's agitation became a tumult; some discharged their weapons without halting and without aim. And all the while the red line in front, silent and motionless, though we had got within 300 metres, seemed unaffected by the gathering storm.

The contrast was striking; more than one among us began to think that when the enemy's long-reserved fire *did* begin it might be inconvenient presently. Our ardour began to cool. The moral influence of apparently unshakable calm is irresistible, in action against disorder which strives to make up by noise what it lacks in firmness. It used to sit heavy on our hearts. Then, at the time of most painful expectancy, the English muskets would come down—they were 'making ready'. An undefinable impression nailed to the spot a good many of our men, who would halt and open a desultory fire.

Then came that of the enemy, volleyed with precision and deadly effect, crashing upon us like thunder. Decimated, we turned half round, staggering under the blow and trying to regain our balance, when the long-pent-up silence of the enemy was broken by cheers. Then came a second volley, and perhaps a third, and with the third they were down upon us, pressing us into a disorderly retreat. (Note of Marshal Bugeaud, quoted in Trochu's *Armée Française en 1867.)*

The fact was that a column, with its two first ranks and half its flanks (which were exposed because of its narrow frontage) blown to pieces, was in a miserable plight. It speaks well for the 1st Léger at Maida that they stood three volleys, and that even from one battalion a few desperate men staggered on to cross bayonets with the two companies of the 35th and the "Light Bobs" of the 20th. There is said to have occurred in this quarter a little of that rarest of things in the Napoleonic Wars—bayonet fighting.

The British light infantry, with a headlong impetus, charged straight after the flying mass, which scattered and went up-hill in the direction of the French camp. This was the sort of pursuit that Wellington would never have allowed: his rule was to re-form before doing anything more. But Kempt forgot or failed to restrain his men; they went up-hill, shooting or making prisoners of all the slow runners among their adversaries. The 1st Léger was absolutely half destroyed; of 1,810 present at Maida only 953 were under arms when the next regimental muster was taken a month later. Four hundred and thirty were prisoners, (in September the regiment acknowledges 562 prisoners, but 133 of these were taken at Reggio later on), four hundred and twenty-seven were killed or wounded there—176 of the former, 254 of the latter apparently. Of sixty officers present only thirty-five survived at the roll-call of September 18th; seven were killed, fourteen wounded, one an unwounded prisoner.

The rout and pursuit swept through the French camp, along the hill-side beyond, and for a mile or more; till, at the village of Maida, Kempt at last succeeded in checking and rallying his scattered men. Undoubtedly, they had done their share in the battle, but the rest of it went on without their aid; they were a "spent force", and took no further part in the action, when their intervention might have had incalculable results. For want of a general directing mind each section of the British Army fought its own battle apart.

We must now return to the plain by the Lamato. At the very minute when the 1st Léger had begun to break up and retire, the second echelon on each side had come into action. Acland with the 78th and 81st got level with Kempt's original front at the very moment that the French 42nd Ligne came up on the flank of the 1st Léger. Here the British brigade had the advantage in numbers, having 1,300 men against 1,050, so that the victory of the line over the column would have been much more easy even if the disaster to Compère's first echelon had not had its effect. The firing began at 300 yards; the French battalions advanced till they had received two shattering volleys, and then broke up and fell back, demoralised, as it appears, as much by the sight of the disaster to the 1st Léger on the left as by their own losses. Reynier merely writes that:

> The 42nd saw the flight of the 1st Léger, and at a moment when they were only at a very short distance from the enemy commenced to hesitate, and followed the example of the other

regiment.

They had not suffered nearly so much. Of 1,046 bayonets present they had 656 left at the next regimental muster—much more than half. They had three officers killed and nine wounded out of forty-three present. Of the men, it seems that 379 were lost, of whom 250 were left wounded on the field—figures that show a far less bitter fight than that of the 1st Léger. The 42nd retired, not like its left-hand neighbour up the hill-side, but along the Catanzaro road, directly in its own rear. Acland, following the routed regiment for some way, soon came into contact with its supports, the three foreign battalions—900 Poles and 600 Swiss, a fresh force outnumbering him by 200 men. Here he had a second but a very short fight to sustain—the Poles broke at the first shock, though Reynier himself had ridden up to them and was using all his efforts to keep them steady.

Their rout was disgraceful—their casualty list shows only one officer hit but four taken prisoners unwounded: of the men, it would appear that nearly 250 were captured, nearly all without a wound. This was the work of the 81st, while the Highland regiment at their side got engaged with the Swiss. This battalion was dressed in red, like all the other Swiss corps in the French Army. According to the regimental history of the 78th, they were at first mistaken by the Scots for de Watteville's Swiss regiment of the British force, whose uniform was very similar. They were allowed to approach within a very short distance, and their first volley did the 78th much harm and even forced it to recoil.

But after ten minutes of close fighting the Swiss gave back-though not in disorder, and fell off towards their right. Acland did not pursue them, and they took refuge with Digonet's troops on the west end of the field, where they rallied and re-formed. Acland was prevented from moving after them by the French cavalry. According to Bunbury, he was threatened at this moment by one or two squadrons of *chasseurs* à *cheval* and two guns. His battalions being much disordered by the two fights that they had gone through, the brigadier bade them form squares, and kept them halted for some time under artillery fire, by which they sustained some loss. When the French cavalry moved off, it was found that the battle on the left, no less than on the right, was over. Acland's brigade suffered, in its two successive victories over the 42nd and the three foreign battalions, a heavier loss than any other part of the British Army. The 2/78th had eighty-five killed and wounded, the 1/81st eighty-four—together more than half the total loss at Maida, which only came to 327 casualties.

We must now pass on to the left wing. Cole's brigade, composed of the 27th and the six grenadier companies, had been detained in its advance by the demonstration of the French cavalry, and therefore only reached the battle-ground twenty minutes after Kempt and Acland had come into action. Cole then found himself in front of Reynier's right, which had been delayed, like himself, by the distance it had to cover in descending from the camp. This body consisted of the two battalions of the 23rd Léger, 1,260 bayonets, and (unless I am mistaken) of the rallied Swiss battalion which had retired from Acland's front. Here, too, were French cavalry and four horse guns.

Cole had with him about 1,300 men and the three field guns of the army. He had also in his rear Oswald's reserve, eight companies of the 58th and four of de Watteville's regiment, which were available for his help as they were not needed elsewhere. In this part of the field, therefore, the British, when Oswald came up a quarter of an hour later, had a slight superiority of numbers, apparently 2,200 infantry and three guns, against 1,800 infantry, two squadrons (about 200 men) of cavalry, and four guns.

But they were terribly handicapped by their entire want of horse. Every time the *Chasseurs* threatened a charge Cole had to prepare to form square and lost time. Digonet, the French officer who commanded in this part of the field, had deployed the 23rd on one side of his guns, the Swiss battalion on the other, and stood on the defensive on a slightly rising ground. He threw his two *tirailleur* companies into the rough bushy ground on his right, and tried to encircle with them the left flank of the 27th regiment, while a squadron of cavalry followed the *tirailleurs* to protect them from any scattered advance of Cole's skirmishers. There resulted a fierce frontal fire-engagement between the 27th and grenadiers on one side and the two battalions of the French 23rd on the other; both suffered severely.

Presently Oswald came up with his 850 men and into a similar bicker with the Swiss. The four French and three English guns seem to have paired off against each other, while the 9th Chasseurs were threatening Cole's left. The battle seemed to be standing still; yet Reynier was, as a matter of fact, only fighting a rear-guard action, as he himself confesses, in order to allow his routed left time to get off. If he had ordered an advance, or tried to turn the English left, he says that the 23rd Léger would have been smashed up *(abîmé)*.

At this moment the battle came to a sudden end by the unexpected arrival of a small additional British force. The 20th regiment, or rather its eight weak "battalion companies", about 600 men, had arrived too late to join in the march of the main army. By the advice of Sir Sidney Smith, who came out to meet their three transports on his frigate, Colonel Ross landed not where the first disembarkation had taken place, but near the mouth of the Lamato, directly behind the battlefield and two miles from it. As the landing began, the firing in front made itself heard, and Ross, leaving his last men still on shipboard, for the disembarkation was very difficult owing to the heavy surf on the shore, hurried off across the marsh.

On his way to the front he fell in with Bunbury, Stuart's quartermaster general, who told him that he could strike in to the best effect by coasting along behind Cole's line and turning the French extreme right in the bushy tract which lay beyond it. He did so, and, thrusting aside a few *tirailleurs*, found himself looking down the French line, with a squadron of *Chasseurs* just in front of him which was demonstrating against the left of the 27th regiment. Ross, forming line in the bushes as best he could, delivered a volley at fifty yards against the cavalry, which sent them in confusion to the rear. He then emerged from his shelter, and advanced, forming in line against the flank of the nearer battalion of the French 23rd. This finished the day. The enemy were already yielding before Cole's and Oswald's fire—the latter had just come up, and was getting into effective action at the same moment that the 20th appeared from the bushes.

Reynier gave the order for an instant retreat, and his last three battalions went off across the open plain to the east, covered by the two remaining squadrons of the *Chasseurs* and the four horse guns. Bunbury writes:

> If we had owned 200 good cavalry we should have destroyed the whole of them, but we could do little more with our jaded infantry. We followed them until they abandoned the plain of Maida, and retreated rapidly up the valley through which runs the road to Catanzaro.

The French right wing had suffered severely, though not in the same proportion as their left. The 23rd Léger had two officers killed, eight wounded, and one taken prisoner without a wound. Of 1,200 bayonets present at Maida, 780 were effective in September—they had left ninety-one prisoners behind, and had about eighty killed and

250 wounded. Their Swiss auxiliaries suffered in about the same proportion to their number, with their 106 prisoners and 100 killed and wounded, more than a third of their number. The 300 *Chasseurs* had one officer killed, thirty five prisoners, no doubt men whose horses had been shot, and about thirty killed and wounded.

So, ended the Battle of Maida. You will notice that I have not had occasion to mention Sir John Stuart once during the narrative, though Reynier's name is perpetually occurring. The explanation seems to be simply that he allowed the battle to fight itself, and gave no further orders after he had once launched his echelon of brigades against the French. His quartermaster general, Bunbury, writes as follows:

> But where was Sir John Stuart? And what part did he play in this brilliant action? To say the truth, he seemed to be rather a spectator than the person most interested in the result of the conflict. He formed no plan; he declared no intention; and scarcely troubled himself to give a single order. Perfectly regardless of personal danger, he was cantering about the field, indulging himself in little pleasantries, as was his wont. He launched forth with particular glee when a Sicilian *marchese*, whom he had brought as an extra *aide-de-camp*, betook himself to shelter from fire behind a haystack. But after the charge of Kempt's light infantry and the utter rout of the French left wing a change came over the spirit of Sir John. He still dawdled about, but broke into passionate exclamations: 'Begad, I never saw a thing so glorious as this! There was nothing in Egypt to equal it! It's the finest thing that I ever witnessed.' From that moment he was an altered man, full of visions of coming greatness; as I found that I could get no orders from him, I made it my own business to go round to the leaders of brigades, to give them what information they wanted.

This picture of fussy incompetence, written by a man whom Stuart himself, in his dispatches, praises for his zeal and activity, is probably little exaggerated. For Sir John's subsequent actions give evidence of the most extraordinary want of military insight and enterprise—as we shall soon see. His first order was that there should be no pursuit, and that the whole army should return to the beach for repose, save Kempt's light infantry, who were completely out of call; but orders were sent to search for them in the Maida direction and to bring them back.

They only returned next morning, and not all of them then, for the light company of the 20th under Colborne, who had been directed by Kempt to go ahead and keep touch with the flying enemy till the main army should come up, had outstripped its commander and continued to dog the steps of the demoralised French, not only on the afternoon of the 4th but for the whole of July 5th, till it reached the town of Borgia, right on the other side of the Calabrian peninsula and only ten miles from Catanzaro, where Reynier finally rallied his routed host. Then, hearing that not a man was following in his support, Colborne had to turn back.

Sir John Stuart spent the evening of his victory in dining on board Sidney Smith's flagship the *Pompée*, where he received many compliments, heard the whole story of the siege of Acre from his self-centred voluble entertainer, and was finally invested with a shawl of honour, after the Oriental fashion, by his host. At daybreak he re-landed, and marched his force to Maida and the French camp, where a certain amount of valuable camp equipage was picked up. Stuart slept at Maida that eve, having (according to his quartermaster general) spent the greater part of the day in the agonies of composition of his dispatch. This seems corroborated by the fact that it is dated on the morning of July 6th, while the battle had taken place on the morning of the 4th. Bunbury bitterly remarks that for forty-eight hours after the victory the whole army was kept "kicking their heels and eating grapes about the hill-sides of Maida". while the enemy was on his way towards a place of safety, unmolested save by the brigands of the hills.

Stuart's losses, which he carefully sums up in his dispatch, had been astoundingly small. One officer only had been killed, a Captain McLean of the 20th light company, who had served in Kempt's battalion. I know no other case where a battle of such importance was fought with the loss of one single officer to the winners. There were also the moderate number of forty-four men killed, and thirteen officers and 269 men wounded—a total casualty list of 327. It is notable to see how the losses were distributed; Kempt had fifty-nine killed and wounded, including the Corsicans. Acland showed by far the heaviest proportional losses in the whole army—169 killed and wounded, more than half the total list. Cole had eighty-four casualties, while Oswald and the 20th, who came up only at the very end of the fight, lost five and seven men respectively.

Still, it is an astounding fact that with a loss of 327 men Stuart's troops had killed, wounded, or taken a full 2,000 Frenchmen. Reynier in his dispatch acknowledges a loss of 1,300, but this figure is too low.

He had sixteen officers killed, forty wounded, and apparently eight unwounded prisoners, (I have discovered their names at the Record Office—one staff officer, four Poles, one each from the 1st and 2nd Léger); of rank and file a full 900 were prisoners—more than half of them wounded—nearly 500 were killed (Stuart says that he had buried 700, but this is probably inaccurate, for that number of killed would by all battle averages presuppose at least 2,800 wounded, and the French lost nothing like that total). The full number of wounded who were not captured must have been about 900, for 200 were afterwards taken at Cotrone, and Reynier had 500 in his hospitals on September 1st over and above his normal sick. Besides these we must allow for deaths and recoveries in August. If we put the total loss at 2,000 and a trifle over, we are certainly very near the mark.

Reynier's dispatch, which he wrote at Catanzaro on July 5th—twenty-four hours before Stuart got his completed—is a curious document, in that he shows no notion whatever of the reason why he was beaten. He throws all the blame on his men; he had, he says, only 5,350 men (understating by a thousand), but that ought to have sufficed to throw 6,000 or 7,000 English into the sea. He thinks he acted for the best:

> But I was not well seconded either by the number or the morale of the troops. Many of the soldiers did not conduct themselves with the vigour of regiments who had so distinguished themselves in earlier battles. A part of them are still so demoralised that I could not count on their standing in face of the enemy again. *Combien je suis malheureux d'avoir été abandonné par mes troupes au moment où elles devroient décider la victoire.*

And then he proceeds to say that they will disgrace them selves, if not strengthened at once by reinforcements whose morale is intact. He had no news from Verdier at Cosenza; his only hope was in prompt aid from Naples. Of the character of the English tactics or the effectiveness of their fire there is not a word. All blame is thrown on the cowardice of the rank and file.

Berthier, Joseph Napoleon's Chief of the Staff at Naples, found an easier way to account for Reynier's defeat than did that general himself. He had the effrontery to write to Napoleon that there were 9,000 English at Maida, and that they had already been joined before the battle by 3,000 or 4,000 Calabrese brigands. "*Ils étaient treize mille et nous avions cinq mille et cinquante!*" His 9,000 British were manufactured by counting as present every battalion quartered in Sicily, crediting Stuart with the 35th, 61st, and Corsican Rangers, whose light companies only were with Kempt, and with the 39th and *Chasseurs Britanniques*, of whom not a man sailed at all. Moreover, Ross's disembarkation during the action is said to have brought 2,500 men to Stuart, in addition to his other forces—it really, as we saw, consisted of 600 bayonets, one depleted battalion. But that was the way in which history was written to please Napoleon. He did not, however, believe it, since he read the London papers with deep interest and generally believed them when it came to a conflict of evidence. I have noted several clear examples of this—especially after Talavera.

After Maida had been fought the campaign took a most strange aspect. I know of no other war in which, after a decisive victory, the victors and the vanquished turned their backs on each other and proceeded to place 150 miles between them. That Reynier should turn northward from Catanzaro and fight his way along the east-coast road towards his base at Naples was but natural. The peasantry were already up all over northern Calabria, and Stuart might be manoeuvring (for all Reynier knew) to go north by the west-coast road, and place himself between Catanzaro and Naples. He soon found that this was not the case, yet continued to fall back, harassed but not seriously harmed, by the "*Masse*", as the insurgents called themselves. By the first days of August he was in the Basilicata at Cassano where he was, as he found, in safety. But when we reflect that it took him nearly a month to get to Cassano and that Stuart could have taken a road *via* Cosenza, which was fifty miles shorter than that of Reynier, we see that there was every chance for the British commander to cut him off.

Stuart had three choices before him on the day after Maida. There was the obvious and immediate plan of either following Reynier hotfoot to Catanzaro, or marching by Cosenza to cut him off from his retreat. If either alternative had been adopted, it would probably have resulted in the complete destruction of the French division. Secondly, a less obvious but a grander scheme presented itself. The whole object of divisions in Calabria should have been to draw off the French from the great task which they had in hand—Masséna's siege of Gaeta, which had been making such a splendid defence for six months and was detaining in front of it the largest section of the French Army. What if Stuart and Sidney Smith, leaving Reynier to force his way as best he could through the insurgents, and treating him as a negligible quantity—which he was—had tried to do something for the relief of Gaeta?

I am here taking up Bunbury's suggestion, which seems to me absolutely conclusive. If Sidney Smith had sailed with his squadron for Gaeta, announced the victory, and landed his marines, if he had used his energy to hearten up the long-deserted garrison of the Prince of Hesse-Philipsthal, if at the same time Stuart with his transports had arrived in front of Naples and presented himself before the city, after making a base in Capri, the isle in front of it, which was in British hands, it is practically certain that King Joseph, who had only 3,000 men with him, would either have abandoned Naples—which was seething with discontent and ready to rise—or have called on Masséna to help him. But Masséna could not have helped him (having only 12,000 or 15,000 men), save by raising the siege of Gaeta, which would have meant the abandonment of all northern Naples and general insurrection in the Abruzzi, Molise, and Campania. In either case the result would be splendid—either the capture of Naples, or the raising of the siege of Gaeta.

What Sidney Smith and Stuart found to do was something very different. The naval hero went off to make a dash at the insignificant Castle of Scilla on the Straits of Messina. He was beaten off with loss by the garrison of 250 men, the place being impregnable on the side of the sea. No news was sent to Gaeta. What Stuart did was to make up his mind, in his own words, "to begin a march southwards, preparatory to returning to Sicily". He actually handed over the Calabrias to his brigand allies, and devoted himself during the next fortnight to a march back to the Straits, sweeping up on the way the garrisons that Reynier had left in southern Calabria. The half-battalion of Poles at Monteleone surrendered to him without firing a shot; so, did the single company at Tropea. Reggio, where there were 600 men of the 23rd and 42nd in a weak medieval castle, gave in almost as easily. There only remained the inaccessible fastness of Scilla, which gave more trouble, as it lay on a rocky point connected with the land by a narrow isthmus.

The governor held out until heavy guns had been hoisted with infinite trouble to a commanding point on the mainland, and then laid down his arms on July 23rd. There were now no more French in southern Calabria, and the bag of prisoners had been swollen by 1,300 men. Even this was ultimately increased for Stuart sent the 78th regiment by sea to pounce on Cotrone, on the east coast of central Calabria, where Reynier's last outlying post, his central hospital guarded by 250 Poles, had been left isolated. The governor surrendered at once, and some 600 men, sick or hale, were sent to Messina. Of Reynier's whole division, after this last disaster, there were left only 4,681 effective and 1,106 sick, out of 9,191 effective and 689 sick who had existed on July 1st. Four thousand one hundred and three men had disappeared, of whom 2,732 were prisoners, and the rest dead or deserters.

But what was the use of this, when the news arrived that Gaeta had surrendered on July 18th, a full fortnight after Maida, when its governor had been mortally wounded, and its garrison reduced to complete demoralization. Masséna's army was set free; he marched to deliver King Joseph from the danger of insurrection in Naples city, and then detached 8,000 men to join Reynier and Verdier, whose position was thus made secure. There was an end to any general scheme for the reconquest of Naples, and the English abandoned Calabria to the enemy, who nevertheless took many months to subdue the fierce but ill-led bands of the mountaineers, even when they were unsupported by a single British soldier. It was not till the next year that the French had, after infinite trouble, got back to the position that Reynier had held in July 1806. Meanwhile the better part of the English Army of Sicily had been sent out on the unhappy second Egyptian campaign, which proved such a fiasco under General Frazer.

The Maida campaign then had, as its sole good result, the confirming in the minds of the more intelligent British officers who had taken part in it, of the great truth of the superiority of line tactics over column tactics. It was of no small importance that a very appreciable number of the men who were to take an honourable part in the Peninsular War had their first experience of fighting on a considerable scale on the Calabrian shore. We have already noted the names of Cole, the celebrated leader of the 4th division all through the Spanish War; of Kempt and Oswald, who afterwards commanded brigades in Spain, the former at Waterloo also; especially of Colborne, who, as a brigadier, fought so desperately at Albuera, and made the final attack on the French Guard at Waterloo, also of Ross, a distinguished officer in the Peninsula, but better remembered as the captor of Washington. It was invaluable to the British Army, two years later, to have many officers of high rank who had been eyewitnesses of this first typical clash of line with column, and who could foresee from experience what would be the result of the application of similar tactics on the battlefields of Spain and Portugal.

LEONAUR
ALSO FROM LEONAUR
AVAILABLE IN SOFTCOVER OR HARDCOVER WITH DUST JACKET

THE FALL OF THE MOGHUL EMPIRE OF HINDUSTAN *by H. G. Keene*—By the beginning of the nineteenth century, as British and Indian armies under Lake and Wellesley dominated the scene, a little over half a century of conflict brought the Moghul Empire to its knees.

LADY SALE'S AFGHANISTAN *by Florentia Sale*—An Indomitable Victorian Lady's Account of the Retreat from Kabul During the First Afghan War.

THE CAMPAIGN OF MAGENTA AND SOLFERINO 1859 *by Harold Carmichael Wylly*—The Decisive Conflict for the Unification of Italy.

FRENCH'S CAVALRY CAMPAIGN *by J. G. Maydon*—A Special Correspondent's View of British Army Mounted Troops During the Boer War.

CAVALRY AT WATERLOO *by Sir Evelyn Wood*—British Mounted Troops During the Campaign of 1815.

THE SUBALTERN *by George Robert Gleig*—The Experiences of an Officer of the 85th Light Infantry During the Peninsular War.

NAPOLEON AT BAY, 1814 *by F. Loraine Petre*—The Campaigns to the Fall of the First Empire.

NAPOLEON AND THE CAMPAIGN OF 1806 *by Colonel Vachée*—The Napoleonic Method of Organisation and Command to the Battles of Jena & Auerstädt.

THE COMPLETE ADVENTURES IN THE CONNAUGHT RANGERS *by William Grattan*—The 88th Regiment during the Napoleonic Wars by a Serving Officer.

BUGLER AND OFFICER OF THE RIFLES *by William Green & Harry Smith*—With the 95th (Rifles) during the Peninsular & Waterloo Campaigns of the Napoleonic Wars.

NAPOLEONIC WAR STORIES *by Sir Arthur Quiller-Couch*—Tales of soldiers, spies, battles & sieges from the Peninsular & Waterloo campaingns.

CAPTAIN OF THE 95TH (RIFLES) *by Jonathan Leach*—An officer of Wellington's sharpshooters during the Peninsular, South of France and Waterloo campaigns of the Napoleonic wars.

RIFLEMAN COSTELLO *by Edward Costello*—The adventures of a soldier of the 95th (Rifles) in the Peninsular & Waterloo Campaigns of the Napoleonic wars.

AVAILABLE ONLINE AT www.leonaur.com
AND FROM ALL GOOD BOOK STORES

www.ingramcontent.com/pod-product-compliance
Lightning Source LLC
Chambersburg PA
CBHW021958160426
43197CB00007B/177